John of Fordun's Chronic
William Skene

Introduction

This is a medieval chronicle of the history of Scotland written centuries ago.

From the intro:

"AMID so much that is mythic, uncertain, or matter of controversy, in the early history of Scotland, it may be held as unquestionable that the Scots, from whom the country took its name, had their original seat in Ireland, from whence they migrated to Scotland; and that a line of kings of Scottish race ruled in this country from the middle of the ninth to the early part of the eleventh centuries. The era of the establishment of this Scottish dynasty was the year 850, and it terminated, by the death of the last king of Scottish race, in the year 1034.

It is under this line of Scottish kings that we can trace the rise and gradual formation of the Scottish monarchy, and that we find the first appearance of those ancient chronicles professing to give the succession, and chronology, of the earlier kings, supposed to have reigned in Scotland prior to the establishment of this dynasty.

The direct rule of this line of kings of Scottish descent, and the main seat of their government, was confined to the districts extending from the Firth of Forth to the river Spey. Beyond the river Spey, on the north, lay the extensive district termed Moravia, comprehending the modern counties of Elgin, Nairn, Inverness, and the eastern part of Ross-shire. On the west, and separated from these districts by the great chain of Drumalban or the backbone of Scotland, was Ergadia, Earragaidhel or Argyle, extending from the Firth of Clyde and Loch Long in the south to the point of Coigeach and Loch Enard in the north-west corner of Ross-shire, and forming the western seaboard of Scotland. Over these districts, the kings of this race may have had a nominal sway, but they do not seem to have been incorporated with their proper kingdom. The districts lying to the south of this kingdom consisted, on the west, of the kingdom of Cumbria or Strathclyde, extending from the Firth of Clyde to the river Derwent in Cumberland, and on the east, of the northern parts of Northumbria, which, from the Firth of Forth to the river Tweed, bore the name of Lodoneia or Lothian."

HISTORICAL INTRODUCTION.

AMID so much that is mythic, uncertain, or matter of controversy, in the early history of Scotland, it may be held as unquestionable that the Scots, from whom the country took its name, had their original seat in Ireland, from whence they migrated to Scotland; and that a line of kings of Scottish race ruled in this country from the middle of the ninth to the early part of the eleventh centuries. The era of the establishment of this Scottish dynasty was the year 850, and it terminated, by the death of the last king of Scottish race, in the year 1034.

It is under this line of Scottish kings that we can trace the rise and gradual formation of the Scottish monarchy, and that we find the first appearance of those ancient chronicles professing to give the succession, and chronology, of the earlier kings, supposed to have reigned in Scotland prior to the establishment of this dynasty.

The direct rule of this line of kings of Scottish descent, and the main seat of their government, was confined to the districts extending from the Firth of Forth to the river Spey. Beyond the river Spey, on the north, lay the extensive district termed Moravia, comprehending the modern counties of Elgin, Nairn, Inverness, and the eastern part of Ross-shire. On the west, and separated from these districts by the great chain of Drumalban or the backbone of Scotland, was Ergadia, *Earragaidhel* or Argyle, extending from the Firth of Clyde and Loch Long in the south to the point of Coigeach and Loch Enard in the north-west corner of Ross-shire, and forming the western seaboard of Scotland. Over these districts, the kings of this race may have had a nominal sway, but they do not seem to have been incorporated with their proper kingdom. The districts lying to the south of this kingdom consisted, on the west, of the kingdom of Cumbria or Strathclyde, extending from the Firth of Clyde to the river Derwent in Cumberland, and on the east, of the northern parts of Northumbria, which, from the Firth of Forth to the river Tweed, bore the name of Lodoneia or Lothian.

The first four kings of this race, viz., Kenneth mac Alpin, the founder of the dynasty, his brother, and his two sons, though of Scottish descent, are termed in the Irish Annals "Reges Pictorum,' and, in the oldest chronicle, the districts under their direct rule are termed 'Pictavia.' There is then a break in the line, when Eocha, the son of Run, king of the Britons of Strathclyde, and grandson of Kenneth by a daughter, reigns jointly along with Grig, whose descent is unknown. The male line is again established in the person of Donald, a grandson of Kenneth by his eldest son, and the remaining kings of this dynasty are termed in the Irish Annals 'Ri Albain,' the Irish equivalent of 'Reges Albaniæ,' while, in the same chronicle, the name of Albania is now applied to their kingdom. Under Constantine, the second of the kings termed 'Ri Alban,' his brother was elected king of Cumbria, which placed the Scottish race on the throne of that British kingdom; and upon Malcolm, his successor, the kingdom of Cumbria or Strathclyde was bestowed in 946, by Edmund, king of Wessex, who had conquered it in that year. His successor, Indulph, added the district extending from Stirling to Edinburgh.

Kenneth, the son of Malcolm, who reigned from 971 to 995, is said by some of the English historians to have acquired Lothian, but the statement is of doubtful authority. In his reign, however, was compiled the oldest of the Chronicles we now possess, viz., that usually termed the Pictish Chronicle.

His son Malcolm was the last king of this race. He reigned from 1004 to 1034, and he certainly acquired from Eadulf Cudel, Earl of Northumbria, as the result of a battle fought in 1018, the northern districts of that Earldom, comprehended under the names of Lodoneia and Tevethdale, or Lothian and Teviotdale. In his reign, between the years 1014 and 1023, was compiled the Synchronisms of Flann Mainistrech or Flann the Ferleighin of the monastery called Mainister Boice, who died in 1056. This work contains a list of the kings of Ireland, synchronized with tie provincial kings, and with those of foreign countries, and among them are the kings who ruled in Scotland.

In the same reign was born, in the year 1028, the chronicler Marianus Scotus, who was thus almost a contemporary writer, and he terms Malcolm 'rex Scotiæ.' He was thus the first king to whom this title was applied; and the districts which formed his kingdom proper, and which had previously been termed, first, Pictavia, and afterwards Albania, now usually appear under the designation of 'Albania, quæ modo Scotia vocatur.' They are however still distinguished from Moravia, on the north, Ergadia or Argyle on the west, and Lothian and Cumbria, or Strathclyde, on the south.

Malcolm was thus the first king who bears the title of 'rex Scotiæ.' Prior to his reign, the name of Scotia had not been applied to the whole, or to any part, of the kingdom of Scotland, but was held to belong exclusively to Ireland.

Fordun is probably reporting a genuine tradition when he states that, towards the end of this dynasty, an alteration had been made in the law of succession. The succession to the throne had hitherto been regulated by the Irish law of tanistry, which limited it strictly to males, and preferred even an illegitimate male to a female. By this law, the senior male capable of ruling was chosen in preference to the direct descendant, a rule which placed brothers on the throne before sons, and it appears to have assumed a form not unusual in Ireland, where the succession was vested in two families, and passed alternately from the one to the other. These families were descended from the two sons of Kenneth mac Alpin, the founder of the dynasty, as well as its first king. An attempt seems to have been made, after the death of the second of his two sons, to introduce the son of a sister, even though of a different race (Eocha son of Run, king of the Britons of Strathclyde by the daughter of Kenneth), according to the Pictish law of succession, which preferred the sons of sisters in preference to the brothers' sons; but after his reign the male line was firmly established by the accession of Donald, followed by Constantin, the grandsons of Kenneth by his two sons. Fordun states that this old law of succession lasted till the time of Malcolm, the last king of the race, "when, for fear of the dismemberment of the kingdom, which might perhaps result therefrom, that king, by a general ordinance, decreed, as a law for ever, that thenceforth each king, after his death, should be succeeded in the government of the kingdom by whoever was, at the time being, the next descendant, that is, a son or a daughter, a nephew or a niece, the nearest then living. Failing these, however, the next heir begotten of the royal or collateral stock should possess the right of inheritance." If such an alteration ever were formally made, it was in fact a substitution of the Teutonic for the Celtic law of succession, and the increasing influence of Saxon institutions, or the anticipation of a failure of the dynasty in the male line, may have led to its introduction. Malcolm was the last king of this line, and appears to have been the last legitimate male descendant of Kenneth mac Alpin, the founder of the dynasty; and the recent acquisition of Lothian with its Saxon population may have rendered such an alteration necessary, as the only means of maintaining the integrity of the kingdom. He had two daughters, one married to Crinan, the lay abbot of Dunkeld, by whom she had a son, Duncan; the other to Sigurd, the Norwegian Earl of Orkney, by whom she had a son Thorfinn, afterwards Earl of Orkney. On his death, Malcolm was succeeded by his grandson Duncan; but a war immediately arose between him and Thorfinn, who probably claimed half the kingdom in right of his mother. This war ended in the establishment of the power of Thorfinn over the northern provinces, which he maintained for thirty years, and in the death of Duncan, who was slain in 1040 by Macbeth, who succeeded him on the throne of Scotland, and reigned seventeen years. Marianus Scotus, a contemporary writer, calls Macbeth the commander of Duncan's troops (*occiditur a duce suo Macbethad*), but it appears, from the Irish Annals, that he was of the race of the Celtic Mormaers of Moray, one of the provinces subjected by Thorfinn. It is probable, therefore, that he had committed this act of treachery in Thorfinn's interest, and was placed by him on the throne of the southern half of the kingdom. Cumbria and Lothian with their British and Anglic populations no doubt adhered to the fortunes of the family of Duncan, and an invasion of Scotland by Siward the Earl of Northumbria in 1054 prepared the way for the accession of Malcolm, the eldest son of Duncan, who, four years afterwards, drove out and slew Macbeth, and his successor Lulach, a member of the same family.

Malcolm, surnamed Canmore, reigned thirty-five years, from 1058 to 1093. His kingdom was nearly co-extensive with the modern kingdom of Scotland, and he seems, during his reign, to have maintained his power over all the different races which formed its population. This probably resulted from the peculiar advantages which he possessed, and from the union in his person of qualities, which commended to each his claim to the throne. His pedigree in the male line cannot be pushed further back than his grandfather Crinan, but there are indications that Crinan was of Cumbrian descent, while his position as abbot of Dunkeld must have secured for his descendants the powerful support of the Church. Through his grandmother, Malcolm represented the Scottish line of kings. Through his mother, who was a sister of Siward Earl of Northumberland, he was connected with those powerful Earls, and soon after his accession he married Ingibiorg, widow of Thorfinn Earl of Orkney, which must have conciliated the Norwegian population of the north, while his second wife was Margaret, the sister of Edgar Ætheling, the last scion of the Saxon royal family. There is little indication, therefore, of discontent on the part of any of the different races under his rule. His reign adds some further documents throwing light on the earlier history of Scotland. In the early part of his reign, in the year 1072, died Gillacaemhan, who translated the Latin work of Nennius into Irish, and made considerable additions to it, taken from both Irish and Pictish sources. He is also, in all probability, the author of the historical poem usually termed the Albanic Duan, which bears to have been compiled while Malcolm was king. Towards the end of his reign, in the year 1088, died Tighernach of Cloinmacnois, compiler of the Irish Annals which bear his name, and which contain a number of notices, of the highest interest, of events which took place in Scotland.

These five historical documents, viz., the Pictish Chronicle, and the Synchronisms of Flann Mainistrech, which belong to the period when the Scottish dynasty still reigned in Scotland; and the Irish and Pictish additions to Nennius, the Albanic Duan and the Annals of Tighernac, which belong to the reign of Malcolm Canmore, form the first group of authorities for the early history of Scotland. They are entirely consistent and in perfect harmony with each other. The same chronology runs through the whole, and they stand apart, and far above all other chronicles in authority,—first, from their superior antiquity; secondly, because they emerge from the native races themselves, whose early annals they profess to give; and thirdly, because they were compiled before any of those controversies, whether secular or ecclesiastic, arose, which, like all controversies involving matters of national or clerical interest, in which the patriotic feelings of the country or the ambition of ecclesiastical parties are enlisted, led to the falsification of records and to the perversion of history.

What then do these ancient documents tell us of the history of the country prior to the establishment of the Scottish dynasty under Kenneth mac Alpin?

The Pictish Chronicle, after a preface consisting in the main of extracts from Isidore of Seville, and after stating that the Scots and Picts derive their origin from a Scythian people mentioned by Isidore, termed Albani, gives a long line of Pictish monarchs from "Cruidne filius Cinge, pater Pictorum habitantium in hac insula" to "Bred," whose successor is "Cinadius filius Alpini" and one of the additions in the Irish Nennius contains the same list. Cruidne, who is evidently the *eponymus* of the Picts, the Irish or Gaelic equivalent for whom is *Cruithne*, is said to have had seven sons, whose names are given. An ancient stanza, quoted in the Irish Nennius, and attributed to St. Columba, states that Alban was divided by these seven sons into seven provinces, and that the name of each man was given to his territory. Five of them can still be identified, viz., Caithness, the Mearns, Fife, Stratherne, and Atholl, so that the Pictish kingdom, whose ancient kings are here given, must have extended from Caithness in the north to the Firth of Forth in the south, as is indeed expressed in an old poem contained in the Irish Nennius, and from the German Ocean on the east to the range of hills which forms the western boundary of Atholl and divides it from Argyle, and was known by the name of "Dorsum Britanniæ" or *Drumalban*, on the west.

The Synchronisms of Flann Mainistrech state, on the other hand, that twenty years after the battle of Ocha, "the children of Erc, son of Eochaidh Muindremhair, passed over (from Ireland) into Alban or Scotland,—viz., the six sons of Erc, two Anguses, two Lorns and two Ferguses." The battle of Ocha was fought either in 478 or 483, and this gives either 498 or 503 as the date of this colony from Ireland. The Irish Nennius and the Albanic Duan state that Britus, the *eponymus* of the Britons, and Albanus his brother, first possessed Alban—that then came a colony called the *Clan Nemhidh*—then the *Cruithnigh* or Picts— and then the sons of Erc, son of Eachach; and Tighernac has under the year 501, "Feargus mor, the son of Earca, held part of Britain with the people of Dalriada, and died there." All these authorities therefore agree that, about the end of the fifth or beginning of the sixth century, a colony from Ireland, termed the 'gens Dalriada,' settled in Alban or Scotland under the sons of Erc, son of Eachach.

Flann Mainistrech and the Albanic Duan give a list of the kings of this colony, extending from Fergus son of Erc, the founder of this kingdom, to Eoganan, son of Angus, the last king, who is immediately succeeded by Kenneth mac Alpin. The boundaries of their kingdom can be pretty well ascertained from the statements of two writers whose works were compiled while it still existed. Adomnan, who died in 704, states in his Life of Saint Columba that the Scots of Dalriada were separated from the Picts by the 'Dorsi montes Britannici,' which exactly corresponds with what we gather from the Pictish Chronicle and the Irish Nennius; the chain of hills which separates Perthshire from Argyllshire, and divides the eastern from the western waters, being thus the western boundary of the one population, and the eastern boundary of the other. The Firth of Clyde was their southern boundary; for Bede in describing this Firth says that it formerly divided the nation of the Picts from the Britons, but that the Scots arriving on the north side of this bay settled themselves there. The northern boundary is more difficult to ascertain. We gather, from Adomnan, that the inhabitants of Lochaber were Pictish, and Bede says that Iona was given to Saint Columba by the Picts who inhabited the neighbouring districts, while Tighernac states, as distinctly, that Iona was given to him by the Scottish king of Dalriada. It is probable that the actual kingdom of Dalriada was bounded on the north by the Linnhé loch; for the only districts mentioned in the Irish annals, as under their rule, are Lorn, Cantire, Cowall, and the island of Islay; but there is reason to believe that the tribe of Lorn occupied part of the district of Morvern, and this district, with the island of Mull, to which Iona belongs, may have been a sort of debateable land between the Picts and Scots, and have been partly occupied by both.

The kings of Dalriada are given by Flann Mainistrech, the oldest authority, without adding the years of their reign, but they are grouped together, and each separate group is made to synchronize with periods in Irish history, so that there is no difficulty in fixing the period within which each king must have reigned, keeping in view that, when the period of the Irish kings named does not quite correspond with that of the reigns of the Dalriadic kings, there is occasionally a discrepancy of a few years. The list of kings in the Albanic Duan, with the exception of an occasional omission, exactly corresponds with that in Flann, and, as the length of the reign of each king is given, a calculation founded upon the years of the reign of each shows that the chronology is the same, while both agree with that of Tighernac.

The first four groups, consisting of twenty kings, extend from the arrival of the sons of Erc to the death of Aeda Allain, king of Ireland, in 743; but this latter date exceeds the real date by about twenty years. These kings appear all as descendants of Fergus mor, son of Erc, with the exception of three kings in the last of the four groups, viz., Ferchar

Fada, whose father is not given, and his two sons, Ainbhceallach and Sealbach, who appear from Tighernac to have been chiefs of the tribe of Lorn. Thus Tighernac has at 678 "Slaughter of the tribe of Lorn in Tirinn in a battle between Fearchar Fada and the Britons, who were victorious;" and in 719, "Battle of Finglinne between the two sons of Fearchar Fada, in which Ainbhceallach was slain on a Thursday in the Ides of September. Maritime battle of Ardeanesbi between Duncan Beg with the tribe Gabrain and Selbhac with the tribe of Lorn and Selbhach, was defeated on the second day of the Nones of October on a Tuesday, in which many of his followers perished;" and in 723 "Selbhach, king of Dalriada, becomes a cleric." The Cinel Loarn, or tribe of Lorn, were the descendants of Lorn, son of Erc, and had now probably established a right of alternate succession to the throne of Dalriada with the Cinel Gabhran, who were the descendants of Fergus, son of Erc, through his grandson Gabhran, according to one form of the law of tanistry.

The next group of kings, according to Flann Mainistrech were thirteen in number, and reigned for 132 years, from the death of Aeda Allain, king of Ireland in 743, to the death of Aeda Finnleith, king of Ireland in 879; but the last king of this group is "Cinaet mac Alpin," and, as his death certainly took place in 858, according to the Irish Annals, or in 860, according to the Pictish Chronicle, the period is here also post-dated twenty years.

With this group a singular connexion commences between the kings of Dalriada, as given by Flann and the Albanic Duan, and the kings of the Picts, as given in the Pictish Chronicle—a connexion on which the Annals of Tighernac throw great light.

The first two kings in this group of thirteen kings of Dalriada given by Flann, are Dungal son of Selbaigh and Ailpin son of Eachach. In the list of Pictish kings given by the Pictish Chronicle, we find at the same period two kings, Drest and Elpin, who reign together five years, and in the Annals of Tighernac, under the year 726, we have "Dungal expelled from his kingdom, and Drust from the kingdom of the Picts, and Alpin reigns in their stead." The Alpin therefore who succeeds Dungal in the one list and Drust in the other, thus appears to be the same. His patronymic connects him with the Scottish line, but his own name is Pictish. The law of succession among the Picts, by which, according to Bede, whenever the succession was in doubt, the female line was preferred to the male, seems to have admitted persons of foreign descent by the male line, if they were of Pictish descent by the female line, to the Pictish throne. In the list of Pictish kings we find brothers succeeding each other, but in no instance is a father succeeded by his son. The Pictish rule of succession seems, therefore, after the brothers, to have preferred the son of a sister to the son of a brother; and when the husband of the sister was a foreigner, the son succeeds notwithstanding, but under a Pictish name. Thus we have Talorgan, son of Ainfred, succeeding three kings who were brothers, in 653, and his father Ainfred was the son of the Anglic king of Northumbria, who had taken refuge among the Picts, but eventually became king of Bernicia. Again, the Pictish king who defeated Ecfrid, king of Northumbria, in 686, was Brude, son of Bile, who also succeeds two kings who were brothers, but his father, we are told in a poem contained in the Life of Saint Adomnan, was the British king of Alclyde, while his grandfather (by his mother of course) is stated in another poem to have been a king of the Picts.

Alpin, therefore, was probably a descendant of the Scottish kings of Dalriada, in the male line, who had a claim to the Pictish throne through the female line; and as an Angle and a Briton by male descent had already occupied the throne, there could have been nothing in the Pictish system to exclude a Scot.

His right, however, seems to have been fiercely contested, for, two years after, we find two battles recorded in the Annals of Tighernac, under the year 728. The first is the "battle of Moncrieff in Strathearn between the *Piccardach* (Picts) themselves. Angus and Alpin fought that battle, and the victory was with Angus, and the son of Alpin was slain there, and Angus took his power." The other battle was fought in the same year. It is thus recorded: "A miserable battle between the

Piccardach at the Castle of Belief (Scone), and the victory was against the same Alpin, and his territories and all his men were taken, and Nechtan, the son of Derili, obtained the kingdom of the *Piccardach*."

The struggle seems to have resulted in Angus, the son of Fergus, suppressing all resistance and seating himself firmly on the Pictish throne, and then entirely subjecting Dalriada to his power. In 729 Tighernac has "the battle of Drumderg Blathmig between the *Piccardach*, that is, Drust and Angus, king of the *Piccardach*; and Drust was slain there on the twelfth day of the month of August;" and in 736 he has "Angus, son of Fergus, king of the Picts, lays waste the regions of Dalriada, seizes Dunad (the capital), burns Creich, and puts the two sons of Selvach, viz. Dungal and Feradach, in chains." From this period Flann gives us eleven kings of Dalriada. Of these, the fourth, Domnall mac Custantin" has, from his name, apparently a Pictish father. The fifth, seventh, and eighth, viz., "Conall," "Custantin mac Fergusa," and "Angus mac Fergusa," are also found in the list of Pictish kings at the same period. The ninth and tenth are "Aed mac Boanta" and "Eoganan mac Angusa;" and the latter also appears in the list of Pictish kings at the same time.

There is, unfortunately, a hiatus in the Annals of Tighernac from 765 to 973; but a fragment in the Book of Leinster, a compilation made in 1160, states that in 838 a fleet of the Galls or foreigners plundered Dublin, Leinster, and Bregia, and that "the Dalriatai gave battle to this fleet, for they went, with the left hand to Erinn northwards, after the plundering of Leinster and Bregia. Eoghanan, son of Oengus, king of Dalriatai, was killed in that battle;" and the Annals of Ulster, which generally repeat the Scotch entries in Tighernac, has, in 838 (*recte* 839), "Battle by the gentiles against the men of Fortrenn, in which Euganan, son of Oengusa, and Bran, son of Aengusa, and Aed, son of Boanta, and many others were slain."

The expression, "men of Fortrenn," shows that these two kings, "Aed mac Boanta" and "Euganan mac Aengusa," were Picts; and it may be remarked that the other kings in the list of kings of Dalriada, who correspond with kings of the same name in the list of Pictish kings, appear in the Irish Annals as kings of the Picts only, while of the eleven kings of this group only two, viz., Aed Aireatec and Fergus, appear in the Irish Annals, as kings of Dalriada, no corresponding names appearing in the Pictish list. It seems therefore very plain that the attempt of Alpin to obtain possession of the Pictish throne led to the invasion and conquest of Dalriada by the Pictish king, and that it was, at this time, a province subject to the Picts.

The last king of this group is Kenneth mac Alpin, whose chronology is well known, and corresponds in the main with his place in the Synchronisms of Flann.

As both the lists of the Pictish kings, and of the Dalriadic kings, combine in him, and are succeeded by his dynasty, he must have acquired possession of the thrones both of the Pictish kingdom and of Dalriada, now apparently a Pictish province. Of his own antecedents we know nothing, except that he was of Scottish race and bore the patronymic of "mac Alpin," which is a Pictish name. A narrative of his conquest of the Picts seems at one time to have been contained in the Pictish Chronicle, but it is omitted in the only copy that has come down to us. This Chronicle however says that, two years before he entered Pictavia, he had obtained the kingdom of Dalriada. As the Chronicle gives him a reign of sixteen years, and he died in 858, this gives 842 as his accession to the Pictish throne, and 840 to that of Dalriada, which is the year following the great battle with the Scandinavian pirates, recorded in the Book of Leinster and Annals of Ulster, and the death of Euganan, king of Dalriada, his immediate predecessor, according to the Synchronisms of Flann and the Albanic Duan. Flann adds the important statement, that "he was the first king of the Gael (or Scots) who possessed the kingdom of Scone," showing that Scone was then the capital of the Pictish kingdom, over which he established his power.

It is difficult now to ascertain the exact nature of the revolution by which this was accomplished. The Pictish Chronicle indicates that there was an ecclesiastical element in it, when it says that "God vouchsafed to make them (the Picts) aliens and vain in their inheritance, on account of their malice, for they not only despised the worship and precepts of the Lord, but refused to allow others to participate equally, according to the law of equity." This obscure allusion refers probably to the expulsion of the Columban clergy from the Pictish territories in 717, thus recorded by Tighernac: "Expulsion of the family of Iona across Drumalban by King Nectan," and the introduction of a secular clergy in their place from Northumbria, as indicated by Bede. The Scottish clergy, no doubt, never lost the hope of regaining their position as the Church of Pictavia, and of recovering their possessions there. The occurrence of a Scottish prince having a claim to the Pictish crown by the Pictish law of succession, accompanied by the invasion of the Danes, and the crushing defeat sustained by the Pictish army which opposed them, probably afforded a favourable opportunity; and, while Kenneth, his brother and two sons, though of Scottish descent, appear to have occupied the throne as Pictish kings, the substitution of the law of tanistry for the Pictish law of succession, which they succeeded in effecting, perpetuated the succession in this Scottish race. The re-establishment of the Scottish Church, and the predominance of the Scots over the Picts, was thus gradually accomplished in the districts extending from the Forth to the Spey, of which Scone was the chief seat. These districts, first known as Pictavia, and then as Albania, eventually assumed the name of Scotia, and this name gradually spread over the rest of the country.

Such is the aspect in which the early history of Scotland is presented to us by these ancient authorities, and such was the received account down to the end of the reign of Malcolm Canmore. They exhibit to us prior to 850, a Pictish monarchy in the eastern and northern districts of Scotland; a colony of Scots from Ireland forming in the sixth century the small kingdom of Dalriada in the west; the expulsion of the Scottish clergy from the Pictish territories in 717; the attempt of Alpin, the last king of Dalriada, of the Scottish race to mount the Pictish throne in 726, followed by the conquest of Dalriada by the Picts in 736, and their subjection to them for a century under princes partly of Pictish race; and the final union of both kingdoms under a king of the Scottish race in the year 850. It becomes therefore necessary to trace the causes which led to the gradual corruption and manipulation of the Chronicles, and laid the foundation of that fictitious history of the early period, which superseded this earlier received account and threw it into oblivion. The country generally, and the different races which composed its population, appear to have in the main acquiesced in the government of Malcolm, and his reign seems to have given birth to something like a national spirit. The tie which united the districts south of the Firths of Forth and Clyde, with their Welsh population in Cumbria, and their Anglic population in Lothian, with Scotland north of the Firths, must still have been a slender one, and there can have been but little community of feeling between them. The heart of the kingdom still consisted of the districts extending from the Forth to the Spey. There the Crown had its chief power, and were brought most directly in contact with the people; but the connexion of the reigning house with the Saxon Royal family, must have given them a peculiar hold upon the population of the southern provinces; while the Gaelic people of the provinces beyond the Spey, viz., those of Moravia or Moray, and Ergadia or Argyle, as well as of the southern province of Galwedia or Galloway proper, and the Norwegian possessors of Caithness, Orkney, and the Western Isles, must have maintained a position of semi-independence.

On the death of Malcolm Canmore in 1093, these interests again clashed, and the different laws of succession once more came into collision. By the law which governed the succession to the southern provinces, Malcolm ought to be succeeded by his eldest son, Duncan, but, by the law of tanistry, his brother Donald was the heir, and he succeeded in obtaining possession of the crown for six months, when he was driven out by Duncan with the aid of a Northumbrian army. Duncan, after a reign of six months, was slain by the head of one of the great Celtic tribes, the men of the Mearns, who frequently appear in the Scottish annals, and Donald again came in; but he seems to have claimed only Scotland north of the Firths, and to have tried to conciliate the southern provinces by placing Edmund, a son of Malcolm by the Saxon Princess Margaret, over them. Finally, after a reign of three years and a half, Edgar, the eldest son of Malcolm by the Princess Margaret, was firmly established as king of the whole country by a Saxon army led by Ædgar Ætheling, Margaret's brother.

Edgar's reign seems to have been undisturbed, but under his successors the northern and southern districts were once more separated. Edgar appears to have assumed the right claimed by the Saxon kings, of regulating the succession to the throne by testament, where no direct descendants existed, and bequeathed to his brother Alexander the kingdom of Scotland north of the Firths of Forth and Clyde with the title of king; and the districts south of the Firths to his youngest brother David with the title of Earl. On the death of Alexander, however, without lawful issue, David succeeded to him, and the northern and southern districts were once more united under the same king.

It is with the reign of David that the work of concentration really commenced. Early in his reign, the Earl of Moray, the head of the principal Celtic tribe in the north, invaded the kingdom, and penetrated as far as Stracathrow in Forfarshire, but by his defeat and death in 1130, David brought the people of Moray under his authority. Nothing can better show the heterogeneous elements that made up the aggregate of the population under his rule, and with which he had to deal, than the account which Ailred gives of the composition of his army at the battle of the Standard in 1138. The army was ranged in four divisions; the first consisted of the 'Galwenses,' or people of Galloway, usually termed Picts, but who were a Gaelic people; the second division consisted of the 'Cumbrenses' and 'Tevidalenses,' or the British people of Strathclyde and Teviotdale; the third division consisted of the 'Laodonenses,' or Anglic population of Lothian, with the 'Insulani' and 'Lavernani,' or people of the Isles and Lennox; and the king had in his own division the 'Scoti,' or people of the districts extending from the

Forth to the Spey; the 'Muravenses,' the newly conquered Gaelic people of Moray, and a body of 'Milites Angli et Franci,' or Anglic and Norman knights, who formed his own body-guard. David had passed his youth at the Court of England, and had married the daughter of the Earl of Northumberland and the widow of the Norman Earl of Northampton. He had ruled the provinces south of the Firths as earl for seventeen years before he became king, and his whole training and leanings were Norman. He endeavoured to effect the work of concentration by the introduction of a powerful Norman baronage into the kingdom, and the establishment of branches of the most influential of the monastic orders. His reign is the true commencement of feudal Scotland. Prior to his accession, the various Celtic branches of the population north of the Firths properly represented the kingdom, and were under the rule of a line of princes who, descended from the Saxon royal family in the female line, had been maintained on the throne by Saxon support, and seem to have considered themselves as to all intents and purposes Saxon kings; but David ruled as a feudal monarch, and based his power on the feudal vassals of the Crown. The Celtic element became one to be controlled and kept down, and any attempt to vindicate ancient Celtic rights and privileges, to be suppressed, as rebellion against the Crown.

The great power and force of character of David appears to have controlled these discordant elements in the population of his kingdom and materially advanced the work of their amalgamation, when the sudden death of his only son, Prince Henry, leaving three sons under age, threatened its stability. David foresaw that the succession to the throne would again lead to a collision between the Celtic and Teutonic branches of the people, and to a renewed conflict between their laws of succession. The sons of Malcolm Canmore had succeeded each other in strict accordance with both laws. The Teutonic population appear not to have recognised any right to the throne in the family of Duncan the eldest son, though unquestionably legitimate, in competition with the sons of the Saxon Princess Margaret, and the Celtic law preferred brothers to sons; but the succession of a grandson to a grandfather was repugnant to the Celtic notions, as long as an elder branch of the royal family could be resorted to. The essence of their law was the preference of every male member of the older generation before any of the next generation could be called to the succession. In order to strengthen the position of his grandson, Malcolm, the eldest son of Prince Henry, David prevailed upon the Earl of Fife, whose functions and privileges in connexion with the election and coronation of the kings were derived from the older Celtic constitution, and from his position at the head of the seven Earls of Scotland, to make a progress with Malcolm through the kingdom and to obtain his recognition by all classes, as heir to the throne. David, however, died in the following year, and his forebodings were realized, for Malcolm, who was probably supported by the southern districts, had to encounter the opposition of the entire Gaelic population of the country. He had no sooner been crowned at Scone, in 1153, than Somerled, the Celtic lord of the extensive province of Ergadia, along with his nephews, who claimed to be descendants of Angus Earl of Moray, invaded the kingdom. In 1160 he was besieged in Perth by the Earl of Stratherne and five other earls, no doubt six of the seven Earls of Scotland, the seventh, the Earl of Fife, being committed to his cause, and, in the same year, Galloway, under its Celtic lord, Fergus of Galloway, rose against him. Malcolm has always been regarded as a weak prince, and his reign productive of no great events, but certain it is that he succeeded in overcoming this great opposition, and in more effectually reducing his Gaelic subjects to submission, than any king before or after him. He took Donald, the son of Malcolm Macbeth, the claimant to the Earldom of Moray, prisoner in the year 1156. He made peace with Somerled in 1157, and, by releasing Malcolm Macbeth, the father of his nephews, from prison, and bestowing upon him the Earldom of Ross, he neutralized the claims of his family. He defeated the attempt of the six earls who besieged him in 1160, and, in the same year, he thrice invaded Galloway, completely subdued it, and compelled its lord to take the monastic habit and retire to Holyrood. In the next year, following the policy of his grandfather, he deprived a part of the inhabitants of Moray of their lands, and bestowed them upon Norman barons; and finally, in the last year of his twelve years' reign, Somerled was slain in an attempt to invade his kingdom.

Malcolm was succeeded in 1165 by his brother William the Lion, and, in that year, the first of the later chronicles makes its appearance, but in a very different shape from the earlier historical documents.

In this chronicle the long list of Pictish kings is not to be found. The title of the chronicle is "Cronica regum Scottorum ccc et iiij annorum." It commences with Fergus son of Erc, and adds that he was the first of his race who reigned in Scotland from Drumalban to the Irish Sea; then follow the kings who succeeded him, down to Alpin son of Eochadh. The kings, however, who reigned over Dalriada from Alpin in the early part of the eighth century to Kenneth mac Alpin in the middle of the ninth, during which time it appears to have been a Pictish province, and governed to some extent at least by Pictish princes, disappear; the history of that century is suppressed; and the earlier kings, from Fergus mac Erc to Alpin mac Eachach, are extended, by the introduction, in the latter part, of five fictitious kings between Aincellach and Selvach to make up the additional time added to the true date of Alpin, and he is brought down and made the immediate predecessor of Kenneth mac Alpin, thus identifying him with the father of Kenneth. The effect of these alterations is to present a continuous Scottish kingdom, with a succession of kings of the Scottish race, from Fergus mac Erc to Malcolm the Second, but the fictitious character of this alteration is apparent from the compiler having inadvertently preserved Kenneth mac Alpin's designation of "primus rex Scotorum." In this chronicle appears for the first time a long Celtic pedigree of the kings of Scotland, deducing the descent of William the Lion from Gaidhil Glas, the *eponymus* of the Gaelic race, through a long line of mythic Irish kings, and probably equally imaginary kings of Irish Dalriada, down to Fergus mac Erc, the part of the genealogy representing the kings of Scotch Dalriada being in strict accordance with the reconstructed chronicle. At the same time that this chronicle was given forth, there also appeared a legend of the foundation of St. Andrews, in which that event, which really took place in the suppressed century of Dalriadic history, viz., the latter half of the eighth and first half of the ninth, is put back and synchronized with the removal of the relics of St. Andrew from Patras to Constantinople in the fourth century. The object of all this manipulation was probably to present William to the Gaelic population, as the heir of a long line of Scottish ancestors, and to enhance the claims of St. Andrews, as the ecclesiastical church, by whose Bishop he was crowned; and, as this long genealogy first appears in the year of his accession, it is not impossible that the ceremony was first introduced at his coronation which Fordun describes at the coronation of Alexander III., when a Highland sennachy recites this Celtic genealogy before the king, when placed upon the Coronation Stone at Scone, on which so many of his Scottish ancestors had been crowned.

William the Lion had not reigned nine years when events occurred which introduced a new and important element into the political history of Scotland, and materially influenced the form of its chronicles. In 1173, William took the part of the young Prince Henry against his father, Henry the Second, king of England, and invaded England. In 1174 he repeated the invasion, entered Northumberland at the head of a select body of troops, and was taken prisoner near Alnwick, and the Scots purchased his liberty by surrendering the independence of the kingdom. With the consent of the Scottish barons and clergy, William became the liegeman of Henry for Scotland and all his other territories; and, in the following year, he, with his clergy and barons, did homage to Henry at York. In 1189, Richard I., the successor of Henry, restored to Scotland its independence for payment of a sum of ten thousand merks.

The question regarding the independence of Scotland, and the supremacy of England, had hitherto been merely a speculative one. If the English chronicles contained entries to the effect that the king of Scots did homage to the English king, the Scots maintained that the homage applied only to the districts south of the Forth, derived originally from the English monarchs, and in no way concerned the more ancient kingdom of Scotland proper. There had been as yet no serious controversy between the two countries on the subject, and, if the discussion which took place in the reign of Alexander I. with the English Archbishops, as to the independence of the Church of St. Andrews, indirectly involved that of the kingdom also—for Alexander did not possess Lothian and Cumbria, and there could have been no question about them,—the Scottish king stoutly asserted and practically maintained the independence of his kingdom. There had been as yet, in fact, no reality in the question, and the Scottish kings, whether as regards Scotland proper, or the districts south of the Firths, had acted, to all intents and purposes, as the monarchs of an independent kingdom.

Giraldus Cambrensis, a contemporary writer, and who may be considered as unbiassed on this question, clearly implies this.

In his tract "De instructione principum," completed about 1214, he says, "Having taken William prisoner, he (Henry II.) subjected Scotia, and thus adding nobly to the Anglican crown an unexpected increase, greatly extended the bounds of his kingdom from the Southern Ocean to the northern Isles of Orkney, comprehending the whole island, as it is enclosed by the ocean, with a powerful hand in one monarchy. Because, from the time when the Picts and Scots first occupied the northern parts of the island, it is not recorded in any authentic writing that this was done by any one after the time of Claudius Cæsar, who not only added Scotia to the Britannic kingdom, but also the Orkney Isles to the Roman empire. But such, alas, and so great an honour, sold by his immediate successor by a vile commerce and irreparable loss, vanished from the Anglican Crown, and thus, for a passing price, was extinguished a perpetual and invaluable lustre."

Giraldus's statement, that no act of homage had as yet been recorded in any authentic writing, is remarkable, and goes far to invalidate the passages to that effect now found in English Chronicles and historians, and his belief evidently was that the subjection of Scotland to Henry the

Second was the first time in which any king of England really possessed any supremacy over Scotland.

The surrender of the independence of Scotland, and its recovery, naturally led to a serious controversy between the two countries, with its usual results of the manipulation of chronicles, and falsification of records on both sides; and we find that shortly before the restoration of the independence of Scotland, the chronicles assume a new form adapted to meet that question.

A chronicle, which appears to have been issued in 1187, has been preserved, unfortunately in a very inaccurate transcript so far as proper names are concerned, but sufficiently distinct for our purpose, especially when compared with the subsequent chronicles of the same type. In this chronicle, which is the second of the later chronicles, the kings of Dalriada, from Fergus mac Erc to Alpin, according to the altered form in which they are found in the chronicle of 1165, are placed before the long line of Pictish kings, so as to give them a remote antiquity; and this kingdom of the Scots is said to have commenced 443 years before the Incarnation. After Alpin, the last of these kings, we have the expression "et tunc translatum est regnum Scotorum in regnum Pictorum." We then have the list of Pictish kings, beginning, "Cruchine filius Kyan clemens judex accepit monarchiam in regno Pictorum;" but this list has not either escaped manipulation. It in the main agrees with the Pictish Chronicle down to Nectan, son of Derili, whose reign terminates in 724. But, just where the connexion between the Pictish kings and the Scottish kingdom of Dalriada commenced, we find it disguised by artificial alterations. The names of Drust, and Alpin, the Dalriadic king who succeeded him, disappear. The first part of the reign of Angus mac Fergus, during which the conquest of Dalriada takes place, is likewise eliminated, and the last sixteen years of his reign only given, and the interval is filled up by an imaginary Garnard, son of Ferath, who reigns twenty-four years. The subsequent reigns likewise undergo alteration, and three additional kings are added, the last of whom is "Drust filius Ferat." Of him it is said, "Iste occisus est apud Fortheviot, secundum quosdem Sconam, a Scottis;" and he is followed by "Kynat mac Alpin," who reigns "super Scottos, destructis Pictis."

The object of thus throwing back the kings of Dalriada to a period before the commencement of the Pictish monarchy was evidently to oppose to the English claims, founded upon the early traditions of Britain as one monarchy, an ancient Scottish kingdom, as the origin of the Scottish monarchy, and by thus clinging fast to their Scottish descent, which merged from Ireland, to fall back upon an early independence. It was necessary, however, to connect Kenneth and his Scots with these early Scots, from whose kings he is in this Chronicle separated by the entire duration of the Pictish monarchy, and this was done by adding to the account of his reign the statement, "Hic mira calliditate duxit Scotos de Ergadia in terra Pictorum." The statement that Kenneth was not only of Scottish descent, but that he led the Scots out of Argyle, and established them, after destroying the Picts, in the kingdom of the Picts, appears in this Chronicle for the first time, and is perhaps little less bold than a statement likewise inserted in it for the first time, in the reign of Grig, the fourth successor of Kenneth: "Hic subjugavit sibi totam Hiberniam et fere totam Angliam." If this statement were true, it certainly disposes very summarily of any question of the subjection of Scotland to England.

The surrender by the English monarch of the rights which had been extorted from the Scotch by the capture of their king, two years after the appearance of this Chronicle, threw the question again into abeyance. Fordun records the important fact that, at the coronation of Alexander II., the successor of William, the seven Earls of Scotland appear as a body to have taken a part; but, if any Chronicle was then compiled, it has not been preserved. At the coronation of Alexander III. however, of which he gives a more elaborate account than of any other, and his narrative of which is very graphic, he tells us that, when Alexander was placed on the coronation stone, consecrated king, and received the homage of the earls and other nobles, "a certain Scotch mountaineer, suddenly kneeling before the throne with bent head, saluted the king in his mother tongue, in these Scottish words: Benach de Re Alban Alexander mac Alexander mac William mac Henri mac David, and thus, repeating the genealogy of the Scottish kings, rehearsed them to the end." In the earliest compilation of his work, Fordun does not insert the genealogy itself, but merely says that it was deduced from Scota, daughter of Pharaoh, King of Egypt, from whom the Scots derived their origin; but, in the subsequent editions of this part of his work, the genealogy is inserted as far as Fergus, son of Feredach, who he says is by others called Ferechere, and he tells us (in B. v. cap. 50) that he obtained this genealogy from Walter de Wardlaw, Bishop of Glasgow.

The genealogy, however, is precisely the same as that which appeared for the first time at the accession of William the Lion; and, as on that occasion, a chronicle of the kings of Scotland appears about the same time. This is the Chronicle which was preserved in the Register of the Priory of St. Andrews, and is the third of the later chronicles. The form of this Chronicle differs from that of the Chronicle which appeared at the accession of William the Lion, but resembles in every respect the Chronicle which appeared in 1187, and is in close accordance with it. The two Chronicles are in fact the same, and we have likewise the latter only in a later transcript, with a very inaccurate rendering of the proper names. A comparison of the two, however, enables us to restore this form of the Chronicle with sufficient accuracy. The form of this and the preceding Chronicle is, however, quite inconsistent with the genealogy which was framed in accordance with the form of the Chronicle of 1165. That Chronicle makes the Dalriadic kings from Fergus, son of Erc, to Alpin the immediate and direct predecessors of Kenneth mac Alpin, and the genealogy in accordance with it, takes the pedigree up to Kenneth, and then through Alpin to Fergus mac Erc. But the Chronicle of 1187 and that of St. Andrews, which is in similar form, remove the Dalriadic kings from Fergus to Alpin to a remote period before the commencement of the Pictish monarchy, and again dissever them from Kenneth.

This inconsistency seems to have become apparent to the framers of these chronicles, for the next chronicle which appeared, the chronicle introduced into the Scalachronica, which is the fourth of the later chronicles, and appears to have been originally compiled in the year 1280, two years after Alexander III. had for the second time done homage to the English king, has some important variations. The Dalriadic kings are here also made to precede the line of Pictish kings, but the name of the first of these is changed from Fergus son of Erc to "Fergus son of Ferthair of Ireland, descended from Scota." This is obviously an attempt to adapt this form of the chronicle to the genealogy. Fergus mac Erc appears in the genealogy twelve generations before Kenneth mac Alpin, but in the same genealogy, thirty-five generations higher up is a "Forgo son of Feradaig," and in some copies now lost the names seem to have been "Fergus son of Ferethar." This name accords better in point of time with the commencement of the line of the Dalriadic kings when removed to this remote position, and thus, in this chronicle, Fergus son of Erc becomes Fergus son of Ferethar. His successors are the same down to Alpin with this exception, that only two of the five interjected kings are given. After Alpin, instead of the "Tunc translatum est regnum Scotorum in regnum Pictorum," it is said, "He was the last of the Scots who at that time reigned immediately before the Picts." Then follows an account of the origin of the Picts taken apparently from Geoffroy of Monmouth, and a list of the Pictish kings, which in the main agrees with the Chronicle of 1187, and that of St. Andrews, but with the same suppression of the reigns of Drust and Alpin and fourteen years of the reign of Angus mac Fergus, and the introduction of a fictitious Garnard, son of Feradach. After the last king, Drust son of Feradach, is the statement, "He was the last king of the Picts and was killed at Scone by treason." He is not however immediately followed by Kenneth mac Alpin, as in the two previous chronicles. Another difficulty seems also to have become apparent, viz., how to connect Kenneth and his Scots with the previous Scottish kingdom when removed to so remote a period; and, in order to remove this difficulty, the framer of this chronicle introduces here another colony of Scots from Ireland who, under Redda the son of a king of Ireland, colonize Galloway, and spread from thence to Argyle and the Isles, and then conquer the Picts, and thus the chronicler adds, "the kingdom of the Scots recommenced, which had commenced before the Picts, 443 years before the incarnation." Then follows the statement: "The Picts destroyed in this manner, Kynet son of Alpin reigned over the Scots and was the first king of the Scots after the Picts." There is no equivalent statement to that in the previous chronicles: "Hic mira calliditate duxit Scotos de Ergadia in terram Pictorum," but, in place of it, after stating, as in the other chronicles, that Kenneth was buried in Iona, where Fergus, Loern, and Angus were buried, this chronicle adds, "three brothers who brought the Scots into Archady (Argyle) upon the Picts." The statement that Grig "subjected to his government all Ireland and a great part of England" is repeated in this chronicle.

The death of Alexander III. without male issue and that of his granddaughter, the Maid of Norway, the heiress of the crown, terminated this line of kings, and, as is well known, led to a competition for the crown and the revival of the English claims. In the course of the steps which Edward I. took to bring the kingdom of Scotland under subjection to him, he produced in 1290 a vast body of Extracts from Chronicles collected from the monasteries in England, including the very important Chronicle of Huntingdon. In these extracts every instance in which a Scottish king did homage to the king of England is quoted; and, in 1301, a discussion took place at Rome before the Pope, in which it was assumed on the English side that these acts of homage were for the whole kingdom, while the argument on the Scottish side is contained in two documents which Fordun has preserved, viz., the "Instructiones" sent by the Scottish Government to their Commissioners in Rome, and the "Processus contra figmenta regis Angliæ," by Baldred Bisset, one of their Commissioners. The Pope again interposed in 1317, but this was after the battle of Bannockburn had been fought, and Robert Bruce had firmly established himself as independent king of Scotland. The Pope's interposition was on behalf of England, but he was met by an assertion of the independence of Scotland. At the same time, another chronicle makes its appearance, and, in this chronicle, which is the fifth of the later chronicles, the form is again altered and a different attempt made to reconcile the conflicting statements between the chronicles in their later form and the genealogy.

This chronicle places the list of the Pictish kings from "Gruchne filius Kenne" to Drust son of Ferach first, but, with the three previous chronicles, contains the alteration by which the reigns of Drust and Alpin, and part of that of Angus son of Fergus, are suppressed, and the fictitious Garnard son of Ferath, with a reign of twenty-four years, substituted. Then follows "Summa annorum quibus regnaverunt ante Scotos mille ducenti et xxxix anni et iiii menses." Then follow the kings of Dalriada with this title "Summa regum lxv." These kings begin with "Fergus filius Herc," and go down to "Alpin filius Heochet." They contain the five kings interjected between Ainbhcellach and Selvach. After Alpin comes the sentence, "Et tunc translatum est regnum Scotorum ad terram Pictorum," which betrays the artificial character of the differences in this chronicle; for this passage, appropriate when the Dalriadic kings were placed before the Pictish kingdom, is no longer so when they come after, and are followed immediately by the Scottish kingdom founded by Kenneth mac Alpin. We have then this sentence, "Summa annorum a tempore Fergus filius Herc ad tempus Alpin ccc et vii anni et tres menses," and then follows "Kenneth filius Alpin" and his successors down to the death of Alexander III. After Kenneth we have the sentence, "Hic mira calliditate duxit Scotos de Ergadia in terram Pictorum," and, in place of the broad assertion that his fourth successor. Grig, conquered all Ireland and nearly all England, we find the sentence thus expressed: "Hic subjugavit sibi totam Berniciam et fere Angliam," and the chronicle concludes with this sentence, "Summa annorum a tempore Kinet usque ad tempus Alexandri ultimi Dlxvii. et siluit terra sine rege tot annis quot intervenerunt."

This chronicle corresponds closely with the chronicles of 1187 and of St. Andrews in the lists of the kings, but alters their relative position, by bringing back the Dalriadic kings to the period in which they were placed by the chronicle of 1165; but the alteration is not a genuine one, as appears from the chronicle itself, and the change of Hibernia to Bernicia rather indicates the influence which dictated it, as proceeding from the Gaelic part of the population.

The appearance of this chronicle was followed three years after by the celebrated letter of the Barons of Scotland to the Pope in 1320, vindicating the independence of Scotland. In this letter the statement is made that the kingdom of Scotland "had been governed by an uninterrupted succession of one hundred and thirteen kings, all of our own native and royal stock, without the intervening of any stranger," and that the Scots were converted to Christianity by St. Andrew the Apostle, the introduction of whose relics, according to the tract which appeared in 1165, had been removed back to the fourth century. As the number of kings who reigned in Scotland during what may be termed the historical period, from Kenneth mac Alpin to Robert Bruce, in whose reign this letter was written, did not exceed, under any computation, thirty, this leaves upwards of eighty kings to be accounted for. It is obvious, therefore, that this computation is founded upon the genealogy and not upon any list of kings, and assumes that to a remote period, even beyond the era of Forgo or Fergus son of Feradaig, who is only forty-five generations removed from Kenneth mac Alpin, these names represented ancient kings of Scotland, an assumption that gave a latitude for such statements, of which the barons availed themselves without much moderation.

Seven years after this, in the year 1327, peace was finally concluded between England and Scotland, and the English king, by a formal instrument ratified by the English Parliament, renounced all claim of superiority over Scotland, and declared "that the said kingdom, according to its ancient boundaries observed in the days of Alexander III., should remain unto Robert king of Scots, and unto his heirs and successors, free and divided from the kingdom of England without any subjection, right of service, claim, or demand whatever; and that all writings which might have been executed at any time to the contrary, should be held as void and of no effect." This practically and to all real intents and purposes terminated the great controversy between the two countries, and the question involved in it passed from the field of political discussion into the domain of historical speculation, and became more a subject of theoretical inquiry, though still one of national interest, in which national feeling was keenly involved though the independence of the kingdom no longer depended on it.

The chronicles then which appeared from the accession of William the Lion in 1165 to this event in 1327, viz., the Chronicles of 1165, and of 1187, the Chronicle of St. Andrews, that contained in the Scalachronica and the Chronicle of 1317, form the second group of historical documents, and the sketch which has just been given of them and of the various changes they underwent during the 160 years which elapsed from the one event to the other, and the influences which gave rise to these changes, will show how little they are to be depended upon in attempting a reconstruction of the early history of Scotland. They may possibly contain, in their statements, a germ of historic truth. So far as they preserve the lists contained in the older documents, they may be trustworthy, but the connexion in which they are recorded is quite artificial, and they have been constructed in order to present the early history of the country in a false aspect.

Upon these chronicles, however, the early history of Scotland has been based by all the more recent historians of Scotland who have entered upon that portion of the history at all, from the ponderous *Caledonia* of George Chalmers down to the latest history of Scotland. The only historian who has estimated correctly the value and superior claims of the earlier documents, and saw somewhat of their true bearing upon the early history, was John Pinkerton, but they were to a very limited extent accessible to him. He obtained a correct copy of the Pictish Chronicle, but the Synchronisms of Flann Mainistrech were unknown to him. Of the Irish additions to Nennius, he had an imperfect and incorrect extract, and their meaning was perverted by a bad translation. The Albanic Duan he possessed, but unfortunately he altered the order of the stanzas, and the position of the two kings Dungal and Alpin, and placed the stanza containing them immediately before that in which Kenneth mac Alpin appears, from an idea that one of the leading differences between it and the later chronicles arose from a mistake of the transcriber,—an idea which the Synchronisms of Flann would have corrected, if he had possessed them, and thus prevented him from missing the full bearing of the Duan. The great work of Doctor O'Connor, containing the Annals of Tighernach, Inisfallen, Ulster, and the Four Masters, had not been published, and he only knew what the Annals of Tighernac contained through an inaccurate transcript of the Annals of Ulster which usually repeat his statements, in the British Museum, and a translation published by Johnstone in his "Antiquitates Celto-Normanicæ." Still it is remarkable how near to the truth he came, and his conclusions would probably have met with more general acceptance had he not identified himself so thoroughly with a theory of early Teutonic settlements, and of the Teutonic origin of the early population, and displayed so unreasoning a prejudice against everything Celtic, that the calmer and more elaborate production of George Chalmers, with its quiet adoption of the later chronicles as the basis of the history, has recommended itself more to the general reader, and more greatly influenced the views of later historians. These later chronicles, with the genealogy which first appeared in 1165, formed part of the materials which Fordun endeavoured to weld into a consistent narrative, by which the highest antiquity was to be given to the Scottish nation.

John of Fordun must have been born not long before or after the commencement of the fourteenth century. The last of these Chronicles appeared while he was a young man, and he was probably already in priest's orders, when the claims of England to a superiority over Scotland were finally surrendered in 1327. The circumstances which led him to devote himself to the work of compiling a history of his native country, we are not sufficiently acquainted with his life to be able to guess, but the Church of St. Andrews had always been associated with the production and preservation of these early historical documents, and his name indicates his connexion with that diocese. The great Register of the Priory of St. Andrews had been compiled between 1313 and 1332, and contained documents connected with the early annals of Scotland, as well as a "Historia" which may have attracted his attention, and the work of Ranulph Higden, which appeared at intervals from 1327 to his death in 1363, and gave to the world a general history of England which acquired at once great popularity, may have led him to plan a similar work, and to do for Scotland what Higden had done for England.

But he did not at once attempt so great and laborious a work as to compile a complete and systematic history of the country from the earliest period. The object he seems first to have proposed to himself was a history of the descendants of the Saxon princess Margaret, who by her marriage with Malcolm Canmore had brought into the Scottish Royal line the representation of the ancient Saxon monarchs. This work was based upon Ailred's "Genealogia regum," which Fordun seems at first to have attributed to Turgot, and contained copious extracts from that work, to which is added the events of the reigns of Margaret's sons to the death of David I., and this was followed by Annals of Scotland from the accession of Malcolm IV. to the year 1363, in which it appears to have been compiled—curiously enough both the year in which Higden died, and at which the contemporary work called the "Scalachronica "terminates. He then seems to have enlarged his plan so as to make it form a complete history of Scotland from the accession of Malcolm Canmore, and to have thrown the earlier part prior to the death of David I. into the form in which it now appears in the fifth book, and this he termed "Chronica regni Scotiæ; " and finally, he seems to have resolved to compile a complete history of Scotland from the earliest times, and to have taken as his model Higden's Polychronicon which had now become very widely known. For this purpose, he had to commence by an extensive research into the materials available for such a work, and research in those days meant visiting all the monasteries and other repositories of manuscripts, and laboriously collecting local materials from place to place. Nearly twenty years appear to have been spent in this work, and then John of Fordun compiled the first four books, added three chapters to the fifth book, and would probably have elaborated the Annals into two more books, thus throwing the whole into seven books in imitation of Higden, when he seems to have been arrested in his work by death, in the year 1385, leaving his materials in the shape in which they now appear in the first volume of this edition.

In constructing his scheme of the early history of Scotland, Fordun has evidently taken for its basis the genealogy deducing the kings of Scotland through a long line of Celtic ancestors from Gaedil Glass, whom he calls Gaythelos, the *eponymus* of the Gaelic race, which first appeared at the accession of William the Lion and again at the coronation of Alexander III. To this, as a connecting link, he adapts the later chronicles which appeared from time to time in their various forms—the earlier and more authentic documents he either was ignorant of or ignored—and endeavours to form one uniform scheme out of them; and he harmonizes this scheme with such notices as he can adapt to his purpose from the Roman writers, and such authors as Giraldus Cambrensis, *Geoffroy* of Monmouth, and others. In doing so, he uses to a considerable extent the same class of writers and the same kind of materials, as were employed by Higden in his Polychronicon, and very much in the same manner. And wherever he finds the word Scotia in these writers, he applies it to Scotland, and thus adopts into his history events which properly belong to Ireland, while by this process he materially aids his scheme of an early settlement of Scots in this country.

It is only when we follow in detail the manner in which he has worked out this plan that we see the great skill with which it has been done, considering the limited extent of real information he possessed, and the scanty materials at his disposal.

Beginning with Gaedil Glass, or Gaythelos, the *eponymus* of the race, and Scota their female ancestor, by which the country in which they settled is usually typified, he connects the names in the genealogy with a fictitious narrative of the emigration of the race from Egypt to Spain, and thence to Ireland, based to some extent upon the Irish traditions, but differing in several leading particulars from them. He then brings the Scots over from Ireland to Scotland under a leader, Ethachius Rothay, whom he finds in the genealogy several generations before Forgo or Fergus son of Feradaig—the resemblance of the name of Rothay to that of Rothesay in the island of Bute having apparently suggested it. His object was of course to give the Scots as early a settlement in Scotland as he could. He adopts the statement of the Chronicle in the Scalachronica, that the first king of the Scots who preceded the Picts was Fergus son of Ferchard, whom he identifies with this Forgo son of Feradaig in the genealogy; but, instead of giving him, as his successors, the Dalriadic kings of the sixth and seventh centuries according to that chronicle, he merely states generally that he was succeeded by forty-five kings, but he refrains from giving their names or the events of their reigns, except in two instances. Finding in the genealogy three generations below Forgo, the name Rether, he identifies him with the Reuda of Bede, who states that the Dalriads came over from Ireland to Scotland under him, and places a second colony of Scots from Ireland under Rether. He then, under a supposed king Eugenius, brings this colony to an end at a time when he finds it stated that Maximus the Roman emperor had defeated the Picts and Scots; states that Maximus slew Eugenius, and expelled the Scots from Britain, under his brother Ethodius; and takes them over to Ireland in order that he may bring them back under Fergus mac Erc forty-three years afterwards.

Fordun thus harmonizes that form of the Chronicle which places an early settlement of the Scots before the Christian era with the other forms of it which retain the foundation of the Dalriadic colony at its true period in the sixth century. He solves the difficulty by supposing two colonies, one at an early date under Fergus son of Ferchard which, after lasting till the fourth century, under a series of kings with two exceptions unnamed, comes to an end; and a second under Fergus son of Erc, followed by the line of Dalriadic kings contained in the Chronicles in both forms. The attempt, however, to connect the termination of the first colony with Maximus the Roman emperor obliges him to antedate the second colony about one hundred years, otherwise he would have left too long an interval between the two.

In the history of the second colony, he follows closely the order of the kings as given in these chronicles, interpolating in the early part a few fictitious kings in order to obtain the additional hundred years he had added to its commencement; much in the same manner, and with as easy a conscience, as the compiler of the first of these chronicles, that which appeared at the accession of William the Lion, had interpolated five kings towards the end of the list, in order to obtain the additional time necessary to bring Alpin down, so as to synchronize with the father of Kenneth. Fordun thus suppresses, as the chronicles had done before him, the period of time, extending to a century, between Alpin and Kenneth, in which the Pictish king Angus mac Fergus had conquered Dalriada, and subjected it to his kingdom; but it is remarkable enough that Fordun transfers some of the events which took place in this period to the fictitious interval which he has placed in the fourth century, between the first colony and the second. We there find also a Hurgust, son of Forgso or Fergus, who founds St. Andrews; but feeling the incongruity of taking back a war between him and an Athelstane king of the Saxons to so early a period, he divides the narrative given in the Legend of St. Andrew into two, and relegates the latter part to the ninth century.

Fordun has also constructed the personal history of Kenneth mac Alpin, and the supposed revolution which placed him on the Pictish throne, with great skill, by weaving together the very valuable narrative in the Chronicle of Huntingdon with the more questionable statements in the other chronicles, so as to make a consistent narrative of a conquest of the Picts by the Scots of Dalriada, under their leader Kenneth, the last of a long line of kings of the Scots, and the first Scottish monarch of the whole kingdom, formed by the junction of the territories of the Scots, which he had inherited, with those of the Picts, whom he had subdued and destroyed.

It is thus only the early part of Fordun's work which is tainted with this artificially constructed history. With the reign of Kenneth mac Alpin the historical period of Scottish history, in the true sense of the term, may be said to commence, and he had little motive to pervert the history of his successors, while that part of his history which is based upon the work he originally compiled, extending from the accession of Malcolm Canmore to the year 1363 when he put it together, and contained in his fifth book, and in the annals which follow, is one of great value and authority, and must form the basis of any continuous narrative of the history of that period.

With these few remarks, sufficient to indicate the character of the later chronicles and other historical documents, and of the first detailed and systematic history of Scotland, founded upon them, we shall now leave John of Fordun to tell his own tale.

WILLIAM F. SKENE.

20 INVERLEITH ROW,
EDINBURGH, *November* 27, 1872.

JOHN OF FORDUN'S

CHRONICLE OF

THE SCOTTISH NATION.

JOHN OF FORDUN'S

CHRONICLE OF THE SCOTTISH NATION

BOOK I.

CHAPTER I.

Antiquity of the Origin of the Scots—Their Exploits—The Material World: that is to say, the Earth, and its Four Principal Points, East, West, South, and North.

WE gather from various writings of old chroniclers that the nation of the Scots, one of most ancient descent, sprang from the Greeks, and from the Egyptians who survived the overthrow of their fellow-countrymen and king in the Red Sea. I, therefore, think it fitting to describe the local position of the countries of Greece and Egypt, where they were fostered, as well as of the other places they traversed, and of the site of their modern habitation, so that the reader may more clearly understand in what part of the globe these are situated, and their geographical bearings. Almighty God, the Creator and Euler of all things, willed in his Creation, according to the philosophers, that the World should be round, and in its midmost region He placed the Earth, the mother, nurse, and abode of all animate, material, and rational things; separated, as a central point, from all parts of the heavens by an equal interval. But the material world, that is, the Earth, is girt in on all sides by the waters of the boundless sea, called the Ocean, and is encroached upon, broken into, and indented, by variously shaped arms of this sea; with the moisture of which it is soaked through hidden passages, lest it should be altogether reduced to dust through excessive drought. The World, moreover, has four principal points or parallels equidistant from each other—that is, East, West, South, and North; and from these are said to proceed the four Cardinal Winds, with their eight Collateral Winds.

CHAPTER II.

The Four Cardinal Winds, with their Eight Collaterals; and the Summit of the Material World, the Terrestrial Paradise in the East.

THE first point, or cardinal wind, is in the east, where the sun rises, under the vernal equinox, and is called Subsolanus. This wind has two collaterals, Vulturnus towards the north, and Eurus towards the south. The second point, or cardinal wind, is situated in the west, where the sun sets, under the autumnal equinox, and is called Favonius; which also has two collaterals, namely, Circius towards the north, and Zephyrus towards the south. The third point, or cardinal wind, is Auster, and is situated under the antarctic pole of the summer solstice, where the sun rises highest at mid-day; it has two collateral winds, viz., Nothus towards the east, and Africus towards the west. The fourth point, or cardinal wind, is Boreas, under the arctic pole of the winter solstice, where the sun descends lowest at midnight; and this has likewise two collateral winds, Aquilo towards the west, and Chorus towards the east. The Earth, or material world, begins in the east, under the cardinal point Subsolanus, its summit being the terrestrial paradise, a most delicious place of flowers and trees, redolent with all sweetness. It is uninhabitable for men, however, on account of Adam's sin; but it is accessible to good spirits and glorified souls. This spot rises so high above the level of the earth, that the universal Deluge, which far overtopped the peaks of the mountains, could not reach it.

CHAPTER III.

The Three unequally divided Portions of the World, and the Inland Sea.

The world, according to *Isidore*, is divided into three unequal parts: Asia, Africa, and Europe. It is thus said to be divided, because a very large gulf of the ocean, flowing in from the westward, or Favonius, and, dividing its north-western from its southern shore, reaches nearly to the middle of the world, and, forming there an angular gulf, directs its course straight to the ocean northwards, towards the arctic pole, between Asia and the eastern boundary of Europe. Asia, which is believed to be one half of the globe, is named after a certain woman, who, according to *Isidore*, formerly ruled the East; stretching from the north, through the east, as far as the south, it is bounded on the east by the rising sun, on the south by the ocean, on the west by the inland sea, and on the north, nearly under the pole, by the lake Mæotis. Europe is said to be named after Europa, daughter of Agenor, king of Lybia, whom Jupiter carried off from Africa and brought to Crete; and he named one of the three portions of the earth after her. It begins at this same lake Mæotis, and stretches through the northern ocean as far as the west and the sea of Gades, while its eastern and southern portion, starting from Pontus, is washed along its whole extent by the Inland Sea, and is terminated at these same straits of Gades. Africa, the remaining third part of the world, is said to be opposite Asia and Europe, although it is smaller in extent, according to Isidore, than either, but richer and of more admirable quality, in proportion to its size. It is so called from Afer, one of the descendants of Abraham and Keturah, who is said to have led an army against Lybia, and, after having vanquished his enemies, to have settled there, and called his descendants Africans. It commences at the confines of Asia, in the south, and stretches through the southern ocean as far as Mount Atlas. It is bounded on the north by the Inland Sea, and terminates also at the straits of Gades. And thus Asia by itself occupies one half of the world, while Europe and Africa occupy the other, being cut in two by a great sea which flows in between them from the ocean.

CHAPTER IV.

Division of the Three Portions of the World among the Three Sons of Noah: Shem, Ham, and Japhet—Position of certain Regions of Asia and Africa.

THE sons of Noah shared the world among themselves, after the Flood, in the following manner:—Shem, with his descendants, took possession of Asia, Japhet, of Europe, and Ham, of Africa. From them was the whole human race distributed in nations and kingdoms over the earth. From Shem sprang the Jews, and the Saracens, or rather Hagarenes; from Japhet, the Gentiles, the greater part of whom are the

Christians; and from Ham, the Canaanites, who, by the curse of Noah, are doomed to expulsion from the place of their habitation. These three portions of the world contain many different regions, the whole of which I by no means propose to describe, but those only which seem necessary to the work I have undertaken, or which, on account of the reverence due to their patron saints, deserve especial honour; as, for instance, the holy city of Jerusalem, and the city of Rome. The first region of Asia, on the east, is, according to Vincentius, the Terrestrial Paradise; but it is unknown to us. Then comes India, under the rising sun. In the extreme north is Upper Scythia; and, in the extreme south, Egypt, whence, as old chroniclers have written, the Scots partly had their origin. Between these countries, that is, Egypt and Scythia, is situated the district of Jerusalem, where is the site of the holy city Jerusalem, in which the Son of God, God and Man, Jesus Christ, Our Lord, suffered for the salvation of all men. The first region of Africa, on the east, is Cyrenian Lybia, adjoining the borders of Egypt. On the south is Upper Ethiopia, and the last land towards the west is Lower Ethiopia. For Ethiopia is threefold: its western portion being mountainous, beginning at Mount Atlas; its middle portion, sandy, and its eastern, a desert. By the Inland Sea, on the northern coast, is the country of Zeugis, where Carthage formerly stood, and this is Africa proper.

CHAPTER V.

Position of certain Regions of Europe: namely, Scythia, Greece, and the City of Rome.

I MUST NOW endeavour to describe certain regions of Europe, of which *Ptolemy*, in his *Tripertita* Nova, speaks as follows:—Europe comprises, next to Asia, most of the habitable earth; nay, in proportion to its size, it is more populous than any other part of the earth. The first region of Europe is Lower Scythia, which begins from the Riphæan mountains and the lake Mæotis, at the arctic pole, between the Danube and the northern ocean, and extends as far as Germany. On the east of it is the Inland Sea, which is there called the Baltic, from Balth, the place where it flows into the land from the ocean. From this region, according to some, came forth the Plots of Albion. Next, on the shores of the Inland Sea, and in the sea towards the south, are the seven provinces of the Greeks, which were formerly kingdoms, namely, Dalmatia, Epirus, Hellas, which is also called Attica (where stood Athens, the mother of the liberal arts, and the nurse of the philosophers), Thessaly, Macedon, Achaia, and Crete, in the sea, which was formerly also called Centopolis; and the islands of the Cyclades, fifty-three in number, the metropolis of which is Rhodes. On the Achaian gulf, too, is Arcadia, which is also called Sicyonia. From one of these countries went forth some turbulent Greeks, and being intermixed with the Egyptians, formed one people, that of the Scots, as will appear in the sequel. On the same sea, likewise, towards the south, on an angular gulf which trends back northwards, are situated the chief Roman countries, adjoining the sea on either side. These are Italy, Tuscia, Etruria, Calabria, and Apulia. Nearly in the centre of these countries is situated the renowned city of Rome, to which the greater part of the world was formerly subject; and in which suffered, and were buried, the glorious Apostles Peter, Christ's Vicar over the Faithful, and Paul, the teacher of the Gentiles, with numberless other holy martyrs, confessors, and virgins.

CHAPTER VI.

The same continued—The greater Islands of Europe: Albion and Hibernia.

THE farthest country of Europe, on the west, is Hispania (Spain), or rather, the islands of Gades, which are in the ocean, 120 paces distant from the mainland of Spain; on these formerly Hercules fixed his pillars. There are two Hispanias, a nearer and a further, comprising the various regions of Legio, Castellum, Navarre, Arragon, and Portugal, and the provinces of Galicia, the natives of which, according to *Isidore*, claim a Greek origin; and Celtiberia on the river Hyber. The Scots settled in this country first, for some time. Europe comprises also many large islands, the largest of which, Albion, lies in the ocean, to the north-west. Its southern, and larger, part was formerly inhabited by the

Britons, and was called Britannia, but is now known as England. Its northern portion, in like manner, being inhabited by Scots from an early period, was called Scotia; and it is now, by the help of God, the chief kingdom of the island. The Scots possess numerous islands, a hundred or more, which have belonged to them from ancient times, and beyond the shores thereof no land is found to the north-west, except, it is said, an island called Thule, at a distance of seven days' sail from them. A day's sail beyond this, the sea is said to be sluggish and thick. Beyond Britain, also, in the ocean between it and the west, is situated the island of Ireland, where the Scots first fixed their abode. Let this topographical description suffice for the present, as a preface to my task; and let us pass over to the Ages of the world which elapsed before our Lord's Incarnation, and which must be introduced into this work.

CHAPTER VII.

The Number of Years from the Beginning of the World to the Birth of Christy divided into Five Ages.

THE old fathers divide the years elapsed from the beginning of the world to the Birth of Christ into five Ages, varying, however, in their estimate of the duration of each. In the Ages, therefore, which will be hereafter recorded in this Chronicle, the computation of years of the old translation, which is held by Holy Church, will be observed, until He who is the Source and Beginning of all goodness. Himself without a beginning, and the end thereof. Himself without end, through whom this work has been begun, shall have brought it to an end. Now the first of these Ages, from the beginning of the world to the Flood, comprises 2242 years; the second, from the Flood to the birth of Abraham, 942; the third, from Abraham to the reign of David, 940; the fourth, from the reign of David to the Babylonish captivity, 485; the fifth, from the last removal of the children of Israel into Babylon to the Incarnation of our Lord, 590. Thus, from the beginning of the world to the Incarnation, the sum-total is 5199. Whence some one has put it metrically:

"The years of man, from our first father, shall appear.
To Christ, two hundred and five thousand, less one year."

CHAPTER VIII.

The First Occasion of the Origin of the Scots; and their First King Gaythelos.

IN the third Age, in the days of Moses, a certain king of one of the countries of Greece, Neolus, or Heolaus, by name, had a son, beautiful in countenance, but wayward in spirit, called Gaythelos, to whom he allowed no authority in the kingdom. Roused to anger, and backed by a numerous band of youths, Gaythelos disturbed his father's kingdom by many cruel misdeeds, and angered his father and his people by his insolence. He was, therefore, driven out by force from his native land, and sailed to Egypt, where, being distinguished by courage and daring, and being of royal birth, he married Scota, the daughter of Pharaoh. Another *Chronicle* says that, in those days, all Egypt was overrun by the Ethiopians, who, according to their usual custom, laid waste the country from the mountains to the town of Memphis and the Great Sea; so that Gaythelos, the son of Neolus, one of Pharaoh's allies, was sent to his assistance with a large army; and the king gave him his only daughter in marriage, to seal the compact. It is written in *The Legend of St. Brandan* that a certain warrior, to whom the chiefs of his nation had assigned the sovereignty, reigned over Athens in Greece; and that his son, Gaythelos by name, married the daughter of Pharaoh, king of Egypt, Scota, from whom also the Scots derived their name. And he, that is, Gaythelos, who was conspicuous for strength and boldness, exasperated his father, and every one, by his waywardness, and, departing on account of the failure of his cause, rather than of his own accord, retired into Egypt, supported by a spirited band of youths. Another *Chronicle*, again, says:—But a certain Gaythelos, the grandson, it is said, of Nembricht, being unwilling to reign by right of succession, or because the people, assisted by the neighbouring nations, would not submit to his tyranny, left his country followed by a great crowd of young men, with an army. At length, harassed by many wars in various places, and compelled by want of provisions, he came to Egypt, and, having joined King Pharaoh, he strove, together with the Egyptians, to keep the children of Israel in perpetual bondage; and he finally married

Pharaoh's only daughter, Scota, with the view of succeeding his father-in-law on the throne of Egypt.

CHAPTER IX.

The successive Kings of Egypt, down to Pharaoh, Scota's Father, who was drowned in the Red Sea.

THE kingdom of Egypt, originally called Etherea, is, according to *Vincentius*, the oldest of all kingdoms but that of the Scythians; for we read that its rise, as well as that of Scythia, took place in the time of Ragau, Abraham's great-great-grandfather. Thence there has long been a dispute between the Scythians and Egyptians, as to the antiquity of their respective races. The Scythians, however, seem to be the more ancient. This kingdom of Egypt lasted from the time of Ragau to Octavianus Augustus, not, however, continuously, but with a few interruptions. Some have it that the first who reigned over this kingdom was Pharaoh, who, as we read, built the city of Pharus, and after whom the subsequent kings were called Pharaohs. After him reigned Zoes. At the time of the birth of Abraham, the kingdom of Egypt was ruled by powers which were called dynasties. In the seventeenth dynasty, then, reigned the Pharaohs, one of whom, by Commestor called Nephres, promoted Joseph. This Pharaoh, Nephres, died in the thirteenth year of the administration of Joseph. He was succeeded by—

The Pharaoh Amosis, who reigned twenty-five years.

The Pharaoh Chebron, thirteen years.

The Pharaoh Amenophis, twenty-one years.

The Pharaoh Mephres, twenty-two years, in whose ninth year died Joseph.

The Pharaoh Mispharmotosis, twenty-six years.

The Pharaoh Authomosis, nine years.

Ammenophis, thirty-one years, whose daughter Theremuch, in the twenty-sixth year of his reign, took the infant Moses out of the water, and adopted him as her son; after which this Ammenophis reigned five years.

The Pharaoh Horns, thirty-eight years.

The Pharaoh Accentris, twelve years.

The Pharaoh Athorisis, seven years.

The Pharaoh Chencres, eighteen years. He was swallowed up in the Red Sea, while pursuing the children of Israel. His daughter was Scota, wife of Gaythelos before mentioned.

CHAPTER X.

The Period at which the Scots had their Origin, and from whom; and their Outlawry from Egypt.

THREE thousand six hundred and eighty-nine years after the beginning of the world, in the five hundred and fifth year of the third Age, three hundred and thirty years before the taking of Troy, seven hundred and sixty years before the building of Rome, in the year 1510 B.C. (or as others put it—

"One thousand and five hundred years, and seventy, less one,

Before the birth, as I have found, of God's incarnate Son,

Was Pharaoh, following the Jews, in the Red Sea undone")

the above-mentioned Pharaoh was swallowed up, with his army of 600 chariots, 50,000 horse, and 200,000 foot; while the survivors, who remained at home, hoping to be released from the tax of grain formerly introduced by Joseph in the time of famine, suddenly drove clean out of the kingdom, with his followers, lest he should usurp dominion over them, the king's son-in-law Gaythelos Glas, who had refused to pursue the inoffensive Hebrews. Thus, then, the assembled villagers cruelly expelled from their midst, by a servile insurrection, all the nobles of the Greeks, as well as those of the Egyptians, whom the greedy sea had not swallowed up. We read in another Chronicle:—After the army was gone, Gaythelos remained behind in the city of Heliopolis, by a plan arranged between him and King Pharaoh, in case he should have to succeed him in his kingdom. But the remainder of the Egyptian people, perceiving what befell their king, and, at the same time, being on their guard lest, once subject to the yoke of a foreign tyranny, they should not be able to shake it off again, gathered together their forces, and sent word to Gaythelos that, if he did not hasten, as much as possible, his departure from the kingdom, endless mischief would result to him and his without delay.

CHAPTER XI.
Gaythelos is elected King, and sets out for the West.

NOW Gaythelos, since he was the king's son-in-law, and the most noble of all, is set up as king over them by the expelled nobles of both nations. But, although attended by a numerous army, he cautiously came to the conclusion that he could not withstand the hosts of so great a multitude of furious enemies; and knowing, also, that the path of his return into Greece was closed to him, on account of the crimes he had formerly perpetrated there, he decided, to a certain extent, indeed, by the advice of his officers, that he either would seize from some other nation a kingdom and lands, and dwell there in continual warfare, or, by the favour of the gods, would only seek out some desert place to take possession of, for a settlement. This they all in concert swore to put into due execution, as far as they were able. Having, therefore, appointed Gaythelos their leader, the banished nobles, impelled to some extent by a youthful craving for adventure, soon made ready a good-sized fleet, laden with provisions in store and the other necessaries for an expedition, to go in quest of new lands to settle in, on the uttermost confines of the world, hitherto, as they imagined, unoccupied. Another *Chronicle* says:—Gaythelos, therefore, assembled his retainers, and, with his wife Scota, quitted Egypt; and as, on account of an old feud, he feared to retrace his steps to those parts whence he had come into Egypt, he bent his course westwards, where, he knew, the inhabitants against whom he would have to struggle with his men, unskilled as these were in the use of arms, were fewer and less warlike. Another *Chronicle* has the following account:—At length all was ready; and Gaythelos, with his wife and whole family, and the other leaders, trusting to the direction of their gods, embark, in boats, on board ships prepared for them; and when the sailors, with busy diligence, had weighed anchor, and cast off the warps, the sails are spread wide to the blasts of the winds. Then, sailing out into the inland channel, they made for the western tracts of the world, with prows cutting the waves of the sea between the southern limits of Europe and Africa.

CHAPTER XII.

Stay made by Gaythelos in Africa; and cause of his first repairing to Spain.

GAYTHELOS then, having wandered through many provinces, and made various halts in such spots as he found convenient, because he knew that the people he led, burdened as they were with wives and children, and much baggage, were distressed beyond measure, entered Africa by the river Ansaga, and rested in quiet, for some time, in a province of Numidia, though the dwellers in that country have no habitation where they can be sure of quiet. For the forty years, therefore, that the children of Israel dwelt in the desert, under Moses, Gaythelos himself, also, with his followers, wandered, now here, now there, through many lands; but at length, leaving Africa, he embarked in such ships as he could then get, and went over into Spain, near the islands of Gades. Another *Chronicle* tells us:—Thus, indeed, wandering hither and thither, they kept traversing, for a long time, many unknown parts of the sea; and, forasmuch as they were driven about by the violence of contrary winds, they were exposed to many dangers, and various risks, until, at length, just as they were being pinched by want of provisions, they unexpectedly arrive safely in some part of the coast of Spain. There the ships were laid up, made fast to moorings which had been laid down.

CHAPTER XIII.

Reason alleged by some for the Departure from Egypt of Gaythelos, and the rest who went away from the same cause.

IT is maintained, however, elsewhere, that many Egyptians as well as Greek foreigners, panic-stricken, not through fear of man only, as said above, but rather by dread of the gods, fled far from Egypt and their native country. Seeing the terrible plagues and wonders with which they had been afflicted, through Moses, they feared exceedingly, neither durst they remain there longer. For, as the regions of Sodom and Gomorrah, with their people, had, of old, been reduced to ashes, on account of their sins, so they expected that Egypt, with its inhabitants, would suddenly be overthrown. This is also evident from the *Historia Scholastica*, where it is said:—Many of the Egyptians, indeed, fearing that Egypt would be destroyed, went forth; of whom Cecrops, crossing over into Greece, built the town of Athen, which was afterwards called Athens. It is believed, also, that Dionysian Bacchus, in that season, going forth out of Egypt, built the city of Argos, in Greece, and gave to Greece the use of the vine. Whether, indeed, she was led, in this wise, of her own accord, by fear of the gods, or forcibly compelled by her enemies (but it was certainly in one or other of these two ways), it is taught that Scota, with her husband, followed by a large retinue, went forth in terror out of Egypt. *Grosseteste* says:—In the olden time there went out of Egypt Scota, the daughter of Pharaoh, with her husband, by name Gay el, and a very large company. For they had heard the evils which were to come upon the Egyptians, and thus through the commands or the answers of the gods, flying from plagues which were to come, they launched out into the sea, intrusting themselves to the governance of their gods. And they, cruising thus, for many days, through the seas, with wavering minds, at length, on account of the inclement weather, were glad to bring up on a certain coast.

CHAPTER XIV.
How Gaythelos obtained his first Settlement in Spain.

IN the meantime, being harassed by the long fatigues of the sea, they hastened to the land of Spain, for the sake of obtaining food and rest. But the natives hastily assemble from every side; and, brooking ill the arrival of the new-comers, propose to withstand them by force of arms. They are soon engaged in battle, and, after a desperate struggle, the natives are overcome and put to flight. The victory thus gained,

Gaythelos pursues the natives; and, having plundered part of the surrounding country, he returned to the shore, and pitched his tents, surrounded by a mound, on a certain hillock on rising ground, where he could more safely oppose the attacking columns of the enemy. He there afterwards, the natives having been subdued for a while, built by degrees a very strong town, by name Brigancia, in the middle of which he erected a tower of exceeding height, surrounded by a deep ditch, which is still to be seen. He thus passed all the days of his life there, harassed by the continual assaults of war, and perpetually entangled in the various chances of fortune. *The Legend of Saint Brandan* says:—But Gaythelos, driven out of Egypt, and thus sailing through the Mediterranean Sea, brings to in Spain; and, building, on the river Hyber, a tower, Brigancia by name, he usurped by force from the inhabitants a place to settle in.

CHAPTER XV.

On Account of the continual Slaughter of his People there, Gaythelos sends out Explorers to search for Lands out at Sea—Their Return when they had discovered a certain Island.

MEANWHILE, being there troubled by annoyances of many kinds, Gaythelos, whose whole attention was engrossed in the guardianship of his people, as became a useful and careful chief, foresaw that there was no other fate in store for him there than that he himself, with his tribe, should either be blotted out from off the face of the whole earth, or subjected to the yoke of a perpetual slavery, by the powerful tribes of Spain; for though it very often had happened that he had inflicted very great slaughter on his adversaries, he had never, however, gained even one victory without loss to his small tribe, which, far from increasing, he foresees will rather be diminished by daily and continual wasting; and thus, forecasting with watchful care, he pondered in his mind this continual slaughter, which even threatened dispersion, and what steps he should take in consequence; and at length, debating within himself, he perceived that he deserved to suffer the difficulties he had incurred; for, inasmuch as he had renounced the design he had originally formed, on consideration, namely, to seek out unoccupied lands, without bringing injury upon any one, and had besides insulted territory held from heaven by another people, he feared that he had thus given manifold offence to his own gods. Minded, therefore, to return to the plan he had before conceived in Egypt, he, with the advice of his council, calls the seamen together, and straightway directs them, being provided with arms, and boats provisioned with victuals, to explore the boundless ocean, in search of some desert land. They duly put off to the ships, set sail, and leave the coast of Spain; and, leaving behind them the places they knew, enter an unknown sea. After a most speedy passage, by the favour of the gods, they perceive, looming up afar off, an island washed by the sea on all sides; and having reached it, and put into the nearest harbour, they make the circuit of the island, to explore it. When they had examined it as thoroughly as they could, they row quickly back to Brigancia, bringing their King Gaythelos tidings of a certain most beautiful tract of land, discovered in the ocean.

CHAPTER XVI.
Same continued—He exhorts his Sons to go to that Island.

NOW Gaythelos, since he was unacceptable to the inhabitants, looking forth, one clear day, from Brigancia, and seeing land far out at sea, arms some active and warlike youths, and directs them to explore it in three boats; and they commit themselves to the high seas. They, at length, against a northerly wind, came in a body to the island, and, rowing round it to reconnoitre, attacked the inhabitants they found, and slew them. And, thus, having explored the land, and admired its goodliness, they return to Brigancia. But Gaythelos, overtaken by sudden death, exhorted his sons, and impressed upon them that they should do their best to get possession of the aforesaid land, charging them with both slothfulness and cowardice if they gave up so noble a kingdom, and one which they could penetrate into without war or danger. "Whatever happen to me," said he, "you will be able, they say, to make this island your habitation. When we, driven by want of food, arrived in this country, our gods gave us the victory over the opposing inhabitants; and justly so, had we, as soon as our ships had been provisioned, set sail and gone to this island, which the gods now offer us, or to one, like it, devoid of inhabitants. We therefore deserve to suffer these adversities of ours, because we have been nowise careful to obey the just wishes of the gods. In these parts, I think, the possession of property is difficult to acquire, unless it be purchased at too dear a price, namely, by slavish subjection, or by the death of us all—far be it from us! But it is both pleasanter, and more praiseworthy, for us to suffer death bravely in battle, than, barely dragging on an ignoble existence, to die daily, miserably fettered under the burden of an execrable subjection. For he, on whose neck, as on that of the ass, is imposed the yoke of continual slavery, is by no means worthy the name of man. Now, therefore, my sons, gratefully accept the gift the gods offer you, and go without delay to the island prepared for you, where you shall be able to live noble and free; for it is the highest nobleness of man, and the one delight, of all things most desired by every gentle heart, nay, the one gem which deserves to be preferred to all the jewels in the world, to endure the sway of no foreign ruler, but to submit voluntarily to a hereditary power of one's own nation."

CHAPTER XVII.

Hyber, the Son of Gaythelos, goes to the Island and takes Possession of it—It is afterwards called Hibernia after him,

HYBER, therefore, having heard his father's words, went, with his brother Hymec, to the foresaid island, with a fleet, and took it, not by force, but untenanted, as some would have it, by a single inhabitant; and, making it over, when taken, to his brother and his family, he returned to Spain. Some, indeed, relate that giants inhabited that island at first; and this, also, is Geoffroy of Monmouth's account in his Chronicle, when commemorating the deeds of Aurelius Ambrosius, in the seventh book, where he writes as follows: *Geoffroy*.—"Send for the Giants' Ring," said Merlin to Aurelius, "which is on Gallaraus, a mountain in Ireland," etc. At these words of his, Aurelius burst into laughter, saying, "How is it possible to convey the vast stones of that Ring from so distant a country, as if Britain lacked stones?" To this Merlin retorted: "Do not, oh king! indulge in idle laughter, for my words are not idle. Those stones are mystical, and of a medicinal virtue. The giants of old brought them away from the farthest coasts of Africa, and placed them in Ireland, while they inhabited that country. Their design was to make baths under them, when they should be taken with any illness." Thus spake he. *The Legend of St. Brandan* says:—Now one of the sons of Gaythelos, Hyber by name, a young man, but valiant for his years, being incited to war by his spirit, took up arms, and, having prepared such a fleet as he could, went to the foresaid island, and slew part of the few inhabitants he found, and part he subdued. He thus appropriated that whole land as a possession for himself and his brethren, calling it Scotia, from his mother's name. *Grosseteste* writes:— And because their princess herself, the most noble of all who were present, was called Scota, they called that part of the land which they reached first, that is, Oylister (Ulster), Scotia. But afterwards, says a *Legend*, from that same King Hyber, or rather from the Hyberian sea, they called it Hibernia. From *Chronicles* we learn:—Hyber, therefore, by his frequent voyages to the island, and back again as often through the sea, left an eternal designation, from his own name, to that same sea, as well as to the island. That is, just as the sea was thenceforth called the Hyberian sea, so also was the island, either from that very king, or from the sea, always, up to the present day, called Hibernia. Some writers, again, relate that the river Hyber, which, also, took its name from that very king, as we read, gave to the whole of Spain the name of Hyberia. But *Januensis* has written that the nearer Spain was at first called Hyberia, but the farther, Hesperia, either from the star Hesperus, which shines in that part of the heavens, or from the brother of Atlas, King Hesperus, who, driven out by his brother, occupied Italy, and called it Hesperia from his own name, or the name of the former region which he had left.

CHAPTER XVIII.

What the learned Isidore and the Venerable Bede have written about Hibernia.

Januensis, it is true, lays it down that Hibernia is derived from Hiems, because the winter is there peculiarly severe. All the historians, however, who make mention of this island, have written otherwise. *Bede* says:—Hibernia is the largest island of all, next to Britain, and is situated to the west of it. But as it is shorter than Britain towards the north, so, on the other hand, stretching out far beyond its confines to the south, it reaches as far as opposite the north of Spain, although a great sea lies between them. But this island much excels Britain, both in being broader and in the wholesomeness and serenity of its climate. For the snow rarely lies there more than three days; no one either cuts hay, in summer, for winter's provision, or builds stables for his beasts of burden. There no reptile is wont to be seen, no serpent can live. For, if serpents are brought thither from elsewhere, as soon as they begin to scent that air, they die. On the contrary, almost all the produce of the island is good against poison. It is an island rich in milk and honey, nor devoid of vineyards and birds, and it is renowned for the chase of deer and goats. Hibernia, writes Isidore, is an island of the ocean, in Europe, near the island of Britain, narrower in extent, but a more fertile region. This island stretches from south to north, its southern parts extending into the Hyberian, or Cantabrian sea. It is exceeding fruitful in cornfields, watered by springs and rivers, pleasant with meadows and woods, in metals plentiful, and yielding precious stones; for, there, is produced the Hexagon stone, that is, the Iris, which, being held up to the sun, forms a rainbow in the air. And as for wholesomeness of climate, Ireland is a very temperate country. For, there, the summer and winter are moderate. There is, there, no excess in cold or heat. It is a region where there are no snakes, few birds, and no bees; so that, if one should scatter amongst beehives pebbles, or dust, brought from thence, the swarms desert the combs. There are, there, no serpents, no frogs, no poisonous spiders; nay, the whole land is so adverse to poisonous things, that earth brought thence and sprinkled, destroys serpents and toads. Irish wool, also, and the skins of animals drive away poisonous things. There are, there, marvellous springs and lakes, whereof I will say nothing at present. But, in that land, there are many other wonderful things, whose properties I will not describe, as it would, I think, beget weariness in the reader.

CHAPTER XIX.

The Laws which Gaythelos first taught his People.

GAYTHELOS taught his people to observe the laws which King Phoroneus gave to the Greeks. *Commestor* tells us:—At the time when Jacob, by his mother's advice, fled to Laban, that is within the space of the fourteen years during which he served for his daughters, Phoroneus, son of Inachus and Niole, first gave Greece laws, appointed that causes should be pleaded before a judge, and established a distinct office of judge. He called the place of traffic *forum*, from his own name. His sister Isis, sailing to Egypt, gave certain forms of letters to the Egyptians, and after her death was there received into the number of the gods. But Phoroneus' son, king of the Argives, who was called Apis, when he had set his brother Ægialeus over Achaia, himself, with his people, sailed to Egypt, and, having died there, was deified by the Egyptians. At that time, the Egyptians had nearly the same laws and language as the Greeks, although they differ in many things, according to the different manners and customs of their respective countries and nations, as is found in various writings. Whence *Isidore* tells us, in the ninth book of the *Etymologia*, about the language of the Greeks: For the Greek language, which in the mode of pronunciation is clearer than the others, is divided into five parts. One, indeed, is mixed or common, which is used by all. The second is the Attic, which is called the Athenian, which all the authors or philosophers of Greece have used. The third, the Doric, which the Egyptians and Syrians used. The fourth is the Ionic. The fifth, the Æolic, which the Æolists used. And each of these languages has many species, or varieties. So in the Latin language, also, are comprised Ecclesiastical Latin, Italian, French, and

Spanish. But amongst these languages, again, a subdivision is made according to the mode of speaking, and the peculiar idioms, of provinces. Another *Chronicle* says: Gaythelos, indeed, having his memory well stocked with the laws which King Phoroneus had imposed on the Greeks, and which were, in his time, practised amongst the Egyptians, imbued therewith the people which followed him, and by the regulations of these laws he managed them wisely, and with moderation, as long as he lived; whence our Scots have boasted that they have had the same laws up to this day.

CHAPTER XX.

Hyber, the son of Gaythelos, succeeds to the Throne of the Scots dwelling in Spain after his Father's death.

To the government, however, of the Scots remaining in Spain after his father's death, succeeded Hyber. His son Nonael succeeded him; then, indeed, the nation set up as their king him on whom the government had devolved by right of succession. For about two hundred and forty years, says another *Chronicle*, they made a stay, with sorry sustenance and mean clothing, amongst the Hispani, who molested them continually. For desert and forest lands in the Pyrenean mountains were granted to them by the Hispani, so that they could scarcely live, sustaining life only with goats' milk and wild honey. In this misery, then, or worse, much time did that people live, dwelling in woods and hidden places, having nothing but what they were able to get by rapine and plunder (on account of which they were exceedingly detested by the nations around them on all sides); going barefoot, ill-fed, most meanly attired,—for they were nearly naked, but for furs, or hairy garments, which were their unshapely covering. And, in all these sufferings and straits, they could never be prevailed upon to be subject to, or to obey, a strange king; but always, on the contrary, humble and devoted under their own king, they elected to lead only this beastly life, in freedom. The Scots, also, says *Grosseteste*, have always had, nearly from the beginning, a distinct kingdom, and a king of their own.

CHAPTER XXI.

Mycelius, King of the Scots of Spain, and his Sons set out for Ireland.

At length, the supreme authority came to a man equally energetic and industrious, that is. King Mycelius Espayn, one of whose ancestors had won for himself and his tribes, with their liberty, a place of abode, free, indeed, but too small for tribes so strong in numbers. The people, truly, at this time, enjoyed the tranquillity of a long-desired peace, which they had obtained from all around, and for which they had long contended. Mycelius had three sons, named Hermonius, Pertholomus, and Hibertus. These then, when he had prepared a fleet, he sent with a numerous army to Ireland, knowing that they would find there a spacious, but nearly uninhabited, land to dwell in, though it had been settled, of old, by some small tribes of the same race. And when they had, a short time after, arrived there, and had easily taken possession of it, whether by force of arms, or with the consent of the inhabitants, Hermonius returned to Spain, to his father, while his brothers, Pertholomus and Hibertus, with their tribes, remained in the island. Another Chronicle writes as follows:—After the death of Gaythelos and Scota, and of their sons, the next of kin always succeeded to the chieftainship in his turn, as occasion arose, down to one whose proper name was Pertholomus. He, being as sagacious in spirit as active in understanding, began to lament that he and his people could not increase nor multiply in those parts, on account of the very grievous and frequent molestations of the hostile Hispani. They, therefore, determined to escape from so barren a soil, which, too, they had held in misery, among such as reputed them the vilest of men, and to pass over to some more roomy place of abode, if possible. Having, at length, eagerly taken counsel with the elders, they come to the Gallic sea with bag and baggage, and having prepared ships, or procured them wherever they could, they commit themselves to the dangers of the deep, seeking, wherever fortune might lead them, a sure and perpetual home, in freedom. Thus Pertholomus, with his family, set out for

Ireland with a fleet, and, having subdued the natives, obtained it as a perpetual possession for himself.

CHAPTER XXII.
Geoffroy of Monmouth's account of Bartholomus, Son of Mycelius.

AMONG the other incidents of the History of the Britons, however, this voyage of Pertholomus to conquer part of Ireland is found thus fabulously written in the third book; in which *Geoffroy* says:—Gurgunt Bartruc, king of the Britons, son of King Belinus, when he was returning home with a fleet, by the Orkney islands, after a victory obtained over the Dacians, who had denied him the wonted tribute, came across thirty ships full of men and women; and, when he had inquired the cause of their coming, their leader, Pertholomus by name, came up to him, and making obeisance to him, desired pardon and peace. For, he said, he had been driven out of a district of Spain, and was wandering about those seas; and he begged of him a small part of Britain to inhabit, that he might bring to an end his tedious wanderings at sea; for a year and a half had already elapsed since, driven out of his own country, he had sailed about the ocean with his companions. When, therefore, Gurgunt Bartruc had gathered that they had come out of Spain, and were called Vasclenses, and what their request was, he sent men with them to the island of Ireland, which was then wholly uninhabited, and assigned it to them. There they increased and multiplied, and they have held the island to the present day. Such is Geoffroy's account.

CHAPTER XXIII.
Discrepancies of Histories.

BUT this seems altogether incompatible, both in fact and in date, with the foregoing narrative, in which it is related that Ireland was inhabited, and not the reverse, before the arrival of Pertholomus; and that he did not get the island through the gift of a strange king, but that, on the contrary, being accepted as king, either by the power of his sword, or simply by the wish of the natives, he freely possessed those places, having been the second to form a colony there. Our histories, too, are far from making these kings contemporaries; for the reign of Pertholomus is related by the Chronicles to have begun in the third Age, about, or a little before, the days of Abdon, a judge of Israel, in whose sixth year the destruction of Troy is recorded to have occurred; while it is said that King Gurgunt reigned in the fifth Age, after the first capture of the city of Rome. For, as Geoffroy relates. King Belinus, father of King Gurgunt, together with his brother Brennius, took all the chieftains of Gaul prisoners, or forced them to lay down their arms, within one year, thus bringing the provinces into subjection. Then, having accomplished this, they went to Rome with a strong army, and took it by assault, after a siege of some days, in A.U.C. 364, according to Eutropius. Now, according to Eusebius, the year of this capture is thus calculated. In the seventeenth year of Artaxerxes II., king of the Persians, who in the Hebrew tongue is called Assuerus, in whose reign, also, the history of Hester was written, that is in the 198th year of the fifth Age, the Senones Gauls, led by Brennius, attacked Rome, and took it, except the Capitol, and they would have taken that also in the darkness of night, had not a goose prevented them. The ascent of Gauls, writes *Isidore*, was detected in the Capitol by the clamour of a goose. For no animal perceives, so readily as a goose, the scent of man. Whence *Ambrose* apostrophizes Rome as follows, in derision of the gods of the nations:—Oh, Rome I thou justly owest it to geese, that thou reignest; for thy gods slept, while geese kept watch. To them shouldst thou sacrifice, rather than to Jove. Let thy gods, therefore, yield the palm to geese; for they are conscious they were themselves defended by them from capture by the enemy. After the capture of Rome, then, says *Geoffroy*, King Belinus left his brother Brennius there, and returned to Britain, where he reigned some time. For the remainder of his life, he repaired dilapidated towns, and built new ones; and, on his death, he was succeeded by his son, Gurgunt Bartruc. It thus appears clearly that the latter reigned after the capture of the city.

CHAPTER XXIV.

About the Time of the First Capture of Rome, not Scots, but Picts, attempting a Settlement in Ireland, are sent by the Scots to Albion.

You must know, however, that in these days—that is, at the time of the capture of Rome—when, as is propounded by *Geoffroy*, that king lived, the Picts, journeying forth with their kindred from Pictavia, went across the British channel, in ships, to Ireland, that they might obtain from the Scots a residence there. The latter, by no means willing to admit them, sent them over to Albion, as will appear below. And of these, if I am not mistaken, may be understood what was written above, by Geoffroy, about the Scots, through the blunder of his informant. For these, I think, did the king, by chance meeting them wandering through the seas, advise that they should sail to the island. Whence the foolish babbling of the British people, glorying highly, perhaps, in this advice, would assert that Ireland had been given by their own king as a gift to this people (the Scots). Of this King Gurgunt, I find that a certain historian has written as follows:—One must admire, he says, the boldness of this modest and prudent King of the Britons, who had tribes of his own nation in such numbers at his command, that he undertook to subdue, or at least to harass, in perilous wars, very remote regions beyond the sea, regions which it was a terror, of old, even to the Romans to invade, and left desert and uninhabited the fertile island of Ireland, so renowned as it was (for it was said by historians much to excel Britain), and gave it up to be possessed by stranger tribes. Earety are kings known to offer kingdoms to kinsmen they know; more rarely to strangers they do not.

CHAPTER XXV.

Discrepancies of Histories excused.

CHAPTER XXVI.

Third Expedition of the Scots to Ireland, made by Smonbricht—His Genealogy.

IN process of time there came, besides, as the Chronicles teach, from the confines of the Hispani to the above-mentioned island, a third colonist of Scottish race, whose name was, in Scottish, Smonbricht, but in Latin, Simon Varius, or Lentiginosus, and, there, seizing the reins of government, greatly increased the population of the island with fresh inhabitants. At that time, they say, Manasses, son of Hezekiah, reigned in Judæa. He began to reign in the year 364 of the fourth Age, and reigned fifty-five years. He was a detestable idolater, and made the streets of Jerusalem crimson with the blood of the prophets. Among his other misdeeds, he even caused Isaiah, his maternal grandfather, according to the Hebrews, but certainly a kinsman of his, to be cast out of Jerusalem, and to be sawn through the middle, with a wood saw, beside the pool of Siloam. When he was in anguish, as they began to saw him through, Isaiah asked them to give him water to drink; and when they would not give him any, the Lord sent water from on high into his mouth, and he expired; nevertheless, the executioners desisted not from their sawing. From this sending down of water, the name Siloam was confirmed, which is, being interpreted, *sent*. In the time of Manasses, likewise reigned Numa Pompilius, the second of the Roman kings, who succeeded Romulus, and first gave laws to the Romans. Now the above-mentioned Simon was the son of King Fonduf, who at that time reigned over the remainder of the Scots who dwelt in Spain, and he was

    The son of Etheon,
    The son of Glachus,
    The son of Noethath Fail,
    The son of Elchata Olchaim,
    The son of Sirue,
    The son of Dein,
    The son of Demail,
    The son of Rothotha,
    The son of Ogmam,
    The son of Engus Olmucatha,
    The son of Frachach Labrain,
    The son of Emirnai,

The son of Smertha,
The son of Embatha,
The son of Thernay,
The son of Falegis,
The son of Etheor,
The son of Jair Olfatha,
The son of Hermonius,

The brother of Bartholomus and Hibert. These three were the sons of Mycelius Espayn, mentioned above. About this Smonbricht and his acquisition of this kingdom, we find somewhat in the *Legend of Saint Congal*, in the following words.

CHAPTER XXVII.

Smonbricht—The Throne of Stone, and the Prophecy concerning it.

THERE was a certain king of the Scots of Spain, who had several sons; one, however, whose name was Smonbret, although not the eldest, nor the heir, he yet loved above the rest. So his father sent him with an army to Ireland, and gave him a marble chair, sculptured in very antique workmanship by a careful artist, whereon were wont to sit the Scottish kings of Spain; whence it was diligently preserved in their territory, as the anchor of the national existence. Accordingly this same Smonbrec, accompanied by a great crowd of men, went over to the foresaid island, and having subdued it, reigned there many years. But that stone or chair he placed on the highest spot in the kingdom, which was called Themor (Tara), and it was thenceforth said to be the seat of royalty, and the most honoured spot in the kingdom; and the succeeding kings of his line were, for many ages, wont to sit there, when invested with the insignia of royalty. Gaythelos, some say, brought this chair and other regal ornaments to Spain with him from Egypt. Others, again, that Smonbret made fast his anchors, which he had let go, in the sea near the coast of Ireland; and when, pressed by contrary winds, he had striven hard, with all his might, to haul them in again from the billowy waves, he brought on board, with the anchors, a stone raised from the depths of the sea, carved out of marble into the shape of a chair. Accepting this stone, therefore, as a precious gift offered by the gods, and a sure presage of a future kingdom, and carried away by too great a joy, he gave worship unto his gods as devoutly as if they had altogether given him over a kingdom and a crown. He there accepted this occurrence as an omen from his gods that it would be so, because, as some writings assert, the soothsayers had bidden him hold as certain that he and his would reign wherever, in time to come, they may find, in any kingdom, or domain, a stone which had been carried off from them, against their will, by the might of their adversaries. Whence some one, predicting from their divination, has prophesied metrically as follows:—

> "Unless the fates are false, the Scots will reign.
> Where'er the fatal stone they find again."

And this, as common belief asserts to this day, proved true in their frequent early wanderings; for they themselves, when this stone had been carried off by their enemies, not only the princes of Spain, but also their own countrymen of Ireland, recovered it by force of arms, and took their territories, according to the prophecy noticed above. Afterwards, however, since this mixed people derived their origin from the Greeks and Egyptians, lest the memory of their first chiefs should, perchance, perish from amongst men, through the lengthened course of time, they applied their names as designations for themselves. The Greeks, that is to say, thenceforth called themselves Gaythelians, from the name of their chief Gaythelos; and the Egyptians, likewise, from Scota, called themselves Scots, which name alone afterwards, and at this day, both races in common are proud to bear. Whence it has been written:—

"The Scots from Scota take their name, all Scotia from those;
While Gaythelos, their leader's name, less common daily grows."

CHAPTER XXVIII.

The first King of the Scots inhabiting the Islands of Albion.

So this people increased and multiplied exceedingly on the earth. For it stretched out its branches from sea to sea, and its offshoots to the islands of Albion, tenanted by no inhabitants before, as it is related. But the first leader of those who inhabited them, Ethachius Rothay, great-grandson of the aforesaid Simon Brek, by the interpretation of his name, gave a name to the island of Rothisay; and it bore this name, indeed, for the space of no little time, until, when the faith of our Saviour had been diffused through all the ends of the earth, and the islands which are afar off. Saint Brandan constructed thereon a booth—in our idiom, *bothe*, that is, a shrine. Whence, thenceforth, and until our times, it has been held to have two names, for it is by the natives sometimes called Rothisay, *i.e.* the isle of Rothay, as also sometimes the isle of Bothe (Bute).

CHAPTER XXIX.

The Picts, arriving in Ireland to settle there, are driven off by the Scots, and sent to Albion.

AFTER the lapse of some little time, while the Scots lived in prosperous quiet and peace, a certain unknown people, afterwards called Picts, emerging from the confines of Aquitania, brought their ships to on their coast, and humbly requested the council of chiefs to let them dwell either by themselves, in a desert place, or together with them, all over the island. For they said that they had been lately driven out of their own country, though undeservedly, by the strong hand of their adversaries, and had, until now, been tossed on the sea, in the great and terrible dangers of tempests. They would not, however, allow them to remain among them in the same island. On the contrary, admitting them to a friendly peace, and taking them under their protection, they sent them across, with some they gave them as companions, to the northern coasts of Albion, hitherto a desert. When these began, accordingly, to inhabit the land about there, as they had with them no women of their nation, the Scots gave them their daughters to wife, under a compact of perpetual alliance, and a special agreement as to dowry. The arrival of the Picts in this island, however, is variously described by various authors, some of whom relate that the Picts took their origin from the tribes which King Humber brought with him from Scythia to Britain, when he was drowned in the river by Locrin, the son of Brutus, on account of the slaughter of his brother Albanact. For these tribes did not retire from the island when deprived of their king, but for a long time decided their causes by judges, in its extreme confines. Another *Chronicle* says: The Picts indeed, sprung from Scythia, accompanied the flight of Agenor, and, under his leadership, settled among the nation of the Aquitanians. To this assertion of ours bears witness the town Agenorensis, constructed by Agenor, and the country of the Pictavi, in which the Picts built the city of Pictavis, named after them. Now these are said to have afterwards assembled a fleet, and, having sailed to Albion, to have remained with the Scots to this day.

CHAPTER XXX.

Bede's Account of the Arrival of the Picts.

BUT in the Ecclesiastical History of the English Nation, which the Venerable Bede has compiled with his usual faithfulness, it is taught that the Picts did not, as Geoffroy relates, first come to Albion by reason of a grant from the Britons, but from the Scots, or through their advice only; and that they settled in the lands there, under the shelter of their protection. The following are his words. *Bede*:—When the Britons, beginning at the south, had got possession of the greatest part of the island, it happened that the nation of the Picts from Scythia, as is reported, putting to sea in a few long ships, were driven about by the blowing of the winds, and arrived in Ireland, beyond all the confines of Britain, and put in on the northern coasts thereof, where, finding the nation of the Scots, they asked, for themselves, also, a settlement in those parts, but could not obtain it. The Picts, then, having arrived in this island with a fleet, asked that a settlement and habitation should be granted to them also therein. The Scots answered that the island could not contain them both. "But we can," said they, "give you wholesome advice, what you may do. We know there is another island, not far from ours, to the eastward, which we often see at a distance, on clear days. If you will go thither, you can settle there, or, if any should oppose you, you shall have our assistance." The Picts, accordingly, sailed over to the island, and began to settle there throughout its northern parts: for the Britons occupied the southern. Now the Picts, having no wives, asked them of the Scots, who consented to give them on this condition only, that, when there should be any doubt, they should choose themselves a king rather from the female race of kings, than from the male. And this custom is well known to be preserved among the Picts even to this day. These are Bede's words.

CHAPTER XXXI.

Original Cause of the Arrival of the Scots in the Island of Albion.

Now the daughters and wives of the Scots, whom the Picts had taken to wife, when their husbands took them with them, one after another, to their own homes, were followed by their numberless kinsfolk—their fathers, that is, and mothers, their brothers, also, and sisters, their nieces and nephews. Many, however, of the rest followed, not only urged by affection for a child or a sister, but, rather, strongly allured by the grassy fertility of the land of Albion, whither they were bent, and its most ample pasturage for their flocks. So great a number, indeed, of the rabble of either sex as followed them, bringing their herds with them, and went forth in the interval of a little time, to remain with the Picts, is not recorded to have left their own native land, before, without a leader. Continual arrivals of proscribed malefactors, likewise, increased their numbers; because whoever feared to undergo the discipline of the law went to live secure with the Picts, and, having then sent for his children and wife, remained there in peace, and never went back afterwards. But the Picts, in the meanwhile, brooking ill the arrival of so great a multitude, for they became imbued with fear of them, caused it to be published by proclamation that no stranger should thenceforth obtain a place of abode anywhere within their boundaries; and even to those who contended that they remained with them, at the first, at their desire, they gave repeated opportunities of departing. For, when they were first entering the island, they gathered from the oracles of their gods, or, rather, demons, to whom they sacrificed before doing anything in any undertaking, that it would come to pass that, if they did not do their best to subdue the Scots, they would themselves be utterly annihilated by them; and thus, seeing their number amongst them increase, they began to fear more and more, and most harshly drove them forth from their territory. This, however, turned out true, not immediately afterwards, but a thousand years after, as the race and language of the Picts were entirely destroyed by the Scots at that time.

CHAPTER XXXII.
The Gods, or rather Demons, of the Gentiles.

CHAPTER XXXIII.
Same continued—Folly of the Gentiles therein.

CHAPTER XXXIV.
The First King of the Scots holding sway in Albion.

MOREOVER, while the Picts were afflicting the Scottish settlers with annoyances and difficulties of this kind, it was secretly announced to the council of chiefs of the Scottish nation in what misery they were living amongst the Picts. In the meantime, also, came forward certain men who acquainted them with the amenity of so broad and so fertile a region, in which were only fowls, wild beasts, and animals, although it might easily be brought under cultivation. When, therefore, a certain youth, noble, and of unbounded prowess, Fergus, son of Ferechad, or Farchardus, begotten of the race of the ancient kings, heard this, namely, that a leaderless tribe of his own nation was wandering through the vast solitudes of Albion, without a ruler, having been cast out by the Picts, his heart was kindled with wrath. He was, moreover, much allured by the praises he heard of that country, where, perhaps, he aimed at reigning; for those who had seen it boasted that it was exceedingly rich, in spite of the whole ground being covered, at that time, by very dense woods; whereof a sure token is manifest to us, even until now, in this wise: it happens that, in places, often the most level, in which the ground has, by chance, been dug up, or excavated, enormous subterranean roots and trunks of trees are found—yea, even where you would never have said, from any sign, that forests had grown before. Stimulated by these exhortations, therefore, and by the ambition of reigning, he assembled a great multitude of youths, and at once proceeded to Albion, where, establishing, in the western confines of the island, the Scottish settlers, sifted out from the midst of the Picts, together with those whom he had brought with him, he there constituted himself the first king over them.

CHAPTER XXXV.

The Northern Parts of Albion first possessed by the nations of the Picts and Scots.

DIVERS ancient histories of the nation teach that Scotia was first possessed by these two nations, and that their arrival therein, respectively, was without any, or with only a little, space of time intervening; whilst, however, some maintain that the Scots reigned for many years before the Picts. But even in this, even if they had arrived in the island simultaneously, do histories by no means so much disagree; for, while kings reigned over the Scots continuously from their origin, that is, during the course of two hundred years at least, the Picts had, not kings, but judges, even until the son of Clement, one of the judges, who was named Cruchne, seizing upon the insignia of royalty, by force, reigned over this nation. *Bartholomæus* even seems to wish to make out, in his fifteenth book, *De Proprietatibus Rerum*, that the Scots were conjoined with the Picts from the beginning, and that the two nations entered Gallia Narbonensis together. *Bartholomæus*:—Pictavia is a province of Gallia Narbonensis, which the Picts and Scots, of old, attacked with a fleet, and inhabited; and they finally left, for the future, from their ancient stock, a name to the country and nation. These, preparing a fleet, go from the coast of Britain round the shores of the ocean, and, at length, invade those of the Aquitanian gulf. Then, obtaining, not without risking the chances of war with the inhabitants, a footing in their country, they build the town of Pictavum, named from the Picts, and thenceforth call the adjacent country, Pictavia. No history that I have read, however, favours this view. The *Policraticon* says:— The bird Pica or Picta (magpie) conferred its name on the town of the Pictavi, typifying, both by its colour and by its voice, the levity of that nation. Some maintain that the people of the Picts were called Picti, or *Painted*, either from their beauty of form, or the elegant stature of their bodies, or from their particoloured garments; for they were, so to speak, *decorated* by a certain variety and novelty of bright clothing, beyond the rest of the surrounding nations; or that, perchance, other nations called them Picti in derision, by antiphrasis, because they were of most sorry appearance.

BOOK II.

CHAPTER I.

Situation, Length, and Breadth of this Island of Albion—Its Change of Name into Britannia and Scotia.

NOW let us briefly survey the whole course of the wanderings of the Scots, how they passed from nation to nation, from one kingdom to another, until, at length, they reached, in God's name, the land they now live in, the name of which was, of old, according to some writers, Albion. Let us speak of its various changes of name, as each fresh nation subdued it in turn, and of the position and boundaries of the countries it comprises. Albion is an island of the ocean, situated in Europe, between the north and west; stretching, along its length, from the south, first, northwards, it afterwards assumes a somewhat curved shape, inclining a little to the north-east. Its southern and middle parts have Ireland to the west of them, while its northern lie open to the boundless ocean, over against the arctic pole. It has, also, Iceland on the north, and Norway towards the northeast; on the east, Dacia; on the south-east, Germany, or Alemannia; more to the south, Holland and Flanders; on the south and south-west, Gaul and its dependencies; and Spain further westwards; and it lies hedged round by these countries, with a greater or less interval of ocean between. It is reported, also, to be eight hundred miles in length, or a little under; and in breadth across, in some of the broadest places, two hundred; in others, much narrower; for, nearly in the middle, it is only sixty-four miles from sea to sea; and it is there so much cut up by large rivers, that their head waters are nearly drawn together, but for some intricate passes over rough land, for the space of twenty-two miles, with groves, brushwood, and marshes interspersed. Whence it arises that, from the flowing down on either side of rivers so large, although they do not quite touch each other, some historians have written that it is, as it were, divided into two islands, as will appear more clearly from the following passages. This island of Albion, therefore, after the giants, having lost its first name, had, consequently, two names, according to these two divisions, that is, Britannia and Scotia. The first settlers, indeed, in its southern part were Britons, from whom, since that region was first inhabited by them, it got the designation of Britannia. Its northern part, likewise, had Picts and Scots for its first colonizers, and to it was afterwards given, in like manner, from the Scots, the name of Scotia.

CHAPTER II.

Divers passages of Geoffroy, affirming that Britannia is divided from Scotia.

NOW this original and ancient division of these countries is corroborated by the writings of many. *Geoffroy of Monmouth*, peculiarly the historian of the Britons, writes in his Chronicle as follows:—Leil, king of the Britons, enjoyed a prosperous reign, and built a town in the north of Britain, from his name called Karleil (Carlisle). Now that town of Karleil is certainly in the north of Britain, but by no means in the north of Albion, for it is situated nearly in the middle thereof. King Belinus, says he again, wishing to clear the law of all ambiguity, caused a road to be constructed of mortar and stones, which should cut the island in two, along its length. Now the truth of the matter is that this paved road, or ditch, does not extend farther than to the shore of the Scottish sea; for its track is visible until now, nor will it, in all time to come, be obliterated from the view of beholders. *Geoffroy* says further:— Severus, after several cruel engagements, drove into Scotia, beyond Albania, that part of the British nation which he could not subdue. Again:—The Saxons, however, for fear of Aurelius, betook themselves beyond the Humber, into Albania; for the vicinity of Scotia afforded them a safeguard, as that country used to watch for every opportunity of molesting the people of Britannia. Again, he says:—After these kings had been slain by Cadwallo, Oswald succeeded to the kingdom of Northumbria; but, as he became turbulent, Cadwallo drove him, like the rest, out into the outlying country, to the very wall which the

Emperor Severus had formerly built between Britannia and Scotia. Again, in the introduction to his book, commending Britain for its rivers, he says:—Further, Britannia is watered by rivers abounding with fish; for, besides the channel on the southern coast, which one sails over on the way to Gaul, it stretches out three noble rivers, the Thames, the Severn, and the Humber, like three arms, by which the commerce of various nations beyond the sea is imported into it. What then? Are there not any other famous rivers in Albion? But, in truth, if he had called the whole of Albion, Britannia, he would certainly not have passed over in silence the rivers of Scotia, which are much broader than those above mentioned, more full of fish, better, and more useful in every way; such as the river Forth, which is also called the Southern Firth, or Scottish Sea; the river Esk, which is called Scottiswath or Sulwath (Solway); as also the river Clyde, and the river Tay, and the river of the Northern or Crombathy (Cromarty) Firth, which, by reason of the excellence of its holding-ground, gets the name of Zikirsount from seamen. And, besides these, there are many others which are more useful to seamen than the above-mentioned rivers of Britain, from their shell-fish, and sea, and fresh-water, fish—and safer, too, as they are incomparable places of refuge from the perilous tempests of the ocean.

CHAPTER III.

Passages of William of Malmesbury and the Venerable Bede affirming the same thing.

William of Malmesbury likewise, a faithful historian of the English, and one, they say, above suspicion, would not allow that all Albion was called Britannia; nay, he states plainly, in his writings, that only the territory of the Britons, by itself, like an island distinct from Scotia, was Britannia, as it were the Britons' land, or the country which they ruled over and inhabited. He says:—The Saxons, involving, by their fleet, the tribes of the Orkneys, together with the Scots and Picts, in equal calamity, settled, at that time, and thereafter, in the northern part of the island, now called Northumbria. Therefore, Northumbria is the extreme portion of the island of Britain, towards the north. He says again:—Bede, a venerable man, whom it is easier to admire than worthily to extol, was born and educated in the most remote tract of Britannia, near Scotia (in fact, in the territory of the monastery at Wearmouth). That is, therefore, the most remote tract of Britannia. Saint Cuthbert, as the story goes in his History, appeared to King Alfred, while watching in bed, saying, "Henceforth love mercy and judgment, for, at my request, the empire of the whole of Britannia is yielded to thee;" and, not long after, he obtained the empire which the saint had foretold. Now *William*, again, describing what manner of empire the king afterwards obtained, says:—Alfred, by his courage, "had subdued the whole of England, save what the Danes possessed. *Bede* writes:—After that, they began to come, for many days, from the country of the Scots into Britannia, and to preach the Word of God to the Angles. Again:—Meanwhile Bishop Colman, who was from Scotia, left Britannia, and returned to Scotia. He then retired to a lonely island not far from Ireland. *Bede* says further:—But Saint Oswald was slain beside the wall wherewith the Romans fenced the whole of Britannia, from sea to sea, in order to keep off the attacks of the barbarians. The kingdom of Scotia, says *Tholomœus*, is a promontory, separated from Britannia by mountains and arms of the sea, and has manners and a language and mode of life quite distinct from those of the Angles; it is a region, indeed, in all things similar to Ireland. *Bartholomœus* tells us:— The progeny of the Angles possess the island of Britannia. He says again:—Britannia, which is now called Anglia, is an island over against Gaul, etc. Again:—It was called Britannia, from Brutus, but finally, from the Angles who took possession of it, it was called Anglia.

CHAPTER IV.

Passages from the same Writers affirming the reverse of this—History very often distorted and falsified by rival Transcribers.

BUT, although these and numberless other passages, found in the works of these writers, refer to Scotia as separated from Britannia, from the beginning, it may be acknowledged, on the other hand, that, in some of their writings, the whole of Albion is called Britannia. Thus Bede says:—Britannia is an island in the ocean, formerly called Albion, eight hundred miles long. Now this is, in fact, the length of the whole of Albion. He says again:—And then Britannia groaned, for many years, under the scourge of two very savage transmarine nations,—the Scots from the northwest, and the Picts from the north-east. We speak of these nations as transmarine, not because they were located out of Britannia, but because they were remote from the part of it possessed by the Britons. *Geoffroy* writes:—Britannia, the best of islands, situated in the western ocean, is eight hundred miles in length. *Geoffroy* says again:—Albanactus, son of Brutus, possessed the country which in our times is called Scotia; and he gave it, from his own name, the name of Albania. Now, do not these passages seem to differ entirely from the preceding? Verily, they do differ. But histories do not hold consistent language, either one way or the other; for, frequently, in the very same work, various passages are intermingled with others of contrary import, so that clauses incompatible with each other are sometimes inserted even in the same chapter. Although, however, discrepancies of this sort are very often found in chronicles, they should by no means be imputed to their skilful, nay, holy, authors, who have taken care to write their histories in strict conformity with truth, and with an unswerving regard for their original authorities; but, rather, to transcribers of a rival nation, by whose envy, lest the power of adjoining kingdoms should be strengthened, certain chronicles are entirely perverted, corrupted, violated, and, very often, indiscreetly so changed that the assertion of one chapter seems to annul the purport of the next. But, in truth, whatever variations of this sort, in the definition of the boundaries of Britannia, may be found in histories, through the fault of transcribers, the common opinion of modern time is that the whole of Albion was called Britannia, from Brutus, who only colonized its southern regions; just as of old one third of the world received an eternal name from Europa, Agenor's daughter, although it was over only a small part of it that she was the first, at that time, to exercise dominion.

CHAPTER V.

Brutus under whom the Britons first arrived in the Island of Albion.

WE have thus, in the foregoing pages, reduced to some sort of order the accounts of the entrance, first, of the Scots into the island; and it now remains for us to clear up briefly the various accounts given by historians of the arrival of the Britons therein. The Britons, then, first settled in the island of Albion under the leadership of a certain Brutus; but who this Brutus was, and of what race, historians are not all agreed. For some hold that Britain was named and peopled by a chieftain of Trojan race, Brutus, and his followers, as is related by Geoffroy and those who favour his version. Some, also, assert that the Britons were named after one Brutus, son of Isichyon, the eldest born of the leader Alanius. Now Alanius was of the race of Japhet, and was the first, with his three sons, Isichyon, Armenon, and Neguo, to traverse the Mediterranean Sea and arrive in Europe. From these, it is said, sprang four nations, the Latins, Franks, Alemanni, and Britons, Some again make out that the Britons were called, in Latin, *Britones*, or brutish men, so to speak, from their savage condition, as the Franks were so named from their ferocity; and Isidore favours this view. Others, on the other hand, disparaging the theories of the ancients, have derived the name of the Britons from the Roman consul Brutus. We, however, passing over other less known assertions, pin our faith upon the words of a page better known to us; and, following Geoffroy's chronicle in this particular, we may fitly begin our account of the Britons from that Brutus who was the son of Silvius, the son of Ascanius, the son of Æneas, the fugitive from Troy, whose father, Anchises, was the son of Troius, the son of Dardanus.

CHAPTER VI.

Division of the Three Kingdoms of the Britons among the Sons of Brutus.

NOW this Silvius, during his father's lifetime, begat Brutus, of a woman of noble birth, the niece of Queen Lavinia. Brutus was born in a.m. 4032, as appears from the following rhyme:—

"Four times a thousand years, and three times ten,
Came Brutus, after Adam, first of men,"

that is, in the year 848 of the third Age. He left" Italy a youth of fifteen years, and began to reign in the southern provinces of Albion at the age of thirty-five. Of his wife, the daughter of Pandrasus, king of the Greeks, he begat three sons, on whom were bestowed these names:— Locrinus, Albanactus, and Camber. He reigned twenty-four years, and then died, and was buried by his sons in the city of London. After his death his sons apportioned amongst themselves their father's realm, which, after him, or his Britons, was called Britannia; dividing it into three kingdoms, and prescribing boundaries to each, and a designation after their own names respectively. The kingdom of Locrinus, accordingly, was Locria, and, beginning from the southern shore of the island, that is, the Totonian shore, it was bounded on the north by the river Humber and the Trent. Then Cambria, the territory of his younger brother Camber, adjoined the kingdom of Locria, lying, not on its southern frontier, as some assert, nor yet on its northern, but on its western side; and, though divided from it by mountains and the estuary of the Severn, as it were side by side with it, over against Ireland. Likewise Albania, the kingdom of Albanactus, the third region of the country of the Britons, stretching from the aforesaid river Humber and the estuary of the Trent, is terminated by the northern bounds of Britannia, as above described; and such provinces of this kingdom of Albania as were between the Humber and the Scottish sea were the most northerly possessions of the Britons, who never gained a footing farther north. Having so far dealt with the entry of the Britons into this island, and the ambiguity as to the line of demarcation of the kingdoms it comprised, it only remains for us to explain what sort of country is Scotia,—the land of the Scots and the name which moderns have given to Albania,—and what is, or was long ago, its extent.

CHAPTER VII.
Scotia: its Nature and Extent, now and formerly.

SCOTIA is so named after the Scottish tribes by which it is inhabited. At first, it began from the Scottish firth on the south, and, later on, from the river Humber, where Albania also began. Afterwards, however, it commenced at the wall Thirlwal, which Severus had built to the river Tyne. But now it begins at the river Tweed, the northern boundary of England, and, stretching rather less than four hundred miles in length, in a north-westerly direction, is bounded by the Pentland Firth, where a fearfully dangerous whirlpool sucks in and belches back the waters every hour. It is a country strong by nature, and difficult and toilsome of access. In some parts, it towers into mountains; in others, it sinks down into plains. For lofty mountains stretch through the midst of it, from end to end, as do the tall Alps through Europe; and these mountains formerly separated the Scots from the Picts, and their kingdoms from each other. Impassable as they are on horseback, save in very few places, they can hardly be crossed even on foot, both on account of the snow always lying on them, except in summertime only; and by reason of the boulders torn off the beetling crags, and the deep hollows in their midst. Along the foot of these mountains are vast woods, full of stags, roe-deer, and other wild animals and beasts of various kinds; and these forests oftentimes afford a strong and safe protection to the cattle of the inhabitants against the depredations of their enemies; for the herds in those parts, they say, are accustomed, from use, whenever they hear the shouts of men or women, and if suddenly attacked by dogs, to flock hastily into the woods. Numberless springs also well up, and burst forth from the hills and the sloping ridges of the mountains, and, trickling down with sweetest sound, in crystal rivulets between flowery banks, flow together through the level vales, and give birth to many streams; and these again to large rivers, in which Scotia marvellously abounds, beyond any other country; and at their mouths, where they rejoin the sea, she has noble and secure harbours.

CHAPTER VIII.

Lowlands and Highlands of Scotia, and what is contained in them.

SCOTIA, also, has tracts of land bordering on the sea, pretty level and rich, with green meadows, and fertile and productive fields of corn and barley, and well adapted for growing beans, pease, and all other produce; destitute, however, of wine and oil, though by no means so of honey and wax. But in the upland districts, and along the highlands, the fields are less productive, except only in oats and barley. The country is, there, very hideous, interspersed with moors and marshy fields, muddy and dirty; it is, however, full of pasturage grass for cattle, and comely with verdure in the glens, along the water-courses. This region abounds in wool-bearing sheep, and in horses; and its soil is grassy, feeds cattle and wild beasts, is rich in milk and wool, and manifold in its wealth of fish, in sea, river, and lake. It is also noted for birds of many sorts. There noble falcons, of soaring flight and boundless courage, are to be found, and hawks of matchless daring. Marble of two or three colours, that is, black, variegated, and white, as well as alabaster, is also found there. It also produces a good deal of iron and lead, and nearly all metals. The land of the Scots, says *Erodotus*, in the fertility of its soil, in its pleasant groves, in the rivers and springs by which it is watered, in the number of its flocks of all kinds, and its horses, where its shore rejoices in inhabitants, is not inferior to the soil of even Britain itself. *Isidore* tells us:—Scotia, with respect to the wholesomeness of its air and climate, is a very mild country; there is little or no excessive heat in summer, or cold in winter;—and he has written of Scotia in nearly the same terms as of Hibernia. In Scotland, the longest days, at midsummer, are of eighteen hours, or more; and, in midwinter, the shortest are of not fully six; while in the island of Meroe, the capital of the Ethiopians, the longest day is of twelve hours; in Alexandria, in Egypt, of thirteen; and in Italy, of fifteen. In the island of Thule, again, the day lasts all through the six summer months, and the night, likewise, all through the six winter months.

CHAPTER IX.

The nations of Scotia, and their Languages, distinct—their different Manners and Customs.

THE manners and customs of the Scots vary with the diversity of their speech. For two languages are spoken amongst them, the Scottish and the Teutonic; the latter of which is the language of those who occupy the seaboard and plains, while the race of Scottish speech inhabits the highlands and outlying islands. The people of the coast are of domestic and civilized habits, trusty, patient, and urbane, decent in their attire, affable, and peaceful, devout in Divine worship, yet always prone to resist a wrong at the hand of their enemies. The highlanders and people of the islands, on the other hand, are a savage and untamed nation, rude and independent, given to rapine, ease-loving, of a docile and warm disposition, comely in person, but unsightly in dress, hostile to the English people and language, and, owing to diversity of speech, even to their own nation, and exceedingly cruel. They are, however, faithful and obedient to their king and country, and easily made to submit to law, if properly governed. *Solinus*, the historian, in describing the manners and customs of the Scottish nation of the olden time, says:—In its social observances, the Scottish nation was always rugged and warlike. For, when males were born to them, the fathers were wont to offer them their first food on the point of a sword, so that they should desire to die not otherwise than under arms, in battle for liberty; and when, afterwards, they are grown up, and able to fight, the victors, after drinking of the blood of the slain, besmear their faces with it. For they are a high-spirited race, of sparing diet, of a fierce mettle, of a wild and stern countenance, rugged in address, but affable and kind to their own people, given to sports and hunting, and to ease rather than toil. The Scottish nation, writes *Isidore*, is that, originally, which was once in Ireland, and resembles the Irish in all things—in language, manners, and character. For the Scots are a light-minded nation, fierce in spirit, savage towards their foes, who would almost as soon die as be enslaved, and account it sloth to die in bed, deeming it glorious and manly to slay, or be slain by, the foe in the field; a nation of sparing diet, sustaining hunger very long, and rarely indulging in food before sunset; contenting themselves, moreover, with meat, and food prepared from milk. And though they are, by nature, a people of, generally, rather graceful figure, and goodly face, yet their peculiar dress much disfigures them.

CHAPTER X.

The Islands of Scotia, apart from the Orkneys.

THERE are also many islands, both great and small, at the back of Scotia, between it and Ireland, separated from the Orkneys by a great intervening firth; and the names of some of these are as follows:—

Beginning first from the south, there is an island, formerly called Eubonia, now Man, whose prince is bound to furnish to his lord, the king of Scotland, ten piratical galleys, as often as shall be necessary; besides other regal services. Here is the episcopal see of Sodor.

Arran, where are two royal castles, Brethwyk (Brodick), and Lochransa.

Helantinlaysche (Lamlash, or Holy Island).

Rothesay, or Bute, where there is a fair and impregnable royal castle.

Great Cumbrae, a rich and large island.

Little Cumbrae, renowned for sport, but thinly inhabited.

Bladay (Pladda).

Inch Marnoch, where there is a monastic cell.

Aweryne (Sanday), where is the chapel of Saint Sannian, and a sanctuary for transgressors.

Rachryne (Rathlin), distant only six miles from Ireland.

Gya (Gigha).

Helant Macarmyk (Eileanmore), where is also a sanctuary.

A large island called Ile (Islay), where the Lord of the Isles has two mansions, and the castle of Dounowak.

Helant Texa, with a monastic cell.

Colonsay, with an abbey of canons-regular.

Dura (Jura), twenty-four miles long, with few inhabitants, but affording very good sport.

Scarba, fifteen miles long, where there is a chapel of the Blessed Virgin, at which many miracles are performed. Beside this island rushes down the mighty whirlpool of Corrievrekan.

Lunga.

Luing.

Shuna.

Great Seil.

Little Seil.

Helant Leneow (Eilean-na-naomh), that is, the Isle of Saints, where is a sanctuary.

Garveleane (Garveloch), near the great castle of Donquhonle, at a distance of six miles out at sea from the other islands.

Mull, where are two castles, Doundowarde (Dowart), and Dounarwyse (Aross).

Out at sea, at a distance of four miles from Mull, is Carneborg (Cairnaburgah), an exceeding strong castle.

Hycolumbkil, or Iona, where are two monasteries, one of monks and the other of nuns. There is also a sanctuary there.

Saint Kenneth's Island (Inchkenneth). His parish church is there.

Kerrera.

Lismore, where is the episcopal see of Argyll at Lismore.

Coll.

Tiree, where there is an exceeding strong tower, and great plenty of barley.

Helantmok (Muck), that is, the Isle of Swine.

Barra, where there is a chapel of the Holy Trinity.

Uist, thirty miles long, where whales and other sea-monsters abound. There also is the castle of Benwewyl (Benbecula).

Rum, a wooded and hilly island, with excellent sport, but few inhabitants.

Fuleay.

Assek.

Skye.

Lewis.

Hirth (St. Kilda), the best stronghold of all the islands.

Near this is an island twenty miles long, where wild sheep are said to exist, which can only be caught by hunters.

Tyreym (Eileantirim).

Thorset, where there is a very strong tower.

Stroma, near the whirlpool of the Orkneys.

Durenys, where, at midsummer, the sun is visible at night, not shining, indeed, but as it were piercing through the gloom.

These above-mentioned islands, as well as many others, lie scattered about in the sea, on the western confines of Scotia, between it and Ireland; and some of these, to the north-west, look out upon the boundless ocean; whence it is believed that the inhabited world is bounded by this region of Scotia.

CHAPTER XI.

The Orkneys.

THERE are also the Pomonian islands, called the Orkneys, situated at the northern extremity of Scotia, in the ocean between it and Norway; and these are separated from the aforesaid islands by a considerable expanse of sea, although it is maintained by some that the other islands, as well as these, are called Orkneys. Their name Orkneys, or Orcades, is derived from the Greek *Orce*, "to receive;" for, there, a vortex, or whirlpool, of the ocean continually sucks in and pours forth again the waters of the sea. Orcas, writes *Isidore*, is an island near the British sea, and the neighbouring islands have derived from it the name of Orcades. These are thirty-three in number, of which twenty are desert, and thirteen inhabited. But, in truth, if along with the Orkneys themselves we number the rest of the islands of Scotia, both inhabited and uninhabited, to wit, they will be found to be more than two hundred; while, in modern times, forty or more of the Orkneys are inhabited. In order, therefore, that these islands may be more clearly distinguished, the names of the Orkneys are given below:—

The main island, called Pomona, or Orcadia.

North Ronaldsha.	Lamholm (Lamau).
Great Papa (Westra).	Glowmisholm (Glims).
Little Papa (Stronsa).	Boroway (Burra).
Stronsa.	South Ronaldsha.
Sanda.	Flota.
Auskerry.	Swona.
Eda.	Switha.
Stromholme (Green Holm).	Wawys (South Walls).
Westra.	Hoy.
Fara.	Little Fara.
Egilsha.	Gremsa.
Rollisay (Rowsa).	Risa.
Weir.	Cava.
Enhallow.	Calf of Flota.
Gairsay.	Pentland Skerries.
Swynay (Swain Holm).	Sowliskery.
Scalpandisay (Shapinsha).	Brough of Birsa.
Heleneholm (Eller Holm).	Brough of Dernes.

Colbansay (Copinsha).   A third Papa.

CHAPTER XII.

Fergus, Son of Ferchard, the first King of the Scots, begins to Reign in Scotia—The Arms he bore.

FERGUS, having, as above recorded, come over to the island of Albion, was created first king of the Scots therein, and having given them laws and statutes, he extended his kingdom from the western ocean, and the islands, to Drumalban, and there established the boundary-line between the kingdoms: for the Picts inhabited the country on the eastern seaboard. The beginning of the reign of this king, and the arms he bore, have been thus commemorated:—

"The first of Scottish kings that Albion boasts,
Who oft to victory led the Scottish hosts,
Was Fergus, Ferchad's son, whose mighty shield
Bore a red lion on a yellow field.
Three hundred years and thirty was his reign
Before Christ came to break Sin's deadly chain."

At this time, that is, in the year 255 of the fifth Age, Alexander the Great succeeded his father Philip; and afterwards, in the sixth year of his reign, he slew Darius, king of the Persians, and took Babylon. At this time, likewise, amongst the Romans, Lucius Papirius was made Dictator; and so generally was he then held to be one of the most warlike soldiers of the city, says *Eutropius*, that, when Alexander was said to be crossing over into Italy, the Romans chose him, in preference to the rest, to withstand in battle the onset of Alexander. Then a good while afterwards, as we read in the *History of Saint Congall*, there came over from Ireland a certain king, Fergus by name, the son of Ferchad, bringing with him into Scotia the regal chair carved out of marble, and, in it, he was there crowned their first king by the Scots. All subsequent kings who succeeded to the throne followed his example, and duly assumed the crown in that same chair. This was the chair which Smonbrec first brought to Ireland, as has been already related.

Now after the death of Fergus and that of some other kings, his great-great-grandson Rether, called Reuda by Bede, succeeded to the throne of the Scots of Albion, and, during his reign, was unwearied in his exertions to extend the frontiers of the country; and he even managed to annex to his kingdom some parts of that of the Picts. But he was not content with the gift of so much good fortune smiling upon him, for, too much given to hankering after the extension of the frontiers of his kingdom, he also undertook the task of subjugating some of the northern border provinces of the territory of the Britons.

CHAPTER XIII.

King Rether, the Great-great-grandson of Fergus, called Reuda by Bede.

KING RETHER, then, assembling a great multitude of men from Ireland, as well as the Scots inhabiting the islands and the land of Albania, marched into the territory of the Britons with a strong force; and from his sojourn there, with his followers, for some little time, that part of the country where he pitched his tents derived, from his name, its present name of Retherdale, or, in English, Rethisdale, that is, the "dale," or "deal" (part) of Rether. Some of the British writers, however, relate that, while he was ravaging their country, he was slain in that valley, which got its name from that circumstance. We read therefore, that, under this king, a second incoming of Scots from Ireland into Albania took place, for nearly all those whom he had called thence to his assistance swore fealty to him of their own accord, and joined the Scots of Albania, never more to return. The Scots, says *Bede*, migrating from Ireland under their leader Reuterha, appropriated, either by fair means, or by force of arms, those settlements among the Picts, which they still possess. At any rate, while this king was on the throne, he restored peace between the Picts and his Scottish subjects, both of the islands and of the mainland, and skilfully concluded a fast treaty of fellowship between them; providing that they should thenceforth, by common consent, combine both defensively and offensively against the hostile aggression of any foreign nation, when the contingency should arise. And this treaty was, for a long time afterwards, strengthened by the ties of frequent intermarriage amongst them, and by many mutual offerings for the sake of perpetuating the kindliness of reciprocal affection between themselves, and between their descendants.

CHAPTER XIV.
Julius Cæsar sends an embassy to the Kings of the Scots and Picts, exhorting them to submit to the Romans.

ACCORDINGLY, the Scots and Picts were set at one by this reasonable peace, and reigned, for a long time subsequently, each content with the limits of their respective kingdoms, and neither inflicting any annoyance or injury on the other. The Britons, again, at that time, had monarchs who, far from harassing the nations around them, on all sides, by lawless hostilities, preserved, by their unvarying clemency and kindness, mutual harmony with all men. While, then, all the island nations in the north-west enjoyed such peaceful harmony. Gains Julius Cæsar, who, together with Lucius Bibulus, became Roman consul in A.U.C. 693, having made a bridge, crossed the Rhine, and struck terror throughout all Germany, and nearly the whole of Gaul lying between the Alps, the Rhone, the Rhine, and the sea; and after he had, in nine years, subdued that most ferocious nation of the Gauls, he turned his arms against the Britons, to whom, says *Eutropius*, the Romans had not theretofore been known, even by name. *Bede* writes:—Britannia, indeed, had never been visited by the Romans, and was unknown to them before the time of Gains Julius Cæsar; who, being consul with Lucius Bibulus, after having daunted or subdued the nations of the Germans and Gauls, compelled Cassibellaunus, the king of the Britons, to surrender. Cassibellaunus, says *Geoffroy*, promised Julius Cæsar a yearly tribute of three thousand pounds of silver. In A.U.C. 703, or B.C. 49, Cæsar, after having conquered the Britons, wishing to subject the kings of the north country to a similar yoke, first sent envoys on before, to expound the conditions he wished them to observe; and, traversing Britannia, he reached the Scottish sea, by which the Britains were, at that time, separated from the Scots, and intrenched himself for some time with a large army on the shore of that tide. In the meantime, he addressed to them, that is, to the kings of the Scots and Picts, by his ambassadors, two letters, one kindly, and the other harshly, worded; with instructions that, if they, as though perchance unmindful of their own welfare, should, with knitted brows, stubbornly reject the former, the ambassadors should present the other, breathing war and discord.

CHAPTER XV.
Answer these Kings returned to Julius by Letter.

NOW, when the kings had heard the ambassador, they were exceedingly indignant, and, having agreed as to the terms of their answer, they curtly wrote back on this wise:—"We, the kings of the Scots and Picts, to Julius, the Procurator of the Roman citizens, with one voice wish, Welfare and Peace—if indeed thou know the things of peace and welfare;"—and so forth, down to this sentence: "Think not, Cæsar, that thou canst entice us, like children, by the blandishments of cajolery like this—that thou canst succeed in leading us astray, to wander in that most loathsome vale of slavery, along a path impassable, crooked, rough, and horrible to every noble-hearted man; leaving the pleasant and noble road of freedom, our birthright, a road wherein our fathers, sustained by help from the gods, were ever wont to walk straight forwards, bending neither to the right hand, nor to the left; more especially as thine embassy came without those gifts which are well suited to those who are unsophisticated in blandishments, to wit, such toys as whirligigs and apples; for shallow fools yearn more strongly for a complimentary offering than for some one, prostrate on his knees, to freely offer them a kingdom. As for the threats which, from thy letter, one might suppose thou hadst just belched forth, we care little, if at all, for them, since we hope that they do not flow from the ordinance of the gods, but, doubtless, rather from the rash arrogance for which thou art notorious; inasmuch as thee, and those whose consul thou proclaimest thyself, we have never offended—nay, we call the world to witness that we do not even know you. Yet, innocent as we are, thou unjustly threatenest us with war forthwith, if we do not pursue these paths of homage to thee—if, casting down the choice garland of our old nobility, which the gods forbid! we kings, blasphemers, as it were, of our own race, and a scorn to all kings, do not, reversing the order of reason, become the servants of citizens, and hasten meanly to submit, to the dismal chain of slavery, heads hitherto accustomed to golden crowns and kingly dignity. As, therefore, what thou hast just addressed to us by thine embassy seems to jar with the laws of both gods and men, we doubt not that the gods will straightway arise to our help, and to thy confusion, if thy words should be followed by deeds. Now, we do not write back this as if, like braggarts, to defy thee to battle; but humbly, with all earnestness, entreating peace and, even more fervently, thy friendship, provided only the traditions of our forefathers are saved harmless. For, the freedom our ancestors have handed down to us, which we must cherish above gold and topaze, and which, in our judgment, far beyond all comparison transcends all worldly wealth, and is infinitely more precious than precious stones; which our high-souled forebears have from the beginning nobly, even to the death, preserved untainted for us, their sons—this freedom, we say, shall we likewise, as not having, in our unworthiness, degenerated from their nature, but as strenuously imitating their standard, preserve inviolate for our sons after our death, and transmit to them unspotted by a single jot of slavishness. Farewell," etc.

CHAPTER XVI.

Sudden Return of Julius in order to quell the repeated Rebellion of the Franks or Gauls—The Stone Landmark, the extreme Limit of the Roman Possessions to the North-West.

WHILE, therefore, Cæsar tarried all this time, with his army, on the southern shore of the Scottish sea, awaiting their answer, there came vessels from Gaul informing him that King Ambio, instigated by the advice of the Treveri, had, with the Eburnaces and Aduatici, surrounded the Roman legates and the entire legion which was advancing against him, and slain them in an ambuscade at Embronæ; and that the Gauls had again conspired and leagued themselves together for relentless warfare against the Romans. Accordingly, apprehending that these matters were of more importance than the subjugation of those kings, Cæsar determined to sail across to Gaul, but being uncertain as to his return, he hastily caused a small round chamber, like a pigeon-house, and of no use, apparently, but as a landmark, to be built, of large smooth stones, without mortar, not far from the mouth of the river Caron; and he wanted to build this little chamber as marking the extreme limit of the Roman possessions to the north-west, almost at the world's end, and as a lasting monument of his military renown; just as Hercules of old planted pillars in the island of Gades, at the western extremity of Europe, as a memorial of his eternal fame and long-drawn labours. Another version, that, especially, of common report, is that Julius Cæsar had this chamber carried about with him by the troops, with each stone separate, and built up again from day to day, wherever they halted, that he might rest therein more safely than in a tent; but that, when he was in a hurry to return to Gaul, he left it behind, with the intention of coming back without delay; and it was built up with one stone merely laid upon another, as is to be seen to this day. On the east side of this chamber, there is an entrance so large that an armed soldier on horseback can pass in, without touching the top of the doorway with the crested helmet on his head.

This Julius, says *Richard*, defeated the fierce nation of the Gauls in many battles, and finally, sailing over into Britannia, extended the Roman empire beyond the barrier of the ocean; all which he accomplished within ten years.

CHAPTER XVII.
Julius Cæsar, first Emperor—His Usurpation of the Sovereignty of Rome.

NOW as the rumours of this league of the Gauls grew more frequent, Cæsar, thinking a matter of so much importance should not be neglected, lest, by impunity, it should occasion the rebellion of others, deferred for the nonce attacking the aforesaid kings, intending to return in the following spring, and subdue them; so he hastily manned his vessels, and returned to Gaul, taking with him the conquered Britons, after they had given him hostages. And there, according to Orosius and Bede, on his return from Britannia, he was beset and harassed by sudden insurrections and wars on every side. When, therefore, says *Orosius*, Cæsar considered that the whole of Gaul was tranquillized, and durst not compass any disturbances, he sent the legions to Ireland; and he devastated, by dreadful massacres of the inhabitants, the territory of King Ambio, who had instigated so many wars against him. Then, when the rebellion of the Gauls had been stamped out, straightway there broke out among the Romans an execrable and lamentable civil war, which occupied the whole Roman world for four years, even until Cæsar's death, and by which the fortunes of the Roman people may be almost said to have been changed. Meanwhile Cæsar, being opposed by Marcellus, Jubulus, Pompey, and Cato in the earnest request he had sent, by messengers, that he should be reappointed consul without any contest, was ordered to disband his legions, and return to the city without delay. Stung by this insult, he at once, with his army, marched against his native land, from Arantinium, where he had massed his troops. Whereupon the consuls, all the Senate, and the entire nobility, alarmed at his approach, fled from the city into Greece; and, under the guidance of Pompey, the Senate prepared, in

Epirus, Macedonia, and Achaia, for war against Cæsar. Cæsar, however, entered the evacuated city, and, in order that he might place himself above the power of the consuls, he made himself Dictator—an office whose authority dated from the earliest times. Then, after having been occupied with civil war for four years, as has been already said, and having either conquered or slain nearly the whole Senate, together with Pompey and the rest of the nobility, he held the sovereignty of Rome, by himself, for five years; and, during that time, the noble Roman leaders Cato, Scipio, Petreius, and Juva miserably slew themselves in Africa, because they had been vanquished by Cæsar.

CHAPTER XVIII.

The Dates of the Roman Emperors must necessarily he given in this Chronicle—The Four Monarchies of the World.

CHAPTER XIX.

Death of Julius Cæsar—Signal Vengeance on his Betrayers, inspired from Heaven, as I believe.

CHAPTER XX.

Date of the Accession of the Emperor Octavianus, Nephew of Julius Cæsar—Vision revealed to him from Heaven.

CHAPTER XXI.

Conception and Birth of Our Lord Jesus Christ.

IN the first year of grace, which was the forty-second of Augustus Cæsar, the Blessed Virgin Mary, on the annunciation of an angel, became pregnant, in her virginity, of the Redeemer of the perishing world, in the sixth month after the conception of His forerunner; that is, on the 25th of March, when the days begin to lengthen. For Our Lord Jesus Christ, God and Man, who, being in the likeness of God, humbly took upon him, from her, the likeness of a servant, deigned to be born in Bethlehem Judah, the city of David, in the tenth month of that year; that humility might the more fitly be established just at that time when the penalty of pride was already an example to all throughout the world. While, therefore, the tumult of war was everywhere hushed, and everything was wrapped in unbroken silence, when night had run through half its course, the Word of God the Father was made flesh, and began to dwell amongst us, 5199 years after the beginning of the world, 2452 after the crossing of the Red Sea, 1206 after the taking of Troy. Seven hundred and fifty-two years had passed from the building of Rome, when Christ sanctified the world. The reign of the first king of the Scots in Scotia, was three hundred years and thirty before Christ. One hundred and fifty-eight years elapsed from the restoration of the kingdom of the Jews by Judas Macchabæus to the birth of Christ. *Orosius*, in his *Apologeticum* on this passage in the prayer of the prophet Habakkuk—"O Lord, revive thy work in the midst of the years," in describing this event, says:—Christ, the Son of God, in the power and glory of the Father, redeemed in the middle of time, and will judge in the end, those things which He had made in the beginning. And thus the world is divided into three periods, under different laws. For, in Adam began the period of the Law of Nature, which lasted down to Moses, in whom it was terminated; in Moses began the period of the Law of the Scripture, which continued down to Christ, in whom, also, it was terminated; in Christ, likewise, began the period of the Law of Grace, which shall last until the consummation of Time.

CHAPTER XXII.

Various Events after the Incarnation—Tiberius succeeds to the Throne.

CHAPTER XXIII.

Passion and Resurrection of Christ—Various Events.

CHAPTER XXIV.

Accession of Claudius Cæsar—He makes War on the Britons—Accession of Nero.

IN the fourth year of his reign, Claudius, because they refused to pay the tribute, made war on the Britons, whom none had approached since Julius Cæsar's time; and, having slain their king, Guyderius, he compelled his brother Arviragus, who had been raised to the throne in his stead, to surrender, and to pay the tribute. According to Geoffroy, he remained in Britannia the whole winter, and gave his daughter Gewyssa to Arviragus to wife; after which he returned to Rome. *Bede* tells us:—Claudius, without any fight or bloodshed, took the greater part of the island within a very few days, and returned to Rome on the sixth month after his departure. He also, then, with the assistance of the Britons, brought under the sway of Rome the Orkney Islands, which lie between Scotia and Norway. The Britons, however, were not all subdued at that time; for, after his departure, they broke out into a fresh rebellion, which was suppressed by Vespasian, Nero's successor on the throne, who was sent by this same Claudius to Britain, and who, also, then first reduced the Isle of Wight to subjection to Rome. Nero, then, after him succeeded to the throne. He resembled his uncle Caius Caligula. He began to reign in A.D. 56, and reigned thirteen years and eight months. This emperor disgraced and weakened the Roman empire; for he indulged in such extraordinary luxury and extravagance, that he would fish with golden nets, which he would draw up with cords of purple silk. He put to death a great part of the Senate; he was the enemy of every good man; he set the city of Rome on fire, that he might enjoy the sight of a spectacle such as Troy formerly presented when taken and burned. In the sixth year of this emperor, James, the brother of Our Lord, was stoned by the Jews; in the seventh, Mark, the Evangelist, and Mary Magdalene departed this life; and in the last year of his reign, he crucified Peter, and beheaded Paul.

In the self-same year he was adjudged a public enemy by the Senate, and when they sought him, to take him to punishment, he fled from the palace, and killed himself

CHAPTER XXV.

In the Twelfth Year of Claudius begins the War of the Britons against the Scots.

ABOUT this time, therefore, that is, the twelfth year of Claudius, is said to have first broken out the war of the Britons against the Picts and Scots, which lasted one hundred and fifty-four years, to the fifteenth year of Severus, unbroken by any peaceful settlement for any length of time. At any rate, it broke out in the following way: Vespasian was, with several legions, sent over to Britannia by the Emperor Claudius, and, after he had totally suppressed the rebellion of the Britons, and subjected them to a yearly payment of tribute, he returned to Rome, leaving part of his army behind him for the protection of the country, with instructions that it should, with the assistance of the Britons, reduce to servitude, or exterminate, the Irish nation, as well as the Scots and Picts. Ultimately, the Britons did accompany the Romans to Ireland; but, after various losses inflicted and suffered on either side, they made little, if any, way. Returning thence, they everywhere plunder and devastate, with fire and sword, the contiguous lands of the kingdom of the Scots and Picts, because these nations would not submit to the Romans. Meanwhile, as hostilities on the part of the Romans and Britons became more vigorous, these fierce nations, the Irish, the Picts, and the Scots, impelled, by a common need, to come together, bound themselves in a fast league against them, because a threefold cord is hard to break; and they began to lay Britain waste on every side. For the Irish, bursting forth from the westward, the Scots, from the northwest, and the Picts, from the north, parcelled out the country amongst them, and desolated it by deplorable massacres, sparing neither sex nor age, and devouring with fire or the edge of the sword everything they could lay hands upon. The Britons, again, on the other hand, did their best to inflict upon them, and not undeservedly, mischief as great; and, whatever they saw, besides earth and stones, they everywhere either consumed with fire or slew with the sword.

CHAPTER XXVI.

The savage Wars of the Scots and Picts against the Britons, and their first Conquest of the Region of Albania beyond the Scottish Firth.

THEREUPON there broke out between them a most cruel war, the like whereof had never been heard of before; nay, none of equal or greater cruelty, between two nations, has ever been recorded in history. The populace of both nations, whose part it is to give themselves up to agriculture only, and not to war and slaughter, was exposed, on all sides, to widespread war, pillage, and rapine; and, wretched men, the dregs of the people, who could neither help the citizens, at all, nor hurt their enemies, they were massacred without mercy. Accordingly, the remainder of the people, who were able in any way to escape the edge of the sword, being left defenceless, lurked stealthily in mountains, caves, and the recesses of the woods. Here they kept themselves alive in sorry plight, but in perfect contentment, with herb roots, the fruit, leaves, or bark of trees, or only with the milk of some ewe, if at least they happened to have one; whence, also, it came to pass that the citizens who were shut up within strong city walls, and the garrisons of the towns, on the inhabitants of the rural districts being thus cut down by the sword or driven to flight, were brought into such straits of hunger and starvation that, laying no store by their houses, their whole property, and all their furniture, and wishing to save themselves, their wives, and their children, from this calamity, they would take them away to lands far remote. Meanwhile, the enemy would surround the towns, thus very often empty, abandoned as they were by their garrisons, except a few foolish people entirely unskilled in defence; nor would their fierceness be long delayed, but, gathering their columns into one, they would scale the walls with ease, and, breaking them down, without delay, to their very foundations, and scattering the stones thereof down into the ditch, would at once level them with the ground. The strongest towns of the Britons bear witness to this desolation, namely, Agned, which, restored by Heth, king of the Scots, was afterwards called Hethinburgh (Edinburgh); Carlisle also, and Alneclud (Dumbarton), and a large number of towns which were by them razed to the very ground, and have not yet been restored by any one. *Eutropius* in his *Romanorum Historiæ*, in recalling this calamity, says:—Nero ventured on no military exploits, and nearly lost Britannia; for in his reign two or three noble towns were taken and demolished.

CHAPTER XXVII.

The Moravienses driven out by the Romans from their native soil of Moravia—They afterwards join the Picts.

As the folly and sloth of that most wicked emperor, Nero, were not unknown, some hope of recovering their ancient liberty sprang up among the nations. In his days, the Romans suffered innumerable evils. For the Parthians, after having subjected the eastern legions to their yoke, took Armenia, and reduced it to servitude. Britannia, also, was weakened, and nearly devastated, by the surrounding peoples. Moreover, the Germans and Pannonians wanted to engage in a fresh rebellion, but were vanquished by the Roman troops. The people of Moravia, likewise, a district of Pannonia beside the river Danube, were roused by sedition, as they were very often wont to be, and, led by Roderick, they rebelled, and treacherously surrounded and cut to pieces the entire legion which garrisoned that country. These Moravienses had, in truth, before this, been nearly destroyed in a bloody massacre by Augustus Cæsar's stepson Tiberius, before he was emperor. When, therefore, the provincial legions near heard of so wicked a deed, they determined either to punish the ringleaders of the Moravienses by the sword, or to exile them under sentence of perpetual banishment. Accordingly Roderick, panic-stricken, and unable to sustain the onset of the approaching legions, provisioned a fleet, and went an exile with his followers, down the river Danube to the sea; and after going about plundering, as a pirate, various bays in the northern ocean, he betook himself over to the Belgic sea. He there, for some time, made head against the Romans, sweeping the seas, and making constant attacks upon the seaports and ships of the Gauls and Britons; and, at length, wishing to rest, he by treaty submitted to the Picts, among whom he had frequently before made some stay. The Picts, much emboldened and strengthened by the multitude of these people there, exhorted the Scots, without ceasing, to go to war with the Britons; and it so came about. For, combining their hordes into one mass, they swoop into Britannia, without fear of being attacked by any foe; and, after scattering the population on all sides, and grievously devastating the country, they return homewards by forced marches; but, on their way back over the border, laden with spoil and plunder, they were met by Marius, a patrician of the Britons, at the head of the legions of the Roman nation; and, after most ruthless slaughter on both sides, he put them to flight; Roderick, the chief of the Moravienses, having first been slain in the battle. *Geoffroy*, in his writings, has laid it down that these Moravienses were Picts from Scythia; and rightly so, for all the regions from the Baltic Sea to the Danube were formerly called Lower Scythia; and it was from one of these that they came and were permanently united with the Picts. The Pictish people, then, after their defeat, retraced their steps to their homes, in great confusion; and they also gave the nation of the Moravienses, who were deprived of their leader—for their chief had fallen in the battle—their daughters to wife, and a spacious country to bring under cultivation. To this district, according to Geoffroy, they gave the name of their old country of Moravia, that is, to Katania (Caithness); and abode there with the Picts.

CHAPTER XXVIII.

Monument which Marius, leader of the Roman legions, caused to be erected in memory of the battle—Succession of Emperors.

HAVING gained this triumph, this Roman, Marius, wishing to transmit to posterity a perpetual memorial of so great a battle, caused to be erected, close to the scene of the victory, a certain monument in the likeness of a nearly square chamber, but of not much utility, built of hewn stones laid together, without the artificial connexion of mortar, and roofed in with concave cut stones of a workmanship entirely unused before.

CHAPTER XXIX.

Account given by Orosius and Augustine of the rise and fall of the Roman power—Succession of Emperors.

CHAPTER XXX.

Succession of various Emperors.

CHAPTER XXXI.

Alliance of Fulgentius, leader of the Britons in Albania, with the Scots and Picts.

IN the time of the Emperor Commodus, civil discord began to arise in Britannia, amongst the Britons, with reference to the payment of the tribute. For on the death, or, according to others, the want of compliance of their king Lucius, after whom their royal race ceased to reign in Britain, tribunes are appointed, instead of kings, by the Romans. Meanwhile, Fulgentius, the consul of the Britons of Albania, who was sprung from the stock of the ancient kings, asserted that he would on no account pay tribute to the Romans, and even ought not to do so, for that he had never promised either allegiance or submission to them. His fellow-countrymen, then, being on this account excited to envy, determined to force him to contribute by taking his lands; while he repaid them with usury, by not only retaking his own, but also committing depredations upon them, as one maddened against them. Thence, afterwards, followed sore rapine, sedition, and incendiarism, neither side sparing the other, but everywhere consuming everything and each other, as if the northern Britons were totally divided from the southern. The Scots and Picts, however, as they were wont, wasted and devastated, by frequent irruptions, the lands of Fulgentius in their neighbourhood, carrying off unnumbered spoils; so Fulgentius, not able to sustain the shock of wars on all sides, entered into a treaty with the Scots for a time; and, as soon as peace was established by this agreement, he turned all his energies to attacking the Roman patricians who ruled the country at the time, and their British allies. While, therefore, Britannia was labouring under these the evils of civil discord, the amount of the tribute which was wont to be sent over yearly to Rome remained altogether unpaid; and many of the Britons, after him, abjured fealty to Rome, hoping thus to be freed from subjection to taxes.

CHAPTER XXXII.

The Emperor Severus, to shut out the Scots and Picts from invading the Britons, has a wall made across the island.

ON his accession to the government of the empire, Severus, as already said, found the commonwealth everywhere in great disturbance; and he laboured hard to reduce it to order. Thus he slew Pascenius Niger, who was attempting a rebellion throughout Egypt and Syria; he conquered and quieted the Parthians, Arabs, and Azabeni; he smothered the revolt again meditated by the Jews and Samaritans; and, after having quelled many insurrections throughout the whole Roman world, he, at the city of Lugdunum, defeated and slew Clodius Albinus, who had made himself Cæsar in Gaul. When, therefore, civil war had been repressed on all sides with the utmost diligence, Britannia alone remained uncurbed, through the factiousness of Fulgentius. Accordingly the emperor called a council, and asked which of all the military chiefs was prepared to take some legions with him, and go to Britain; and, hearing no one say he was ready, he took up his sword, and said—"Here am I! Prepare ye all to follow me; for with me ye shall go." And he thus set out for Britannia forthwith. The cause of his arrival was not, however, hidden from Fulgentius, who was forewarned thereof by his friends, by means of messengers secretly sent on before, and also that he need not hope in any degree to prevail against the onset of such a multitude of warriors. When he had hastily marched into Scotia, therefore, he and the kings of the Scots and Picts entered into a stable treaty of perpetual peace and eternal fellowship between their respective nations, while he, at the same time, give up his two sons as hostages. He then, supported by a strong army of the Scots and Picts, went back into Britannia, prepared to do battle without delay. And he went backwards and forwards, making expeditions of this sort, very frequently, until impeded by the bulwark of a very broad vallum drawn across the island by Severus; and then only did he become rather more quiet.

CHAPTER XXXIII.

Fulgentius, supported by an auxiliary body of Scots and Picts, besieges the city of York, and slays the Emperor Severus.

NOW the emperor, when he had overcome Fulgentius, and made him flee into Scotia, had, at that time, a vallum made across the island, between two rivers on either side, namely, the Tyne and the Esk, that there might, for the future, no spot seem open for the invasion of the allies by their constant enemies the Scots and Picts, or even by the Britons of Albania themselves, as was their wont. So Fulgentius, knowing that the way to York, by land, was closed to him by the vallum, speedily made ready some small vessels, laden with victuals, warlike engines, and cavalry; while the infantry and the other leaders of his land forces went with him to the river, and set busily to work making coracles, or portable boats, of wickerwork, cunningly sewed round about with skins, each of which could carry across two, or only one, with his arms, and the boatman. Rowing over in these, as well as swimming across, in the darkness of night, they safely crossed the river before daybreak. He then massed the troops together, and laid close siege to the city of York, which he had previously lost, when Severus had assaulted it; and he, at the same time, received again into the bonds of their pristine allegiance to him some of his nobles, who had formerly seceded from him, but who, inspirited by the great multitude of warriors who accompanied him, chose to cleave to him rather than to the Romans. When, therefore, a few days after, Fulgentius was applying himself intently to the siege, and, after having made extensive preparations in the scaffolding of the engines for scaling or breaching the walls of the city, was diligently occupied about the assault, this Roman emperor, like the high-spirited chief he was, suddenly sallied out with his troops, and rushed amongst the enemy; and, engaging in mortal combat with Fulgentius, he was slain. Bede, indeed, relates that Severus died a natural death in this same city; but Geoffroy bears witness, in the following passages, that he was killed by Fulgentius, even as is here related.

CHAPTER XXXIV.

Bede's account of the said Wall, and of the Siege, and of the Death of Severus.

SEVERUS, then, says *Bede*, having been victorious in the civil wars which grievously came upon him all at once, was drawn into Britannia by the revolt of almost all the allies; and, after many a great and serious battle, he thought fit to divide from the other unconquered nations that part of the island which he had recovered—not, as some imagine, with a wall, but with a vallum. Accordingly, he drew this massive vallum, fortified with frequent towers upon it, from sea to sea; and there—that is, at York—he fell sick and died. *Geoffroy* writes:—Severus, as soon as he had arrived in Britannia, gave battle to the Britons, and subdued part of the country; while the inhabitants of the other part, which he could not reduce, were so hard pressed by him that they were forced to flee into Scotia. They, however, resisted him with all their might, under the conduct of Fulgentius, and often inflicted great slaughter upon both their own countrymen and the Romans. For they brought to their assistance all the people of the islands that they could get, and thus often came back victorious. The emperor, therefore, unable to endure the frequent inroads of Fulgentius, commanded a vallum to be built between Deira and Albania, so as to check his further advance; and they built one at the common charge from sea to sea, which, in after time, served more easily to hinder the approach of the enemy. But Fulgentius, when no longer able to resist Severus, crossed over into Scotia, that by the help of the Scots and Picts he might be restored to greatness; and when he had collected all the youth of the country, he returned by sea to Britannia, and besieged the city of York. Upon this news being spread among the other nations of Britannia, the greater part of the Britons deserted Severus, and went over bodily to Fulgentius. However, Severus did not, on this account, desist from his undertaking; but, summoning the Romans and the rest of the Britons together, he marched to the siege, and fought with Fulgentius. The engagement proved very sharp. Severus was slain, with many of his followers, and Fulgentius mortally wounded.

CHAPTER XXXV.

The Pope Saint Victor I., under whom the Scots began to embrace the Catholic Faith.

IN the seventh year of the Emperor Severus, Victor I., the fourteenth Pope from Peter, who was sprung from a nation of Africa, and whose father's name was Felix, ascended the Papal throne, and occupied it ten years two months and twelve days. Under him, the Scots began to embrace the Catholic faith, that is to say, in A.D. 203; whence the following:—

"After Christ's birth two hundred years and three.
His true faith flrst on Scotland shed her rays;
Then the first Victor filled the Papal see,
Who died a martyr in Severus' days."

This Victor, like his predecessor Eleutherius, appointed that the holy Easter should be celebrated on Sunday; and, at the request of the clergy, he held a council at Alexandria of Palestine, on the limits of the celebration of Easter, and other most urgent ecclesiastical matters. There were present, at this council, the holy Pope Victor himself, Narcissus, patriarch of Jerusalem, and Theophilus, bishop of Cæsarea; and it was there determined that Easter should always be celebrated on the Sunday after the fourteenth day of the moon of the month of April. For many bishops, both of the East and of Asia, at that time, and for a long time after, used to celebrate Easter in accordance with the Jews. This Pope also ordained that, in a case of urgent necessity, a man may be baptized in a river, in a pool, or in the sea, provided only he has made open profession of the Christian faith. He received the crown of martyrdom under Severus, and was buried beside Saint Peter, in the Vatican. His feast is held on the 28th of July.

CHAPTER XXXVI.
Succession of many insignificant Emperors.

SEVERUS, says *Eutropius*, left two sons to succeed him, Basianus, and Geta. The Senate conferred the name of Antoninus on Basianus; while Geta was adjudged a public enemy, and speedily put to death. Basianus Antoninus, then, who was also called Caracalla, succeeded his father in A.D. 213, and reigned six years. He paid the debt of nature in the city of Edessa, while attempting an expedition against the Parthians. *Sigibert* relates that Basianus was slain by the Parthians, at the city of Edessa. *Geoffroy* tells us that Basianus was slain by Carausius, in Britannia. But I think we should rather give credit to the histories of the two former; because it is certain that Carausius first usurped Britannia from the Romans in the time of Diocletian and Maximian. For, seventy-two years after the death of this Basianus, Carausius rebelled, in Britannia, against the Romans, and the Emperor Diocletian ordered his associate Adlectus to slay him, as will presently be related below.

CHAPTER XXXVII.
First occasion of the Dissensions which sprang up between the Scots and Picts, in the time of Diocletian, or a little before.

ON Carus having been struck by lightning, Diocletian, the thirty-second from Augustus, succeeded to the throne in the year 287, and reigned twenty years; and, having created Maximian Herculius first Cæsar, then Augustus, he sent him into Gaul. It was in this expedition that the Theban legion suffered. In their time the fury of the persecution of the Christians was so much increased that, within thirty days, twenty-two thousand persons of both sexes, throughout the various provinces, were crowned with martyrdom. In this persecution, Christianity was almost entirely stamped out in Britannia. While, however, such things were being done, by their command, throughout the whole extent of the Roman Empire, the grievous thunderbolts of sudden disturbances crashed upon them. In Britannia, Carausius, who had been set to watch the sea-coast, rebelled, as did Achilleus, in Egypt; while Narseus, king of the Persians, oppressed the east, and the Quinquegentiani, Africa, by their wars. Now, in the time of this Diocletian, or a little before, while the nations of the Scots and Picts reigned together in peace, and everywhere protected their territory with their combined strength, it so happened that, on a day appointed, some nobles of both nations met on the confines of their respective countries, as they were wont, for the purpose of hunting; and, when they had been coursing about hither and thither nearly a whole day, with their dogs uncoupled, in pursuit of game, a certain hound, which was accustomed to follow the blood-stained tracks of the quarry, was stolen away by the Picts, and incontinently found among them. The Scots asked to get it back, but they would not restore it; so they fell out, and the Scots strove to wrest it from them by force. They, on the other hand, taking no manner of trouble to lessen, by reparation, the wrong they had committed, but even more cruelly aggravating it, hastened to battle; and thus many, on both sides, of those who had met together were slain with the sword, one by another. This, then, was the occasion and beginning of the first dissension between them; who, for five hundred years, had lived harmoniously in a united peace, with their united power resisting all other nations whatever. But, not long after, in proportion to the earnestness with which they formerly nurtured the friendship between them, as if they two were one people, by frequent kind turns done to one another; by firm alliances between their children, in connexion by marriage; and often, also, by mutual banquets—was the bitterness with which their enmity thenceforth grew, from day to day, by rapine, fire, slaughter, treachery, and various tumults and raids. And though confirmed peace, and negotiations for a truce, were often agreed upon between them; still things went daily from bad to worse, so that each nation set to work, with all its might, to annihilate the other. However, peace was restored by Carausius, a Briton, whose object, indeed, was to take them with him to fight against the Romans, as will be shown in the sequel.

CHAPTER XXXVIII.

Covenant of Carausius with the Scots and Picts—First Expulsion of the Romans from Britannia.

WHILE fickle Fortune was thus turning her wheel at random, such a change came over the impaired strength of the Romans that the whole of their dominions were disturbed, both by sea and land. Then this Carausius, a man of very mean birth, but of great skill in the art of war, received power from the Senate to restore to order the face of the Belgic sea, and its shores, which were devastated by the piracy of Saxon and Frankish vessels. So he immediately assembled, from all parts, freebooters, always at hand, and ready for sedition; and great was the booty that he many a time took from the enemy. He did not, however, share it equally with his associates, nor restore the natives their own; neither did he give any part thereof for behoof of the commonwealth, or to the Senate, but took good care to keep the whole heap for himself, and enrich himself. On this account, therefore, the Senate secretly, by letter, ordered him to be put to death, for fear he should become too friendly with the barbarians, and, having assembled them, to the prejudice of the Roman interests, bring them into the island. He, however, being in all things prudent and cautious, got a clue to Cæsar's instructions; and, rising with the greatest courage against the Romans, he kept the whole of Britannia for himself, allowing them none of it, and brought it all under his own dominion. He, moreover, without delay, pressingly solicited all the nations of the island, as well as the Scots and Picts, upon whom he had formerly committed the most cruel depredations, to enter into a friendly treaty with him; and, with promises of many gifts, he assiduously besought them to rise, and join him in driving the Romans out of the island. Nor would he have been able to lure them on to contract such a treaty of peace, had he not conceded to them that the possessions they had acquired by the sword, in Nero's time, should subsist in the same peaceful state, and remain theirs, in their integrity, for ever. With the help of these nations, then, he assailed the Romans; and, having wrested from them all their fortresses and towns, he cruelly expelled them, every one, from Britannia, and invested himself with the diadem of the kingdom.

CHAPTER XXXIX.

Ratification of this Covenant, and Treaty negotiated by Carausius between the Island Nations—the Scots, Britons, and Picts—to last for ever.

THE Britons, then, though they all knew that Carausius was of obscure birth, and had risen to fame merely during the late campaign, nevertheless, on account of his practised skill in warfare, gladly accepted him as their king, hoping, through his energy, to be the sooner snatched from the power of the Romans. So they willingly ratified the covenants he had lately entered into with the Scots and Picts; and, to seal the compact, they freely granted him, in perpetuity, the possessions of their late leader Fulgentius, which Gotharius, his grandson through his daughter, had until then, by the help of the Scots, through a long course of years withheld, though with difficulty, from the Romans; and it was settled that, in future, having become, as it were, one people, they should, without treachery, give each other faithful help against the Romans, or any other nations that might wish to make war on them or any one of them. Meanwhile, a Roman force was sent by the emperors into Britannia, under the command of Basianus, to recover it from those barbarous and untamed nations, after Carausius should have been slain or put to flight, and to reduce it to its accustomed condition of a republic; or else dismally to bestrew the fields with the corpses of those of the inhabitants who would spurn them. Accordingly Basianus (not, however, that Basianus Caracalla who had, many years before, succeeded his father Severus in the empire, but another who, on account of his military renown, had at this time been chosen to take command of the legions), on his first arrival, besought the Picts with words of kindness, saying that, if they would make a treaty with him, and exert themselves to help him in warring against the Britons, he, for his part, would not refuse to give them his constant assistance against the Scots. As, however, they were already committed by the covenant Carausius had made with them, they gave no final answer to his promises; but cunningly sent him away under the illusion that they would either give him their help at once, or, at least, withdraw themselves from the war. For, in their disingenuous wariness, they wished first to be able to foresee the result of the war; so that, when certain which side would be victorious, they might then more safely enter into an alliance with the victor. So Basianus arrived, and crushed the Britons by sundry massacres and proscriptions; but he was afterwards, with many of his soldiers, slain in a most hard-fought battle, by Carausius, and the Scots and Picts, who had joined with him.

CHAPTER XL.

Death of Carausius by Treachery, at the hands of Adlectus, a Soldier—His Exhortation, or Instructions, to the Islanders, how they might always defend themselves from the Romans, or any other foreign Foes.

AFTER this victory, then, Carausius, who outshone every one in all military qualities, and was the first, after the Britons had been subdued by the Emperor Julius, gloriously to rule over them, when restored to their pristine freedom on the expulsion of the Romans from their midst, was betrayed, in a measure by the treachery of one of his soldiers, and slain with the sword. Carausius, says *Bede*, possessed himself of Britannia; and, having most valiantly retained it for the space of seven years, he was, at length, put to death by the treachery of his associate Adlectus. This Carausius was remarkable for his faithfulness to his engagements, keeping all his promises to the very letter, and especially the covenants he had made with the Scots and Picts, whom he frequently, by embassies to and fro, and very often by letter, exhorted to mutual and loyal concord. "I do not consider," he would say to them, "that there need be any fear of the Romans in the island, so long as the various nations therein, united in faithful communion under trusty chiefs, firmly keep the peace one towards another. So that, on a sudden arrival of their foes, they should not, without preparation, rush headlong into a hasty war, before being joined by their friends or allies; but, by wisely cutting off the enemy's supplies, they should put off hostilities as long as should be necessary; and thus, after careful discussion of some common plan, seize a fit time for fighting." Meanwhile, the greater part of the British nation renewed the treaty of alliance they had formerly made with the Scots, and strove, if possible, to put Adlectus to death, or drive him out of Britannia, on account of the death of Carausius, their chief. Adlectus, on the other hand, accompanied by the Picts, who had broken the treaty they had previously sworn with the Britons, inflicted many injuries upon Britannia; and at length, a few years after, advancing to battle with them, he himself, after great slaughter on both sides, fell amongst the slain, as he so well deserved. *Eutropius* writes:—After Carausius, Adlectus held Britannia for three years, and was overthrown by the Praetorian troops of Asclepiodotus. Afterwards, as often as the Romans made war on the British nation, the Scots would help the latter, and come faithfully to their rescue; while the Picts would assiduously give their support to the Romans, against the Britons. For the cunning of Adlectus had separated the Picts from the Britons, and these two nations thenceforth wasted each other, with mutual massacres, until the time of Maximus, emperor of Gaul. Let us now return to the enumeration of the emperors, as they succeeded to the throne.

CHAPTER XLI.

Accession of the Emperors Galerius and Constantius—War of Constantius against the Scots and the Britons of Albania.

WHEN, therefore, the commonwealth was in danger, under I the aforesaid emperors Diocletian and Maximian, two men were created their coadjutors: Constantius, father of Constantine the Great, and grandson of Claudius through his daughter; and Galerius Maximin. And the emperors, also, that they might attach these men to themselves by family ties, gave in marriage, Diocletian, his daughter Valeria to Galerius, and Maximian, his stepdaughter Theodora to Constantius. Of Theodora, Constantius begat seven sons, brothers of Constantine. He was afterwards sent by Maximian to Gaul, which was ravaged by the Alemanni, and to Britannia, which was labouring under civil war. Accordingly, after having tranquillized Gaul, he went across into

Britannia, bringing over three legions with him, and easily compelled the southern Britons to make peace—not by war, indeed, but by threats of war. Then, declaring war against the Britons of Albania and the Scots, he stirred up against them the nation of the Picts, who were always prone to harm their neighbours. In those days, the young Constantine, son of Constantius by his former wife Helena, was serving with Diocletian; who, at the instigation of Galerius, was bent upon compassing his death by foul play. The plot was detected by Fausta, Maximian's daughter, whom Constantine had taken to wife; and he hurried back, in safety, to his father. On Diocletian and Maximian retiring from the imperial throne, they were succeeded by the aforesaid Constantius and Galerius, in A.D. 307; and these, after they were raised to the dignity of Augustus, were the first to split up the Roman empire into two divisions, the Eastern, and the Western: so that Constantius got Gaul, Africa, and Italy; while Illyricum, Asia, and the East, fell to the share of Galerius. Constantius, however, content with the dignity of Augustus, and the sovereignty of Gaul, refused to undertake the care of governing Italy and Africa; and, thus, Galerius held the imperial sceptre, alone, for two years. Constantius, writes Bede, who, whilst Diocletian was alive, governed Gaul and Spain, a man of the greatest kindness and courtesy, died in Britannia. He left his son Constantine, begotten of Helen, his concubine, as emperor of Gaul.

CHAPTER XLII.

Accession of the Emperor Constantine the Great—His maternal uncle Traherius slain by the Scots and Britons.

CONSTANTINE, therefore, says *Eusebius*, begotten of Helen, the concubine of Constantius, came to the throne in A.D. 319, and reigned thirty-one years and ten months. Immediately upon his father's death, being minded to usurp the whole empire, he assembled as many as he could of the Gauls and Britons, and set out towards Italy. Meanwhile, an insurrection was stirred up at Rome, and the Praetorian bands conferred upon Maximian's son, Maxentius, the title of Augustus. At that time, writes *Eutropius*, four emperors watched over the commonwealth—Constantine and Maxentius, born in the purple, and Licinius and Maximin, who were upstarts. In the fifth year after he assumed the imperial dignity, Constantine vanquished Maxentius, and took possession of Italy; then, in the ninth year, on Maximin being accidentally overtaken by death, he defeated, by sea and land, Licinius, who had married his sister Constantia, and slew him; and he thus obtained complete sovereignty over the empire. In the tenth year of this reign, the holy Pope Silvester, a Roman by nationality, sat upon the throne of St. Peter, at Rome. He cleansed the emperor from leprosy, by baptism; whereupon the Church had peace for the future. For, according to all historians, it had laboured under a continual whirlwind of persecution ever since Nero's time; although ten years are noted as more cruel than the rest. All the pontiffs, moreover, who had been at the head of the Church at Rome, down to, but exclusive of, this Silvester, had been martyred, save Marcus only. In these days, the Romans in Britannia, and the Gauls whom Constantine had sent over for their protection, were conquered by the Britons—but not driven out; for there were sent to defend them some fresh legions, which brought back the Britons under the yoke, and also wofully defeated the Scots, and cut them to pieces. In the meantime, a certain commander of British extraction, named Octavius, rising unexpectedly, with a few adherents at first, destroyed the commanders of the legions, and the patricians who sat with them in the Prætorium. And, soon, all the natives who wished to ascend the ladder of liberty hastily flocked to his standard, and, having cast out the enemy from the island, unanimously raised him to the throne. Some more legions were afterwards sent against him, under the command of Traherius; and, being vanquished by him, Octavius went into Scotia. He there conciliated into the security of peace the Scots, and even the Picts, whom, until then, the Britons had looked upon as their enemies; and, returning to Britannia, accompanied by them, he slew this Traherius, to whom the whole strength of the Britons had been utterly opposed.

CHAPTER XLIII.

Octavius, King of the Britons, restores the three nations of the island—the Scots, Britons, and Picts—to the unity of peace, as Carausius had formerly done—Accession of the sons of Constantine.

NOW Octavius, being raised to the throne, stood forth as a faithful intercessor, and restored to the unity of peace the three nations of the island—the Scots, Britons, and Picts—as Carausius had formerly done. He further promised that he and his would always be ready, according to agreement, to lend assistance for their defence, if they would come with him and fight against the Romans, whenever necessary; and this they each confirmed to the other with an oath. At any rate, this treaty of alliance was faithfully observed by all parties for some time, even down to the time of a certain tyrant, named Maximus, by the cruel craft of whose tyranny these nations were again separated, and almost annihilated, as the facts of the case will show further on. Upon the death of Constantine, at Nicomedia, he was succeeded by his three sons, Constantius, Constantine, and Constans, to wit, in A.D. 340. Constantius obtained the sovereignty of Rome; while Constantine reigned over Constantinople; and Constans over Antioch. In course of time, Constantine was slain while he was bent on making war on his brother. Constans, also, was put to death by Magnentius, at a castle which bears the name of Helena, in the seventeenth year of his reign. But Constantius, an eminently peaceable man, after he had reigned twenty-four years, devoted his energies to a civil war against Julian the Apostate, and died on the road between Cilicia and Cappadocia. In the sixteenth year of this Constantius, Maximus, above referred to, received from him authority to govern Gaul, and set out with his legions; but being enticed by the treachery of some Britons, he left Gaul at peace, and came to Britannia, with his forces, composed equally of Romans and Gauls. This Maximus was descended from the imperial race, being the cousin of Constantine the Great; and he was accused of aiming at a share in the empire. In a catalogue of the chiefs of Roman lineage who ruled over the Britons, we read that Maximus reigned over the Britons thirty-three years, from the first year of Gratian onwards, that is, from A.D. 381; and he would thus be made out to have lived until the fifth year of the Emperor Honorius. But this we believe will not bear sifting; for, in the second year of the elder Theodosius, that is, in A.D. 388, this Maximus was taken prisoner by Theodosius, at Aquileia, and slain, on account of the iniquitous murder of Gratian, whom he had killed by treachery, rather than in fair fight. The truth thus appears to be that Maximus entered Britannia, with the intention of conquering it by force of arms, in the sixteenth year of Constantius, A.D. 355.

CHAPTER XLIV.
Conan, nephew of Octavius, leads the Scots and Picts to fight against the tyrant Maximus, cousin of Constantine the Great—Maximus, afterwards, by a feigned peace, cunningly separates the Picts from the Scots.

WHEN, therefore, this tyrant Maximus came, to Britannia, the greater part of the Britons cleaved to him, at his first nod—those, especially, who had invited him over to invade their native land; but the remainder were steadfast in their adherence to Octavius. Then was civil war kindled amongst them in Britain, and various were the conflicts between them. Maximus, however, gained the advantage in the end. But Conan, a Briton, who was the nephew of King Octavius, and conducted the war on his behalf, retreated into Scotia; and, assembling his allies, the Britons of Albania, the Scots, and the Picts, and having collected other reinforcements from all parts, he returned, and gave battle to Maximus; but he was beaten. Thereupon King Octavius, in despair, surrendered to the victorious Maximus. Nevertheless, Conan again sought refuge in Scotia; and, again gathering his forces together, he hastened to the theatre of war, and wasted the provinces, across the Humber, of the adherents of Maximus, ravaging them most mercilessly. And thus the horrors of war between them went on interruptedly for the space of three years; until the strength of the Scots was so much exhausted by such great disasters, that they declared they could no longer accompany Conan into battle, as they had, in past battles, lost so many of the noblest men of their nation; but their advice was that he should enter into negotiations for peace, without prejudice to the league between them. The Britons who wished to set up Conan, accordingly, did themselves, as Maximus had more than once besought them to do, make peace with him forthwith, in order to guard against the Scots secretly concluding a treaty with him, without their being parties thereto; and also, because they saw these allies of theirs, without whom they would not have plunged into the war at all, falling away from their side. Maximus, therefore, writes *Geoffroy*, sometimes returned victorious, sometimes retired defeated, from the battles he fought with them. At last, after each had done the other infinite mischief, they were reconciled with the approval of their friends. So Maximus, feigning to have established peace with the Scots for the space of one year, as he had promised Conan on his word of honour in the preliminary negotiations, privily entangled the Pictish king and people in a cunning alliance with himself, and roused them by his wiles to declare war against the Scots. He, indeed, intended to bring both peoples under subjection, so he craftily first parted them asunder, that he might afterwards be able to conquer them more easily. For he knew they were invincible when joined together as one power; and he designed to separate them by outwitting them, and then conquer them. This design was soon after duly carried out.

CHAPTER XLV.

The Britons and Picts, led by Maximus, cast out the Scots from the Kingdom.

UNMINDFUL, then, of the treaty which had formerly been successfully concluded between them and the Scots, through the good offices of Carausius, the Picts, not only those who accompanied Maximus, but also their principal chiefs, with fully more cruelty than the rest, laid waste their provinces there; and, rejecting all offers of ransom, massacred all who fell into their hands during their plundering expeditions, or after a successful engagement; nor spared they the unarmed and peaceful populace. While, however, the whole forces of the British nation combined lost no time in cleaving to the Picts, in order to destroy the Scots, Conan and his followers alone, although they were indignant at the disgrace they had incurred at the hands of Maximus, refrained from pillage and slaughter, and would give the Scots neither countenance nor help. "I am mindful," said Conan, "of the faith I plighted to them, and they to me, for a perpetual alliance, and I can by no means honestly violate it, even as they for their part have hitherto preserved it inviolate." Thereupon there broke out again between them an execrable war, far more savage than ever before; in which, by and bye, neither side had compassion on men worn out with age, or babes suckled at the breast, or women in childbirth; but all of both sexes, all at least who were captured, were destroyed in this deplorable carnage. But why dwell on this?—

> At length proud Victory yields a hard-won smile,
> To the fierce wooing of the Pictish arms.
> The Scots are humbled. They, whose iron hand
> Dealt fear around, struck down the haughty foe,
> Wielded the sceptre o'er the cringing land,
> Yet tempered might with right; whose faithful arm
> Had ne'er refused to strike in friendship's cause,
> Now crouch deserted, none at hand to save
> Or comfort them; the greedy sword pursues them
> To death or banishment; their enemy
> Judges their people; while their high-born chieftains
> Mourn in despair their king and empire dead.

In those days, therefore, there fell in battle the Scottish king Eugenius, with his son, and many chiefs and princes, and common people without number; and the rest who survived the war, being unwilling to be subject to the enemy, as the rabble was, and to serve them, abandoned their estates, and chose rather to live free as strangers in a foreign land, than, in their own, to be subjected to continual slavery. The king's brother, also, Echach, with his son, Erth, and many others, went to Ireland; others to Norway; while some sought refuge in the islands, where they lay hid during the whole time of this affliction. And, with the exception of these islands, they lost the whole kingdom, about the year 360 of our era.

CHAPTER XLVI.

The Emperor Constantius transfers the Relics of the blessed Apostle Andrew from the City of Patras to Constantinople.

ABOUT the same time, also, the emperor Constantius, son of Constantine the Great, who has been already spoken of, induced by his zeal for the Christian religion, and stimulated by the especial devotion he had, long before, conceived in his heart towards the blessed apostle Andrew, wished to satisfy it by some deed. So, in the twentieth year of his reign, he went to Patras, a city in the country of Achaia, where the apostle suffered and was buried; and, carrying off thence his relics by force, he brought them over, with the greatest rejoicings, to Constantinople, on the 9th of May, with hymns and canticles; and he there placed them, with the highest honour, in caskets of gold and silver. Achaia is one of the seven provinces of Greece, and a peninsula; for, save on its northern side, where it adjoins Macedon, it is hemmed in by the sea on all sides. Now the blessed apostle Andrew was one of the first called to the apostleship, and was second, or, at most, third, in order among the apostles. He was dark in complexion, comely in appearance, of middle height, and with a long beard. Some of his bones were brought over from Patras to Scotia, in the following manner. On the third night before the emperor had entered the city, the angel of the Lord came down, by God's command, to a certain holy abbot, a God-fearing man, named Regulus, who was the keeper of the relics, and said to him,—"Take with thee fit brethren, and go to the sarcophagus where the bones of the blessed apostle Andrew are enshrined; and take thence three fingers of the right hand, the bone of the arm hanging down from the shoulder, one tooth, and the knee-cap, and keep them carefully where I shall show thee, until I come again." Thereupon he summoned the brethren he had selected, and, taking away with him all the bones he had been enjoined to take, he concealed them in a secret place assigned by the angel. The emperor, then, came two days after, with his light-armed legions, and captured the city, after having caused it to be evacuated by its troops; and, taking the shrine in which the relics were ensconced, he bade it be brought to Constantinople with becoming reverence, he himself accompanying it with his army.

CHAPTER XLVII.

The Angel of the Lord had commanded the blessed Abbot Regulus and his companions to take part of the relics, and go to the northern parts of the world without delay.

AT length, after the lapse of some years, the angel from heaven returned again to the abbot, and, with awful countenance, gave him the following command, in the name of Almighty God, and in these words:— "Take up again," said he, "the relics of the blessed Andrew, the beloved, which thou didst lately keep back by my instructions, and lose no time in going westwards, to the north-westerly ends of the earth, under the sign of the Lion, attended by a company of saints, worthy to be praised; and, in whatever place the vessel which bears thee shall, God willing, be in danger of shipwreck, though thou and thy comrades shall continue in safety, there thou mayst know that the course of thy labours, or rather of thy lengthened voyage, has come to a prosperous end. Furthermore, take heed, and be not careless nor unmindful of this behest, that thou firmly lay, in that same place, the foundations of a church, to the honour of God's name, and to the praise of His apostle, of venerated memory; for it shall come to pass that, as in days of old the East was adorned by the sound of his living preaching, as thou art well aware, so shalt thou know of a truth that the whole West also will be graced for everlasting by the wonders I which shall be worked by his relics. For that spot, forasmuch as chosen by God, shall be an Apostolic See for ever, and a firm rock of faith; and not undeservedly so, as being that of the brother of the blessed Peter, to whom the Lord said, 'Thou art Peter,' etc.; and it shall likewise be the stanch and steadfast anchor of the kingdom wherein it is situated; and of exceeding renown, for the worship of the apostle, among all the faithful, and especially among the kings and other potentates of the earth, with whose lands and gifts it shall be abundantly enriched. For crowds of the faithful shall wend thither their toilsome way from all the ends of the earth, that they may receive health of body and soul; and shall wondrously obtain their petitions, and return to their own in joy, magnifying God in His apostle, with voice of praise; for He is always glorified in His saints." And with these words the angel vanished from his sight, and the blessed Regulus addressed himself to execute his commands. Wishing, therefore, to comply with the instructions of Heaven, he called to him prudent and religious men, conspicuous for their learning and morality, each of whom also the angel had previously forewarned and exhorted to become a participator in his pilgrimage; and taking away with him the sacred relics on board ship, he went to sea, prepared to go to the north-west. Now, the following are the names of this company of saints:—First, the holy Abbot Regulus, and Saint Damianus, the priest; the deacons Gelasius and Thubaculus; Merinacus, brother of Saint Damianus; Nerius and Elusenius, from Crete; Mirenus, Machabenus, and his brother Silvius; eight hermits, namely, Felix, Sajanus, Matthew, Maurice, Madianus, Philip, Lucius, and Eugenius; and three holy virgins of Colossia, namely, Triduana, Potentia, and Emerea.

CHAPTER XLVIII.

Shipwreck and first arrival in Scotia of Hegulus and his companions, with the relics, in the time of Hurgust, King of the Picts.

ACCORDINGLY, these holy men and virgins embarked on board a small vessel stored with all things needful, and went round the coasts of Europe along the ocean path of the inland sea, until, worn out by many hardships, they came to some islands lying in the ocean to the west. And when they had been wandering about an unknown sea, at the mercy of the winds, for the space of nearly two years, not knowing what to do, a gale of unusual strength suddenly sprang up from the east, and rushed into the sail; and their barque was driven, by its force, on to the kingdom of the Picts, and struck among the rocks of the island of Albion, as had been foretold by the angel. The blessed Regulus, however, fortified by God, safely got to land, in joy, with his companions, on the 28th of September, with the emblem of our Lord's cross borne before them; and he, afterwards, there dedicated a cathedral to the honour of the apostle, in the Swine's Wood, which is called, in the mother tongue, Mucrossis. In that place, by the touch of the relics, many astounding miracles were worked, and are worked to this day, such as had not until that day been seen or heard of in these islands since they embraced the faith; for instance, the blind from their mother's womb received their sight, the dumb were made to speak, the lame to walk, and all who piously bespoke the favour of the apostle were immediately, by God's mercy, healed from any sickness that possessed them. As miracles were thus daily multiplied, people of all nations hastened thither with their gifts, clapping their hands, and humbly sending up boundless praises to God for so great a patron. The king of that country at the time, moreover, Hurgust, son of Forgso, taking delight in the sanctity of the place, built his palace there, close to the cathedral, and granted to the blessed Kegulus and his brethren certain lands to sow produce on, and to be held by them, as alms, in perpetuity. His example was followed by succeeding kings, according as the intensity of their devotion might dictate; so that the property, although by small degrees, still went on increasing, until King Hungus, who reigned over the Picts after A.D. 800, gave the tenth part of the kingdom to the blessed Andrew, on account of the miraculous assistance he had rendered him in an expedition against the Saxons, as will appear in Chapters XIII. and XIV. of Book IV. Having then founded a little cell, after the manner of a monastery, and told off keepers of the relics, these holy men went forth preaching throughout the country, not on horseback, but, like the apostles of old, two and two, sowing the word of God everywhere among the nations, and miraculously working wonders without number. When, therefore, they had imbued these nations with the faith by their heavenly teaching, and had confirmed them therein by various miracles, the blessed Abbot Regulus died full of days, and at a great age, at Kilremont (the name to which that of

Mucrossis had been altered by the king), thirty-two years after his arrival in the isle of Albion, through shipwreck; during which time he laboured at the work of the Gospel, and pleased God exceedingly.

CHAPTER XLIX.

Maximus crushes the Scots in War, after having separated them from the Picts; and subdues the latter also—Succession of Emperors.

BUT the nation of the Picts themselves did not remain long unpunished for breaking the treaty, after they had craftily deceived the Scots, and thrust them out of the kingdom; for they immediately afterwards felt the weight of the tyranny of this same Maximus, and themselves also drank, as they deserved, of the same bitter draught they had wickedly compounded for their allies to drain.' This tyrant Maximus, when he knew that the Scots had been utterly driven out of Scotia, suddenly brought the whole strength of his forces into Scotia; and, after defeating the Picts in many a battle, much weakened as they were by the Scots in the former war, he compelled them to serve him, and captured all their fortresses, as well as those they themselves had taken from the Scots. Meantime, the Emperor Constantius, while engaged in civil war against the son of his father's brother, Julian the Apostate, who was struggling to usurp the throne, died after the twenty-fourth year of his reign, on the way between Cilicia and Cappadocia. On his death, Julian attained the dignity of the empire in A.D. 364, and reigned a year and eight months—others, however, say, three years. *Eutropius* relates that it was seven years. He was the nephew of Constantine the Great, who ordained that Byzantium should be called Constantinople, after him; for Constantine had two brothers by the same father, though not of the same mother, namely, Dalmachius, and Constantius; which Constantius begat this Julian. Under him suffered Saint Damianus, Saint Gordianus, Saint Epimachus, Saint John, and Saint Paul, and many other saints. Then, after the death of Julian, who was slain by the holy martyr and soldier Mercurius, as was revealed to Saint Basil, Jovinian came to the throne, and governed during eight months. Then Valentinian the Great succeeded him in the empire in A.U.C. 1116, according to Paulus Diaconus, and A.D. 368, according to Hugo. In the reckoning up of the Roman emperors, he was the thirty-eighth, and he reigned eleven years. This emperor was conspicuous not only for physical courage, but also for wisdom, temperance, and justice, and for stature of body. He had previously, under the emperor Julian, been tribune of the Scutarii; and, holding the perfect faith of Christianity, on being commanded by the sacrilegious emperor to sacrifice to idols or leave the army, he resigned of his own accord. On Julian being killed, and Jovinian dead, therefore, this Valentinian, who, for Christ's name, had lost his tribunate, obtained the empire, without delay, in the stead of his persecutor. He took his brother Valens to share the throne with him; and, in the third year of his reign, he caused his son Gratian to be raised to the dignity of emperor. At this time, Maximus tyrannously invaded Britannia, and overcame the Scots and Picts, who were making inroads into the country, and after he had taken the daughter of King Octavius to wife, he invested himself with the kingly diadem.

CHAPTER L.

Presumptuous Attempt of Maximus upon the Roman Empire—He is slain—Conan, to whom he had handed over the Kingdom of Armorica, thenceforth called Britannia Minor—Succession of Emperors.

After the death of Valentinian at Brigio (Bregetio), a town of the Squadi (Quadi), of a sudden rush of blood, called apoplexy, his brother Valens, together with his nephew Gratian, governed three years and six months; and on Valens being burnt to death, in a mean hovel, by the Goths, Gratian remained emperor with the young Valentinian, his brother. He began to reign in A.D. 381, and reigned six years. He made Theodosius Augustus coadjutor; and when Gratian himself had been slain by Maximus, Theodosius governed alone, for eleven years, after having already reigned six years in the East, during Gratian's lifetime. He began to reign in A.D. 387. To proceed: Maximus, whose name with good reason meant the *greatest*, if you add of *tyrants*, being exalted to the height of the kingship of Britannia, began to swell with pride when he saw the Scots wickedly beset, and thrust out into banishment, by their allies, the Picts; and the victorious Picts, in their turn, subjected to his domination, and all through his might and crafty wiles; so he began to give his tyrannous spirit scope against the Roman empire. For, as soon as the death of Valens was published, Maximus, notwithstanding that he had long before plighted his faith to Valentinian and his son Gratian while they occupied the throne, and confirmed it with an oath, invested himself with the purple, which he had tyrannously seized upon; and, leaving the tribune Dionotus to be judge over the Britons, he wrested from the empire, and usurped, all the regions of Gaul with the government of which he had been intrusted under those emperors. He called himself the heir of Constantine the Great, and therefore contended that he ought to rule over the Gauls and Britons at least. Then, after he had obtained the kingdom of Gaul, he handed over to Conan Meriodok, in A.D. 386, the kingdom of Armorica, in exchange for Britannia; and, having driven out the natives, he peopled that country afresh with inliabitants of British blood, of both sexes, and thenceforth named it Britannia Minor. For he feared lest, if Conan returned into Britannia, the Britons should rise with him in revolt against the power of his majesty, as they were always wont to do against strangers. He, therefore, brought him, and many other nobles he suspected, over with him to Gaul, and established them in Britannia Minor, together with many thousands of the common people whom he had brought away from the island. Maximus, writes Bede, a man worthy to bear the title of Augustus, had he not broken through his oath of allegiance, crossed over into Gaul, and there ensnared Gratian by a stratagem, and slew him. Theodosius, however, in the second, or, according to others, the first year of his reign, being not unmindful of the benefits he had received from Gratian, slew that stern and terrible enemy of his, Maximus, at Aquileia, and restored Gratian's brother, Valentinian, to the empire of the West. In the time of the elder Theodosius, as we read in *Sigibert*, Saint Patrick, a Scot, was, with his sisters, sold in Ireland; and, while he was swineherd to a certain chieftain there, he oftentimes held converse with an angel.

CHAPTER LI.

The most Christian deeds of the Emperor Theodosius the Elder, and of his wife Placella.

CHAPTER LII.

On the death of the Tyrant Maximus, the Scots begin to win lack their Kingdom—Succession of Emperors.

NOW Theodosius, when the commonwealth was thoroughly tranquillized, went to his long rest by a natural death, at Milan. He was succeeded, in A.D. 397, by his two sons, Honorius and Arcadius, whom he had begotten of Placella; and they reigned together for thirteen years. *Sigibert* tells us that Saint Martin died in the second year of their reign, but Prosper says it was in the fifth. In the time of these emperors, moreover, the Scottish nation, which had long been prostrate, and scattered abroad, began, immediately after the death of Maximus, to raise itself up again, and bethink itself of wreaking condign vengeance on its enemies for the wrongs they had so long inflicted upon it. When therefore Maximus had been put to death by Theodosius, and his son, Victor, whom he had left to govern Gaul while he made for Italy, had also been made away with by him, one of his officers, Count Andragatius, on hearing of this, threw himself headlong into the sea off a vessel; and when his party had no longer any hope of being revived, Gracian Municeps was, by some of the Britons, created emperor in his stead in Britannia. Others, however, who feared his tyranny, lest he should wrong them as Maximus had done, cut him off soon after his elevation. *Paulus* and *Bede* have the following:—In Britannia, Constantine was chosen in Gratian's stead, from the lowest ranks of the soldiery, only because of the hope inspired by his name, without any worth of his own to recommend him. He passed over into Gaul, and did more harm than good to the commonwealth; and he sent his son Constans, whom of a monk he had created Cæsar, into Spain. Honorius, hearing of this, and discerning that the power of the commonwealth was being shaken by continual disasters, sent into Gaul, with an army, his son-in-law. Count Constantius, an energetic man, who, as soon as he had marched thither, put Constantine to death at Aries. His son Constans, also, who, from being a monk, became Cæsar, was slain by Count Gerontius at Vienne. *Geoffroy*, indeed, informs us that these two, father and son, were killed in Britannia by the treachery of the Picts; various histories, however, hold a contrary opinion.

BOOK III.

CHAPTER I.

Fergus, son of Erth, joins the Picts, and regains the Kingdom which had been, through the Treachery of the Tyrant Maximus, held by the Romans and Britons for Forty-three Years.

WHILE, therefore, these and other evils everywhere befell the Romans, and Britannia, moreover, was labouring under civil discord, the Picts, whose fortresses Maximus had previously taken from them and handed over to his own troops to garrison, wishing to be loosed from the chain of slavery, secretly renewed their former treaty of peace and reciprocity with the Scots; exhorting and beseeching them to join their forces to theirs and recover the kingdom and liberties of their forefathers, when a fit opportunity should present itself. The latter, for their part, were prepared to listen to their suggestions; but they made up their minds to beware most carefully of the treachery they had formerly experienced at the hands of that false nation; so as never, in future, to undertake, in concert with them, any general war, or predatory expeditions on a smaller scale, nor to be so rash as to take up a position in the forefront of the battle, between a mistrusted friend and a declared enemy; for the incautious are oftentimes overthrown by their treacherous enemies, after a treaty has just been concluded between them. In A.D. 403, therefore, the sixth year of the emperors Arcadius and Honorius,—that is, the year 733 of the reign of the Scots in the island of Albion, 1903 years having elapsed from their origin and first going forth out of Egypt (namely, from the time of Scota to that of Fergus, son of Erth), in the year 5589, to wit, from the creation of the world, Fergus, the son of Erth, the son of Echadius, who was brother to the King Eugenius who had been overthrown by the tyrant Maximus, being an energetic youth, excelling all others in courage, of great bodily strength and daring, forward withal, and mighty in battle, fearlessly arrived, with his two brothers Loam and Fenegus, and his fellow-countrymen, the Irish and Norican islanders, in the kingdom of Scotia, which was his by right; and he drove the enemy far away out of the country wherein they had long been dwelling.

> The sails are spread to the fast-following breeze,
> And swarming fleets rush through the hissing seas.
> A glittering host of heroes throng the decks,
> Round their proud chief; who toil nor danger recks,
> But hastens to his native soil, to rear
> His prostrate throne, and break the oppressor's spear.
> The dauntless Lion floats above his head,
> Emblem of his fierce valour, bloody red.
> Twice twenty years and three the Scots, forlorn.
> The whirlwind fury of their foes had borne;
> But now their day of hope broke calm and clear,
> A king of their own kith was drawing near,
> And they to freedom fly, to every heart so dear.

Moreover, while Fergus was advancing with his army through the country, which, with its inhabitants, he gradually restored to peace, the Pictish tribes met him, with their columns; and, for fear that a single jot of hatred or perfidy should be supposed to lurk amongst them, they, of their own accord, threw open the gates of all the Scottish castles and fortresses, which, by the permission of Maximus, they had held up to that time, and restored them to the Scots.

CHAPTER II.

The same continued—Expulsion of the Romans and Britons from his Dominions.

BE that as it may, the Scots and Picts fetched over the Vespiliones, from Dacia, and the Huns, to disturb the peace of the British sea, promising them much plunder, and a secure shelter thenceforth, against the Romans, in the harbours of their kingdoms. The above-mentioned nations, therefore, the Scots and Picts, being united, renewed the treaties between them by a solemn oath, for both were in the same predicament; land, ranging through the country, they cast out the strangers from their lands; nor would they grant any delay to any one—for a prudent man will "ne'er delay when fortune serves"—nay, all those, of whatever condition, who did not snatch a hasty departure out of the country, or who did not, on being summoned to do so, willingly surrender the castles they had held up to that time, were immediately besieged, taken, and put to death. So this Fergus united under his dominion, within the space of three years from that time, the whole extent of the kingdom, on hoth sides of the Scottish firth, which had been possessed by his fathers from days of yore,—that is, from the stony moor and Inchegal to the Orkney islands. From the first king of this country, Fergus, son of Ferchard, down to this king, Fergus, son of Erth, inclusive, there reigned, in this island, forty-five kings of the same nation and race; but we refrain, for the present, from specifying the dates of their respective reigns, as we have not found them given fully. From this king onward, then, it will be convenient to insert the years of the reign of every king in succession, down to the present time, according to various chronicles; so that it may be clearly shown forth to posterity who were the kings who reigned, and what the dates and duration of their reigns. This king, therefore, reigned sixteen years in Scotland; during the last three of which he was the first king of Scottish descent to reign in the land of the Picts, beyond Drumalban,—that is, beyond the backbone of Albania, from the mountains to the Scottish sea, where none of his predecessors had held the sovereignty before; but whether he did so by virtue of the sword, or by some other title, I have not been able to ascertain. So the Scots and Picts, after they had conjointly, as above related, driven out the Romans and Britons from their own homes, made frequent raids, in dense bodies, into their kingdom of Britannia, which was, at that time, entirely bereft of the help of fighting men; and, as is noted in divers chronicles, they slew part of the wretched populace, and part, who were left in life, they led off into slavery.

CHAPTER III.

Cruel slaughter of the Britons and the Roman Legion by the Scots and Picts—Building of a dyke, called Grimsdyke, across the Island.

FOR Maximus had taken away with him all the warlike youth of the island that he could find, and left none but unarmed peasants, who, as they could not resist the fierceness of the Scots and Picts, nor cope with them in war, abandoned their lands, and fled from before them as from a fire. Indeed Maximus had, at that time, oppressed them so tyrannically, and dispersed them by his cruel craft, that they had not up to that time,—and have not, to the present day, been able to attain to their former condition, or in any wise to prosper. *Bede* has thus described the cruel disasters of those days, and the building of a second wall across the island:—From that time, Britain, entirely stripped of armed soldiery, and of the flower of its active youth, which had been led away by the rashness of tyrants, never more to return home, was wholly exposed to rapine, as being totally ignorant of the art of war. Whereupon it soon lay, for many years, stunned and groaning by reason of two very savage nations from over the sea, the Scots from the north-west, and the Picts from the north-east. We speak of these nations as being from over the sea, not on account of their being seated out of Britain, but because they were remote from the Britons' part thereof; two gulfs of the sea lying between them, which run in far and broad into the land of Britain, one from the eastern sea, the other from the western. The eastern has in the midst of it the town of Guidy; the western has above it, that is, to the right of it, the town of Alcluit, which in their language signifies the Rock of Cluit (Clyde), for it is beside the river of that name. On account of the troublesomeness of these nations, the Britons sent messengers to Rome with letters, imploring assistance with tearful prayers, and promising perpetual subjection, provided the impending enemy were driven away from them. An armed legion was at once told off for this service; and, on arriving in the island, engaged the enemy, swept down a great multitude of them, and drove the rest out of the territory of the allies; and, having thus delivered them from the most cruel oppression, the Romans advised them to construct a wall, in the meantime, across the island, between the two seas, for a bulwark to keep off the enemy; and then they returned home with great triumph. But as the wall the Britons constructed across the island, as they had been directed, was not of stone,—as they had no artist capable of such a work,—but of sods, it was of no use. However, they drew it between the two firths or inlets of the sea, which we have spoken of; to the end that, where the protection of the water was wanting, the vallum might serve as a bulwark to defend their borders from the irruption of the enemy. Of which work there erected,—that is, of the vallum,—there are most evident remains to be seen to this day. It begins at about two miles distance from the monastery of Abircornyng, that is, Abercom, on the east, and stretching westwards, ends near the city of Alcluit (Dumbarton). After the death of Arcadius, Honorius reigned fourteen years with his brother's son Theodosius, a boy of eight years of age, after having already reigned thirteen years with his brother Arcadius. He began to reign in A.D. 411.

CHAPTER IV.

Victory of the Roman Legion and the Britons over the Scots and Picts, in a War in which fell King Fergus and a great number of his People and of the Picts.

THESE events, indeed, are thus related by *Paulus*:—At this period, the Britons, unable to endure the molestations of the Scots and Picts, sent to Rome to entreat assistance against their enemies. A legion of soldiers was, accordingly, immediately sent to them, and swept down a great multitude of the Scots and Picts, driving the rest out of the borders of Britannia. As soon, therefore, as these had been thrust out of Britannia, the Britons, who, by the help of the Romans, had the upper hand in the war, constructed the aforesaid wall from ocean to ocean, as they had been ordered to do; and finished it off, at enormous expense, by strengthening it with towers, at intervals, such that the sound of a trumpet could reach from one to the other. It begins, on the east, upon the southern shore of the Scottish sea, near the town of Carriden; then stretches on across the island, for twenty-two miles, with the city of

Glasgow to the south of it, and stops on the bank of the river Clyde, near Kirkpatrick. After this frightful and ruinous struggle, already noticed, in which the Romans and Britons were victorious, and Fergus, the renowned king of the Scots, and a great multitude of his people, and of the Picts, were destroyed, those of the Scots who survived would not on any account submit to the Romans and Britons; but, with the exception of a few of the common peasants, they left their native land desert, and fled. For they durst not linger beyond the southern firth any longer—although certain seers of that time, notwithstanding so great a disaster had befallen both nations in the war, sang that the Scots would, without doubt, gain possession of the whole island. Fergus left there sons under age, Eugenius, Dongardus, and Constantius, whom he had begotten of the daughter of Gryme, the Briton, descended from the stock of the leader Fulgentius. The emperor Maximus had warily driven this Gryme from his dominions, as being the never-failing abettor of Conan and the Scots. When, however, Eugenius was raised to the sovereignty of the kingdom upon the death of his father, as he was young, and of tender years, the chiefs appointed his grandfather Gryme governor to him and his brothers, and protector of the kingdom, inasmuch as he excelled in the art of war, and had also himself derived his origin from the race of their own ancient kings. Since, therefore, they knew him to be well fitted for the government, in time of peace as well as in time of war, they chose him out to be their leader, until his grandsons should have attained to years of puberty, and become able to govern.

CHAPTER V.

Accession of King Eugenius, son of Farchard—He, together with his grandfather, Gryme, breaks down Grymisdyke—A second legion drives the Scots and Picts back across the Tyne.

KING EUGENIUS, being at length raised to the throne of the kingdom, began to reign, with his grandfather, the consul Gryme, in A.D. 419,— that is, in the ninth year of the emperor Honorius, and reigned thirty-three years. Meanwhile the Roman legion had gone back, after the building of the wall; so he first carefully set in order the matters pertaining to the peace of the country, and then turned his thoughts to war. For, unable to brook that the Romans and Britons should unjustly keep back the lands to the north of the Humber, some of which had, by rights, before the war, belonged to him by hereditary succession (those formerly of Fulgentius, to wit), and to other nobles of the Scots and Picts, he gathered reinforcements from all directions, and went, in great strength, to the said wall; and, having first duly ordered his engines, he broke it down to the very ground, while its guards either escaped by flight, or were slain. Of this dyke, or wall, there are evident signs and genuine traces to be seen to this day. It got its name from Gryme, and is called Grymisdyke by the inhabitants. In short, having broken down the wall, they gained possession of the lands they had formerly held, and brought the natives under their sway, as of old. *Bede* has the following:—But soon their former enemies, when they saw that the Roman soldiers were gone, came by sea, and broke into their borders, slaying all things, and trampling, overrunning, and mowing down, like ripe corn, everything in their path. Accordingly the Britons again sent messengers to Rome, imploring aid with tearful voice, lest their wretched country should be utterly blotted out,—lest the name of a Roman province should, through the forwardness of stranger nations, be dimmed in the lustre wherewith it had so long shone among them, and become contemptible. A legion is again sent, and arriving unexpectedly in the autumn, made great slaughter of the enemy, obliging all those who could escape to flee beyond the seas; whereas before, these were wont to carry off their yearly booty across the seas, without any soldiery to withstand them. This legion also was sent by Honorius; and those nations, forasmuch as they had in their various incursions been overawed by it, durst not hazard a pitched battle; but retreated, though not far, beyond the northern banks of the rivers Esk and Tyne, to seek shelter, where they could lie hid until that legion should go back.

CHAPTER VI.

The Wall which the Emperor Severus had formerly commanded to be built across the island, between Gateshead and Carlisle, repaired—Return of the Legion—Election of the first King of the Franks.

THEN the Romans, says *Bede*, declared to the Britons that they could no longer be troubled with such toilsome expeditions for their protection. They advised them rather to take up arms themselves, and undertake the task of coping with their foes, who could prove too strong for them for no other reason than their being themselves relaxed in slothfulness. Thinking, too, that it would also be of some advantage to the allies whom they were forced to abandon, they set up a strong stone wall, in a straight course from sea to sea, between the towns which had been built there for fear of the enemy, and where Severus had formerly made a vallum. This well-known wall, which is still plainly to be seen, they constructed at the public and private expense, the Britons also lending them a hand. It is eight feet in breadth, and twelve in height; and they built it in a straight line from east to west, and put a row of towers at intervals, as is to this day evident to beholders. As soon as this wall was speedily built, they gave that slothful people brave advice, and furnished them patterns for a supply of arms; and so they bid the allies farewell, as though never more to return. Now, in the ninth year of Honorius, according to *Sigibert*, on the death of Samno and Marcomirus, leaders of the Franks, that people resolved, in a general meeting, that they also would have a king, like other nations. So they appointed Pharamund king, the son of their leader Marcomirus; and he reigned eleven years. But the emperor Honorius, after thirteen years had gone by, during which he had ruled with his brother Arcadius, and again other fourteen years with his nephew Theodosius, departed this life.

CHAPTER VII.

The Scots destroy the Wall, and bring slaughter upon the Britons.

WE read in *Paulus*:—But when the Romans went away, the enemy came over again by sea, and trampled and consumed everything they came across. Meanwhile, says *Bede*, the Romans returned home; and the Scots and Picts, on their side, learning their refusal to return, immediately became more confident than their wont, seized upon the whole of the extreme northern part of the island, as far as the wall, and settled there. A slothful body of troops, therefore, was stationed on the top of the fortification, where day and night they pined away with trembling hearts, benumbed with fear. The enemy, on the other hand, attacked them unceasingly with hooked weapons, with which the cowardly defenders were miserably dragged from the walls, and dashed to the ground. Why dwell on this? They forsook the cities and the wall, fled, and were dispersed; while the enemy pursued, and massacres more cruel than any before followed thick. For as lambs are scattered abroad by wild beasts, even so were the wretched citizens by their enemies. Accordingly, being cast out from their homes and possessions, they mitigated the threatening danger of famine by robbing and plundering one another; augmenting external calamities by domestic broils, until the whole country was left entirely destitute of the sustenance of food, save such relief as was afforded by the chase. Meanwhile this famine distressed the Britons more and more, and left to posterity a lasting memory of its ravages; compelling many of them to yield as vanquished men to these troublesome robbers. Now this above-mentioned wall starts, on the east, from the southern bank of the river Tyne, at Goat's Head, which is pronounced *Gateshead* in the English tongue, where formerly Severus commanded a wall and vallum to be made, opposite Newcastle; and stretching onwards for sixty miles, ends, on the west, at the river Esk, otherwise called Scotiswath (Solway), near Carlisle. After the death of Honorius, this Theodosius the younger, his nephew through his brother Arcadius, succeeded to the empire in A.D. 425, and reigned by himself three years. In the third year, he created

Valentinian, the son of his aunt Placidia and Constantius, emperor, to reign with him; and they reigned together twenty-three years.

CHAPTER VIII.

Arrival in Scotland of Saint Palladius, the first bishop and teacher of the Scots, although these had long before embraced the Faith.

IN the second year of Theodosius, likewise, Celestinus I. being a Roman by nation, and begotten of one named Prisons, his father, sat eight years, one month, and eight days, as forty-first Pope of the Roman Church. This Pope appointed that the Psalm "Judge me, Lord, etc." should be said before the Introit of the Mass; and that the one hundred and fifty Psalms of David should be chanted by all antiphonally before the sacrifice. This was not previously done—only the Epistle of Paul and the Holy Gospel were said. By this ordinance, the Introit of the Mass, the Gradalia, and the Hallelujah, were taken from the Psalms; and the Offertory before the sacrifice, and the prayers while communicating, began to be sung with modulation at Mass, in the Roman Church. In the year 429, according to *Sigibert*,—or, according to others, 430,—Saint Palladius was ordained by Pope Celestinus, and sent, as their first bishop, to the Scots who believed in Christ. To which also *Bede* bears witness. Socrates, however, has these prefatory words:—Saint Palladius was the disciple of Evagrius, who was the disciple of the two Macharii—of whom, as of the other holy fathers of Egypt, his book has a full account. He says, too:—It behoves us both to learn what we know not, and faithfully to teach that we do know, etc. We read in the Polychronicon:—In A.D. 430, Pope Celestinus sent Saint Palladius into Scotia, as the first bishop therein. It is, therefore, fitting that the Scots should diligently keep his festival and Church commemorations; for, by his word and example, he with anxious care taught their nation,—that of the Scots, to wit,—the orthodox faith, although they had for a long time previously believed in Christ. Before his arrival, the Scots had, as teachers of the faith and administrators of the Sacraments, priests only, or monks, following the rite of the primitive Church. So he arrived in Scotland with a great company of clergy, in the eleventh year of the reign of king Eugenius; and the king freely gave him a place of abode where he wanted one.

CHAPTER IX.

Account of Saint Palladius continued—Saint Servanus—Saint Kentigern—Saint Ternan—Saint Ninian.

MOREOVER Palladius had as his fellow-worker in preaching and administering the Sacraments a most holy man, Servanus; who was ordained bishop, and created, by Palladius, his coadjutor—one worthy of him in all respects—in order to teach the people the orthodox faith, and with anxious care perfect the work of the Gospel; for Palladius was not equal to discharging alone the pastoral duties over so great a nation. In the *History of Saint Kentigern* we read:—This Servanus was the disciple of the reverend Bishop Palladius, almost in the very earliest days of the Scottish church. Palladius himself was, in the abovementioned year of our Lord's incarnation, sent by the holy Pope Celestinus to be the first bishop of the Scots, who had long been believers. On his arrival in Scotia, he found Saint Servanus there, and called him to work in the vineyard of the Lord of Sabaoth; and when, afterwards, the latter was sufficiently imbued with the teaching of the Church, Palladius appointed him his suffragan over all the nation of the Scots. So runs the story in that work. The holy bishop Terranan likewise was a disciple of the blessed Palladius, who was his godfather, and his fostering teacher and furtherer in all the rudiments of letters and of the faith. Kentigern, again, was a disciple of Saint Servanus, by whom he was washed in the font of holy baptism, and thoroughly indoctrinated in all the dogmas and learning of the Christian religion. He afterwards, while yet a youth, was endowed with so much perfection and grace vouchsafed from above, that God deigned to work great and astounding miracles through him. *Sigibert* tells us:—Moreover, in the fifth year after Palladius arrived in Scotia, this same Pope Celestinus sent Saint Patrick to the Irish Scots, a man of British descent, the son of Chonches, sister of Saint Martin, bishop of Tours. He was named Suchat at his baptism, Magonius by Saint Germanus, and Patricius by

Saint Celestinus, by whom also he was ordained bishop; and, during sixty years, in which he excelled in learning, miracles, and holiness, he converted to Christ the whole island of Ireland. They say that the bishop Saint Ninian died in the time of this emperor Theodosius the younger; for we know of a truth, from passages in various histories, that he flourished uuder the administration of that emperor's father and uncle, Arcadius and Honorius; because it was in the fifth year of their reign that the blessed Martin, bishop of Tours, died; in healthful conversation with whom, while yet living in the flesh, Saint Ninian was privileged to be solaced. He also preached to the tribes in the southern parts of the country, beyond the Scottish firth, which had not yet been found worthy, like the northern Scots, to receive Christ's law. He was a man of wondrous virtue and holiness before God and man, and during his life, nay, after his death, even until now, a marvellous worker of numberless miracles. Hence *Gregory* says:—No wonder the elect can work many marvels while abiding in the flesh, when their very dead bones oftentimes live in miracles!

CHAPTER X.

The Wall broken down by the Scots and Picts, whence its name—The Britons of Albania subjected to the sway of the Scots.

NOW, during the want occasioned by the aforesaid famine, the Scottish and Pictish chiefs were joined by some of the Irish, and, rowing across the rivers Tyne and Esk, in ships of divers kinds, to both ends of the wall, they overran, destroyed, and consumed all the country round about. After some little time, having brought under their sway some of the natives there, put some to flight, and others to the sword, they received the whole country, from sea to sea, under the shelter of their sway; and it has hitherto been found impossible to drive them out thence. O vengeance of Heaven, exclaims *Geoffroy*, for past wickedness! O madness in the tyrant Maximus, to have brought about the absence of so many warlike soldiers! If they had been at hand in this disastrous overthrow, there could not have come upon them any people they would not have driven to flight. Meanwhile, indeed, as we saw in the above passage from *Bede*, the enemy plied them unceasingly with hooked weapons, wherewith the wretched populace were dragged off the walls, and cruelly dashed to the ground. Why dwell on this? The cities and the lofty wall were forsaken, and flight, dispersion, much more than usually hopeless, pursuit by the enemy, and cruel slaughter, came thick upon the citizens, in quick succession. Thus the conquerors won the country on both sides of the wall, and began to inhabit it. Then they speedily summoned the peasantry, with whose hoes and mattocks, pickaxes, forks, and spades, they all, without distinction, set to work to dig broad clefts and frequent breaches through the wall, whereby they might everywhere readily pass backwards and forwards. From these breaches, therefore, did this structure take its present name, which in the English tongue is Thirlitwall—in Latin it would be *murus perforatus* (drilled wall). In the twelfth year, also, of the reign of King Eugenius, the devil appeared to the Jews in the Isle of Crete, in the likeness of Moses, and promised to lead them dry shod through the sea to the promised land. Great numbers were thus killed and drowned, and the remainder were converted to Christ.

CHAPTER XI.

The Britons yet again write to the Romans, Litorius and Aëtius to wit, for Succours, which they do not obtain.

WHILE, therefore, the British people were attacked on either side by these and like disasters, Gryme, the chief of the forces and first consul to King Eugenius, died a natural death, at an advanced age, after he had fulfilled the duties of protector for nineteen years, during which he had not only ruled the kingdom nobly, but even more nobly restored it to its olden state. Then, after his death, the king reigned fourteen years alone. He, likewise, combining with the Picts, lost no time in stirring up a cruel war against the Romanized Britons; and he attacked them with the whole strength of the combined forces. The Britons, on the other hand, unable to withstand him, speedily sent to the Roman patricians, who were vicegerents of the commonwealth under the emperors Theodosius and Valentinian—namely Aëtius, and Litorius, whose authority was second only to that of Aëtius—beseeching them not to refuse to vouchsafe them such help against their fierce enemies, the Scots and Picts, as other subjects of the Romans would obtain. To Aëtius, says *Bede*, the remainder of the poor Britons sent a letter, which began thus:—"To the Consul Aëtius, the groans of the Britons." And in the course of the letter they thus unfolded their woes:—"The barbarians drive us back to the sea; the sea drives us back to the barbarians. Between them, two kinds of death are in store for us: we are either murdered or drowned." Yet neither could they, for all that, get any assistance from him, forasmuch as he was at that time engaged in very serious wars with Bledla and Attila, kings of the Huns. As, therefore, they got no aid from them, they sorrowfully returned home, and announced their rebuff to their fellow-countrymen. *Paulus* tells us:— The Britons, likewise, being again hard pressed by the ravages of the Scots and Picts, sent Aëtius a letter full of tears and distress, imploring aid from him as soon as possible. When, however, Aëtius would not listen to them, seeing that he was engaged against enemies nearer home, some of the Britons made an energetic resistance, and drove away the foe; while others were forced by the enemy to submit. Finally, the Scots and Picts subdued the uttermost part of this island, and made it their habitation; wherefrom it has hitherto been found impossible to expel them. Meanwhile, the emperor Theodosius, after reigning sixteen years, besides the one-and-twenty years he had already reigned with his uncle Honorius, of which time he had spent twenty-five years associated with his son-in-law Valentinian, died at Milan, wasted by sickness, and was buried there. At this time Saint John the Baptist revealed his head, near what had formerly been the dwelling of King Herod, to two eastern monks who came to Jerusalem.

CHAPTER XII.

The Britons and their King Vortigern, in despair, invite the heathen nation of the Saxons to help them against the Scots and Picts.

SOME Chronicles have the following:—The rest of the Britons, however, being in constant fear of the onslaught of the Scots, and no longer trusting to the protection of the Romans, by the advice of their king invited over the nation of the Saxons, under two leaders, Hors and Hengist, to help in their defence, in A.D. 447, or, rather, 449, the thirty-third year of King Eugenius. After Maximus had drained the island of Britannia of soldiers to guard it, says *Sigibert*, the Scots and the Picts, and the other nations with them, poured into the island, and began to waste the unwarlike population and the whole land, by slaughter and pillage. Then a further mischief was added to this; for King Vortigern invited over the nation of the heathen Saxons, to provide for his own safety, and attack the enemy. Some Chronicles again say:—In the year stated above, when the wickedness and weakness of mind of Vortigern, the king of the Britons, became known to all the nations round about, there rose up against him the Scots on the north-west, and the Picts on the north, who assailed the kingdom of Britannia with the most galling outrages and molestations. For, consuming everything with fire and sword, pillage and rapine, they crushed that sinful nation, who abetted the pride and extravagance of their king; so that the masses, as corrupt as their king, were overthrown in a common vengeance; while those of that miserable people whom the inroads of the enemy had not reached, were clean consumed by the severe famine. And thus the multitude, as if rolled and crushed between two millstones, were assailed by pestilence, and attacked by the sword, so that the living were not even enough to bury the dead. So the king, with his people left desolate and worn-out by the inroads of war, knew not what to do to oppose the irruptions of the enemy, and sank forlorn. They entered into consultation, says *Bede*, as to what should be done, and where they should look for protection, to avoid or repel the incursions, so fierce and so frequent, of the northern nations; and they all, with their king Vortigern, agreed to call over the Saxon nation to their aid, from the parts beyond the sea—which, as the issue of the matter more clearly proved, was surely contrived by the will of God, that evil might come upon the wicked. For, in the year above noted, the nation of the Angles or Saxons came over at first in three long ships, on the invitation of

Vortigern, king of the Britons, and took up their abode in a place in Kent, as though prepared to fight for the country. These came over from the three strongest nations of Germany, that is, the Saxons, Angles, and Jutes. Moreover, from the Angles, that is, from the tribes sprung from that country which is called *Angulus*, all the other nations of the Angles derived their name.

CHAPTER XIII.

First arrival of the Saxons—Various reverses inflicted and suffered on both sides.

Accordingly, as the Romans stood aloof from the defence of the Britons, the Saxons were deliberately called in by the general voice. These, being earnestly desirous of renewing afresh, in conjunction with the Britons, the war against the Scots, after their arrival proceeded at once to Albania; and, having made a hostile attack upon it, they carried off a great deal of plunder. The Scots, also, on the other hand, together with the Picts and that part of the Britons which was subject unto them—for in those days they were permanently settled throughout Albania—gathered their columns together, and plundered the country across the Humber, in their wonted manner. Thereupon the Saxon barbarians, says *Geoffroy*, on the ratification of the treaty, abode with Vortigern at his court. But the Scots and Picts formed an exceedingly large army; and, issuing forth from Albania, began to lay waste the northerly parts of the island. When, therefore, Vortigern heard of this, he assembled his own troops and the Saxons, and, marching against them across the Humber, forthwith routed the enemy, who were accustomed to victory. So Vortigern gave Hengist broad acres in the region of Lindissey. Now, although, for the space of nearly two years, frequent reverses were inflicted on either side, still no pitched battle was fought. But the Saxons craftily suggested to Vortigern that if he could contrive to get some more stipendiaries from their country, they would easily enable him to overcome his aforesaid enemies. This was accordingly done. For, as *Bede* relates, swarms of those before-mentioned nations poured eagerly into the island; and the numbers of the strangers began to increase so much that they became a terror to the natives themselves who had invited them. *Geoffroy* resumes:— When the Britons saw this, fearing their treachery, they told the king to drive them out of the borders of his kingdom; but Vortigern evaded acquiescence in their advice, as he loved the Saxons above all other nations, on account of Hengist's daughter Rowen, whom he had taken to wife some time before. Thereupon the Britons deserted Vortigern, and suddenly set up as king, to drive out the barbarians, Vortimer, the king's son, whom he had begotten before. Now Vortimer, the son of Vortigern, says *William*, perceiving that he and his Britons were being undone by the craft of the Saxons, turned his thoughts to driving them out, seven years after their arrival.

CHAPTER XIV.
Accession of Dongardus, brother to Eugenius—Alliance of Vortigern's son, King Vortimer, then King of the Britons, with the Scots, against the Saxons—Their Struggle for Britain.

So Eugenius, when the days of his unhappy reign were fulfilled, died of a severe illness—or, as is related in a certain history, fell in battle with the Britons and English, south of the Humber; and his brother Dongardus was raised to the throne of the kingdom in his stead, and reigned five years. He began to reign in A.D. 452, in the first year of the emperor Martian, who succeeded Theodosius; which Martian, likewise, reigned six years and six months. Now, in the second year of Dongardus, Vortimer, of whom we have spoken above, being, on a sudden, proclaimed king during his father's lifetime, felt that it would be unsafe rashly and precipitately to come into collision with the Saxons, before making friends with the Scots, for fear those two nations should combine their strength, and make an onslaught together upon the Britons; so he despatched messengers to King Dongardus, to induce him, in security of mind, to renew, against the heathen Saxons, the wonted treaty they had formerly concluded against the Romans, and to observe it faithfully in all respects. The king, accordingly, joyfully acceded to all their demands on every point; and they reported to their own king, in due order, all that was done and agreed upon. Vortimer, however, seized a fit opportunity, and, with his men, suddenly fell upon the Saxons, slaying their leader Hors, Hengist's brother, with many others, in the first battle. On the death of the chief Hors, the Saxons set up as king his brother Hengist, who is reported to have fought against the Britons three times in the same year; but, unable to withstand the prowess of Vortimer, he took refuge in the Isle of Thanet, where he was harassed by daily sea-fights. At length the Saxons barely managed to embark on board their boats, and return to Germany, leaving their wives and little ones behind. On Vortimer being afterwards taken away by fatal destiny—who so loathed his father's indolence that he would have governed the kingdom mightily, had God permitted it—Vortigern was again promoted to the government of the kingdom, and the Saxons came back to Britain. The emperor Martian died in the sixth year of his reign, and after an equal number of months had gone by; and to him succeeded Leo the Great, who reigned sixteen years. But Dongardus died in the fifth year of Martian.

CHAPTER XV.
Return of the Saxons after Vortimer's Death, with a greater multitude of the Heathen—Death of the British Chieftains by Treachery.

IN A.D. 461, therefore, Hengist, having heard of the death of Vortimer, who was cut off by poison administered by his stepmother, Rowen, came over to Britain, accompanied by three thousand armed men. When, however, the arrival of so great a multitude was announced to Vortigern, who had been again created king, and to the chiefs of the kingdom, they were extremely indignant, and determined to do battle with them. This was secretly hinted, through messengers, to her father Hengist by his daughter, whom Vortigern had previously unlawfully married; and Hengist bethought himself of betraying the British nation under a show of peace. So he sent ambassadors to the king, saying that it was not to offer any violence to him or his kingdom that he had brought so great a multitude with him; but that he might put himself and his people at his disposal, so that the king might retain in the country those he wanted, while the rest would sail back to Germany. When, therefore, this was announced to the king, and it was likewise proposed that a day and place should be fixed upon beforehand for adjusting these matters by common consent, the king commanded his subjects and the Saxons to meet on the first of May, at the village of Ambrium (Ambresburgh), to adjust these matters accordingly. Meanwhile Hengist instructed his comrades to have every one a long knife in his boot; and while the Britons were holding converse with them in all security, each one was to be ready, at a given signal "Nemet zoure Sexes," to draw his knife and stab the Briton next to him. And it came to pass thus: Hengist held back Vortigern by the cloak, while the rest stabbed the Britons present, who little suspected such a thing, to the number of about four hundred and sixty persons, barons and consuls. Then, soon, the Saxons wasted and overran all the country, and suddenly attacked the inhabitants, as wolves pounce upon sheep when abandoned by their shepherd; pulling down the churches, and everything belonging to them, to the very ground; murdering the priests beside the altars; and burning up the sacred Scriptures with fire. Men of religious orders and married men leaving behind them their substance, their wives and children, and, what is more their freedom, betook themselves to foreign lands beyond the sea. Some, likewise, of the miserable remainder, who managed to escape from this slaughter, betook themselves to caves and wooded spots, some to the north, others to the south—that is, to Scotia, Wales, and Cornwall. Others, again, spent with hunger, came forth and submitted to the enemy, to get some relief in food; though destined to undergo perpetual slavery, even if they were not murdered on the spot.

CHAPTER XVI.

Accession of King Constantius, and the division of Britannia, in course of time, among the Saxons, into eight Kingdoms.

IN A.D. 457, Dongardus was succeeded by his brother Constantius, who reigned twenty-two years. On Vortigern, king of the Britons, being struck by lightning, or, as *Geoffroy* maintains, burnt to death in his own tower by Aurelius Ambrosius, this Aurelius was raised to the throne, by the Britons. For, as *William* tells us, after King Vortimer's death, the British strength dwindled away; and they would then have altogether perished, had not Ambrosius, the sole survivor of the Romans, been monarch of the kingdom after Vortigern. But the Britons, says *Bede*, had at that time, for their leader, Aurelius Ambrosius, a man of great moderation, who alone, probably, of the Roman nation, had survived the storm described above, in which his parents, who bore a royal and distinguished name, had been slaughtered. Under his guidance, the Britons began to gain strength; and, from that time, now the inhabitants, now the enemy, prevailed; until the year of the siege of Mount Badamor, when they made no small slaughter of those enemies of theirs, about the year 44 after their arrival in Britannia. When, therefore, Britannia was brought under the yoke of the Saxons, eight kings of the Saxons began to reign over the country, which they shared among them. These sought, above all, to root out Christ and the worship of Christians; extending their kingdoms, and assigning each, according to his ability, boundaries to their realms, whereof the following are the names. The first kingdom was certainly Kent; the first kings whereof were Hors and Hengist.

The second, Sussex; whereof the first king, Ellen, began to reign in A.D. 477, while Aurelius ruled over the Britons.

The third, Wessex, took its rise, in the time of Uther, from King Cerdic.

The fourth, Essex, took its rise, in the time of King Arthur, from Erkenwyn.

The fifth, Anglia; the first king whereof was Ulfa.

The sixth, the kingdom of the Mercians, began with King Creodda.

The seventh, the kingdom of Deira, began with Alle.

The eighth is the kingdom of Bernicia, which took its rise from Adda. These last two kingdoms grew out of the disruption of the kingdom of Northumbria, which was afterwards restored as one kingdom. Let the reader, for the present, be satisfied with thus much concerning the first arrival of the Saxons.

CHAPTER XVII.

Alliance of Aurelius Ambrosius, King of the Britons, with King Constantius, against the Saxons—Merlin the Seer.

AURELIUS AMBROSIUS, then, the king of the Britons, sent greeting to King Constantius, and earnestly besought him, by means of messengers, to take up arms without delay against the heathen Saxons, the restless foes of the true God and the Christian religion, and do his part in coming to the assistance of his allies the Britons, in consideration of the former alliance between them. The king, accordingly, acknowledged the treaty lately concluded with Vortimer, and moreover renewed and ratified it, with the greatest solemnities, to last in perpetuity—if, at least, Aurelius would do the same. So, as all things had sped prosperously according to their wishes, the messengers returned home again, together with some ambassadors of the king's. At the same time, Aurelius also sent messengers, charged with the same business, to Drostanus, king of the Picts, who, however, was already bespoken by the messengers of Hengist, to whom he had promised a friendly alliance against the Britons, and a safe repair in case of need; nor did he care any longer to offer Aurelius even the assurance of peace. Accordingly, when Hengist had established his kingdom within the borders of Kent, trusting to the promise of the Picts, he sent forth his brother Octa, and his son Eubusa, men of tried prowess and boldness, to seize the northern parts of Britannia; and to withstand the Scots, and check their attacks. On the arrival of these soldiers, therefore, they were received by the Picts with looks of gladness; and, being strengthened in numbers by them, they made war for a time against both the Scots and Britons. The Britons thenceforth combined with the Scots, and they always fought together against the Picts and Saxons. Now, in the days of Aurelius and his predecessor Vortigern, a certain seer from Cambria, named Merlin, chanted many socalled prophecies, dark to the understanding, the meaning of which could never or seldom be discerned by any one until they were fulfilled; but which, on being fulfilled, or after they had come to pass, many very often believed they recognised. These predictions of his, which will be found in the Sixth Book of *Geoffroy's* Chronicle, towards the end, have suggested the following:—

> "Weak Vortigern sits pranked with royal show;
> Great Merlin stands and bodes the coming woe."

The prophecy begins thus:—As Vortigern was sitting upon the bank of a drained pool, etc. He openly declares, however, among other things, that the Britons were to be driven out of the country by the Saxons; and that the Saxons were first to be overcome by the Danes, and then overthrown by the Neustrians, that is, the Normans,—which things, indeed, are, in our own days, known to have been truly fulfilled in all respects. He likewise foretold that the Britons, accompanied by the Armorican and Albanian nations, would wrest back their kingdom of long ago, from the Normans, who now reign in Anglia, and would thenceforth hold sway therein. After all, the fulfilment of divination of this kind, which has not yet, it is believed, come to pass, or which has still to come to pass, is it not surely under the control of Him to whom the past and the future are alike continually present?

CHAPTER XVIII.

Accession of King Congal—Renewal of the Treaty between the Scots and Britons—Internal strife of the Britons, whereby they lose the Kingdom, and the Saxons everywhere prevail.

BUT after the death of Constantius, who lay for a long time lingering in sickness, Congal, his nephew through his brother Dongardus, assumed the kingdom in A.D. 479, the sixth year of the emperor Zeno, who had succeeded Leo, and taken his daughter to wife. This king also reigned twenty-two years, like his uncle who had preceded him. With Congal also, as soon as he was crowned king, was the friendly alliance renewed and ratified through the messengers of King Aurelius. For the Saxon wars against the Britons began to grow more serious, as fresh swarms kept unflaggingly coming upon them on all sides, in such great numbers, that the latter, do what they could, were unequal to the task of driving them out of the country—nay, from day to day they increased more and more in numbers and wickedness, and waxed strong. Out of all the lands of the heathen, but mostly from Germany, armed vessels flocked together, as crows to the carrion; whereby their numbers were largely increased, while those of the Britons were daily lessened. The strength also of the latter was so much taken up with continual and calamitous intestine quarrels, and so much split up into several parties, that had not the prudence and firmness of Aurelius come to their rescue, they would then doubtless have lost the kingdom. But during the whole of his lifetime the Britons maintained friendship with the Scottish tribes, and these with the Britons in return. For, thenceforth, no subtlety of their adversaries could part them, never after could the fierceness of aliens break up their peaceful covenant, nor the foreign quarrels or wrongs of their respective nations thenceforward sever their friendship—nay, rather, the speedy renewal of the treaty between them welded them in closer unity of love. Thus the Saxons and Picts on the one side, and Scots and Britons on the other, fought against one another continually; until the Scots had got the upper hand, and laid the Picts even in the dust; and the Saxons had wrested Britain from the Britons, through the apathy of that people. Wherefore *William* tells us:—At length the Britons combined with the Scots, and fought many a battle against the Saxons and Picts. Meanwhile, says *Bede*, the Saxons and Picts, whom one and the same necessity drew together into the field, took up arms with their united forces against the Britons and Scots.

CHAPTER XIX.

Clovis, the first King of the Franks who was baptized—Origin of the Franks.

CHAPTER XX.

Same continued—Period when they first had a King—Succession of their Kings down to this Clovis—Saint Gyberianus Scotus.

CHAPTER XXI.

Accession of Gonranus—Renewal of the Treaty with Uther—Saint Brigida.

MOREOVER, we read that, in the time of Congal, there was no open war, though the Saxons and Picts made various inroads and attacks upon the country. At his decease, however, in A.D. 501—the ninth year of the emperor Anastasius—he was succeeded by his brother Gonranus, a man of advanced age, also a son of Dongardus. Gonranus reigned thirty-four years. At the outset of his reign, war broke out between him and the Britons. For as soon as that noble chief of the Britons, Aurelius, was taken away from their midst, having been treacherously poisoned by the Saxons, the Britons were altogether at a loss any longer to maintain peace with their friends and allies, or concord among themselves. And that excellent historian of the Britons, Gildas, has spoken his praises above all their other kings—nay, he has left to posterity his deeds faithfully recorded in well-chosen language. For he was mighty on foot, and mightier still on horseback; bountiful and bold; diligent in the service of God; moderate in all things; and well versed in commanding armies. At length, upon his death, he was succeeded by his brother Uther, a man excessively given to stirring up civil war among his subjects. For, at the instigation of certain persons, he endeavoured to wrest from the Scots the district of Westmeria (Westmoreland) and other adjoining districts, the peaceful possession of which they had so many years enjoyed. But being assailed on all sides by the inroads of his heathen enemies, he consented to renew the old treaty with the king; and, by the intervention of ambassadors from both parties, they were again restored to harmony. In the eighth year of King Gonranus, the aforesaid pagans—Cerdix and Kenrik—in one day slew 5000 Britons, with their king Nathanleod. In his fourteenth year, also. Stuff and Wythgar, heathen Saxons, sailed over to Britain with a few ships, and giving battle to the Britons at Cerdixore, were all routed. In his eighteenth year died Saint Brigida, a holy maid, beloved of God, and was buried at Dunum (Down). In the same year, Cerdix and Kenrik fought against the Britons at Cerdixforde, and were victorious; and thus they obtained the supreme power in Wessex.

CHAPTER XXII.
Gildas the Historian—Some Metrical Prophecies of his.

ABOUT this time died Gildas, a sound and elegant historian, and was buried at an old church in the Isle of Avallon. The Britons owe it to him, as divers histories bear witness, that they were of any renown among the other nations. Some maintain that he was Arthur's chaplain; others that he was not, but that he flourished in the beginning of his days, and earlier. Delighting in the holiness of the place, which he loved not a little, he tarried long in this same Isle of Avallon, and, leading there a solitary life pleasing to God, he attained to so much grace, that he was found worthy to be invested with the power of working miracles, and, oftentimes, with the spirit of prophecy. Indeed, he uttered many prophecies, some in prose and some in verse, which turned out true. A few of these predictions of his in verse, which, according to the expounders of our day, are not believed to have as yet come to pass, we have thought fit to insert below, in the present chapter. First, we give the following passage, on the continuance of the treaty concluded between the Scots and the Britons—first broached by Carausius, then faithfully observed by Conan, renewed by Aurelius Ambrosius, and continued, likewise, until now by many chiefs, though not by all. *Gildas* says,—

> "The sons of Brutus, banded with the Scot,
> Fair Anglia's beauty shall with slaughter blot.
> Her streams shall flow red-stained with hostile gore;
> Her faithless sons shall fall to rise no more.

The thirsty ground shall drink the Saxon's life,
Shed by the Briton's, and the Albanian's, knife.
The friendly Scots shall see the Britons reign.
The land shall bear its ancient name again.
An eagle from a ruined tower foretold:—
These nations shall the ancestral kingdom hold;
Their foes cast out, they shall with blissful sway,
Together reign until the Judgment Day."

CHAPTER XXIII.

These Prophecies continued—Saint Brandan—Saint Machutes.

AMONGST other things, Gildas also sang the following, concerning certain misfortunes which should befall the Scots:—

"Scotia shall weep a noble chieftain's fate,
Who o'er the sea-girt land shall hold his state.
While twice three years, and moons thrice three, roll by,
Under no prince the widow'd land shall lie.
Scotia shall mourn her famous kings of old—
Her kings so just, rich, bountiful, and bold.
For an unkingly king—so Merlin sings—
Shall wield the sceptre of victorious kings.
Then shall Albania wail for ruin nigh.
Her people, self-betray'd, shall slaughter'd lie.
Alas! Albania, conquered by her guile,
A king of Anglic birth shall serve a while.
But after, when a miser king is dead,
She shall revive—so the ancient Sibyl said.
White Alban's treachery shall bruise the land;
His countrymen shall perish by his hand.
The northern king, with his wild sailor horde.
Shall scourge the Scots with famine, fire, and sword.
The stranger nation, by their friends betray'd,
At length, shall grovelling in the dust be laid;

Their Noric chief, on the lost battle-field,
Shall to the avenging sword his life-blood yield.
The realm shall be enrich'd by one from Gaul,
Who by his brother's sword, alas! shall fall.
Pale woe shall then give way to thriving weal.
And o'er the land a peaceful calm shall steal.

Gildas, unveiler of the olden time,
These mighty things enshrines in lowly rhyme."

Justin, the elder, a most Christian emperor, succeeded the faithless Anastasius in A.D. 518, and governed ten years, dying in the twenty-eighth year of King Gonranus. In that same year—namely, A.D. 528—he was succeeded by Justinian, his nephew through his sister, who reigned thirty-eight years. This emperor made a digest of the books of the Roman laws, in one volume, called the *Justinianum*. In the thirtieth year of King Gonranus, Cerdix, and Kenrick, his son, took the Isle of Wight, and gave it to Stuf and Wychtgare, the nephews of Cerdix. At this time, also, Dionysius composed, in the city of Rome, the Paschal cycles of nineteen years, beginning from A.D. 532. Saint Brendan flourished in Scotland at that time—a man of great abstemiousness, and conspicuous for his virtues. He was the father of nearly 3000 monks. Moreover, he went a seven years' voyage in quest of the Fortunate Isles, and saw many things worthy of wonder. Saint Machutes, also called Macloveus, who was baptized and regularly educated by him, and accompanied him on his voyage, lived in Britain, renowned for his miracles and holiness.

CHAPTER XXIV.

Death of King Gonranus—Arthur ascends the British Throne.

GONRANUS, after he had completed his thirty-fourth year on the throne, was ensnared in an ambuscade at Innerlochy, by his brother's son, Eugenius or Eochodius Hebdre, and put to death. His body was taken to the church of Saint Oran, at Hy (Iona), to be buried, where repose the remains of his father and grandfather. After his death, however, his wife, the queen, fled secretly to Ireland, with her sons Rogenanus and Aydanus, and remained there while Eugenius and his brother reigned, even up to her death; though her sons, when they had attained unto the full age of puberty, and unto strength to fit them for military service, on the king's spirit being softened by the prayers of mediating friends, returned to their native land, and thenceforth abode in peace. Of these we shall speak at greater length in their proper place. Now, on the death of Uther, king of the Britons, by poison, through the perfidy of the Saxons (like his brother Aurelius of happy memory), his son Arthur, by the contrivance of certain men, succeeded to the kingdom; which, nevertheless, was not lawfully his due, but rather his sister Anna's, or her children's. For she was begotten in lawful wedlock, and married to Loth, a Scottish consul, and lord of Laudonia (Lothian), who came of the family of the leader Fulgentius; and of her he begat two sons—the noble Galwanus and Modred—whom, on the other hand, some relate, though without foundation, to have had another origin. It is certain, at all events, that Arthur reigned in the days of the reign of Gonranus, and for seven years after his death; for Arthur died A.D. 542, as is shown in sundry writings; but I have not come upon the year when he took upon him the kingly dignity. But why Arthur was adopted as king, and the lawful heirs were passed over, may be seen from *Geoffroy*; for, as he says, on the death of Uther Pendragon, the nobility from the several provinces were gathered together in the city of Silchester, and suggested to Dubricius, Archbishop of Caerleon, that he should consecrate Uther's son, Arthur, to be their king. For they were pressed by necessity, because the Saxons, on hearing of the aforesaid king's death, had invited over their countrymen from Germany, and, under the command of Colgerin, were endeavouring to exterminate the Britons.

CHAPTER XXV.

Arthur.

DUBRICIUS, therefore, grieving for the calamities of his country, did, with some of the bishops, invest Arthur with the diadem of the kingship. Arthur was then a youth of fifteen years, of singular courage and bounteousness, to whom his innate goodness lent such a charm that he was beloved by almost all men. When he had thus been consecrated with the insignia of royalty, he, observing his wonted custom, gave way to his liberality; and so large a number of knights flocked to him, that even what he distributed among them ran short. But the man in whom bounteousness and valour are inborn, though he may be in want for a time, yet poverty shall not harm him for ever. Thus speaks *Geoffroy*. But let us return to the subject—where it is said that they were impelled by necessity—which has no law, both with gods and men; for necessity makes that lawful which otherwise were not lawful. But much depends on what and what manner of necessity that was. We can, however, gather quite well, from the progress of *Geoffroy's* narrative, that at that time Gualwanus, who is also called Waulwanus, and his brother Modred were boys under the age of puberty. For we start with the understanding that Arthur, as we have mentioned above, was fifteen years of age when he was adopted as king; then sundry hostile outbreaks were, in the meantime, brought about by him against the Saxons; and *Geoffroy*, after declaring the battles which were so fought from the time of his accession to the throne, goes on to speak thus:—After these events, when, etc.—and a little further on:—Walwanus, the son of the aforesaid Loyth, was then a youth of twelve years, and was handed over to the service of Pope Sulpicius by his uncle, from whom he received arms. Such are his words. And, therefore, on so strong a necessity suddenly arising, they were justified in electing a youth verging on manhood, rather than a child in the cradle; and it was haply, for this reason, that Modred stirred up against Arthur that war wherehi both met their fate. *Geoffroy*, however, writes that Modred and Galwanus were the sons of Anna, sister of Aurelius, Arthur's uncle. He says: Loth, who, in the time of Aurelius Ambrosius, had married his sister, of whom he begat Galwanus and Modred. But, further on, he calls Arthur the uncle of Galwanus, saying: Walwanus, the son of the aforesaid Loth, was then a youth of twelve years, and was handed over to the service of Pope Sulpicius by his uncle, from whom he received arms. Such are *Geoffroy's* words. But it is clearly certain that neither Aurelius nor Uther survived up to that time; therefore, we may gather that Arthur was this uncle of his. That is *Geoffroy's* account. I, however, refer this point to the sagacity of the reader to deal with; for I do not see my way easily to bring these passages into harmony with each other. But I believe it to be nearer the truth that Modred, as I have read elsewhere, was Arthur's sister's son; and that is the drift of this chapter.

CHAPTER XXVI.

Accession of the three Kings, Eugenius, Convallus, and Kynatel or Connyd—Arrival of Saint Columba.

"EUGENIUS, or Eochodius Hebdre, as soon as his uncle Gonranus was slain, assumed the kingship in A.D. 535, and reigned twenty-three years. In the eighth year of his reign, the fifteenth of the Emperor Justinian, was fought in Britain a battle between the British king, Arthur, and his nephew Modred, wherein both of them fell wounded to the death, with a great multitude of Britons as well as Scots. But Eugenius passed the whole time of his administration in ceaseless struggles with the Saxons and Picts, while fortune yielded the victory sometimes to him, sometimes to them; and, doing his best to keep the peace with the Britons, and the bond of their pristine alliance, he oftentimes, himself present in person, tendered them his help against the heathens. At his death in A.D. 558, the thirty-first year of the emperor Justinian, he was succeeded by his brother Convallus, who reigned ten years. In the eighth year of his reign over the Scots, and the ninth of that of Brude, the son of Mealochon, over the Picts, there came out of Ireland, into Scotland, the holy priest and abbot Columba—a man of a life to be no less admired than venerated, the founder of monasteries, and the father and instructor of many monks. He shared his name with the prophet Jonah: for *Jonah* in the Hebrew tongue is *Columba* in the Latin, and *Peristera* in the Greek. The names of twelve men who sailed over to Scotland with Columba, from Ireland, are these:—

The two sons of Brendinus, Baythenus, also called Coninus, Saint Columba's successor, and Cobthacus, his brother.

Aernanius, the uncle of Saint Columba.

Dormicius, his minister.

The two sons of Rodain, Rus and Fechno.

Scandalaus, son of Bresail, son of Endeus.

Eoghodius.

Thocammeus.

Mocifirus Cetea.

Cayrnaanus, also a son of Brandinus, son of Melgy.

Grillanus.

On a certain day, at the very hour when there was being fought in Ireland a battle, which is called Ondemone in Scottish, this man of God, having audience of the said king Convallus, son of Congal, in Scotland, gave a minute account both of the battle which was being fought, and of the kings to whom God vouchsafed the victory over their enemies. In the second year after Saint Columba's arrival, however, King Convallus died, and was at once, that same year, succeeded in the kingdom by his brother Kynatel or Connyd, who died a year and three months after.

CHAPTER XXVII.

An Angel brings Saint Columba down the Glass Book of the Consecration of Kings—Accession of King Aydanus.

AT this time, says *Adamnan*, while Saint Columba tarried in a certain island named Hymba, in ecstasy of mind, one night he saw the Angel of God bearing in his hand the Glass Book of the ordination of kings, which he held out for Saint Columba to read. As, however, he refused, on the third night, to ordain Aydanus, son of Gonranus, king, as he was in the book bidden to do, seeing that he loved his brother Jogenanus better, on a sudden the Angel stretched forth his hand, and struck the holy man with a scourge; and a livid mark remained on his side, all the days of his life. He likewise addressed these words to him, saying,—"Know thou for certain that I am sent to thee from God with this book, in order that thou shouldest ordain Aydanus king, according to what thou hast read therein; but, if thou shouldest be unwilling to further this behest, I shall strike thee a second time." So when the Angel of the Lord, with the same Glass Book in his hand, had appeared three consecutive nights to Saint Columba, and enjoined the divine behest with respect to the ordination of the said king, that saint sailed over to the island of Iona; and on the arrival of Aydanus there, in those days, as he was bidden, Saint Columba laid liis hand upon his head, and blessed him, and ordained him king; prophesying, among the words of the ordination ceremony, what should befall his sons, grandsons, and great grandsons. Aydanus, therefore, having been thus ordained king, to the joy of his nation, through the warning of an angel, ruled the kingdom in great prosperity. He began to reign in A.D. 570—the fifth year of Justin the younger, who succeeded Justinian on the imperial throne in A.D. 566, and governed twelve years; and the king reigned thirty-five years. He devoted himself beyond measure to warlike enterprises, even against the warnings of the blessed Columba; so that he not only utterly vanquished all the nations round about; to wit, the Noricans, Picts, and Saxons, as often as they burst into his kingdom, but also overcame these Picts on their own ground. It is written, however, that his army was twice defeated: on one occasion, under Brendinus, the chief of his host; and on the other, under himself. The manner of one of these discomfitures—the former—follows in the next chapter. It came to pass thus:—

CHAPTER XXVIII.

Aydanus sends assistance to Malgo, King of the Britons—Victory of the Heathens—Parentage of Saint Furseus, Saint Foylanus, and Saint Vultanus.

IT came to pass that Malgo, king of the Britons, hearing the prowess of Aydanus extolled, sent messengers to him beseeching him not to be unmindful of their late covenant and friendship, nor refuse to help him against a heathenish and wicked nation. He, on his side, readily inclining his ear to so just a request, and giving effect to it, sent off his son Griffinus, a distinguished soldier, and Brendinus, prince of Eubonia, his nephew by his sister, with a mighty host, in the fifteenth year of his reign. Nor would he, in this case, have intrusted to those men the care of so great a matter, notwithstanding that they had many a time before been wont to discharge the duty of leader of armies wisely; for he took steps to direct this expedition himself, and would have done so, had not the nobles, with sounder judgment, most earnestly recalled him back from his purpose. As soon, therefore, as these set out with their army, they were joined by the northern Britons; and with forces thus combined, they hastened in all security, as if afraid of nothing, to meet Malgo. But lo suddenly, on the third day after they had crossed the stony moor, they fell, though not unawares, right among the squadrons of the heathens, led by Cenlinus, king of the West Saxons, at a place called Fethanlege; and, after a severe struggle there, for the space of a full day, Cutha, the son of Cenlinus, was slain, with the whole of the first line, which he commanded. The remaining ranks of the heathen host did not, aught afraid on that account, retreat from the field. Nay, they exerted themselves to press on more bravely until, with cruel slaughter, they fearfully routed both our men and the Britons, who seemed at first to be winning the battle. In these days, says *Vincentius*, the prince Brendinus had a brother in Scotia, named Adelfius; of whose daughter, called Gelgehes, Philtanus, king of Ireland, begat Saint Furseus, and his brothers, Foylanus and Ultanus, exceeding great saints before God. In the ninth year of King Aydanus died Justin, and was, in A.D. 578, succeeded in the empire by Tiberius, who was six years emperor. On the death of Tiberius, he was succeeded, in A.D. 584, by his daughter's husband, Mauricius, who reigned twenty-one years.

CHAPTER XXIX.

This King Aydanus sets out to the assistance of Cadwallo, King of the Britons, against the Saxons—Issue of the Battle—Saint Columba's Prophecy about this battle—Saint Kentigern and Saint Convallus.

KING Aydanus, in the twenty-third year of his reign, on being asked by the Britons and their King Cadwallo for assistance against the aforesaid King Cenlinus, advanced with his army as far as Chester, where he was joined by the Britons, massed in line by squadrons, and prepared to give battle to Cenlinus. The latter, hearing this, prepared for action, and marched to meet them; and a severe battle was fought at Wodenysborch, where, on the side of Cenlinus, the leaders Cealinus, Quichelm, and Cryda, and great numbers of the soldiery of his army, perished utterly; while he himself was wounded and fled, and was thereupon deprived of his kingdom. At the very time of the battle, the holy man Columba, tarrying in the island of Iona, as he relates in his works, suddenly called his minister, and said to him, "Ring the bell." By the sound thereof the brethren were hurried to church, and came running quickly, the saint himself going on before and leading them. And, when they had knelt down in the church, he said unto them, "Now, let us earnestly pmy for King Aydanus, and this people; for, this very hour, they are going into battle." After a short interval, he walked out of the church, and looking up to heaven, he said, "Now the barbarians are being put to flight; and to Aydanus, unhappy though he otherwise be, yet doth God grant the victory." The holy man, also, prophetically and truly, told them of the number of three hundred and three men who were slain of the army of Aydanus. Now, contemporaneously with Saint Columba, there flourished the most blessed Kentigern, bishop of Glasgow, a man of wondrous sanctity, and a worker of many miracles; whose revered bones there rest entombed, illustrious for many miracles to the praise of God. The utmost boundary of his bishopric southwards was, at that time, as it ought by rights to be now, at the royal cross below Stanemor. And one of his chief disciples was Saint Convallus, renowned for miracles and virtues, whose bones likewise rest buried at Inchenane, near Glasgow.

CHAPTER XXX.
This Aydanus is driven from the field by Ethelfrid, King of the Northumbrians—Augustine preaches the Faith to the English.

AT another time, also—that is, in the thirty-third year of his reign—the army of King Aydanus was vanquished while he was himself present. For in the eleventh year after he had discomfited Cenlinus, king of the Saxons, it was at length agreed upon between Aydanus and the Britons to make a twofold attack upon the Northumbrian people, ruled at that time by Ethelfrid, a powerful and wise king, who committed constant outrages upon the Britons and Scots. Aydanus was to come in from the north, and the Britons from the south, until they met at a point agreed upon by a solemn pledge. The king, accordingly, when the stated time arrived, hoping that the Britons would, on their side, do as they had stipulated, marched into the territory of Northumbria, although he was of advanced age; and while his army was daily engaged in burning and despoiling, one day King Ethelfrid, with a dense body of troops, came upon the Scots (who were dispersed through the towns and fields, plundering in this way), and overcame them, not without great slaughter of his own men. Aydanus, king of the Scots, says *Bede*, being concerned at the advance of Ethelfrid, came against him with an immense and brave army; but nearly the whole of his army was slain, at a place called Degsastan. In this fight Theobald, brother to Ethelfrid, was killed, with the whole force he commanded; but Aydanus was, nevertheless, vanquished, and escaped with a few followers. In the fifth year before this battle, the Pope Saint Gregory sent Saint Augustine with his comrades into the country of the Angles, to be their first teacher and preach the faith to them; and the latter, accordingly, that same year, converted Athelbert, king of Kent, to the faith. Now, in the time of Aydanus, the Franks and Spaniards disagreed as to the celebration of Easter; for the Franks kept Easter on the 18th of April; and the Spaniards on the 21st of March. In his time, also, Saint Gregory was ordained bishop of Tours, and was renowned amongst all men. It was he who wrote the history of the Franks. But, to resume—after the said battle King Ethelfrid wofully wasted the nation of the Britons; and, after having exterminated the natives, he made most of their lands tributary, or settled the nation of the Angles thereon.

CHAPTER XXXI.

Saint Columba's prophecy about the sons of Aydanus—His Death—Saint Drostan and his Parentage.

ONCE upon a time, says *Adamnan*, when Saint Columba was asking King Aydanus about the successor to the kingdom, the latter answered that he knew not which of his sons would reign—whether Arturius, or Eochodius Find, or Dongartus. Whereupon the saint prophesied as follows:—"None of these three shall reign, for they shall fall in battle, and be slain by their enemies. But if thou hast any others younger, let them now come to me; and that one of them whom the Lord hath chosen to be king shall at once spring into my bosom." When they were summoned, Eochodius Buyd came up to the saint, as he had prophesied, and nestled in his bosom. So the saint kissed him and blessed him, and said unto his father,—"This is the one that shall survive, and reign as king immediately after thee; and after him, also, shall his sons reign." Moreover, all was, in due time, fulfilled as he said. For Arturius and Eochodius Find were slain, not long afterwards, in the battle of the Maythi, and Dongartus was cut off in battle with the Saxons, like his elder brother Griffinus long before; but Eochodius Buyd, which in our tongue would be Eugenius, succeeded his father in the kingdom the year after. Conanrodus also, the son of the king of Demetia (South Wales), took to wife Fynewennis, daughter of this Griffinus, son of King Aydanus, son of Gonranus; and of her he begat a son greatly beloved by God, Saint Drostan, who donned the monk's habit, and offered himself an acceptable sacrifice unto God. Saint Columba died in A.D. 600, after he had passed in Scotland fully thirty-four years of his excellent life, as appears from the holy man's words. "This present day," said he to the brethren, "thirty years of my pilgrimage in Scotia are completed. But though the Lord granted to me, on my begging for it with my whole might, that I should pass away to Him from the world on this day, yet hearing rather the prayers of many churches for me, He quickly changed His word; and it was yielded by the Lord to their prayers, although against my will, that four years from this day should be added to me to abide in the flesh." But King Aydanus, ever sorrowing after the battle of Degsastan, was so much worn with grief that he died at Kintyre, in the second year after his defeat, so old that he almost reached the term of eighty years, and he was buried at Kilcheran, where none of his predecessors had been buried before. Thereupon Kenethus Kere, son of Conal, immediately took upon him the royal crown; and went to his account a year, or, as is elsewhere stated, three months after.

CHAPTER XXXII.

Accession of Eugenius, son of Aydanus—Saint Gillenius and Saint Columbanus.

KING AYDAN was succeeded in the sovereignty of the kingdom by his son, Eugenius Buyd, or Eochodius, according to some—Aydo according to others—in A.D. 606; who reigned sixteen years. The year before, that is, in A.D. 605, Mauricius was murdered, together with his wife and sons, by one of his soldiers, Phocas, who usurped the imperial throne, and held it eight years. Bonifacius, who was the sixty-fifth pope of the Romish Church, and succeeded Sabinianus, obtained at the hands of this Phocas that the Romish Church should be the head of all the churches; whereas, at that time, the Church of Constantinople styled herself the first of all the churches. Now Eugenius was from the very first, after he had leant his head in the bosom of Saint Columba, his beloved foster-son, most tenderly trained, and, for a long time afterwards, his disciple, most carefully instructed in letters. As soon as he became king, however, amidst the manifold cares of state, the saint's teaching was consigned to oblivion; for, rarely applying his thoughts to peace, but continually to war, he harassed by his inroads the country of the Saxons, and sometimes that of the Picts. He was harsh in his government, and exceedingly pitiless and fierce towards all those who offended the majesty of his power; thinking, in his pride, to overcome the highminded or wanton rather by cruelty than by courtesy. Towards his conquered enemies, and loyal subjects, however, he was beyond measure merciful and mild, and readily extended his favour and kindness to those who asked forgiveness for their offences; so that in this he might be said truly to take after the noble-natured lion, whose device he bore on his arms; for—

"The lion's rage will spare the grovelling prey."

In the eighth year of Eugenius, the emperor Phocas, in the midst of his furious raging against his followers, was put to death by order of Heraclius, patrician of Africa, who, after his death, seized the commonwealth, which he found dismembered and wasted. He began to reign in A.D. 613, and reigned thirty years. At that time Saint Gillenus, a Scot, by his sound teaching, gained over to Christ, and drew to him by his signal miracles, the province of the Atrebatii. One day, when this saint was taking some refreshment with Saint Pharaoh, the glass cup for drinking wine fell out of the cupbearer's hand by chance, and was broken. Whereupon the blessed Gillenus, seeing the servant's face turn pale, privily beckoned to him to give him the broken piece of the cup; and when he had said a prayer over it, the glass was at once restored whole. In the days of Eugenius, Saint Columbanus, a Scot, was distinguished for his many virtues, and built the convents of Luxeu and Bobio in Gaul. He was afterwards driven out of France by King Theodoric, at the instigation of his grandmother Brunechild; and, leaving his disciple Gallus in Germany, he subsequently built a convent in Italy.

CHAPTER XXXIII.

Cadwallo, King of the Britons, takes to flighty and comes to Scotland for assistance— Arrival of Saint Oswald, and his Brothers baptized there—Burial of the Right Hand and Sword of King Eugenius in the stony moor.

IN the tenth year of Eugenius, Crugillus and Quichelmus, kings of the West Saxons, fought a battle at Beautonum against Cadwallo, king of the Britons, and forced him to take to flight, with the loss of two thousand and forty-six killed. Cadwallo afterwards came secretly to Scotland with a few followers, to get help from the king; whereof he obtained a welcome promise. From Scotland, he repaired to Ireland; and thence he went off to Armorican Britain, where he speedily obtained a good-sized band of warriors from the king, whose name was Salamon; and on his return home, he harried the Saxons with numberless calamitous massacres. In the eleventh year of Eugenius, Redwald, king of the East Angles, slew Ethelfrid, king of Northumbria, in battle; whose successor, Edwin, banished from his father's kingdom the seven sons of Ethelfrid, to wit, Andefrid, Oswald, Oslaf, Oswiu, Offa, Oswud, and Oslac, and one daughter, Ebba. All these, accordingly, having, with many nobles, escaped by flight, through the exertions of friends, arrived in Scotland, driven by sore need; and though their father had overcome his own in battle, yet the king kindly harboured these heathens in his kingdom for a long time after, in such honour as was meet. Moreover, a few years afterwards, they were drawn to the Christian faith by his exhortations, and by the teaching and preaching of the holy fathers, whose zeal and glorious lives at that time shed their lustre over Scotland; and they were born again, through the water of sacred baptism, in the name of the Holy Trinity. In the twelfth year of this king's reign, the fifth of the emperor Heraclius, Palestine was overthrown in battle by the Persians; and the holy city of Jerusalem, after 90,000 Christians had been slain therein, was taken, and Our Lord's Holy Cross itself carried off. Consequently, five years after this, on Easter Monday the 4th of April, the emperor, being stirred up, set out against King Cosdroes; and, having quickly put him to death, he brought the Holy Cross back to Jerusalem, breaking out into praises thereof, and singing this antiphon, "O cross more bright," etc. King Eugenius, however, who nearly all the days of his reign eschewed peace, having at length reached the goal of life, wished to be, even after his death—as he had been in life—a continual terror to the enemy. So, in order that the people of the kingdom might not, in future, be in need of a defender, though he himself were dead, he appointed by will, which his loyal chiefs were sworn to carry out, that on his death, they should at once cut off his right arm at the shoulder, and bury it, decked with the war device of the lion, and with sword in hand, as a strong bulwark for them ever after. A certain chronicle, however, has ascribed the burying of the king's hand in this way to King Eugenius, the son of Congal, and not to this one. It is left to the reader's judgment whether it should be ascribed this one, or rather to the other.

CHAPTER XXXIV.

Accession of King Ferchardus, and his brother Donaldus, blessed, while yet a boy, by Saint Columba—Return of Saint Oswald to his Fatherland.

IN A.D. 622, the tenth year of the chief Heraclius, Eugenius was succeeded in the kingdom by the elder of his sons, Ferchardus, who reigned ten years, and in whose time nothing worth remembering happened. About the beginning of his reign, Mahomet, the magician and false prophet, led astray the Arabs, who are also called Saracens, and many peoples. When this Ferchardus had been buried in the island of Columba (Hycolumbkill or Iona), his brother, Donenaldus Brek, took upon him the kingship, in A.D. 632, the twentieth year of the said Heraclius, and reigned fourteen years. Adamnan relates that this same Donenaldus, while yet a boy, was brought by merchants to Saint Columba in the island of Dorcete; and when Saint Columba had looked upon him, he strictly inquired of them, saying, "Whose son is this whom ye have brought?" They answered, "This is Donenaldus, son of Eugenius; and therefor is he brought unto thee, that he may return enriched with thy blessing." Whereupon the saint blessed him, saying, "He shall outlive all his brethren, and shall become a very famous king.

Nor shall he ever be betrayed into the hands of his enemies; but, in old age, he shall die a peaceful death in his bed, at home, in presence of a crowd of friends and retainers." And all this was verily fulfilled, according to the foreshowing of the holy man. In the second year of this king, Edwin, king of the Northumbrians, who had driven the above-mentioned sons of Ethelfrid out of the kingdom, was slain by Cadwallo, king of the Britons, and Penda, king of the Mercians. Whereupon his brothers Andefrid and Oswald, and the other nobles, who had then sojourned seventeen years in exile in Scotland, being certified of his death from trustworthy information, came into the king's presence, and begged him to grant them their liberty, and graciously deign to vouchsafe them some help whereby to win back their father's kingdom. The king, accordingly, freely gave them full leave to go away or come back,—and even promised them help against Penda or any of the Saxons; but he altogether refused it against Cadwallo and the Britons, who had long been bound to the Scots by the friendship of a faithful alliance. Moreover, though less moved thereto by liking for the Saxon race than by zeal for the Christian religion, he sent with them a strong body of warriors, to the end that they might safely cross the marches of his kingdom. Being, therefore, supported by so large a host, they entered their father's kingdom, and were gladly welcomed by the inhabitants. Their eldest brother, Andefrid, was, likewise, at once crowned king of Bernicia. At that time also, Osric, who was baptized by Bishop Paulinus, took upon him the kingdom of Deira. For the kingdom of Northumbria was then divided into the two countries of Bernicia and Deira. These kings, however, Andefrid and Osric, when they had recovered their kingdoms, abjured the Catholic faith, and went back to the service of idols.

CHAPTER XXXV.

Saint Oswald—Saint Aydan chosen to convert the Saxons.

All the time that Edwin reigned, says *Bede*, the sons of the aforesaid King Ethelfrid, with many of the youth of the nobility, lived in banishment among the Scots, and were there taught the doctrine of the Scots, and regenerated by the grace of baptism. Upon the death of the king, their enemy, they were allowed to return to their native land. Andefrid, the first of them, assumed the sovereignty over the Bernicians, while Osric, as above related, was set over the kingdom of Deira. Both these kings, as soon as they had obtained the badge of an earthly kingdom, forswore the sacraments of the heavenly kingdom, and again gave themselves over to be defiled and ruined by the abominations of their former idolatry. Nor was it long before Cadwallo, king of the Britons, slew both these kings—with impious hand, indeed, but through the just vengeance of God. Then when Saint Oswald had held the provinces of the Northumbrians for a whole year after the murder of his brother, he advanced with a small army, but fortified with faith in Christ, and slew King Cadwallo himself, with his immense forces. The field of battle is near that wall, in the north, which is called Thirlwall—wherewith the Romans formerly fenced the whole of Britain from sea to sea, to ward off the attacks of the Scots. This same King Oswald, when he assumed the sovereignty, desiring that the whole nation over which he had just been set should be imbued with the grace of the Christian faith, sent to the elders of the Scots—among whom he himself, and those soldiers who were with him, when in banishment, had received the sacraments of baptism—and asked them to send him a bishop, through whose teaching, the nation of the Angles which he ruled might learn the benefits of faith in the Lord, and embrace its sacraments. Nor was it long before he got what he wanted. For there was first sent, to preach to them, a certain man of harsh disposition, who, after he had preached for some time to the nation of the Angles, and met with no success, returned to his native land, and, in an assembly of the elders, reported that he had not been able to do any good in teaching the nation to which he had been sent, and that they were untameable and stubborn-minded men. Thereupon they began to have great debate in the council as to what should be done; for they were anxious to forward the well-being of that nation in what it sought, but grieved that the preacher they had sent had not been received. Then said Saint Aydan—for he also was of the council—to the priest in question, "It seems to me, brother, that thou wast harder than was right upon thy unlearned hearers, and didst not, according to the apostolic discipline, first offer them the milk of more gentle doctrine; till, being, by degrees, nourished by the Word of God, they should be able to receive the more perfect, and practise the more sublime, precepts of God." Having heard these words, all who sat with him turned their eyes and countenances upon him, and began diligently to discuss what he had said; and they resolved that he was worthy of the office of bishop, and should be sent to instruct the unbelievers and unlearned.

CHAPTER XXXVI.

Preaching of Saint Aydan—Death of the holy King Oswald.

Bede goes on to say:—Saint Oswald, then, received the holy bishop Aydan, a man of the greatest meekness, godliness, and moderation, and having the zeal of God; and granted him a place for his episcopal see in the island of Lindisfarne, where he himself wished to have it. The king also humbly and willingly in all things gave ear to his admonitions, and applied himself most diligently to build up and spread the Church of Christ in his kingdom: indeed, when the bishop, who had not a perfect knowledge of the Anglic tongue, preached the gospel there, it was often beautiful to see the king himself interpreting the Word of God to his generals and thanes; for he had naturally, in the long period of his banishment, perfectly learnt the language of the Scots. From that time they began to come for many a day out of Scotland into Britain, and to preach most devoutly the word of faith to those provinces of the Angles over which Oswald reigned; and those among them who had received priest's orders administered to the believers the grace of baptism. Churches were built here and there; the people joyfully flocked together to hear the Word of God; possessions and lands were given, of the king's bounty, to establish monasteries; the little ones of the Angles, as well as their elders, were, by their Scottish masters, imbued with learning, and the observance of regular discipline. The holy bishop left to the clergy, among other lessons for a good life, a most wholesome example of fasting and continence; and it was, with all men, the highest commendation of his teaching, that he taught not otherwise than he himself, and his followers, lived. His life was so different from the slothfulness of our times, that all who walked with him, whether tonsured or laymen, were bound to *meditate*—that is, to spend their time in reading the Scriptures, or reciting the Psalms. In the eleventh year of King Donaldus, this same Saint Oswald was killed by Penda, king of the Mercians, and was succeeded by his brother Oswiu, who had also been instructed in the Catholic faith, and baptized by the Scots. The self-same year died the emperor Heraclius. His son Constantine reigned in his stead, and was, in the fourth month of his reign, poisoned by his stepmother, Martina, and the patriarch Pirrus; whereupon Martina and her son, Heraclonas, seized the imperial throne. But, the next year, Heraclonas and his mother, Martina, were banished—he with his nose cut off, and she with her tongue cut out; and Constans, also called Constantine, son of the aforesaid Constantine, mounted the imperial throne in A.D. 644, and reigned twenty-six years.

CHAPTER XXXVII.

Accession of King Ferchardus—Saint Finanus, Saint Furseus, Saint Foilanus, and Saint Ultanus.

FINALLY, after a reign of fourteen years, Donaldus died, and his nephew Ferchardus Fode, son of Ferchardus, was raised to the government of the kingdom, and crowned. He began to reign in A.D. 646, the third year of Constans, or Constantine, and held the kingship for eighteen years, during the whole of which time he reigned in peace. In the sixth year of his reign, Aydan, the holy bishop and teacher of the Angles, passed away to the Lord, after having gloriously administered the bishopric of Northumbria for seventeen years. He was succeeded by Saint Finan, also a Scot, who was bishop ten years. By the latter, just after his arrival there, the king of the midland Angles, Peada, son of

Penda, was baptized, and all the earls and thanes who had accompanied him, together with all their households. About the beginning of the reign of this king. Saint Furseus, of whose parentage we have spoken above, full of shining virtues, went forth out of Scotland on a pilgrimage for Christ's sake, and got as far as Gaul; where, being received with honour by King Clodoveus, son of Dagobert, he founded the convent of Lagny. Not long after, his brothers, Saint Foilanus and Saint Ultanus, having likewise vowed to go on a pilgrimage, followed him, and lived illustrious lives in Gaul. Of these, Foilanus afterwards founded the monastery of Fosse, through the bounty of the virgin Gertrudis; and he lies there, crowned with martyrdom. In the time of this king, likewise, Dido, bishop of Poitiers, was sent into banishment to the king in Scotland, who received him with honour, and entertained him for a time; but he afterwards sent him back to the aforesaid King Clodoveus, who received him again into favour.

CHAPTER XXXVIII.

Saint Colman—He preaches for three years—His return to Scotland.

THE holy bishop Finan died in the sixteenth year of King Ferchardus, and was succeeded by Saint Colman, likewise sent and ordained by the Scots. Colman, however, exercised his office there but three years; for, unable to bear the envy of those Angles who were lettered, he left his bishopric, and hurried back to his native land. Now Colman, says *Bede*, after he had presided over the Northumbrian nation as bishop for three years, took with him part of the bones of the holy father Aydan, and returned to Scotland. How thrifty, how continent he himself and his predecessors were, the place which they governed bare witness. There were there, at that time, many of the nobility as well as of the middle class of the Angles. These, in the time of the bishops Colman and Finan, had forsaken their native land and retired thither, for the sake either of divine studies, or of a more continent life. And some of them soon devoted themselves faithfully to the monastic life, while others chose rather to go about from cell to cell, attending the lectures of the masters. The Scots most willingly received them all, and took care to supply them with daily food, free of cost, and also with books to read, and gratuitous teaching. Meanwhile, Colman, who had come from Scotland, quitted Britain, and returned again to Scotland, taking along with him the Scots he had gathered together, and about thirty men of the English nation, who were imbued with the teaching of the monastic life. With these he came to an island called Hybofynd, not far remote from Ireland; and, building a monastery there, he placed therein the monks of both nations, whom he had brought over. These, however, could not agree among themselves. So he established another monastery, in a place called Mageo, and leaving the Scottish monks in the former, he appointed that the English should remain by themselves in the other.

CHAPTER XXXIX.

Number of Kings of the Angles whom the Scots baptized—Bishops by whom they were baptized.

THROUGH these most holy men, therefore, the bishops Aydan, Finan, and Colman, furthered by the Scottish kings and the elders of the clergy—at least either through them, or through others whom they had consecrated and given to the Angles as bishops and priests, as they had also given them some as teachers—were the two kingdoms of the Northumbrians, those of the Mercians and Middle Angles, and one half of the kingdom of the East Saxons, almost to the banks of the river Thames, converted to Christ; and their kings and inhabitants baptized in the name of the Holy Trinity, and faithfully taught the works of faith, and moulded thereto.

The first king of the Angles baptized by the Scots was Eanfrid—although he returned to his idols as a dog to his vomit.

Then his brother, the holy King Oswald; at whose request, as stated above, the catholic faith was preached to the Northumbrians by the blessed Aydan.

Also, King Oswy, Oswald's brother, and successor in the kingdom.

Oswyn, king of Deira; who was betrayed by his own men, and slain by this same Oswy.

Peada, Penda's son, king of the Middle Angles; to whom Dwyma, the Scot, was given as bishop, to be over the Middle Angles and the Mercian people—for the scarcity of priests made it necessary that one bishop should be set over the two peoples of two different countries.

Sigbertus, king of the East Saxons, who had lately driven out Mellitus, and abjured the faith. To this king, Cedda was sent as bishop to teach the heathen. Cedda likewise baptized King Swythelmus, the successor of this Sigbertus. But the first of the Scottish bishops who preached the faith to the Angles was Saint Aydan; who, at his decease, was succeeded by Saint Finan; and he, by Saint Colman; who, on his return to Scotland, was succeeded by Tuda, a bishop duly ordained by the Scots. The first bishop, again, of the Middle Angles and Mercians was Dwyma the Scot; then, after his death, he was succeeded by Ceolach, also a Scot; who afterwards, on his return to Scotland, was succeeded by Trumheri, and he by Jarmuan—both, indeed, of Anglic birth, but educated and ordained by the Scots.

CHAPTER XL.

Accession of King Maldwynus—Bishop Tuda succeeds Colman.

NOW after the death of Ferchardus, Maldewinus, son of King Donaldus, attained the throne of the kingdom, in A.D. 664, the twenty-first year of the emperor Constantine. In that year, Saint Colman returned to Scotland, and was succeeded by Tuda. But, throughout the whole time that the Scots preached in England, unshaken peace and communion prevailed, without the din of strife. At length, when the Anglic clergy of native extraction had increased and multiplied, chiefly through the teaching of the Scots, they all ungratefully began to turn against their holy teachers, and to seek frequent and sundry opportunities of forcing them to return to Scotland, or bear the intolerable burden which was laid upon them. Hence, thereafter, for the twenty years that Maldwynus reigned, there seldom, if ever, happened to be peace between the kingdoms; but, on either side, outbreak followed upon outbreak, with almost ceaseless devastation. Nevertheless, no battle worthy of mention is found in the chronicles of either nation, to have been fought during this time. But in the fifth year of this king, the whole of Europe was laid low by the horrible calamity of a most grievous death-sickness among men. *Adamnan*, making mention of this calamity, says:—It is by no means meet to pass over in silence the death-sickness which, in our time, twice wasted the greater part of the earth. For—not to speak of the other more extensive countries of Europe, Italy to wit, and the city of Rome itself, the Cisalpine provinces of Gaul, and the Spaniards, who are shut off by the barrier of the Pyrennean mountains, the islands of the ocean, Ireland and Britain, to wit, were twice utterly devastated by this cruel pestilence; with the exception of two nations, namely, the Scots and the Picts, divided from one another by the mountains of the backbone of Britain (Drumalban) between them. And though neither of these nations are free from great sins whereby the Eternal Judge is oftentimes provoked to wrath, nevertheless He has hitherto patiently borne with them in His mercy, and spared them both. In the seventh year of this king, the emperor Constans, also called Constantine, was murdered in his bath by his servants; and Mezentius, the Armenian, was created emperor by the soldiery. But not long after, Constantino, the son of this Constans who was murdered, and great-grandson of Heraclius, assumed the purple, and put to a most disgraceful death Mezentius and the murderers of his father. He began to reign in A.D. 670, and was emperor seventeen years. In his fourteenth year died King Maldwynus, and was buried in state in the church of Saint Columba, in the western isles.

CHAPTER XLI.

Flight of Cadwaladr, last King of the Britons, from Britain—Causes why God cast them out of the Kingdom.

AT this time died the last king of the Britons in Britain, Cadwaladr, the son of Cadwallo above referred to. *Geoffroy's* account of this Cadwallo, in his *Gesta Britonum*, is not, as is taught in the chronicles of *Bede* and the other English writers, that he was slain by Oswald, but that he was himself, on the contrary, Oswald's chief persecutor, even unto death; and that he lived long after the latter's decease, ending his life by a natural death in his bed, after a reign of forty-eight years. But, as we find in these and many other histories of the Britons and Angles, the writings of their authors very often disagree as much as do the people's themselves, whose tastes are known to be so contrary, that neither, save under compulsion, would desire the same things as the other. It is expedient, at this point, to notice how the nation of the Britons was rent asunder; that their ceaseless civil strife, their indulgence in base vices, their neglect of divine worship, their wanton choice of new kings, despising the rightful ones—by all which courses they lost the kingdom—may be an example to us and to other nations for ever. Cadwaladr, therefore, assumed the kingly office in his father's stead; and twelve years after, as the inroads of the Saxons became daily more serious, and being sore pressed by that most grievous calamity of the aforesaid death-sickness, he fled out of Britain, weeping, and lamenting in these, or some such words:—"Thou hast given us, Lord, as sheep appointed for meat," etc. "Woe unto us sinners! woe unto us! because of the monstrous wickedness wherewith we have not shrunk from offending God, while we had room for repentance. Therefore the vengeance of His power lies heavy upon us, and hastens to drive us from our native soil—us whom neither the Romans of old, nor the Scots, nor the Picts could drive out; nor yet the Saxons, with their wily treachery, who were always wont to betray, and to keep steadfast faith with no one. But in vain do we struggle to recover our fatherland from them, if it should not be God's will that we should longer reign therein.

For the righteous Judge Himself, seeing that we would in no wise cease from our wickedness, let loose His indignation upon us, to reprove us, unworthy men; who, for our unworthiness, alas! are cast out in crowds from our native country, even as useless tree-branches, tied in bundles, are cast out of the vineyards; that we may be a warning and an example to all nations, lest they should, in time to come, provoke God by such crimes. Whither, oh miserable nation! whither, pray, are gone the strivings and broils of your civil wars? wherewith ye failed not yourselves to bring to nought your most pleasant country of Britain. On the other hand, the Saxons, with their troth belied, now hold such undivided sway therein that they will not let you wage war there, even against the stranger,—far less among yourselves. What then, ye slothful nation!—yea, a nation too truly slothful—what shall ye do? Ye have now no means of waging civil war, nor can ye engage in war against the stranger. For, ever thirsting after civil strife, ye have so far weakened yourselves with internal disturbances, that ye cannot now shield from your enemies your fatherland, your wives and children, or—what is more than these—your freedom. Alas! too late have ye understood the saying of the Gospel, 'Every kingdom which is divided against itself,' etc.; but experience has just taught you that this sentence is too true. For now, therefor do ye see your kingdom desolate, and in the hands of most ungodly heathens, because the frenzy of civil discord, and the fumes of spite have blunted your minds; and because your pride would not let you yield due obedience to one, and that the rightful king, ye see house falling on house, and the whelps of the barbarian lioness snatching from you your towns, cities, and other possessions; wherefrom so miserably are ye driven out that ye shall hardly, if ever, recover your former honourable estate,"

CHAPTER XLII.

These causes continued—Future return of the Britons prophesied by an Angel—Some of Merlin's Prophecies on this event.

CADWALADR, therefore, fleeing out of Britain, came to the region of Bretagne; and there, when, after tarrying some time, he was proposing to return to Britain, an angel instructed him, with voice of thunder, not to carry out what he had conceived in his mind. "For God," said he, "will not have thy nation reign any longer in Britain for the present, before the fated time has come. Then, however, the Britons, through the merits of their faith, shall obtain the kingdom; yet let them not hope that time shall be, until they have possessed themselves of thy remains, and brought them over from Rome into Britain." Having, therefore, heard the angel speak these words, he went to Rome, and died there. *Merlinus Ambrosius* prophesies as follows, on the Britons recovering the kingdom:—"Cadwaladr shall call upon Conan, and take Albania into fellowship. Then shall there be slaughter of the stranger-born; then shall the rivers run with blood; then shall burst forth the mountains of Armorica, and shall be crowned with the diadem of Brutus," etc. To proceed—his son Inor and his nephew Yny got their ships together; and repairing, now to Wales, now to Scotland, they troubled for many years the kingdom of Britain with their savage attacks. From this time— namely, about A.D. 660—Britain lost her ancient name, and from the nations of the Angles took its modern name of Anglia (England). *Bede*, in explaining this name, has written as follows:—Furthermore, from the Angles, that is, the people who came from that part of Germany which is called *Angulus*, the rest of the Anglic nations are named. The Britons, then, being scattered abroad, betook themselves, some, to the kingdom of Armorica, some, to Gaul, some to Scotland, never more to return home; but others, again, to Wales; choosing rather to run the course of their wretched lives in the uttermost ends of their own country, in freedom, than to be subject to the dominion of their foes, in slavery. For, to every one, the hardest lot in slavery, is to serve as a slave in one's native country, where one was wont to lord it in freedom.

CHAPTER XLIII.

Accession of the Kings Eugenius IV. and Eugenius V.—Saint Cuthbert—Saint Adamnan.

On the death of King Maldwynus, he was succeeded by his nephew Eugenius IV., son of Dongardus, son of Donald Brek. Eugenius reigned three years, beginning in A.D. 684, the fifteenth year of the Emperor Constantine. Now in the second year of this king, Saint Cuthbert was ordained bishop, being the third in order after Saint Colman, the Scot of whom we spoke above. The same year Egfrid, king of the Northumbrians, was slain by the Scots. King Egfrid, says *Bede*, rashly leading his army to waste the province of the Scots, much against the advice of his friends, and particularly of Saint Cuthbert, of blessed memory, who had lately been ordained bishop—was drawn, by the feigned flight of the enemy, into the defiles of inaccessible mountains, and slain, with the greater part of the forces he had brought with him. From that time the hopes and courage of the kingdom of the Angles "began to waver and to retrograde;" for the Picts, the Scots who were in Britain, as well as some part of the Britons, recovered the lands that belonged to them which the Angles had been holding. This Eugenius, after his death, was succeeded by Eugenius V., in A.D. 687, the first year of Justinian II., who succeeded his father Constantine, and held the imperial throne ten years. King Eugenius likewise reigned ten years. He was the son of Ferchardus Fode. And, all his days, he had peace with the Angles; but, with the Picts, war, broken by an occasional truce. For, in his time King Alfrid, the illegitimate brother of the aforesaid Egfrid, reigned in Northumbria, albeit not over the same extent of country as his brother had held dominion over; and, forasmuch as he had, for a considerable number of years, devoted himself to literary studies in Scotland and Ireland, he was well known to King Eugenius, as they had seen a great deal of each other. So they steadfastly maintained peace, one towards another, along the borders of their realms. In his days, likewise, flourished Saint Adamnan, the Scot, mighty in virtues and miracles. And during his reign, a rain of blood poured down from on high, for seven days, upon the whole island, both Scotland and Britain, and all the milk and butter was turned into blood.

CHAPTER XLIV.

Accession of King Amrikelleth—His Death—Saint Chillian, the Scot, and his Disciples.

PEACE being thus established with the Picts and Angles, Eugenius, at his decease, left the throne to his successor Amrikelleth, the son of Findan, the son of Eugenius IV. But Amrikelleth, who was crowned the same year, A.D. 697, broke through the terms of peace, and made ready for war against the Picts. And, before that very year was over, while beating the cover of the thick woods, on first marching into their lands, many of his host were shot with arrows; and the king himself was hit by an arrow, and wounded. So returning speedily he died on the tenth day after the wound was inflicted, and vacated the kingly seat in favour of his brother Eugenius. That same year, at Wirzburg, a castle at the entrance to Francia, the holy bishop of that place, Chillian, a Scot, and his disciples Clolaman and Colman, were privily martyred by Geylana, wife of the chief Gothbert, for she was afraid of being separated from her husband, as Chillian had rebuked him for having her to wife, who had formerly been his brother's wife. Moreover, whereas their death was long hidden from all men, Geylana and the murderers were possessed by an evil spirit, and it was divulged by their confession. The self-same year, too, when the emperor Justinian, as has been said, had reigned ten years, the patrician Leo rebelled against him; and depriving him of his kingdom and his nose, sent him into banishment. But, at the end of a year after he had assumed the imperial dignity, Leo was driven from the throne, thrust into prison, and had his own nose cut off by Tiberius; and the latter was seven years emperor. Justinian afterwards, by the help of Crebellis, king of the Bulgari, got back the imperial throne, and slaughtered Tiberius and Leo. Such was the vengeance he took upon his adversaries, that, for every drop of rheum he wiped off, which flowed from his mutilated nose, he ordered some one of the conspirators to be slaughtered. After, however, he had reigned seven years the second time, Philip slew him, as well as his son Tiberius, and reigned a year and a half. Against him rose up Anastasius, and deprived him of his eyes, and drove him from the imperial throne; and he again, two years after, was deposed from the imperial throne, and ordained priest, by Theodosins, who reigned one year. The latter, also, was deposed from the imperial throne by Leo III., who afterwards became a clerk, and passed the rest of his life in peace. And thus, for twenty-one years, the Roman empire was a laughing-stock to all men, even to the unbelievers.

CHAPTER XLV.

Accession of the Kings Eugenius VI. and Murdacus—State of things in Britain at that time.

EUGENIUS VI., son of Findan, as above mentioned, succeeded his brother Amrikeleth, and reigned seventeen years, beginning in A.D. 698, the second year of Leo the patrician. He was a humble king, and of great moderation, who preferred spending his days in peace rather than in war—and would rather disturb wild beasts and birds than men. Thus he drew to him, by a certain sagacity in his disposition, the favour and love of all the neighbouring nations; and, having adorned his reign, while it lasted, with steadfast laws, he ended happily a tranquil life. After his death at Loarno, his body was taken to the islands, and buried in the tomb of his fathers. He was succeeded by Murdacus, his nephew through his brother Amrynkyleth, who ruled the kingdom in peace, like his uncle before him, though by no means finding the same, or equal, favour with his neighbours. He began to reign in A.D. 715, and reigned fifteen years. The *Venerable Bede*, towards the end of his Chronicle, in describing the state of the nations in the whole of the island of Albion, at the time of this king's reign, has made the following remarks:—The nation of the Picts, says he, have, at this time, a treaty of peace with the Angles, and rejoice in being partakers with the universal Church in catholic truth and unity. The Scots that inhabit Britain, content with their own frontiers, no longer hatch plots against the nation of the Angles. The Britons, also, though they for the most part fight against the Anglic nation, through private hate, and through ill-nature, yet, being straightway withstood by the power both of God and man, can in no way succeed in their design. For though they are, doubtless, in part, their own masters, they are, to some extent also, in bondage to the Angles, and what the end of the matter will be, shall be seen in after ages. In the last year of Murdacus, two comets appeared about the sun, striking great terror among the beholders; one of them preceded the rising sun in the morning, and the other followed him, in the evening, as he set; and these presages of awful calamity heralded the spring—one of day, the other of night—to signify that evils were impending over mortals. They turned a face of fire against the north-west, as if bent on setting it on fire. They appeared in the month of January, and lasted nearly a fortnight.

CHAPTER XLVI.

Accession of the three Kings, Ethfyn, Eugenius or Nectanius, and Fergus—Death of the latter by the hand of the Queen.

In A.D. 730, the thirteenth year of Leo III., who deposed Theodosius from the imperial throne, Murdacus was succeeded by the son of Eugenius VI., Ethfyn, who reigned thirty-one years. He was a man worthy of the honour of being raised to the throne; and, for the greater part of his reign, he enjoyed the peace he yearned for, though, in his latter days, the Picts made war upon him. In the second, or, as others maintain, the fifth, year of this reign, died the Venerable *Bede*. In the twelfth year, Saint Eucherius, Bishop of Orleans, while in the attitude of prayer, was rapt into the next world; and, among other things he saw, he perceived King Pipin's father, Charles, tormented in hell, because he took away from churches their substance, and distributed it, and for this alone was he damned. In the thirteenth year, Leo was succeeded by his son Constantine, who was thirty-five years emperor. In the twenty-first year, the French appointed Pipin, the Mayor of the Palace, king, by the authority of Pope Zachary, while King Hilderic received the tonsure in a monastery. Afterwards, King Pipin, his sons, Charles and Carloman, and his daughter, Sigilla, were blessed by the Pope Saint Stephen, at Paris, during the solemn sacrament of the mass, by direction of Saint Paul, Saint Peter, and the blessed Denis. After Ethfyn, the kingly crown, in A.D. 761, the twentieth year of the emperor

Constantine, devolved on the son of Murdacus, Eugenius VII.—called, however, Nectanius, in a certain chronicle—and he reigned two years. He was succeeded, in A.D. 763 (the twenty-second year of the aforesaid emperor), by Ethfyn's son, Fergus, who reigned three years. It is asserted that this king was put to death through poison, by his wife, the queen, who was over-jealous of him for lying with women. She herself afterwards openly confessed it, though no one suspected her of such a deed; and when she looked upon the dead king's corpse, tearing her hair, with mournful cries, she broke forth into these or some such words:—"Oh! most wretched of women, more cruel than any wild beast, traitress most base, what hast thou done? Hast thou not, goaded on by lustful fury, wickedly slain the king, thy lord and husband? Hast thou not, like a viper, with the most savage kind of treachery, slain the most loving of men, and the most beautiful, beyond the love of woman—who alone, of all living, was the delight of thy heart's inmost love? But this wicked crime shall not go unpunished: I myself shall take vengeance on myself. Hasten, then, thou cursed hand! Dare to make ready for my lips that cup which thou didst but now tender to my lord, my sweetest love—ay, that cup, or a more bitter one—and fail not." Then, after she had quaffed the deadly liquid, straightway she went on:—"Nor should this draught be punishment enough for such an evil-doer as I am, or meet reward for one who has been guilty of such a crime! Nay, I should be dragged along, hanging bound to the tails of horses, and my accursed body should be burnt in a fire of thorns, and my ashes scattered to the winds." With these words she grasped in her hand the dagger she had made ready with intent aforethought, and suddenly stabbed herself to the heart before the eyes of the bystanders.

CHAPTER XLVII.

Accession of Selwalchius—King Charles the Great.

The successor of Fergus, Selwalchius, son of Eugenius, son of Ferchardus, began to reign in A.D. 766 (the twenty-fifth year of the emperor Constantine), and reigned twenty-one years. In the days of his reign he had peace with the Picts and Angles, although these indulged in domestic squabbles among themselves. Those Angles, indeed, namely, the Northumbrians, whose country lay nearest to Scotland, were engaged without ceasing in murdering and proscribing their kings, as will more clearly be seen below; while Selwalchius himself, a languid and inactive king, far preferred rest to war—not looking to the increase of the State, but allowing all things to go to wrack and ruin through his wretched slothfulness. Yet it is believed that if the Scottish and Pictisli people had, at that critical time, kept faith and peace towards one another, as they were wont—nay, even if the Scottish nation alone had been led by a warlike chief (in the timely event, of course, of a just cause of war) and had made an armed attack upon the Northumbrians, it could, without doubt, have wrested from them all the tracts of Albania which had formerly belonged to them. Nothing memorable was, however, at that time done against their adversaries, besides a few forays made, at rare intervals, under lowborn military leaders. In the fourth year of this reign, Charles—who, by reason of the success and greatness of his exploits, was called *the Great*—together with his brother Carloman, succeeded his father Pipin, who had begotten them of Berta, the daughter of the Cæsar Heraclius. On Carloman's death, two years after, Charles got possession of the whole of his father Pipin's kingdom, and increased it, moreover, to twice the size of the territory his father had held. In the twelfth year—that is, A.D. 777—Leo, Constantine's son, obtained his father's empire, and was five years emperor. After his death he was succeeded by Irene, a greathearted woman, who, with her son Constantine, ruled the empire nearly ten years, beginning in A.D. 782. As for King Selwalchius, he died a tranquil death at Innerlocho, and lies with his fathers in the island.

CHAPTER XLVIII.

Accession of King Achay, who first entered into an Alliance with the Franks: Cause thereof—The distinguished Soldier Gilmerius the Scot.

SELWALCHIUS was succeeded, in A.D. 787 (the sixth year of the Empress Irene and her son Constantine), by Achaius, the son of Ethfyn, who reigned thirty-two years. His brother, we are told, was that distinguished soldier, Gilmerius the Scot, who long fought vigorously in the service of King Charles, against the enemies of Christ's cross; whence, by his splendid deeds of arms, he won an everlasting name, glorious with military lustre. The friendly alliance between the Scottish and French kings, and their countries—which, God be praised, endures unmarred even to our own days—was originated by King Charles the Great and this Achay; and it was first brought about as follows. Shortly before the reign of Achay, in the time, to wit, of his predecessor, the Anglic kings being puffed up with pride at having overcome the Britons, were not satisfied with disquieting only the neighbouring nations in the same island, the Scots, Picts, and Britons, but they also did their utmost to harass even the French nations beyond the sea, on the seaboard, by frequent plundering expeditions by sea, and to disturb the whole of the Belgic and British seas. In those days, this invincible King Charles was assiduously occupied in war with the heathen, and aimed at securing peace for all Christians, by unwearied toil, and the shedding of his own blood. Since, therefore, the Angles, though repeatedly begged to do so, would not desist from such piratical plundering, and the shedding of the blood of Christians, he busied himself in hunting up his friends on all sides, and those, especially, whom he knew to be most eager for their hurt, to the end that he might curb their fierceness. Accordingly, he sent forth his emissaries in all directions; and some he despatched to King Achay, who, on his side, sent back with them his own agents in this matter, which was in all respects approved by him, to the end that the covenant and compact of the friendly treaty they had entered into should be secured by equitable conditions, and, having been reduced to indented writings, should be mutually signed by both kings. Furthermore, he wrote again and again to his friends, maintaining that it was not unlawful to declare war against any king, Christian though he were, who violently falls upon the rear of a chief at war with the unbelieving heathen. War, however, did not follow upon these fearful threats which were noised abroad; for, on the English submissively promising peace for the future, Charles, with great kindness and goodwill, consented unto them. Of this treaty of peace between them, namely, Charles and the Angles, *Alcwyn* wrote to his companion, saying:—Some say that we are to be sent by the Anglic kings to King Charles, to treat of peace. *William*, likewise, describing some of the acts of Bishop Egbert, says:— As a competent witness to which matter, I cite Alcwyn, who was sent by the Anglic kings to King Charles the Great, to treat of peace; he says:—"For, lately, there has sprung up a slight difference between France and Scotland, whereof the devil feeds the flame; and internavigation has been forbidden and stopped,"

CHAPTER XLIX.
Ambassadors of the Scots sent to Charles, to confirm this Alliance.

William, again, mentioning this difference in another passage, writes:—Offa, king of the Mercians, by repeated embassies, made a friend of Charles the Great, king of the French; though he could find little in the disposition of Charles to second his views. They had disagreed before, insomuch that violent disagreements having arisen on both sides, even the traffic of merchants was forbidden. To the end, therefore, that this difference might be adjusted, Alcwyn, who was in Paris, with some others, wrote back as follows to King Offa, about the aforesaid Scottish ambassadors, who were just leaving Charles, to go back to Scotland:—"Let your esteemed grace be apprised that our lord King Charles has spoken with me lovingly of you, saying that you have a most trusty friend in him; and he sends your grace worthy gifts, and to the several episcopal sees of your kingdom. In like manner he had directed presents to be sent to Ethelred (also called Ethelbert), king of

Northumbria, and for the sees of his bishops; but, alas! just as the gifts were put into the hands of the messengers, there came, by the ambassadors who had come from Scotland, and returned through your country, sad tidings of the faithlessness of the people, and death of the king himself. So Charles took back his bountiful gifts; and is so exceeding wroth with that nation, calling it faithless and perverse, and the murderer of its sovereign lords, and deeming it worse than the heathen, that, had I not interceded for it, he would have already done it every hurt he could contrive, and deprived it of every advantage within his power." And since its treacherous murder of this King Ethelred is mentioned in this place, do not, reader, consider me a calumniator of this my nation, if I bring in here the wicked assassinations, the unheard-of betrayals and proscriptions of the rest of its kings, who preceded this one—as its truthful historians testify in their writings; for I do so, not to slander any nation whatsoever, but for a warning and an example to nations to come, to shrink from the wickedness of such horrible crimes.

CHAPTER L.

Heinous Treachery of the Northumbrians towards their Kings, so that none durst rule them.

Now, in the third year of Achay, this same king of Northumbria, Ethelred, or Ethelbert, or Ethelwald (for he had three names), fell by the foul treachery of his subjects. The names of the other kings of the aforesaid country, who, in like manner, perished through treachery, will be seen below in their order. Oswyn, the son of Osric, and king of Deira (which is one-half of Northumbria), thinking it prudent, says *William*, to abstain from war, owing to the smallness of his army, secretly withdrew to a country seat, where, being betrayed by his own people, he was straightway killed by Oswy. Osred, likewise, the son of Alfred, and king of the whole of Northumbria, died, slaughtered through a plot of his kinsmen, subjects of his—namely, Cenred and Osric; who reigned after him—the former, for two years, and the latter, for twelve, and left only this to be recorded of them, that they expiated the blood of their slaughtered lord, the king, and polluted the air by their foul end. After them Celwlf climbed to the supreme place in the tottering kingdom, and was succeeded by Egbert. Both these kings, unwilling to await the fate of former kings, entered religious orders, and were shorn. Osulf succeeded his father, Egbert, and was slain by his subjects a year after, harmless as he was, thus making room for Mollo. This Mollo discharged the duties of king, vigorously enough, for eleven years, and then fell before the treachery of Alcred. Alcred, likewise, when he had filled, for ten years, the throne he had usurped, was compelled by the inhabitants to retire. Ethelbert, the son of Mollo, having been set up as king by general consent of the people, was, at the end of five years, driven out by them. Olwold was next hailed king; and, eleven years afterwards, he rued the perfidy of the inhabitants, being murdered, though guiltless. His nephew, Osred, the son of Alcred, succeeded him, and was expelled after barely a year; thus vacating the kingdom for Ethelred, who was also called Ethelbert, of whom mention was made before. This man, the son of Mollo, was also called by a third name, Ethelwald. He obtained the kingdom after twelve years of exile, and held it four years; at the end of which time, not having been able to escape the fate of the foregoing kings, he was pitifully murdered in the year stated above. At this, many of the bishops and the nobility were greatly shocked, and fled from their native land. After this Ethelred, none durst ascend the throne; for every one feared that the mischance of the preceding kings would fall to his lot. Thus, being without a ruler for thirty-three years, that province was the laughingstock and prey of its neighbours. Such are *William's* words.

CHAPTER LI.

Rise of the Paris Schools. By whom Established.

ABOUT the same time, during Achay's reign, the Paris schools were first founded by two clerks from Scotland, most learned men—namely, John and Clement—furthered by Charles the Great. *Vincentius* writes in the *Speculum*:—God, the Almighty disposer of things, and ordain er of kingdoms and seasons, when He had, in the Romans, broken off the iron or earthen feet of that wondrous statue, set up, through the illustrious Charles, the golden head of a no less wondrous statue, in the French. For when that king began to reign alone in the west, the study of letters was everywhere sunk in oblivion, and the worship of the true Godhead was therefore lukewarm. But it came to pass that there arrived on the coast of Gaul, with some merchants, two Scottish monks, men of matchless learning, both in secular and in sacred writings. These men, though they exhibited nothing for sale, were daily wont to shout to the crowds who came together to buy:—"Whosoever covets wisdom, let him come to us and get it, for we have it for sale." They kept on shouting these words so long, that they were at length brought to the ears of King Charles—always a lover of wisdom—by such as marvelled at those men, or thought them mad; whereupon he straightway summoned them to his presence, and asked them whether they really had wisdom, so that he might purchase some. "We not only have wisdom," said they, "but are ready to give it to those who seek it in the name of the Lord." On his asking them, then, what they wanted for it, they answered:—"Only a suitable spot, clever minds, and that without which we cannot go through this pilgrimage,—food, and wherewithal we may be clothed." When he had heard this, he was filled with exceeding great joy and he at first kept them both with him for a short time. Afterwards, however, when compelled to go on warlike expeditions, he caused one of them, named Clement, to abide in Gaul—at Paris—and recommended to him a good many boys, of the better, middle, and lower, classes; directing that victuals should be supplied them, as they had need, and dwellings allotted them for meditation. The other, John, he despatched to Italy; and made over to him the monastery of Saint Augustine, near the town of Ticinum (Pavia); so that those who wished to learn might flock thither. John, after he had tarried there some time, returned to Paris, at the king's command; and, having reached a great age, he there ended a glorious life. But Alcwyn, of the English nation, having heard that Charles welcomed the wise gladly, took ship and came to him with his fellows, well trained in all manner of writings; and the king kept him with him until his life's end.—This passage *Vincentius* took out of the Chronicles of the metropolis of Aries, and added it to his writings in the *Speculum Historiale*. In the tenth year of Irene, her son Constantine deprived her of the empire, and was seven years emperor; at the end of which time she deprived him of sight and of the empire, in A.D. 798, and was, for four years, sole empress.

CHAPTER LII.

Charles and his son Louis emperors—Succession of Kings of France, from Clovis up to this Charles.

CHAPTER LIII.

Accession of the Kings Convallus and Dungallus, who revived the long-slumbering War against the Picts.

AFTER King Achay had ended his life, his kinsman Convallus was raised to the government of the kingdom, in A.D. 819—the sixth year of the Emperor Louis; and reigned five years. That same year died Kynwlf, king of the Mercians, and was succeeded by his son Kynelm, who was, while still in his boyhood, harmless as he was, slain by his sister Quendrida, and earned the name and honour of martyrdom, the grace of God besteading him. The following year, there began to be mooted a great question as to the right to the Pictish throne; for it was asserted that the Scots were entitled to it; and it was ventilated in the mouths of all, whether chiefs or churls. They did not, however, proceed to active measures. Full five years after, on the death of Convallus, Dungallus, the son of Selwalchius, straightway began to reign, in A.D. 824—the eleventh year of the emperor Louis; and reigned seven years. By him was renewed the war against the Picts, which had slumbered for nearly fifty years; forasmuch as he said that their throne was his, by virtue of an old covenant. Now, the primitive law of succession of their kings and chiefs, according to *Bede* and other chronicles, is this:—When the Picts first came into this island, they had no wives of their own nation. So they asked the Scots for their daughters; and they consented to give them on this one condition, that, when any doubt should arise as to the succession to kingdom or dominion, the Picts should choose their kings from the female, rather than the male, line; which custom is well known to be constantly observed among the Picts. And this, perhaps, may have been the cause of this claim or dispute. For true it is that it is gathered, from their chronicles and histories, that, in the days of peace, from the very beginning, true friendship was fostered between them to such a pitch, that their kings and chiefs almost always got themselves consorts and wives of the sons and daughters of the Scottish kings and chiefs on the other side—and the reverse. But He, from whom nothing is hidden, knows the ultimate cause of this dispute; and by whose fault was begun this most cruel war, which had no end, until it pleased Him who rules all kingdoms, and scatters them at will, that the Picts should be wholly overcome, and the Scots should finally obtain the palm of victory, together with their kingdom. Then, in the seventh year, died Dungallus, though it is stated elsewhere that he was killed in battle; he was buried in the church of the blessed Columba, and lies in the islands, beside his father.

BOOK IV.

CHAPTER I.

Rule of Succession of foregoing and subsequent Kings of the Scots, down to the time of Malcolm, the son of Kenneth.

WE have shown, above, the true dates of the accessions of the Scottish kings who reigned after Fergus, the son of Erth, in the northern part of Albion, together with the Picts. And now it is fitting to go on to the monarchs who acquired sole dominion over the whole of that part, after the Pictish tribes were overthrown; and to show forth some of their exploits, as well as the dates of their reigns—even as we are taught in the volumes of the ancients. But we must first speak of the rule of their succession. For the question is often asked, why the sons did not commonly succeed their fathers in the government of the kingdom, as the custom of modern times requires, rather than the brothers, as is implied in the succession of the foregoing kings. This, then, was done in those days, for the same law of succession obtained with the Scots, the Picts, and the kings of a great many countries, as well as with certain of the chiefs of the empire—to wit, on each king's death, his brother, or his brother's son, if he had the advantage over the king's son in age or fitness to rule, even though more remote in degree of kinship, came, before him to the throne. For it was not nearness in blood, but fitness as having attained to full puberty, that raised this or that man to the king's throne to reign. Now this arrangement, as to who should reign, first prevailed on account of the scanty numbers of a nation in its early days; which, inasmuch as it is, from its weakness, exposed to war from all quarters in getting, or keeping, a settled home in freedom, shrinks from handing over to youths the government, not only of their kingdom, but also of their persons; and so was established this law we have been treating of. This old custom of the succession of kings lasted, without a break, until the time of Malcolm, son of

Kenneth; when, for fear of the dismemberment of the kingdom, which might, perhaps, result therefrom, that king, by a general ordinance, decreed, as a law for ever, that, thenceforth, each king, after his death, should be succeeded in the government of the kingdom by whoever was, at the time being, the next descendant—that is, a son, or a daughter, a nephew, or a niece, the nearest then living. Failing these, however, the next heir, begotten of the royal, or a collateral, stock, should possess the right of inheritance.

CHAPTER II.

Accession of King Alpin—His Defeat by the Picts—His Death—Example of Hastiness.

AFTER the death of Dungallus, Alpin, the son of Achay, was at once crowned, and assumed the government of the kingdom, in A.D. 831. He reigned three years. With unflagging exertions, he continued the war against the Picts, which was begun by his predecessors, ravaging them constantly with his armies, or by repeated inroads. Accordingly, in the third year of his reign, during the Easter festival, the Scots came to conflict with the Picts, and many of their nobles fell. Whereupon it came to pass that Alpin, being victorious, was puffed up with pride; and, rashly engaging them in a second battle, the same year, on the 20th of July, he was defeated, taken, and, all ransom being refused, beheaded. He was beyond measure prone to war, and in all his actions too hasty and impetuous. Now nothing, almost, so little befits one who carries on a war as impatience, as is shown in the *Historiæ Romanorum*. For *Eutropius* has described the two consuls—Varro, and Æmilius, being sent to fight against Hannibal, and being warned by the Senate to overcome the hastiness of that impetuous leader, Hannibal, by simply staving off a battle; for the consul Fabius had conquered him once before, by putting off fighting. Nevertheless, against the opinion of his colleague Æmilius, Varro fought with him at Cannae, a village in Apulia; and through the impatience of Varro, both consuls were vanquished, and 300,000 Roman warriors perished in that fight. After the said battle, Hannibal offered the Romans that they should ransom the prisoners; but the Senate answered that they had no need of citizens who could be captured with arms in their hands. So he put them to death with various tortures, and sent off to Carthage three bushels of rings, which he had pulled off the hands of the knights, senators, and soldiers. Nor can there be any doubt that this day would have been the last of the Roman state, had Hannibal, after his victory, at once pressed on to occupy the city.

CHAPTER III.

Accession of King Kenneth, son of Alpin—His strange Trick against the Picts.

KENNETH, the son of Alpin, succeeded to his father's throne in A.D. 834; and to that of the Picts, when they had been overcome, in A.D. 839—the twenty-fifth year of the emperor Louis; that is, the year 1169 of the reign of the Scots in the island of Albion, and 2349 years after they went forth out of Egypt, under their first king—the son of Neolus, king of the Athenians—Gaythelos, and his wife Scota. Kenneth reigned nearly sixteen years as sole monarch of these kingdoms. He was a brave and wise man, of keen insight, and remarkable for the daring with which he carried on his war. This king, by a strange trick, brought the Scots into the Pictish kingdom; the reason whereof was this. In the first year of his reign, while the chiefs were gathered together in council, he made it known that he wished to revenge himself for the cruel murder of his father, and of his kinsmen who had lately been slain in the war, many of whom had been killed by the Picts after they had surrendered. He, therefore, earnestly exhorted them to hurry on this business, and, having laid aside all other matters, to get ready, against a given day, for the expedition. They, however, appalled, with exceeding great fear, by the newly-fought struggle, wherein King Alpin and many thousands had fallen, and, moreover, trembling, and altogether fainting in spirit, at the din of this war, answered like cowards or old women, and said, with one voice, unto the king:—"We neither would nor should leave undone, Sir King, anything for the defence of thy kingdom, or any other task thou might appoint us to do—save one. We do not wish to trespass over the landmarks of the Picts; for, in short, we dare not invade them. Fear so great has, until now, filled us, since the time of the war, that though an angel were seat from God to proclaim this to us, we should probably be afraid to comply. For long ago, in the days of our forefathers—ay, even lately, in our own—the bravery of the Scots would exceed the daring of the lion, or of the unicorn,—the nature of the former of which is to be terror-struck at the onslaught of none; that of the latter, never, alive, to come under the power of man—he may, indeed, be slaughtered, but never subdued alive; and if it should, at any time, happen that the hunters have contrived to take him alive, he dies then and there. But the times are changed with us; for we are more timid than women, or, if we may say so, than leverets." The king, therefore, seeing that he could make no way by exhorting them in either smooth or harsh terms, resolved to try a trick. For he bethought himself that they had not positively refused to march forth, but had hesitatingly said that, though an angel were to bid them march against the kingdom of the Picts, they would, perhaps, not obey even him. So he soon devised a scheme in his mind, and secretly revealed the answer of the chiefs to a certain artificer, a great friend of his, instructing him how to work the whole thing through. That artificer, on the other hand, who was a man of ready wit, willingly fell in with the king's wishes, promising, moreover, that all should be faithfully fulfilled to the best of his ability. So he slyly took some scaly fish skins—which, in the darkness of night, shine with a good deal of brilliancy—and cunningly decorated therewith a cloak, so that it flashed as with the flaming wings of an angel; and then he wrapped it round him, his whole body being shrouded thereby. Having thus donned this garment, he slipped privily into the bedchambers of the chiefs, and admirably cheated the senses, nay, the understanding, of such as were awake; and charging them on the part of the Living God, he bade them obey, in all things, their king's instructions, and particularly that they should in nowise be afraid to destroy the Pictish kingdom. The leaders, being led astray by this clever stratagem, went promptly to their lord the king, and promised him full obedience in all things. "For we have," said they, "most surely seen an angel, O king, face to face, who warned us to follow thee whithersoever thou may push on." Their statement was borne out by their chamberlains, who, of their own accord, swore to it with a great oath; and the king likewise swore to it unto them, informing them that he had heard and seen the same angel.

CHAPTER IV.

His Victories against the Picts—He wins their Kingdom.

WHEN, therefore, this turned out according to his wishes, and was brought, in all respects, to the end he had at heart, after general and willing consultation, war was declared against the Picts; and he gathered his forces together, and made his way into their country. So furiously, then, did he rage against not only the men, but even the women and little ones, that he spared neither sex nor holy orders, but destroyed, with fire and sword, every living thing which he did not carry off with him. Afterwards, in the sixth year of his reign, when the Danish pirates had occupied the coast, and, while plundering the seaboard, had, with no small slaughter, crushed the Picts who were defending their lands, Kenneth, likewise, himself also turned his arms against the remaining frontiers of the Picts, and, crossing the mountain range on their borders, to wit, the backbone of Albania, which is called Drumalban in Scottish, he slew many of the Picts, and put the rest to flight; thus acquiring the sole sovereignty over both countries. But the Picts, being somewhat reinforced by the help of the Angles, kept harassing Kenneth for four years. Weakening them subsequently, however, by unforeseen inroads and various massacres, at length, in the twelfth year of his reign, he engaged them seven times in one day, and swept down countless multitudes of the Pictish people. So he established and strengthened his authority thenceforth over the whole country from the river Tyne, beside Northumbria, to the Orkney Isles— as formerly Saint Adamnan, the Abbot of Hy (Iona), had announced in his prophecy. Thus, not only were the kings and leaders of that nation destroyed, but we read that their stock and race, also, along with their language or dialect, were lost; so that whatever of these is found in the writings of the ancients is believed, by most, to be fictitious or apocryphal. It does not, however, seem wonderful to those who read history often, that Almighty God—the Ruler of all kings and kingdoms, and their wondrous Preserver after their merits, but their terrible Destroyer after their shortcomings—has oftentimes allowed strong nations and kingdoms, and will allow them in time to come, to perish when their sins demand it. Whence the prophet David bears witness, saying:—Lo! the sinners have obtained riches abundantly in this world; how are they brought to desolation? They have suddenly failed, they have perished, by reason of their unrighteousness. Their forms are brought to nothing, as a dream when one awaketh.

CHAPTER V.

Subversion of divers Kingdoms for their Sins.

CHAPTER VI.

Same Continued.

CHAPTER VII.

Same continued—Former power of Rome, and her present Helplessness because of her Sins.

CHAPTER VIII.

King Kenneth's final Victory over the Picts—His Death.

KING KENNETH, then, after having, as has been just stated, gained seven victorious battles in one day, overran all the provinces of the Pictish kingdom, and took the un warlike population under the protection of his peace. Many, nevertheless, disdaining to submit their necks to slavery, and with the hope of resistance, followed a new king they had created. Kenneth, however, shortly afterwards, sent forth some columns of foot soldiers against them, and slew some of them, with their king; while others he compelled to surrender, and took them prisoners. But the remainder long roamed, in robber bands, through the vast solitudes, and would neither altogether surrender nor accept but peace; at length, hard pressed, and having nowhere to hide their heads, they sought relief by fleeing to the Angles and Norwegians. And thus God granted that it should come to pass that Kenneth should be the first of all the kings to take the whole of the north-western end of Albion under his sole sovereignty, thus happily welding the two kingdoms into one. He also framed laws, called the Macalpine Laws, and appointed that they should be observed; whereof some remain to this day, and are in vogue amongst the people. When the kingdom had thus been imbued with law and peace, after the many and countless stormy troubles of so long a time, Kenneth passed away to the Lord, at Forteviot, at the end of full sixteen years and eight months of his reign as sole monarch; and he was, with becoming honours, amid the deepest wailing of the Scots, buried in the island of Iona, where, formerly, were laid in the ground King Fergus, the son of Erth, and his two brothers. Loam and Tenegus—may their souls have peace for ever! Now, this Kenneth was the son of King Alpin,

Son of Achay,
Son of Ethfin,
Son of Eugenius,
Son of Findan,
Son of Eugenius,
Son of Dongardus,
Son of Donaldus Brek,
Son of Eugenius Buyd,
Son of Aidanus,
Son of Gowranus,
Son of Dongardus,
Son of Fergus,
Son of Erth.

This Fergus recovered the sovereignty, which had been withheld for forty-three years, by the craft of the tyrant Maximus, and the might of the Picts, and restored it to its olden freedom, as was shown above.

CHAPTER IX.
Preliminary remarks to the Catalogue of Pictish Kings.

AS we have above noticed the overthrow of the Picts, it will not seem out of place to give here the catalogue of their kings, and some other facts we have found in the volumes of the ancients. A clear account of their origin, the reason why they came into these parts, and whence, will be found in Chapters XXIX., XXX., and XXXI. of Book I. It will there be seen that they inhabited part of this kingdom before our Lord's Incarnation—before the Scots, or, at least, at the same time; though there are chronicles which assert that the Scots possessed this country long before the Picts, for an interval of three hundred years. *Geoffroy*, in Book V. Chapter VI. of his Chronicle, states that the Picts had their origin after our Lord's resurrection, in the days of Vespasian; and that the Scots then first grew out of them. But most chroniclers know well enough whether that is so, or not. He would have been nearer the truth had he written that, at that time, the Moravians, uniting with the Picts and Scots, came against the Romans into this country under their leader Roderic—who was certainly a Moravian, and not a Pict; and by the offspring which they begot of their daughters, their multitude was greatly increased. But it could easily be proved, by the duration of their reigns, that they began long before this. For the truth is that they reigned 1100 years, or more, in Albion; and there is no doubt that they perished by the sword of the before-mentioned King Kenneth. So there can be no doubt that they took their origin, not after the Incarnation, but before. But if any one, by chance, should be pleased to object that it is incredible that King Ghede, or his successor Tharan, reigned so long a time that one hundred years are reckoned for the one, and one hundred and fifty for the other, the reader may answer that, though only fifty years were ascribed to either of the kings, it would still be found that the Picts began a hundred years, or more, before the time of the Incarnation. As some, therefore, murmur at so great a number of years being allotted to their reigns, we think fit to leave the computation of the years of both these kings to be corrected by the reader who would search thoroughly into the truth thereof. The duration and order of the reigns of the other kings, however, my pen shall run over, as best it can.

CHAPTER X.

Catalogue of Pictish Kings—Arrival of the blessed Abbot Columba.

THE first king among the Picts was Cruythne, son of Kynne, the judge; and he reigned fifty years.

After him, the second was Ghede.

The third, Tharan; to these two, as was said above, two hundred and fifty years are set down.

King Tharan was succeeded by Dinorthetisy, who reigned twenty years.

Then Duchil reigned forty years.

Duordeghel, twenty.

Decokheth, sixty (forty).

Combust, twenty.

Caranarhereth, forty.

Garnarchbolger, nine.

Wypopneth, thirty.

Blarehassereth, seventeen.

Frachna the White, thirty.

Thalarger Amfrud, sixteen.

Canatalmel, six.

Dongard Nethles, one.

Peredach, son of Fynyel, two.

Garnard the Rich, sixty (forty).

Hurgust, son of Forgso, twenty-seven. In the time of this king's reign, as described in Book II. Chapter XLVIII, some of Saint Andrew's relics were brought to Scotland, by the blessed Regulus.

Thalarger, son of Keother, succeeded Hurgust, and reigned twenty-five years.

Durst, otherwise called Nectane, son of Irb, forty-five years. This king, it is asserted, lived a hundred years, and went through a hundred battles. During his reign. Saint Paladius, the first bishop of the Scots, was sent by the blessed Pope Cœlestinus to teach the Scots, who, however, had been long before believers in Christ.

Thalarger, son of Anile, succeeded him, and reigned two years.

Nectane Chaltamoth, ten years.

Durst Gornoth, thirty.

Galaam, fifteen.

Durst, son of Gigurum, five.

Durst, son of Othtred, eight.

Durst, son of Gigurum, a second time, four.

Garnard, son of Gigurum, six.

Kelturan, his brother, also six.

Tholorger, son of Mordeleth, eleven.

Durst, son of Moneth, one.

Thalagath, four.

Brud, son of Merlothon, nineteen. During his reign. Saint Columba came to Scotland, and converted him to the faith. Saint Columba, says *Bede*, came to Britain during the reign, over the Picts, of Brude, a most mighty king, the son of Meilothon; in the ninth year of his reign, which was the five hundred and sixty-fifth from our Lord's Incarnation.

CHAPTER XI.

Catalogue continued—Conversion of Brude, King of the Picts, by the blessed Columba—The Prince of the Orkneys then a Captive.

WE read in the history of Saint Columba:—In the first toilsome journey of the blessed Columba to visit King Brude, it so happened, by chance, that the king, being jealous of his kingly pomp, did not, in his pride, open the gates of his fortress at the first arrival of the holy man. When the man of God perceived this, he came up to the panels of the gates, with his company; and, having first made the sign of our Lord's cross upon them, he put his hand against the door, and knocked. Thereupon, the bolts were at once forcibly thrust back of themselves, and the doors flew open with all speed. As soon as they were open, the saint and his companions entered, one after the other. When the king learnt this, he and his council were sore afraid; so he went forth out of his palace, and advanced to meet the holy man with all reverence, addressing him most courteously with words of peace; and, from that day forwards, that ruler reverenced the holy and venerable man exceedingly, all the rest of the days of his life, and honoured him highly, as was meet. Now, in these days, while this saint sojourned beyond Drumalban, a certain monk who wished to get a home in the wilderness, after he had launched forth from the shore, full sail through the boundless ocean, was recommended by him to this Brude, king of the Picts, in the presence of the prince of the Orkneys, in these words:— "Some of ours have lately been sailing about the pathless deep, wanting to find a desert. After their long roaming, should they chance to reach the Orkney islands, commend them diligently to this prince, whose hostages are in thy hand; lest any untoward thing be done against them within his borders." This was thus spoken by the saint, because he knew in the spirit that, a few months after, that monk, whose name was Cormack, would come to the Orkneys—which, afterwards, so turned out; and by reason of the aforesaid recommendation of the holy man, that monk was delivered from impending death in the Orkneys.

CHAPTER XII.

Catalogue continued—The King with whom the Pictish Kingdom came to an end.

GARNARD, son of Dompnach, succeeded this King Brude, and reigned twenty years. He founded Abernethy.

Nectane, son of Irb, reigned eleven years.

Kenel, son of Luchtren, fourteen.

Nectane, son of Fode, eight.
Brude, son of Fachna, five.
Thalarger, son of Farchar, eleven.
Talargan, son of Amfrud, four.
Garnard, son of Dompnal, five.
Durst, his brother, six.
Brud, son of Bile, eleven.
Gharan, son of Amfedech, four.
Brud, son of Decili, twenty-one.
Nectane, his brother, eighteen. This king, according to *Bede*, received a letter from England on the observance of the Easter cycle.
Garnard, son of Feredach, succeeded Nectane, and reigned fourteen years.
Oengussa, son of Fergusa, reigned sixteen years.
Nectane, son of Dereli, nine months.
Oengussa, son of Brude, six months.
Alpin, son of Feredeth, likewise six months.
Alpin then reigned, a second time, for twenty-six years.
Brude, son of Tenegus, reigned two years.
Alpin, son of Tenegus, also two.
Durst, son of Thalargan, one.
Thalarger, son of Drusken, four.
Thalarger, son of Tenegus, five.
Constantine, son of Fergusa, forty. He built Dunkelden (Dunkeld).
Hungus, son of Fergus, ten years. During the reign of King Hungus, there reigned in Wessex King Athelwlf, the head of whose eldest son, Athelstan, fixed on a stake, Hungus brought down with him into his kingdom, after he had gained the victory in battle, as will appear more fully in the next following chapter.
Durstolorger succeeded Hungus, and reigned four years.
Eoghane, son of Hungus, reigned three years.
Feredeth, son of Badoc, likewise three.
Brude, son of Feredeth, one month.

Kenneth, son of Feredeth, one year.

Brude, son of Fothel, two.

Drusken, son of Feredeth, three. With this King Drusken, also, the sovereign power of the Picts came to an end, and the kingdom altogether passed over from them to the Scottish king Kenneth, and his successors; and there was formed, thenceforth, one kingdom—that of the Scots.

CHAPTER XIII.

Hungus, King of the Picts, and Athelwlf, King of the Angles, were contemporaries—Athelstan, the son of the latter.

NOW we must show who that Athelstan was, whom King Hungus overthrew in battle. For there were formerly, in England three kings Athelstan, the first of whom was the last king of Kent, whose kingdom was taken over from him, and added to that of the West Saxons; the second was the one in question, the son of Æthelwlf, upon whom his father bestowed all the countries of the English-born nation during his own lifetime, except the kingdom of Wessex, which he retained in his own hands; the third Athelstan, again, was the son of Edward son of Alfred, brother of this Athelstan of ours. King Egbert says *William*, having first subjugated the Britons of Cornwall, made the northern Britons also tributary to him. The kingdom of Kent, with Suthireya (Surrey), the kingdom of the Mercians and East Angles, the East Saxons, and the South Saxons, likewise became subject to him. Thus, by admitting the rest of the English provinces into allegiance to him, or as tributaries, he enlarged the kingdom of the West Saxons. The Northumbrians, however, who saw themselves left alone—both on account of their domestic quarrels, and by reason of their false oaths—and that the finger of scorn was pointed at them by all, gave hostages and yielded to his power. This Egbert, upon his death, was succeeded by his son Æthelwlf, who had begotten five sons during his father's lifetime, Æthelwlf was mild by nature, and would rather live in quiet, than have dominion over many provinces. Content with only his ancestral kingdom of the West Saxons, as soon as he began to reign he handed over to his eldest son, Athelstan, the other dependencies which his father had subjugated. How and at what time, this Athelstan came by his end is uncertain. Such is William's account. But though that Athelstan's end is not shown in William, amongst us it is kept fresh in signal remembrance, both in sundry writings and also in the mouths of the people to this day. For, when King Hungus, with a large army, was wasting with inhuman slaughter the neighbouring nations of the Angles—the Northumbrians, to wit—in those tracts which Athelstan had had granted him by his father while the latter reigned, Athelstan passed out of his own country, and arrived, wearied after several days' march, in a certain pleasant plain to halt in, not far from the river Tyne. So he commanded them to pitch the tents until the army, tired by the length of their journey, should be refreshed by a good meal. Moreover, as that plain was exceeding rich in corn and grass and brushwood, and watered by springs and streams, he decided to tarry there a few days, as fearing nothing.

CHAPTER XIV.

Victory of Hungus, King of the Picts, over Athelstan; whose head he directed to be fixed on a stake.

WHEN King Athelstan had heard this, massing together the strength of the whole English nation, both of the north and of the south, and disposing his battle-array in single companies, he came upon Hungus unexpectedly with his columns, and so beset on every side the place the latter was encamped in, that no outlet lay open to him for escape. Hungus was therefore alarmed, and the chiefs were dismayed in spirit, and feared exceedingly; for they had no hope of being saved betimes by the aid of man. So they fell back upon God's help, which, in truth, is not withheld from those that ask it; and all, both great and small, on their knees, address their vows to God and his saints, and especially to Saint Andrew, the apostle. The king, moreover, promised by a solemn vow that he would give, to the honour of God and the Blessed Virgin Mary, a tenth part of his kingdom to the blessed Andrew, provided he brought him and his army safely back home, and snatched him scathless from the power of that countless and proud nation. The following night the blessed Andrew appeared to the king, saying:—"God, to whom the prayer of the humble always is pleasing, and the vows of the proud displeasing, has, through my intercession, heard thy prayer. To-morrow He shall give thee a gladsome victory, and overthrow thine enemies before thee; neither shall they prevail against thee in battle: for an angel, bearing the banner of the Lord's cross, shall go before thee in the sight of many. When, therefore, thou shalt have prosperously returned into thy kingdom, be thou nowise unmindful of thy vow; but what thou hast thyself promised of thine own free-will, take heed that thou delay not to fulfil it." So the king, awaking from sleep, made known to his officers and people all that he had heard in a vision—how God, through the prayers of his apostle, had granted him a sure victory over his enemies. They all, therefore, through the confidence inspired by this vision, were gladdened beyond belief, and no longer fearful, as on the two previous days; but being made brave, and much bolder than their wont, they dashed forward upon the foe, with shouts and with trumpets sounding, although they themselves were far fewer in numbers. Thereupon so great a panic invaded the hearts of the enemy, that their ranks were broken and they all turned to flee, except a few with the king, who held their ground, and were overcome and slain at the first shock. In memory of so miraculous a discomfiture, the king's head, however, was cut off from the body, and taken away by Hungus, who bade it be fixed on a stake at the top of a rock in the middle of the Scottish sea—a conspicuous object, for several years, to all who crossed there. Now, in the thirteenth year of King Kenneth, sundry fleets of the heathen made frequent piratical attacks on the harbours of England; and, at length, took the city of London, laid it in ruins, and sacked it.

CHAPTER XV.

Accession of the Kings Donald, son of Alpin, and Constantine, son of Kenneth—Death of Donald.

AFTER the solemn celebration of the funeral of King Kenneth the Great, he was succeeded, the same year he died—that is, A.D. 854, the fourteenth year of the emperor Lothaire—by his brother Donald, also a son of Alpin, who reigned four years. He was a renowned warrior, brave, and eager for all warlike deeds; and he likewise achieved many a glorious victory and triumph in vanquishing the Picts. He studied, however, to foster peace and concord with the neighbouring countries and kings, nor did any one presume to molest his territory in anywise, save some outcast Picts, who, in the days of their downfall, seeing the discomfiture of their nation, fled to England. As soon as they had heard of the death of King Kenneth, these being spurred on by the English, as well as swelled by their columns, notwithstanding a treaty of peace that had lately been entered into, began to invade the borders of the kingdom; but, the same year, through the judicious measures of the king and some faithful Picts, they were destroyed, and not one was left. In the third year of this reign, the Emperor Lothaire, having parted his kingdom among his sons, renounced the world; while his son Louis II. was promoted to the imperial throne, and reigned twenty-one years. King Donald, however, went the way of all flesh at Scone, the seat of royalty; and was buried in Iona, beside his brother. He was succeeded, in A.D. 858—the third year of the emperor Louis—by his nephew Constantine, son of his brother Kenneth the Great, who reigned sixteen years. During his time, and the whole of that of his predecessors—his father and uncle, to wit—a great fleet of the heathen, Danes, Norwegians, and Frisians, emerged from the east, and disturbed the whole of the British and Belgic seas. For, in the thirteenth year of the sovereignty of his father, they attacked England by the river Thames, took the city of London, and carried off some precious spoils and treasures. And thus, bursting suddenly upon the two kingdoms of Scotland and England—now here, now there, as they were driven by the winds—they continually, for many days, did a great deal of mischief. In the second year of this reign, frost set in, over nearly the whole of Europe, on the 30th of November, and ended on the 5th of April. In the eighth year, the king of the Bulgari was, with his nation, converted to Christianity, and was so strengthened in the faith, that, not long after, he advanced his eldest son to the throne, while he himself entirely renounced the world, and became a monk. But when his son inconsiderately wished to return to the worship of heathendom, he resumed the knightly belt and royal life; and, having followed after his son, he took him, tore out his eyes, and thrust him into prison. He then placed his younger son on the throne; and, taking again the sacred garb, abode therein until his life's end.

CHAPTER XVI.

Constantine slain by Danes and Norwegians—Accession of King Heth the Wing-footed.

IN the time of the reign of King Constantine, a second fleet of the heathen, larger and more formidable, came from the Danube, and joined the former one; and, combining for no good purpose, but all for warfare and wickedness, they covered the seas—as it were groves planted therein. And thus it came to pass, shortly afterwards, that, landing in both kingdoms, they dwelt there without fear for days and months, as though it were their own home. These, it was now thought, the barbarous Picts, who had not yet been thoroughly tamed, had secretly enticed to Scotland; even as one might not unlikely have suspected from the upshot of the matter. The king had many a time offered them a safe reception among the harbours of his kingdom, and leave to buy provisions to their hearts' content, if only they would cease from their inroads, and faithfully observe the terms of peace. As, however, they could not be appeased by this means, nor by any other treaty of peace, the king—whether on an appointed day, or by chance, unexpectedly, is not known—gave them battle at a spot named the Black Den, and fell there, with many of his men. And no wonder for he had rashly brought with him, to battle, like a snake in his bosom, some of the lately conquered Picts. These fled as soon as they closed in battle, thus giving occasion to the others to do the same. So the king was left on the field by a great part of his army, and beset by the enemy and slain. When the enemy, after their victory there, had retreated to their ships, the rented inhabitants returned; and, after searching the field, they found the king's body, and bore it with deep wailing to the island of Iona, where it was enshrined, with great honours, in his father's bosom. In England, moreover, two years before the king's death, the heathen of the said fleets martyred Saint Edmund, king of the East Angles. Constantine was succeeded, in A.D. 874—the nineteenth year of Louis— by his brother Heth the Wing-footed, who was also a son of Kenneth the Great, and who reigned one year. This king was so distinguished for vigour and nimbleness of limb, that all men called him Heth *the Wing-footed*, that is, Heth with wings on his feet; for he had earned a name for swiftness above all others of his day. But ought he to be set above the runners of Alexander the Great—Anisius the Laconian, and Philonides—for nimbleness, those men who, according to *Solinus*, went through, in one day, from Lapnum to Sicion, a distance of twelve hundred stadia (about 138 miles)? A certain Ladas, however, seems to have outstripped them in speed, as the same Solinus relates; for he ran so swiftly on the white dust, that he left no trace of a footprint on the sand. Enough for the king that he bore the palm for swiftness in his time. Now, according to the rule of the kingship, Gregory, son of Dungallus, should have come before him; wherefore, the chiefs of the kingdom being divided amongst themselves, a battle was fought at Strathallan, wherein the king was mortally wounded at the first shock, and died two months after; while a few of the chiefs on either side were slain in the fight. King Heth was buried in the island of Iona, beside his father.

CHAPTER XVII.

Accession of King Gregory, who brings tender his Yoke the whole of Ireland and nearly the whole of England.

NOW this Gregory, when he had, with the approval of most of the chiefs, obtained the government of the kingdom, was solemnly crowned at Scone, in A.D. 875—the twentieth year of Louis—and reigned nearly eighteen years. When the ceremony of his coronation was over, he forthwith firmly established peace throughout all the ends of his kingdom; and granting full forgiveness to all who, he knew, had withstood him in battle, he brought them round to true friendship with him. Neither was he, from the beginning of his reign, forgetful or neglectful of divine worship—nay, he even, with the consent of the chiefs, granted the Church of God, and churchmen, their freedom for ever, confirmed by Pope John VIII., who held the fifth synod at Constantinople. For, until then, the church had been subject to servitude, according to the custom of the Picts. Moreover, he brought the whole of Ireland, and nearly the whole of England, under his yoke. And though Ireland belonged to him by right of succession, he did not get possession of it without war on the part of some who withstood him. The sovereignty of his possessions in England he won partly by his arms, and partly by kindness. In his days—even as before, and long afterwards, pirates of various nations, as was shown above—to wit, Danes, Norwegians, Goths, Vandals, and Frisians—sharing one and the same lawless bent, were scattered over the harbours and lands of the English; and, in their fury, unceasingly laid waste, with most woful desolation, the districts, especially, on the seaboard, until they had reduced them, in great part, under their dominion, and gained possession of them. Moreover, King Gregory himself, also, subdued the upper and western districts, even as they had those on the sea-board; and he brought upon them desolation not far short of that those men had spread around. The natives of some provinces, however, before he had reached their borders, gave themselves of their own accord, with their lands and property, into his power, after having sworn fealty and homage. For they deemed it a more blissful lot, and more advantageous, willingly to be subject to the Scots, who held the Catholic faith, though they were their enemies, than unwillingly to unbelieving heathens. All the provinces, says *William*, were burning with fierce ravages, because each king cared more to withstand the enemy in his own territory, than to extend help to his fellow-countrymen in their struggles. In the first year of Gregory, two Norican, or Danish, kinsmen—Rollo and Gello—forced their way into Neustria, and seized Rouen, and the other towns in the neighbourhood. In the third year, the emperor Louis died, and was succeeded by his uncle, Charles the Bald, who held the empire two years. After his death, Charles the younger was emperor twelve years. Now Charles, since he was unable to drive Rollo and his comrades from the fatherland, took counsel, and, after having received a solemn promise from Rollo that he would embrace Christianity, gave him his daughter Gilla to wife, and the whole of Neustria—which Rollo called Normandy, after the Normans.

CHAPTER XVIII.

Gregory—His Death—Martyrdom of the blessed King Edmund—Nearly the whole of England at that time subject to the Scots and Danes.

The English had then—in the time of Gregory, to wit—no defender, or, at all events, a feeble one; for they were bereft of all their kings—of old, eight in number—except Alfred, king of the West Saxons, who, alone surviving, attacked the enemy with all possible courage, though with little success. Being, however, much more often attacked by them, and having to avoid the snares of enemies raging on every side, he soon fell into so forlorn a state that, with fearful heart, he knew not where to turn for a place where he could hide in safety in England. The Northumbrians, again, had more than once before, by their own fault, driven out their kings from their midst, but were now driven, by force of circumstances, to take back a king whom they had previously cast out—namely, Osbert; and, shortly afterwards, they were, together with him, cruelly slain or burnt, under the walls of the city of York, by the enemy, who thenceforth held their lands by right of conquest. Burthred, likewise, king of the Mercians, being driven from his kingdom by the enemy, repaired to Rome, nevermore to return; while Saint Edmund, king of the East Angles, having gloriously suffered martyrdom at the hands of the heathen, as above described, exchanged his earthly for a heavenly throne; and thenceforth his foes possessed his kingdom. The rest of the chiefs, too, who were left over, being in bondage either to the Scots or the Danes, did service for their lives and property. But the upper provinces, bordering on the kingdom of Scotland, unwillingly submitted to King Gregory. And thus, in those days, and for a long time after, the whole of England, whirled round through the various chances of fortune, wretchedly succumbed to various lords—

The Dane had part; the greatest part the Scot;
And one small part fell to King Alfred's lot.

But Alfred, says *William*, was at last driven to such a pitch of distress (scarcely three counties standing fast in their allegiance to him— namely, Huntingdonshire, Wiltshire, and Somersetshire) that he sought refuge in a certain island called Adlingia (Ely) which, from its marshy situation, was hardly accessible. In the time of Gregory, the County of Flanders took its rise. Before that, it used to be ruled by the French king's foresters; the first of whom was Lideric, the second Ingerlam, and the third Audacer; and these, though they were not counts, were the rulers of Flanders under Pipin, Charles the Great, and Louis. Afterwards, Charles the Bald, who was mentioned above, gave Flanders to Baldwin, the son of Audacer, and his daughter Judith, for an inheritance. But this glorious King Gregory, after a vigorous reign of eighteen years, all but a few months, closed the last of his days at Donedoure, and lies buried in the island of Iona. In the thirteenth year of Gregory, died the emperor Charles, and was, in A.D. 887, succeeded by Arnulph, who filled the imperial throne fifteen years.

CHAPTER XIX.

John Scotus, the philosopher—The Emperor Arnulph, who was eaten up by lice.

IN the time of this Gregory flourished John Scotus, a man, according to *Helinandus*, of penetrating genius, and honeyed eloquence. While the din of war was crashing around him, he crossed over into France, to Charles the Bald, where, after a thorough examination of sundry books, he, at Charles's request, translated the *Hierarchia* of Dionysius the Areopagite, word for word, out of the Greek into Latin. He also composed a book which he entitled *Peri physicon merismou*, that is to say, *On the Division of Nature*, very useful for solving the wearing-out study of certain indispensable questions. In after years, allured by King Alfred's munificence, he came to England; and, shortly afterwards, suffered martyrdom at the monastery of Malmesbury, being stabbed by the boys he taught—with their writing-styles, it is said. His illustrious memory is handed down by his tomb, on the left side of the altar, and by the verses of his epitaph:—

"The holy sophist John here buried lies,
  In life endowed with wondrous wealth of lore.
He earned, at last, by martyrdom, to rise
  To Christ, and reign with saints for evermore."

The Emperor Arnulph—the date of whose reign was noted in the foregoing chapter—smote down by a terrible blow the Normans who were wasting Gaul, Lorraine, and Dardania (Dordogne?), about Liège and Mentz; and then began to cease the yoke of the Normans and Danes, who, for forty years, had laid France waste. This Arnulph, afterwards, languishing in a long sickness, was, in spite of all the physician's art, eaten up by lice. In the sixteenth year of Gregory died Guthrum the Dane, king of Northumbria and East Anglia, to whom Alfred had stood godfather, naming him Athelstan. He was succeeded by his son Ranald, and Sithric, one of his kinsmen.

CHAPTER XX.

Accession of King Donald, son of Constantine—His Death.

WHEN the mourning for the death and burial of Gregory was ended, Donald, who was the son of the above Constantine, son of Kenneth the Great, obtaining the sovereignty of the kingdom, was crowned at Scone in the same year that Gregory died, that is to say, in A.D. 892, the sixth year of the emperor Arnulph. He reigned eleven years, with vigour indeed, but with huge and restless trouble, now in the parts of northern Scotland, now in those of England which had been lately conquered; lest at any time, having grown to pleasure and careless ease, he should ingloriously lose what his predecessor had won by his watchful prudence, and with great trouble. For

'Tis no less praise to keep than to acquire.

But the heathen of the Danish nation offered Donald—as they had, formerly, his predecessor Gregory—to enter into a treaty of peace with him against the English, so that these, being assailed on all sides by their combined strength, might the more easily be overcome. Both kings, however, utterly declined this, answering that it would never do for a Christian chief to afford help to unbelieving heathens, or be bound by any sworn treaty with them, against Catholics, even though his enemies. Finally, after some years, a certain Danish king of Northumbria and East Anglia—Gurmund—was, with his followers, baptized by King Alfred, and bound himself to the same by an oath. Nevertheless, he immediately afterwards, by his pressing entreaties, obtained of Gregory, who was then still alive, that the treaty of fealty and friendship he had before desired, should be concluded. After Gurmund's death, moreover, when his son Ranald, and his kinsman, Sithric, his successors, kept on importuning King Donald for a similar treaty engagement, he granted it quite willingly, although he undoubtedly knew they had, like Gurmund, already plighted their troth to Alfred. About the same time, also, while the king was making a stay in the south, some mischievous robbers began to disturb the country beyond the hills, by frequent secret murders and open rapine. In order, therefore, to put down their outrages, he sent out escorts of soldiers southwards in detachments; and as soon as he had set foot in their borders, he shortly fell sick and died, almost suddenly, in the town of Forres—whether worn out by toil, or poisoned by the treachery of those villains, is uncertain. He was buried in the island of Iona. May he rest in peace for ever, awaiting the last day! In the tenth year of Donald, Alfred, king of the West Saxons, died, and was succeeded by his son Edward. In the eleventh, that is to say, the last, year of this reign, the emperor Arnulph died, and his son Louis began to reign. Louis, however, did not attain to the imperial crown. Ten years are allotted to him. With him the empire came to an end, as regards the posterity of Charles, owing to their own shortcomings.

CHAPTER XXI.

Accession of King Constantine, son of Heth the Wing-footed—He gives the Lordship of Cumbria to Donald's son, Eugenius, his expected next heir.

CONSTANTINE, son of Heth the Wing-footed, succeeded Donald in A.D. 903—the first year of Louis—and reigned forty years. During his reign, two English kings—the aforesaid Edward, to wit, and his illegitimate son Athelstan—who reigned in succession, repeatedly warred against him: both because of the help he had afforded the Danes, and because he protected, with all his might, the natives of his Cumbrian territory, and other possessions in England, who faithfully cleaved to him even until the battle of Brounyngfelde (Brunanburh). The kings of the Danish nation, indeed, more fickle than the wind, were united with him in the same sworn treaty, and show of friendship, as with his predecessors; but, remaining faithful scarcely two years, they were led away by the treacherous promises of Edward, and made a peace with him against the Scots, to their own hurt. Nor did the stipulations of this covenant hold long; indeed, four years after, there sprang up some estrangement between them—by what chance, is not certain; but, it is believed, by Edward's wickedness, who made a hostile invasion of their territory, and wasted it with piteous slaughter for a whole month. They, on the other hand, driven by force of circumstances, saw no hope of help anywhere but in again conciliating the Scots, and renewing the former friendly treaty with them, from fellowship with whom Edward's craft had lately made them withdraw. In order, therefore, to soften the settled hatred of Constantine towards them, they sent messengers, humbly begging pardon and peace, and promising by an oath never again, through fault of theirs, to break any treaty, if only he would be pleased to renew this one. So the messengers joyfully brought back word that all had been arranged according to their wishes, the king's wrath having been turned into pity. Now Constantine, in the sixteenth year of his reign, gave Eugenius, the son of Donald, his expected next heir, the lordship of the region of Cumbria to rule over, until he should, on Constantine's death, obtain the diadem of the kingdom; and, on his being crowned king, his next heir was to succeed to that lordship; and thus the lordship was in future, by this rule of succession, always to be transferred from the heir, immediately on his being crowned king, to his next successor. In the twenty-second year of this reign, Edward died, and was succeeded by his illegitimate son Athelstan, begotten of the daughter of Opilio; his brother Edwin, who should, by rights, have reigned, having been set aside, and afterwards delivered over unto a wretched death; for he was sent to sea alone, but for one man who accompanied him, in a vessel without an oarsman, and rotten with age, and was drowned. But a certain chief, Alfred, being exasperated at what he saw done, speedily bound himself with King Constantine and the aforesaid Sithric, in a close and faithful alliance against Athelstan. In the eleventh year of Constantine, the emperor Louis died, and was succeeded by a certain Conrad, a German, who was seven years emperor; though he is not numbered with the emperors, as he lacked the imperial blessing. Conrad was succeeded by Henry, in A.D. 920, the eighteenth year of Constantine. He was emperor eighteen years; but he is not reckoned either among the emperors, as he also was not crowned by the Pope.

CHAPTER XXII.

Constantine—Woeful and cruel Battle of Brounyngfeld.

WHEN, however, Athelstan had heard rumours of the alliance above touched upon, he was moved beyond measure; for he knew that the strength of his adversaries was increased, while his had diminished. So, on mature reflection, he began to think that it would be better to manage the matter in an underhand way, in secret, than openly to try the doubtful event of a battle. So secretly sending forth his tale-bearers, who craftily instilled deceit into Sithric's ear, he cheated him into forgetting his former oath, and falsely marrying Athelstan's sister, though utterly against the wishes of his own sons. Whence it came to pass that he lived barely nine months after, having been, it is deemed, wickedly put to death. *William* relates that Sithric's life being cut short a year after, gave Athelstan occasion to join Northumbria to his dominions. Athelstan soon after laid siege to York; and after urging the townsmen, now by prayers, now by threats, to surrender, and in neither way speeding according to his wishes, he retired. But the Northumbrian and Cumbrian nations, having already been long straitly cemented with the Scots and Danes, as one nation, were anxious to be subject unto them rather than to the English. So, on Sithric being taken away from their midst, as above narrated, the Northumbrians willingly took his sons, Analaf and Godofrid, to be their chiefs; and these, being straightway joined unto Constantine, made war upon Athelstan with their whole strength. In the thirty-sixth year of his reign, therefore, King Constantine, Analaf, and Godofrid, having gathered together an exceedingly large army, invaded the English territory to the south, wasting everything in their path, until they arrived in the place where Athelstan had pitched his tents, which is called Brounyngfelde. Athelstan's last battle, says *William*, was with Sithric's son Analaf, and the Scottish king Constantine, who had crossed the Borders in the hope of seizing his kingdom. Athelstan purposely retreated, that he might conquer gloriously; and the assailants had already passed far into England, when suddenly, the columns and ranks of the two sides were mixed up together, and there was fought a most cruel battle, far more savage than any handed down in the writings of the ancients, or intrusted to the memory of men now-a-days. For there were slain, on the side of the victorious Athelstan, two chief leaders—Eldwyn and Ethelwyn—and two other leaders, as well as two bishops and many nobles. On the other side, the Prince of Deira, Eligenius, and three other princes, nine leaders; and a countless multitude of the rabble of either side.

CHAPTER XXIII.

Loss inflicted upon the Scots by this battle—Death of Constantine in the monastic garb.

THAT was an unlucky day for the Scots: for all the domains they had conquered in the time of Gregory, or down to that time—which, moreover, they had held fifty-four years or more—were, in this day, lost to them by right of conquest. Constantine, king of the Scots, says *William*, fell there, a man of high spirit, and a vigorous old age; five kings, etc. Various truthful chronicles, however, advance the opposite of this statement of Williams. For, after the fatal overthrow of this battle, he wielded the sceptre for four years; and then he resigned the crown, and, serving God in the monastic garb at St. Andrews, was made Abbot of the Culdees, and lived there five years; where he also died, and was buried. The monks of Hy (Iona) then straightway dug up his bones, and took them away and buried them in the tomb of his fathers, in the chapel of the blessed Oran, in A.D. 947. It does not, therefore, hold good that he was slain in the battle of Brounyngfelde, as he outlived the battle nine years. In the *Legend of the miracles of Saint John of Beverley*, I have found the following passage, among others, about the aforesaid king Athelstan:—King Athelstan, on his way to fight against the Scots, visited the blessed John of Beverley, upon whose altar he placed a dagger as his bail, promising that, if he came back victorious, he would redeem the dagger at an adequate price. And this promise he also fulfilled: for, during his struggle with the Scots, he asked God that through the prayers of Saint John, He should show him some evident sign, whereby those, in times present and to come, might know that the Scots were rightfully subjugated by the English. Whereupon the king struck with his sword a certain boulder of stone beside the castle of Dunbar; and the stroke made, in the rock, a gash measuring an ell—as may be seen to this day. Such is the story there. But we have heard old hags tell some such fable—that it so happened that one of king Arthur's soldiers—Kay—had to fight with an enormous tom cat; which, seeing the soldier prepared to fight with it obstinately, climbed to the top of a great rock; and, coming down, after having made its claws wondrous sharp for the fight, it gashed the rock with sundry clefts and winding paths, beyond belief. Kay, however, they say, killed the torn cat. But the cleft of Athelstan's rock is not had in remembrance or known by the people, therefore, etc. In the very year of the battle, likewise, died

Henry; and his son Otho was thirty-six years emperor. In the third year of this emperor, A.D. 940, Athelstan died, and was succeeded by his brother Edmund, who held the kingdom nearly seven years.

CHAPTER XXIV.

Accession of King Malcolm, son of Donald—The English King Edmund restores Cumbria to him.

IN A.D. 943—the sixth year of Otho—king Constantine, inspired by the grace of God's mercy, and understanding clearly that all earthly things were subject unto vanity, vacated the throne, as was seen above, and made room for Malcolm, son of Donald, to reign; who accordingly reigned nine years. Furthermore, after the death of Athelstan, the inhabitants of all those lands which he had reduced to his sway by the battle of Brounyngfelde, were restored to their former lords, the Scots and Danes. The Northumbrians, indeed, determined to call back Analaf from Ireland, and set him up as king again. When, therefore, this came to Edmund's ears, being afraid that, perchance, the people of Cumbria would cleave to the Scots, as the Northumbrians had cleaved to Analaf, he preferred winning a friend in exchange for that country, to a cruel enemy's holding it, perhaps for ever, in spite of him. So, desirous of having king Malcolm's help against the Danes, and of conciliating his spirit into close sympathy with his own, he made over to him, for his oath of fealty, the whole of Cumbria, in possession for ever. At this time, says *William*, the Northumbrians, meditating a renewal of hostilities, broke the treaty they had struck with Athelstan, recalled Analaf from Ireland, and appointed him king over them. Edmund, on the other hand, deeming it wrong not to follow up the results of his brother's victory, led his troops against the turn-coat Northumbrians. Analaf, to test the king's disposition, offered to surrender. But his savage mind did not long remain in this resolution: for he violated his oath, and angered the Lord—whereof he paid the penalty by being, the following year, driven into perpetual exile. The province which is called Cumberland, Edmund intrusted to Malcolm, king of the Scots, under fealty of an oath. Such are William's words. So, afterwards, it was straightway agreed between them, and resolved by the councils of both kings, that in future, for the sake of maintaining the peace of both countries. King Malcolm's next heir, Indulf, and the heirs of the rest of the Scottish kings, for the time being, should do homage for Cumbria, and swear fealty to King Edmund and his successors on the English throne. Furthermore, neither of them was to harbour in his kingdom, in any way shelter, hold out help or favour to, or on any account admit to homage or fealty, that savage and faithless nation of the north. And each king bound himself to the other, by the bond of a sworn covenant, steadfastly to observe all these things for the future. In the fourth year of Malcolm, King Edmund was stabbed with a dagger, in the midst of his soldiers, by a certain robber, whom he had one day reproved in court, for his misdeeds; and, dying, was succeeded by his brother Edred.

CHAPTER XXV.
Death of Malcolm—Accession of King Indulf—He is slain by the Danes.

KING Malcolm had peace with Edred, Indulf having first done homage to the latter for Cumbria. Moreover on the Northumbrians conspiring against him, and setting themselves up a new king, Edred, in the fifth year of this reign, supported by succours from King Malcolm, laid them waste with cruel slaughter. This, however, afterwards turned to the great loss of Malcolm's kingdom. For the Norwegians and Danes, who had formerly long been his friends and allies, were stirred up to molest him and his kingdom exceedingly; and for a long time afterwards kept assailing the harbours, and the country around, on the seaboard. Now he was wont every year, unless hindered by more important matters, to traverse the provinces of his kingdom, executing judgment on robbers, and repressing the lawlessness of freebooters; and, in proportion as in this he pleased the good and the sensible, did he displease the evildoers and the violators of the king's peace. At length, through a conspiracy of certain persons, and, as recorded in the *Annales Chronicæ*, by the treachery of the Moravienses, he was killed at Ulrim, after having completed nine years and three months on the throne—

and was buried with his fathers in the island of Iona. Malcolm was succeeded by Indulf, son of Constantine, son of Heth the Wing-footed—who reigned an equal number of years, and began to reign in A.D. 952, the fifteenth year of Otho I. To the Lordship of Cumbria, on the coronation of Indulf, succeeded Duff, son of King Malcolm, after having taken the usual oath of fealty to King Edred. The third year after, that is to say, the fourth of Indulf, King Edred died, and was succeeded by Edmund's son, Edwy, an indolent and useless man, and therefore nearly deserted by his followers, and most others. At that time, a rumour was spread of the return of the Danes and Noricans (Northmen), and terrified the islanders beyond measure—for the Scots were no less hated by them than the English. Nor had the islanders long to wait: for, the next year, in the spring season, what they feared came to pass. The enemy returning with a fleet of fifty ships, repeatedly wasted, with cruel piracy now the southern, now the northern tracts of the country, according as they were driven by the force of the winds; and while the king strove to come upon them in the north, popular rumour noised it abroad that they were wasting the south. At length, while they happened, one day, to be scattered by companies, laying the country waste near a place called Collyn, the king stationed an ambuscade under cover, not far from the coast; for he happened, by mere chance, to be there at that time, with a few followers—but would that he had not been! So while the spoilers were roving about, scattered by companies throughout the fields and towns, he rushed impetuously upon them with shouts, slew a great number, and forced the rest to have recourse to flight. Finally he, high-spirited as he was, having unfortunately thrown away his weapons, so that he might pursue the runaways more swiftly, was struck in the head by a dart out of one of the ships, and died that same night. His body was taken away to Columba's island (Iona), with such honour as was meet, and buried with his forefathers in the customary tomb of the kings.

CHAPTER XXVI.

Accession of King Duff—After his death, his body is hidden under a bridge; and not a ray of sunlight shines on the kingdom until it is found.

AFTER the king's funeral had duly taken place, he was succeeded, in A.D. 961—the twenty-fourth year of the above Otho—by Duff, the son of King Malcolm, who reigned four years and six months. He was a man of dove-like simplicity towards those who loved quiet and peace; but a cruel, terrible, and bloody avenger towards rebels, plunderers, and thieves. He passed the years of his reign at peace with foreign nations, though the inhabitants of the north of his kingdom were molested by plunderers of their own kin, whose wickedness he had before repeatedly quelled by the rigour of the law. In the fifth year of his reign, therefore, being desirous of reducing those districts to order, he went thither with many followers, and tarried awhile at the town of Forres, in Moray, punishing divers evildoers. Now, when he had as usual sent forth his columns and companies to search the wilds of mountain and wood, keeping but few men with him, he told off some of his more intimate followers as his body-guards and watchmen by day and night; but these, as if they had nothing to fear, spent their time in games, plays, and feasting, never thinking about the king. This did not escape the notice of those wicked robbers, who, seizing an hour at the dead of night, entered the king's bedchamber, which had not been carefully bolted, and secretly snatched him away, while reposing in bed, with only one servant of the bedchamber; and dragging him with them through their secret haunts, they slew him. They then put the body of the murdered king into a ditch under the shadow of a certain bridge near Kinloss, and covered it lightly with green turf, without leaving any trace at all of blood. But the wonder was that, from that hour forwards, until it was found, no ray of sunlight gleamed within the whole kingdom—nay, as long as it lay hidden under the bridge, continual darkness miraculously shrouded the whole land, to the amazement of all. But as soon as the body was afterwards found, the sun shone forth more brightly, it seemed, than ever, to reveal the crime of the traitors. His body was then put into a coffin, embalmed with aromatic spices, and taken to the island of Iona, to be there honourably buried.

CHAPTER XXVII.

Accession of King Culen—His Death—Fable given in the English Chronicles.

CULEN, son of King Indulf, was set up as king, in A.D. 965,—the twenty-eighth year of Otho—and, like his predecessor, reigned four years and six months. He was useless and slack in the government of the kingdom; and nothing kingly or worthy of remembrance was done in his days. For, spurning the advice of men of sense, he cleaved in all things to the paths of the young: being sore given to violating maids; a lustful adulterer with the wives of nobles and private persons; in many things, an imitator of Edwy, king of the English, who was just dead, and who, according to *William*, on the very day he was consecrated king, burst suddenly from the midst of a full assembly of the nobles, who were deliberating on weighty and urgent matters of state, and darted wantonly into his chamber, to sink into the arms of a harlot. But Culen, forasmuch as he gave up his whole mind continually to shameful vices of this kind, and could not be reclaimed therefrom by the exhortations of any of the chiefs or clergy, provoked the indignation of all the inhabitants against him. Meanwhile, among other most heinous deeds of his, he snatched away, against her will, and violated, the lovely daughter of a certain chief, named Radhard, who would not, of his own accord, betray her to him; on account of which he was shortly afterwards slain by the father, to the great joy of many, and the grief of very few. Nevertheless, they took away his body, and buried it with the other kings in the island of Iona. A certain wonder which formerly happened to the Scots, I should have described under the reign of Gregory; but, having hitherto—I will confess—left it out by an oversight, I will insert it here, word for word, as it is described in a certain legend. Some little time after A.D. 883, the Scots gathered together a countless host to fight against the king of Northumbria, and among the rest of their cruel misdeeds attacked and plundered the church of Lindisfarne, and infringed the privileges of Saint Cuthbert; whereupon the earth suddenly opened and swallowed them up, so that they vanished in a moment. For when it was morning, the king and his men charged the enemy; but—strange as it may seem—of those men whom they had just seen hurling javelins at them, straightway, in that same moment, never a one did they find. For—as Cuthbert, the man of God, had foretold to the king, in the spirit—the earth had swallowed them all up alive before their eyes. But why should a historian ply his pen in such apocryphal tales, in which every man of sense refuses to pub faith?

CHAPTER XXVIII.

Accession of Kenneth, son of Malcolm—lowers Disputes—Unsteadiness in the Rule of Succession of the Emperors, as well as of Kings.

CULEN was succeeded, in A.D. 970—the thirty-third year of the Otho so often mentioned—by Kenneth, the son of Malcolm, and brother of King Duff—a brave and prudent man,—the second of that name since the monarchy was established. He reigned, in peace and happiness, twenty-four years and nine months. During the whole time of his reign, he and the English kings, his contemporaries, Edgar and his two sons—the blessed martyr Edward, to wit, and Ethelred—mutually esteeming one another, faithfully preserved the fellowship of the most steadfast peace and friendship. As soon as Kenneth was crowned, Edgar willingly received Malcolm, the son of Duff, as prince of Cumbria, under the usual oath of fealty—for, had he lived, he would have been the next to succeed his father. This covenant of mutual peace and friendship between the kings and the countries (first happily entered into by Malcolm, king of the Scots, and Edmund, king of the English) lasted, without any noisy wrangle, unbroken and continuously for one hundred and twenty years, or more—even until William the Bastard invaded England, and took it. For Edgar was a king most fortunate, peaceful, open-handed, and imparting his bounty to neighbouring kings and chiefs; and no wonder—seeing that he did not depart from the admonitions of his most holy teacher as well as governor, Dunstan, In the fifth year of King Kenneth died Otho I., and was succeeded on the imperial throne by his son Otho II., who held it ten years. In these days—and previously, as well as long afterwards—a great many difficulties began to crop up in sundry parts of the world, with reference to the unsteadiness in the rule of succession of kings and chiefs. For, in the fifth year of the reign of this Otho I.—as we read in the *Speculum Historiale*—such a question of succession arose among the chiefs of the empire: whether, that is to say, while their grandfathers were still surviving, the grandsons should inherit after their father's death, or whether, being disinherited, the inheritance should revert to the father's brothers. Otho, indeed, and all the chiefs decided that the finding out of the truth should be intrusted to trial by combat. The victory went to those who said that the sons of brothers should succeed their fathers. In the fifteenth year of King Kenneth died Otho II.; after whose death, there likewise arose a dissension among the princes of the empire, about setting up an emperor in his stead. Some contended that the imperial throne should go to his son Otho; others wished to pass it on to Duke Henry, brother to Otho I. Now this Henry had factiously kidnapped the boy Otho, and kept him in custody; but the chiefs wrested him out of his hands, and raised him to the throne; and he reigned nineteen years. In France, likewise, on the death of King Louis, the French wished to pass on the kingdom to Duke Charles, brother of King Lothaire, and uncle to Louis himself; but while he was referring the matter to the Council, the kingdom was usurped by Hugh, sou of Hugh, Count of Paris, and Hawyde, sister of Otho I.

CHAPTER XXIX.

Kenneth—Novel Change in the Ride of Succession of the Emperors, and of the Kings of Scotland.

To the end, moreover, that the dangers involved in the succession of the emperors might be avoided, the chiefs of the empire laid down, by unanimous consent, that, after the death of that Otho III., who was then reigning, and sitting as president at that Council, no one, in whatever degree of blood-relationship or kinship he might be related to the emperor, should thenceforth presume to mount the imperial throne, unless elected by set officers of the empire. These officers are seven, namely, three chancellors—the one at Mentz, Chancellor of Germany; the one at Treves, Chancellor of Gaul; the one at Cologne, Chancellor of Italy; the Marquess of Brandeburgh, Chamberlain; the Palatine, Steward; the Duke of Saxony, Swordbearer; the King of Bohemia, Cupbearer. Whence this rhyme:

"Mentz, Trèves, Cologne, three Chancellors afford;
Palatine, Steward; Duke that bears the sword;
The Marquess, Chamberlain; Bohemia's king.
That bears the cup; to these, for aye, shall cling
The right to constitute a sovereign lord."

Having heard rumours of these changes in the rule of succession. King Kenneth wished that the law of succession of the ancient kings of his country—who had hitherto reigned in entangled disorder—should be abolished; and that, after each king, his offspring of legitimate birth should, in preference to the rest, be decked with the kingly diadem. He himself had an illustrious son, named Malcolm; and he proposed to use every endeavour to have the throne assigned to him. He therefore appointed, with the consent of all his chiefs, with the exception of a few supporters of the old rule of succession, that, thenceforth every king, on his death, should be succeeded by his son or his daughter, his nephew or his niece; or by his brother or sister, in the collateral line; or, in short, by whoever was the nearest survivor in blood to the deceased king, surviving him—even though it were a babe a day old; for it is said, "A king's age consists in his subjects' faith;" and no law contrary to this has since prevailed. In the sixth year of Kenneth, Edgar, king of England, died, and was succeeded by his son. Saint Edward, who reigned three years and a half, and was crowned with martyrdom: being stabbed with a dagger, through the treachery of his stepmother Elfrida. After him, his brother Ethelred obtained the kingdom, and—as *William* puts it— besieged, rather than ruled, it, for thirty-seven years. The course of his life, he says, is asserted to have been fierce in the beginning, wretched in the middle, and shameful in the end. Dunstan, indeed, had foretold his worthlessness. For when he was plunging the little child into the baptismal font, it defiled the sacrament with the discharge of its belly; at which Dunstan, being troubled, said, "By God and his mother! this will be a sorry fellow."

CHAPTER XXX.

Baldred, Abbot of Rivaulx, recites the Sermon of Edgar, King of the English, against those who lead had lives in the Church of God.

CHAPTER XXXI.

Sermon continued.

CHAPTER XXXII.

Strange Instrument of Treason, to deceive King Kenneth—A wily Woman's Flattery.

BUT the chiefs who favoured the other rule of succession, hated King Kenneth and his son, asserting that they were now deprived of the accustomed ancient title to the succession. The principal of these were Constantine the Bald, son of King Culen, and Gryme, son of Kenneth, son of King Duff; and, plotting unceasingly the death of the king and his son, they at length found accomplices for the perpetration of such a crime. The daughter of Cruchne, Earl of Angus, who was named Finele, consented unto their deeds and design, her only son having formerly been ordered to be put to death by the king at Dunsynane, whether by the severity of the law, or for what he had done, or in some other way, I know not. This wily woman, therefore, ardently longing for the king's death, caused to be made, in an out-of-the-way little cottage, a kind of trap, such as had never before been seen. For the trap had, attached to it on all sides, crossbows always kept bent by their several strings, and fitted with very sharp arrows; and in the middle thereof stood a statue, fashioned like a boy, and cunningly attached to the crossbows; so that if any one were to touch it, and move it ever so little, the bowstrings of the crossbows would suddenly give way, and the arrows would straightway be shot forth, and pierce him through. Having thus completed the preparations for perpetrating the crime, the wretched woman, always presenting a cheerful countenance to the king, at length beguiled him by flattery and treacherous words. The king went forth one day, with a few companions, into the woods, at no great distance from his own abode, to hunt; and while pursuing beasts hither and thither with his dogs, as he hunted, he happened by chance to put up hard by the town of Fettercairn, where the traitress lived. She saw him; and, falling on her knees, she besought him with great importunity to come into her house—"otherwise," said she, "I shall, without fail, think myself mistrusted by your Majesty's Grace. But God knows—and thou, my king, shalt soon know—that, although the tattling of the spiteful may repeat many a lie about me, I have always been faithful to thee—and shall be, as long as I live. For, what thou not long ago didst to my most wretched son, I know right well, was justly done, and not without cause;" and tripping up to the king, she whispered in his ear, saying:— "When thou be come with me, I will explain to thee, my lord, who are the accomplices of that accursed son of mine, and the manner of their treachery. For they hoped to get me to join them in their conspiracy to deceive thee; but I straightway refused to countenance their heinous treachery Nevertheless, they forced me to lay my hand on the Gospel and swear never to betray their secret; but, though I promised them this on my oath, still I should be most false anc traitorous towards thee, my lord king—to whom, above al' others, steadfast and loyal fealty is due—were I to conceal the danger to thy person. For who knows not that no sworn covenant holds good against the safety of the king's majesty?"

CHAPTER XXXIII.

Kenneth's Death by Treachery—His son Malcolm promoted to the Lordship of Cumbria.

THUS that crafty woman cunningly misled the king's mind, and drew him, alas! too ready of belief, into the house with her, everything speeding her design. Why say more? Why dwell on so sad a tale? After the king had alighted from horseback, she took his hand, and quickly led him, alone, to the house where the trap was concealed. After she had shut the door behind them, as if with the view of revealing the secrets of the traitors, as she had promised, she showed him the statue, which was the lever of the whole trap. He naturally asked what that statue had to do with him; whereupon she answered, smiling—"If the top of the head of this statue, which thou seest, my lord king, be touched and moved, a marvellous and pleasant jest comes of it." So, unconscious of hidden treachery, he gently, with his hand, drew towards him the head of the machine, thus letting go the levers and handles of the crossbows; and immediately he was shot through by arrows sped from all sides, and fell without uttering another word. The traitress then went hurriedly out by the back-door, and hid herself in the shades of the forest for the time; but, a little after, she safely reached her abettors. The king's companions, however, after having long awaited his return from the house, wondered why he delayed there. At last, having stood before the gate, and knocked persistently at the door, and hearing nothing, they furiously broke it open; and when they found that he had been murdered, they raised a great outcry, and ran about in all directions, looking for the guilty woman—but in vain: they found her not; and, not knowing what to do, they consumed the town with fire, and reduced it to ashes. Then, taking with them the king's blood-stained body, they shortly afterwards buried it with his fathers in Iona, as was the custom with the kings. About the twentieth year of this Kenneth, after he had established the statutes respecting the succession, on the death of Malcolm, the son of Duff, Prince of Cumbria, he wished to make his own son, Malcolm, prince of that lordship; so he sent him to Ethelred, king of the English, who willingly admitted him, under the conditions above touched upon—of fealty and homage.

CHAPTER XXXIV.

Accession of the Kings Constantine the Bald, and Gryme, son of Kenneth.

THE next day after the king's death, Constantine the Bald, son of Culen—of whom mention was made above—came with his supporters, and, despising the State ordinance, usurped the throne; and, backed up by a few of the nobles, he placed the crown of the kingdom on his own head, in A.D. 994—the eleventh year of Otho III. Thereupon there followed a long-lasting division among the inhabitants, with massacres of the populace, and troubling of the clergy. Moreover, there befell the most pitiful slaughter of the great, and even of kings, and much shedding of innocent blood; and, briefly to sum up, the final overthrow of the kingdom, as well as of the whole Scottish race, would have been brought to pass—as many thought it had—if God's pitiful mercy had not deigned to take pity betimes on his people, in spite of their many sins. Meanwhile, these accursed calamities lasted nine years; and the ruin was the greater, seeing that no one had the least idea which of the competitors rather to obey—whether Constantine, who was crowned, or Malcolm, who had the law on his side. Constantine, however, held the kingdom—though not in peace—for a year and a half after he had usurped it. For he was continually harassed by Malcolm, and his illegitimate uncle, named Kenneth, a soldier of known prowess, who was his unwearied persecutor, and strove with his whole might to kill him, above all others. Nor did Kenneth abandon his purpose, until, one day, they met one another in Laudonia (Lothian), by the banks of the river Almond; and, engaging in battle, after great slaughter on either side, both the leaders were killed. It is, however, said that Kenneth had the upper hand. In the meantime, Constantine's guards fled to his colleague Gryme, the son of Kenneth, son of Duff—for he himself was, with Constantine, the chief supporter of the old rule of succession—and Gryme, being joined by those who wished him well; lost no time in taking upon him the badges of kingship, by the same right as his predecessor, in A.D. 996—the thirteenth year of the emperor Otho III.; and he reigned eight years and three months. Now, Malcolm, as luck would have it, had gone to Cumbria a little before this struggle; and, after abiding there a fortnight, he heard from those who had been present at the fight just mentioned, that his uncle and the rest of his faithful friends had been slain, and the kingdom usurped. So he came back at once, and having soon gathered together some reinforcements, kept troubling Gryme (who had then been set up as king), and all who favoured his cause, with all manner of annoyances. The latter, however, withstood him with all his might, and meted out the most grievous loss upon him and his, with the self-same measure, and with no less cruelty; and thus the wretched and helpless multitude long lay crushed and oppressed by them both.

CHAPTER XXXV.

The above-mentioned Prince of Cumbria, Malcolm, son of Kenneth, will not, on behalf of the Cumbrians, pay tribute to the Danes, as the rest of the inhabitants of England do.

IN those days, likewise, and a little before, the English, in return for peace, gave the Danes tribute—first 10,000, next 16,000, soon after 24,000, and lastly, 30,000 pounds. So King Ethelred wrote, by messenger, to the aforesaid Malcolm, prince of Cumbria, commanding him to compel his Cumbrians to pay the tribute, as the rest of the inhabitants did. He straightway wrote back, disclaiming that his subjects owed any other tax than to be always ready, at the king's edict, to fight with the rest, whensoever he pleased. For it was more seemly—he said—and far better, to defend one's liberty with the sword, like a man, than with gold. The king, therefore, carried off a great deal of plunder from Cumbria because of this, and, inasmuch as the prince, in spite of the oath of allegiance he owed to him, sided with the Danes—for so the king asserted in his wrath. Afterwards, however, they soon came to a good understanding in all respects, and were at one, for the future, in steadfast peace. This plundering of Cumbria by King Ethelred took place in A.D. 1000, the fifth year of King Gryme. But, in the seventh year of this reign, this Ethelred, through the advice of the treacherous leader Edric, ordered that all the Danes, throughout all England, should be slain in one day—that of Saint Bricius, to wit—and among them, a noble lady, Gunyldis, sister of Swane, king of the Dacians (Danes). On this account, Swane, maddened with rage, afterwards came to England, and landed at Sandwyk (Sandwich); and, in revenge for so great a crime, he destroyed it all by rapine and slaughter beyond all example, stripping the inhabitants of their substance, and carrying it off, together with hostages, to his ships—not like a lord—according to William—but like a most savage tyrant. In the eighth year of King Gryme, Otho III. was succeeded by Henry, the first elected emperor. We have already treated of this election in Chapter XXVII. (XXVIII.) Henry was twenty-two years emperor. He gave his sister Gilla to wife to the Hungarian king, Salamon, who had hitherto been given over unto idolatry; but, by his wife's exhortations, he and his whole nation embraced Christianity; and, at his baptism, he changed his name, and was called Stephen. His merits are to this day commended throughout Hungary for great and glorious miracles.

CHAPTER XXXVI.
Condition of the English, as set forth in the Polychronicon—A certain Prophecy.

AT the time of the aforesaid Ethelred's coronation, Saint Dunstan, in the spirit of prophecy, foretold these evils, which soon came upon the English; for, according to *William*, he said unto the king:—"Since thou hast aspired to the kingdom through the death of thy brother, hear the word of the Lord. Thus saith the Lord God: The sin of thine infamous mother, and of the men who had a share in her base design, shall not be washed out but by much blood of the wretched inhabitants; and there shall come upon the Anglic nation such evils as it hath not suffered from the time it came into England until then." The *Polychronicon*, Book I., last chapter, has the following passage, on the state of the English:—Pope Eugenius has said that English men would be equal to anything they chose to undertake, were it not for a disposition to trifle; and, as Hannibal declared that the Romans could not be vanquished save on their own ground, so the English nation is invincible abroad, but may easily be overcome at home. In another passage in that work, we read:—That nation loathes what belongs to it, blames its own things, and praises other men's; is hardly ever content with the state of its circumstances; and is eager to show off in itself those qualities which are becoming in others. Nay, more: some of them, going the round of every state of life, belong to none; trying every condition, remain in none. For, in bearing, they are players; in address, fiddlers; gluttons "in feeding; hucksters in business; swaggerers in dress; like Argus for gain; like Dædalus in wariness; like Sardanapalus in bed; puppets at church; thunderers in the courts; while, throughout all the English-born people, such a variety of dress and apparel of all shapes has grown into use, that you cannot tell the sex of any one person. Touching this, a certain holy anchorite, in the earlier days of King Ethelred, prophesied on this wise—as we see in the sixth book of *Henry's* work:—The English, forasmuch as they are given to treachery, drunkenness, and neglect of the house of God, shall be trampled under foot, first, of the Danes—then, of the Normans—and thirdly, of the Scots, whom they hold beneath contempt. And of these three plague-spots, two, those of treachery and gluttony, to wit, have been found out, first by the Danes, and secondly by the Normans; but the third, that of neglecting the house of God—still remains to be found out by the Scots.

CHAPTER XXXVII.
Source of the Calamities brought upon the English by the Danes, who, according to William, repeatedly lay England waste in all directions.

I WILL NOW, as a warning to my hearers or readers in time to come, briefly show by these passages the source of the calamities which, as above described, were brought upon the English by the Danes. In the early English Church, says the *Tabula Londoniæ*, the religious life throve most remarkably: insomuch that kings and queens, chiefs and leaders, earls and barons, and rulers of the churches, had a yearning after the kingdom of heaven kindled within them, and outvied each other in embracing monkhood, voluntary exile, or the hermit's life; and, leaving all, followed the Lord. But, in course of time, all virtue so withered away from among them, that no nation, it seemed, could match them in treachery and guile. Nor was anything so hateful to them as piety and justice; nor cared they for anything so much as wars more than civil, and the shedding of innocent blood. Almighty God, therefore, sent heathen and most cruel nations, like swarms of bees, who spared neither woman's sex nor the age of the little ones—the Danes, to wit, and the Norwegians, the Goths and Swedes, the Vandals and Frisians, who, from the first years of King Ethelwlf, down to the arrival of the Normans—for about two hundred and thirty years, destroyed this sinful land from sea to sea, both man and beast. And thus repeatedly invading England on all sides, they did their best not only to subdue the country and take possession of it, but also to plunder and' destroy it. But, if the English sometimes got the upper hand, it profited them nothing; for a larger fleet and army would unexpectedly and suddenly arrive elsewhere. Of a truth, while the English kings would be wending towards the east coast of the kingdom, to fight against them, before the troops approached the enemy, a messenger would be sure to come flying towards them, saying, "Whither away, O king? Behold! even now a countless heathen fleet have seized the shores of thy kingdom, on the south; and spoiling the towns and villages with the sword, have burned down with fire everything in their way." Such rumours, moreover, coming upon them from the east, west, or north, as well, robbed the natives of all hope of safety; and thus the kings, with their hearts exposed to so many evils and sinister rumours, would divide their forces and enter upon a doubtful struggle against these hostile inroads. Hence it happened that sometimes the inhabitants were beaten, and sometimes their enemies—which suggested these lines:—

"In English story many a plague is seen;
   England bears witness to the captive's woe.
War, pride, fraud, rapine—these the scourge have been
   Wherewith the stranger's hand laid England low."

CHAPTER XXXVIII.

King Gryme slain by the above-mentioned Malcolm, son of Kenneth.

BUT while the quarrel lasted between Malcolm, son of Kenneth—above referred to—and King Gryme, who could fully unfold the losses of the inhabitants of the kingdom, continued through eight years? The people, however, showed more favour to the cause of Malcolm than to that of the king; for, in all knightly deeds, both mimic and in earnest, the former was second renown to hardly any one in the kingdom. Historical annals inform us that he was skilled in brandishing the sword and hurling the spear, and could bear hunger, thirst, cold, and watching, wonderfully long. Roaming, therefore, very often through various districts of the kingdom, and carefully guarding himself against being waylaid by Gryme, he cemented to himself the hearts of many of the aristocracy, and secretly bound them by an oath of fealty to him. Moreover, the common people, who knew him to be endowed with many good qualities, and distinguished for his stalwart and shapely figure, began, with one accord, to extol his name and fame with praises, and declared, even openly, that he was more worthy of the kingship than the rest of men, seeing that he was the strongest. Thus, strengthened by the favour of the people, and at the instigation of some of the chiefs, he forthwith sent to the king, by messenger, bidding him choose one of two things—either that he should vacate the throne, and lay down the crown, which he had, until then, like his predecessor, held unjustly, or that they two should, either accompanied by their warrior hosts, or man to man, if he liked, fight in the open field, and submit it to the just verdict of God, which of them ought, in all lawfulness, to be subject unto the other. Gryme was very indignant at this; for he thought that Malcolm could not withstand him. So, with such of his men as he could trust, he at once set out to give him battle; while Malcolm, on the other hand, with a similar object in view, boldly advanced to meet him, with a small but picked band, and reached a field named Auchnebard—a meet place for a battle. There the two armies engaged one another, and fought a cruel battle, considering their numbers. At length the king was mortally wounded, while fighting bravely, and was straightway led out of the battle by his men; and he died the same night. But when the rest of his party saw this, they all fled; and thus Malcolm was so fortunate as to gain the victory and the kingdom. The day after, however, when he got sure information of the king's death, he bade his own servants take the body away, without fear, and bury, it in the sepulchre of the kings in the island of Iona.

CHAPTER XXXIX.

Accession of this King Malcolm—His daughter Beatrice marries Crynyne, Abthane of Dul.

NOW after Malcolm had gained the victory, as already described, he did not at once take upon himself the name of king; but, having summoned together the chiefs of the kingdom, he humbly requested them to give him the crown, if the laws allowed it—not otherwise. They, for their part, fully ratified the law of the royal succession which had been made in his father's days; and at once appointed him king, crowned with the diadem of the kingdom. He began to reign in A.D. 1004—the second year of the oft-mentioned emperor Henry; and he reigned in happiness thirty years, a brave warrior, and the conqueror of every neighbouring nation which ventured to put his daring to the test. We read that he had no offspring but an only daughter, named Beatrice, who married Crynyne, Abthane of Dul, and Steward of the Isles, a man of great vigour and power. In some annals, by a blunder of the writer, this man is called Crynyne, Abbot of Dul. Abthane of Dul, should properly have been written. Abthane is derived from *abbas,* which means *father* , or *lord,* and *thana* which means *answering,* or *numbering*; so that abthane is the *superior of the thanes*, or their *lord* under the king; to whom they are held yearly responsible for their farms and the rents due to their lord the king. Thus the Abthane has to keep the account of the king's rents, and moneys in his treasury, performing, as it were, the duties of housekeeper or chamberlain. Now this Abthane begat, of his wife, a son, named Duncan; who afterwards, on his grandfather's death, succeeded him on the throne, as will be seen below. But, to resume: this Malcolm, by God's favour, triumphed everywhere with such glorious victories over his vanquished foes, that, in all the writings wherein he is mentioned, he is always called by the title of "the most victorious king." On three occasion did he, by a lucky chance, outwit and defeat the Danish pirates, who often sallied forth on shore from their ships, and ravage the parts of the kingdom bordering on the sea; and once these were routed by the natives, though he was not there. Othred, likewise an English earl, but subject to the Danes, endeavoured to plunder Cumbria—though I know not what was the cause of the hostilities which broke out between them. But Malcolm recovered the plunder, and overcame him in a hard-fought battle near Burgum (Burgie). About the first few days after his coronation, a Norwegian army arrived, with a large fleet, in the north, and made a long stay there, stripping the country. But it was destroyed by him in a night attack; so that few save the sailors escaped that disastrous battle, to bring the tidings to the rest at home. He only lost thirty of his men. Thus the land was freed from their inroads for a long while after this battle. A victory like this fell, of old, to the lot of Cneius Pompey, who had been intrusted, by the Senate, with the prosecution of a war against Mithridates, king of Lesser Armenia. Pompey, says *Eutropius*, vanquished him in a night attack, broke up his camp, and killed 40,000 of his men, losing only twenty men and two centurions of his own army.

CHAPTER XL.

Malcolm—Foundation of a Bishopric at Marthillach, now transferred to Aberdeen.

ONCE, while the Danes and Northumbrians, who were then united as one people, were laying Cumbria waste, King Malcolm, being apprised of their arrival by his grandson Duncan, met them, and swept down great part of their army with woeful slaughter. For he had, before this, given Cumbria to Duncan, though without having got King Ethelred's consent, because one could not safely get across the kingdom to him, as well for fear of the Danes—who wandered through the country at will, so that they carried off plunder to their ships from a distance of fifty miles, without dread of being waylaid by the inhabitants—as on account of the treachery of the natives, who, according to William, did not remain in their allegiance, even towards their king. If, says William, driven by sore need, the king and the leaders had decided on some secret and useful measure, it was immediately reported to the Danes by traitors, the most infamous of whom was Edric, a man whom the king had set over the earldom of the Mercians. He was one of the dregs of mankind, and a disgrace to the English; a wily knave, an artful dissembler, and ready to feign anything. For he was wont to hound out the king's designs in the character of a faithful friend, and spread them abroad like a traitor; and often, when sent to the enemy to mediate for peace, he would kindle war. In the seventh year of his reign, Malcolm, thinking over the manifold blessings continually bestowed upon him by God, pondered anxiously in his mind what he should give Him in return. At length, the grace of the Holy Ghost working within him, he set his heart upon increasing the worship of God; so he established a new episcopal see at Marthillach (Mortlach), not far from the spot where he had overcome the Norwegians, and gained the victory; and endowed it with churches, and the rents of many estates. He desired to extend the territory of this diocese, so as to make it reach from the stream or river called the Dee to the river Spey. To this see, a holy man, and one worthy the office of bishop, named Beyn, was, at the instance of the king, appointed, as first bishop, by our lord the pope Benedict. In the thirteenth year of this reign died King Ethelred—a man, says *William*, born to woes and toil—and was succeeded by his son Edmund Ironside, who was begotten of the daughter of Earl Thoret, and wickedly slain, two years after, by the treachery of the above-named traitor, Edric. We shall speak of this Edmund at greater length in the following Book. After him, Cnuto the Dane, son of Swane, was straightway chosen king by the whole of England, as the true heirs had, in the meantime, been driven out by the treachery of the aforesaid traitor—as the following Book will also show forth. In the twenty-second year, A.D. 1025, the first elected emperor, Henry, died, and was succeeded by

Conrad II., who was fifteen years emperor. In the seventh year of Conrad, King Cnuto went on a pilgrimage to Rome; and having there redeemed his sins by alms, he returned to England some time afterwards.

CHAPTER XLI.

Struggle of King Malcolm for Cumbria with Cnuto the Dane, then King of England— His Death.

DUNCAN, however, though summoned again and again by Cnuto, king of England, to do homage for Cumbria, had not hitherto done so because the latter had usurped the kingdom; for King Malcolm wrote back that, by rights, he owed fealty therefor not to him, but to the English-born kings. Accordingly, on his return from his pilgrimage to Rome, Cnuto speedily set out with a large armed force, and, by easy stages, arrived in Cumbria, to reduce it to his dominion. The king, on his side, equally quite ready for battle, advanced to meet him, supported by a strong escort. But, by God's will, they were brought, by the intervention of the bishops and other upright men, to agree to the following decision: namely, that the king's grandson, Duncan, should thenceforward, in all time to come, freely enjoy the lordship of Cumbria—as freely as any of his predecessors had held it; while, however, he, and the heirs, for the time being, of after kings, should plight their troth, as usual, to King Cnuto and the rest of the English kings, his successors. And thus they departed in peace, fully reconciled. But some, begotten of the stock of the two foregoing kings—Constantine and Gryime, to wit—who had lawfully, it was thought, been slain by the king and his adherents, treacherously entreated his friendship, for fear he should view them with suspicion; and though they swore steadfast faith with him—which it is meet should be observed even towards a public enemy—they were, nevertheless, nothing bound thereby, and conspired to put him to death. He, however, wishing to bring their hearts into kindliness of feeling towards him, took great pains to enrich them with frequent gifts and rents—but in vain: for what is rooted in the hard bone can seldom be torn out of the soft flesh. So it came to pass, afterwards, that when he set out one day, with his usual train of knights, on the road he had to take—I know not whither, nor to transact what business—those disloyal ruffians, who had made diligent inquiries about it, got information thereof; and having, near Glammys, in the darkness of midnight, barred with robbers from among their satellites, the path along which he was to go, they suddenly poured out of their ambush and surrounded him, far as he was from suspecting any such violence. But he, indeed, undismayed, boldly rushed upon them with his followers, and soon overcame their forces, which were three times as numerous as his own; and he slew the ringleaders of the traitors. But it was a mournful victory: for, woe worth the day! the king was wounded in the fight; and after surviving three days, he was, at length, to the grief of all of Scottish birth, released by death of a hæmorrhage, at the age of eighty or more. And thus God gave him freely, even at his death, such meed of success in victory, as He had often bestowed upon him during his life.

CHAPTER XLII.

Vice of Treachery, the most shameful of all Vices, and one execrated by all men—Various examples of accursed Treachery.

CHAPTER XLIII.

King Malcolm's liberality, or, rather, prodigality; for he retained for himself no part of the Kingdom but the Moothill of Scone.

HISTORIES relate the aforesaid Malcolm to have been so openhanded, or rather prodigal, that, while, according to ancient custom, he held, as his own property, all the lands, districts, and provinces of the whole kingdom, he kept nothing thereof in his possession, but the Moothill of the royal seat of Scone, where the kings, sitting in their royal robes on the throne, are wont to give out judgments, laws, and statutes, to their subjects. Of old, indeed, the kings were accustomed to grant their soldiers, in feu-farm, more or less of their own lands—a portion of any province or thanage: for, at that time, almost the whole kingdom was divided into thanages. Of these he granted part to each one at will, or on lease by the year, as to tillers of the ground; or for ten or twenty years, or in liferent, with remainder to one or two heirs, as to free and kindly tenants; and to some, likewise, though few, in perpetuity, as to knights, thanes, and chiefs;—not however, so freely, but that each of them paid a certain annual feu-duty to their lord, the king. As, therefore, he had reserved, it is said, nothing for himself from these lands and annual rents, at length, driven by sore need, he requested, in a general assembly, that out of them some allowance, suitable to the kingly dignity, should be provided—namely, either lands, or rents, or, at least, a meet yearly subsidy, whereby the honour of his majesty might be fully sustained; provided, however, that the poor populace should not, on any account, be weighed down by the heavy burden of a yearly contribution. This was cheerfully approved of and granted by all, both commoners and nobles. Moreover all the nobles, of whatever rank, agreed that the wardship of all their lands and their heirs should remain with the lord king for twenty years, as well as the relief and marriage of every chief or freeholder after his decease. So this King Malcolm, it seems, though magnanimous in peace as in war, bestowed his property unadvisedly: not because he had freely given becoming gifts to those who, having served with him in war, well deserved them, and were worthy of them; but because he left the path of bountifulness, and lavishly squandered, not part of his possessions, but the whole of them, keeping nothing for himself;—for it is certainly unadvised to give away, when one must, of necessity, ask back the gift afterwards. If, says *Bernard*, that man is a fool who makes his share the worse, what must he be who renders himself utterly destitute, so as not to leave himself any share of his goods? *Gregory* writes:—With some, who are unable to bear want, it is better that they should give less, and not murmur at the pinch of want, after their bountifulness. *Seneca*, again, says:—Take heed lest thy beneficence be greater than thy ability; for in such liberality lurks the greed of gain, that one's means may suffice for largess. Such largess is oftentimes followed by rapine. For when men, through giving away, have begun to want, they are driven to 'lay their hands on others' goods; and they incur greater hatred from those they have taken away from, than good-will from those they have given to.

CHAPTER XLIV.

Accession of King Duncan, grandson of the above-mentioned Malcolm—His Death—He was too long-suffering, or easygoing.

AFTER Malcolm was buried with his fathers in the island of Iona, he was succeeded by his grandson Duncan, whom the Abthane Crynyne had begotten of his daughter Beatrice. Duncan began to reign in A.D. 1034—the tenth year of the emperor Conrad II.; and reigned six years. In his second year, died Cnuto the Dane, king of England, and was succeeded by his son Harold Harefote, who reigned five years. The same year, also, died Robert, Duke of Normandy, and was succeeded by his illegitimate son William, called the Bastard, a boy seven years old, who afterwards invaded England. Henry, king of France, William's guardian, vanquished in battle the Normans who opposed him, and shortly appointed him duke. Now Duncan, in his grandfather's days, begat, of the cousin of Earl Siward, two sons, Malcolm Canmore, that is, in English, *Greathead*, and Donald Bane. On this Malcolm the district of Cumbria was bestowed, as soon as his father was crowned. During the short period of Duncan's reign, nothing was done whereof mention should be made; for he enjoyed the security of peace at the hands of all, both abroad and at home, save that a rumour was spread branding certain members of an old family of conspirators as conspiring for his death, as they had done for his grandfather's before him. And though this had more than once been revealed to him by those faithful to him, he refused to put faith in them, saying that it was past belief that those men should dare to undertake the perpetration of so villanous a deed. Hence it came to pass that forasmuch as he would not yield at first to the words of the faithful, which he did not believe, he afterwards suddenly fell into the snares of the faithless, which he had not foreseen. For he had a praiseworthy habit of going through the districts of the kingdom once a year, kindly comforting with his presence his own peaceful people; redressing the wrongs of the weaker unlawfully oppressed by the stronger; putting a stop to the unjust and unwonted exactions of his officers; curbing with judicious severity the lawlessness of freebooters and other evildoers, who ran riot among the people; and hushing the domestic broils of the inhabitants;—and this good quality was inborn in him, that he never suffered any dispute, either in his days or his grandfather's, to spring up in the kingdom, between the chiefs, but he heard it at once, and restored harmony by his good sense. He was, however, murdered through the wickedness of a family, the murderers of both his grandfather and great-grandfather, the head of which was Machabeus, son of Finele; by whom he was privily wounded unto death at Bothgofnane; and, being carried to Elgin, he died there, and was buried, a few days after, in the island of Iona. He was, it seems, too long-suffering, or rather easy-going, a king, in that he did not, by kindness, soothe into friendship men who were accused by hearsay, or in anywise suspected; and in that he did not put them down by the laws, or, at least, even while dissembling, put himself more carefully on his guard against them. In his long-suffering, he was very like the emperor Vespasian; who, with huge dissimulation, despised many conspiracies against him, even when brought to light, though he punished with the penalty of exile—nothing more—some persons guilty of high treason against him. Inasmuch, however, as he inflicted punishment at all, he was harsher than his son Titus, or King Duncan. The emperor Titus, indeed, was a man admired for all manner of virtues, so that he was called the "love and delight of mankind." He was so gentle and mild that he punished no one at all. He forgave those who had been convicted of vowing a conspiracy against him, and admitted them into the same familiarity as they had before enjoyed—though I think he guarded himself, for the future, with more earnest care.

CHAPTER XLV.

Accession of King Machabeus—King Duncan's sons driven out of the Kingdom into England.

THEN this Machabeus, hedged round with bands of the disaffected and at the head of a powerful force, seized the kingly dignity in A.D.

1040, and reigned seventeen years. The same year died the emperor Conrad, and was succeeded by Henry, called *the Pious*, who was emperor also seventeen years. But King Machabeus, after King Duncan's death, went after his sons, Malcolm Canmore, who should have succeeded him, and Donald Bane, seeking, with all his might, to slay them. They, on the other hand, withstanding him as best they could, and hoping for victory, remained nearly two years in the kingdom; while few of the people openly came either to his assistance, or to theirs. When, therefore, they durst struggle no longer, Donald betook himself to the isles, and Malcolm to Cumbria; for it seemed to them, that, had they remained, they would more likely have died than lived. Malcolm afterwards, wishing to have Earl Siward's advice in all his undertakings there, went on to him; and, by his advice and guidance, he sought an audience of King Edward, who was then reigning. The king, who was very merciful and mild, willingly extended his friendship unto him, and promised him help,—for Edward himself had lately been an exile, as Malcolm now was. So Malcolm abode in England about fourteen years, though many a time urged to return, both by friends and rivals;—his rivals, indeed, working for his ruin, and his friends to raise him to the throne. Now, in these days, some of the chiefs of the kingdom talked together in whispers about recalling Malcolm, seeing that he was the true heir to the throne. But they did so with too little secrecy; and, accordingly, it profited them nothing at all: for now and again what was spoken in a man's ear, and passed on from one to another, was openly told the king. Therefore many of them, and those especially whom he knew to be in close friendship with Malcolm, when they had been found guilty of vowing a conspiracy, the king condemned to various hardships. Some of them he delivered over unto death; others he thrust into loathsome dungeons; others he reduced to utter want, by confiscating all their goods. Some, likewise, fearing the king's fierce judgments, leaving their estates, their wives, and children, fled from the country, with the hope, however, of some day returning. Now, in the first year of Machabeus, Harold Harefote, king of England, of Danish birth, was succeeded, after his death, by his brother Hardcanute, who was the last king of Danish birth in England, and reigned two years. This king, immediately after his coronation, dug his brother, the aforesaid Harold, out of his grave, cut off his head, and threw him into the river Thames. After his death, his successor, Saint Edward the Confessor, son of Ethelred, and brother of Edmund Ironside, after having long lived in exile in Normandy, obtained the throne of England, and reigned twenty-four years.

CHAPTER XLVI.
Outlawry of the Thane of Fife, Macduff by name, on account of the friendship he lore towards Duncan's sons, Malcolm, called Canmore, and Donald.

THE greatest and chief of those who laboured to advance Malcolm to the throne was a distinguished, noble, and trusty man, named Macduff, thane of Fife. Macduff kept the unknown purpose of his heart hidden longer and more carefully than the rest; but he was, nevertheless, again and again denounced to the king, until, at length, he was viewed with suspicion. Meanwhile the king, one day, took occasion, I know not on what pretext, first to upbraid him, more cruelly than usual, perhaps on account of his disloyalty, with his shortcomings towards him; and then added plainly that he should stoop his neck under the yoke, as that of the ox in a wain; and he swore it should be so before long. Macduff, however, though seized with exceeding great terror, turned upon him the blithe and merry look of innocence, as the threatening and sudden emergency demanded, with great tact, and soothed his fierceness for the time, with a certain shrewd softness in his words. Then, cautiously going away out of his presence, and stealthily avoiding the court, he went off with all haste, and quickly repaired to the sea; and as the wind did not seem likely to hold fair very long, he embarked on board a little vessel scantily stocked with food. So, after having undergone many dangers of the sea through boisterous weather, he safely landed in England, with bare life, and was there kindly received by Malcolm, on account of the support he had given him. But when his secret departure became known to the king, the latter was furious; and, calling his horses and horsemen every one, he hastily followed after the fugitive, until he had made sure that he saw, out at sea, and clear of the land, the little vessel, in which Macduff had sailed. So, as he had no hope of being able to intercept her, he hastily came back, besieged all Macduff's castles and strongholds, took his lands and estates, commanded everything that seemed precious or desirable to be confiscated, and, taking away all his substance, bade it be placed forthwith in his own treasury. Moreover, he caused him to be proclaimed, by the voice of a herald, an exile for ever, and stripped of all his estates and other property whatsoever. Thereupon there rose great murmuring throughout the whole kingdom, and especially among the nobles (for the thane was beloved by them with kindly affection); for that the king, led rather by wrath than by reason, had been too hasty in rendering so doughty and powerful a man exile, or disinherited, without a decree of a general council, and of the nobles. They said that it was quite wrong that any noble or private person should be condemned by a sudden sentence of exile or disinheritance, until he had been summoned to court on the lawful day of the appointed time. And if, then, when he came, he justified himself by the laws, he should thus go forth free; but if he were worsted in court, he should atone to the king at the cost of his body, or otherwise; or, if he should neglect to come when summoned, then, first, ought he to be outlawed as an exile; or, if he should plead guilty, disinherited.

CHAPTER XLVII.

First Arrival of Malcolm Canmore at the Court of Edward, King of England—Marianus Scotus.

NOW, after kings of Danish birth had held the kingdom of England twenty-four years, and ceased to reign. Saint Edward, son of Ethelred, and brother of King Edmund, called, from his great bodily strength. Ironside, was chosen king by all the people; for the true heirs, sons of that same Edmund, were, until then, and for a long time after, living in Hungary. In the first year, then, of this same King Edward, Malcolm Canmore, driven out of his fatherland, came to England; and the king, knowing that he had been unjustly deprived of the kingly dignity, gladly took him under his protection, and into his own service. In the last days of the foregoing emperor, Henry III., or, as some maintain, in the earlier days of Henry IV., according to Helinandus and Sigebert, lived the famous Marianus Scotus, who came out of Scotland into France, and became a monk at Cologne. He shut himself up first in the monastery of Fulda, in Saxony, which is renowned for the body of Saint Gall, and endowed with most magnificent estates. The abbot of that place furnishes sixty thousand warriors against the emperor's enemies. Afterwards, at Mentz, where he earned the grace of the life to come by his contempt for this life. During his long life of leisure, he examined the chronologers, thought over the discrepancies of the cycles, and added twenty-two years over and above, which were wanting in the aforesaid cycles; but he had few followers in his opinion. William says:—Wherefore I am wont often to wonder why this misfortune besets the learned of our time, that, with so great a number of students, saddening their lives with wan moping, hardly any one gives full praise to knowledge. Time-honoured use pleases so much, that no one, almost, yields a fair assent, according to their worth, to fresh discoveries, even though they can be proved. We make every effort to crawl back to the opinion of the ancients; everything modern is paltry. Thus, since favour alone fosters wit, when favour is wanting, wit is everywhere benumbed.

BOOK V.

CHAPTER I.

Macduff urges Malcolm Canmore to return to the Kingdom—The latter, to try whether he was in good faith, or was deceiving him, falsely asserts that he is Sensual.

AFTER Macduff, therefore, had landed at Ravynsore, in England, he hastened to Malcolm; and, seizing a fit time for an interview, urged him to return, warmly exhorting him to betake himself to the government of the kingdom, a consummation too long delayed through his own sloth, and no one else's. "Do not," said he, "mistrust my good faith. Thy father always held me faithful; and in spite of the many hardships I have borne, to thee also have I been faithful, and am, and shall be all my life. The greater part of the chiefs of the kingdom have, with an oath, plighted their steadfast troth to me, in thy name, and I, in like manner, have also done the same to them, without deceit: so thou mayest firmly believe that we are in heart and soul oath-fellows in loyal obedience to thee. I know, likewise, that thou possessest the hearts of all the common people. They will joyfully hasten together to shed their blood for thee, under thy unfolded banner, pleased to render service to thee, their liege lord." When Malcolm heard this saying, he was very glad in his heart; but turning over and over again in his faltering mind whether Macduff was urging true arguments, in good faith, or false, in treachery, he was somewhat afraid. For this very matter of his return had been cunningly urged upon him before, by some of the opposite side, to deceive him; so he was prudent enough to try him carefully, in the following manner:—"My dearest friend, I thank thee and thy comrades with all my heart; and according to your deserts shall I requite you—and thee above all—as far as I can, under God's guidance. But, being especially sure, in a manner, of thy fealty, I shall reveal unto thee, my friend, some things that lurk implanted by nature in my heart, without hesitating because thou hast concealed them. There have grown up with me, from the beginning, some monstrous besetting sins, which, even though thou should succeed in bringing me to do what thou demandest,—yea, even if every difficulty were swept away, and thou wert to bestow the crown upon me, would not let me reign over you long. The first of these is a marvellous pleasure in detestable lust, which is rooted in my flesh; and thou wouldst not believe what a seducer of maids and women it makes me. And I feel sure that, were I to get the sovereign power, I could not forbear violating the beds of my nobles, and deflowering maidens. I am aware, therefore, that, on a frequent repetition of such shameful wickedness among the people, I should be utterly driven out of the country by the chiefs, as well as the boors, of the kingdom, whose wives and daughters I had wronged. Wherefore it seems to me better to live as a private man, than, after having come by the kingly dignity, to be shamefully degraded therefrom by my revolted subjects, by reason of my faults.

CHAPTER II.

Malcolm adduces various instances of Kings having lost their Kingdoms through Sensuality.

"NOW I will give thee some instances of what evils, and how great, have befallen various mighty kings, in times past, by reason of their unbridled indulgence in lust. Tarquinius Superbus, of old a mighty king of Rome, after having reigned thirty-four years, lost the kingdom, as thou art aware, because his son, also Tarquinius, lewdly violated Lucretia, the wife of Collatinus. For after she had bewailed her wrongs before her father, and her husband, and the rest of her friends, she stabbed herself with a dagger, and killed herself, in the sight of all. Thereupon the citizens were roused to such wrath, that, after they had deposed the king, and shut him out, they never could bear any one who had the name of Tarquin—nor, indeed, would they ever consent to have a king over them any more. A king of Assyria, likewise, Sardanapalus, the last of his race, a man more dissolute than a woman, in order that he might have his fill of lustful pleasures, dressed purple floss with a distaff, in women's clothes, amid bevies of strumpets. For this he was held in such execration by all, that he lost his kingdom as well as his life; so that, in him, the line of his house ceased to reign. Again, a king of the Franks, Chilperic, son of Meroveus, and father of the great Clovis, being too much given to sensuality, and lewdly violating the wives and daughters of his subjects, was deposed from the kingdom; nor was it until eight years were overpast, and then only by chance, at least, on his promising continence, under a bond, that he was taken back to be king. In like manner, Edwy, that late over-wanton king of England, indulged so much in sensual lust, that, on the very day he was consecrated king, while the lords were dealing with matters of importance to the kingdom, he rose from their midst, and burst into his chamber, where he sank into the embraces of a harlot; but Saint Dunstan pulled him off the bed, and thus made him his enemy for ever. On account of such vices, therefore, or greater than these, the nobles of the kingdom always hated him, and held him, as it were, no king. A former king of our own country of Scotland, too, Culen, was he not slain by one of his subjects, through sensuality, to wit, because he had ravished that man's maiden daughter? The kingdom of Hibernia, likewise, came to an end with the lustful king Rodoric (begotten, forsooth, of the stock of our own race), who would have six wives at once, not like a Christian king, and would not send them away, in spite of the loss of his kingdom—though he had often been warned by the whole Church, both archbishops and bishops, and chidden, with fearful threats, by all the inhabitants, both chiefs and private persons. He was therefore despised by them all; and they would never more deign to obey him—neither deign they to obey any king to this day. Besides, as thou seest, that kingdom, so renowned formerly, in our forefathers' time, is now miserably split up into thirty kingdoms, or more. But I need not stop here. I can bring thee forward an hundred instances of kings and chiefs, who, I know full well, have been overwhelmed solely through this vice of incontinence."

CHAPTER III.

Macduff, in answer, adduces the instance of the Emperor Octavian, who was sensual, yet most happy.

MACDUFF, then, said unto him, as it were, scornfully:—"Does this seem to thee a fit and satisfactory answer to make to me? and not to me alone, but to those who wish thee well, to whom I am doing duty as messenger?—to us all, namely, who, for thee, have forsaken country, estates, wives, and children, and the nation of our own blood? who, moreover, lately put our lives in peril of death, as was meet, and would do so again in time to come, if thou boldly do thy part? But I wonder much what this excusing of thyself with empty pretexts would mean? Thou fearest, as I understand, to mount the pinnacle of the kingship, because of thy unbridled love of pleasure, expecting that thou shalt not be able to get plenty of women in the kingdom, without the daughters and wives of the nobles. Does not such an excuse lack reason? Shalt thou not, being king, be able to have, at will, the fairest maidens and the most pleasant women to glut thy wanton lust? I make bold to say thou shalt indeed, even though thou wert twice as sensual as the kings whose incontinence thou hast instanced, as Sardanapalus and Chilperic, or Rodoric,—nay, further, as the emperor Octavian, who was such a slave to lust, as even to be a byword and a reproach. For, as history tells us, he was wont to lie amid twelve maids and as many dissolute women. But he did not, on that account, lose the name of 'the most happy emperor,' or the favour of the people, which mourned him at his death, saying, 'Oh that he had never been born, or had never died!' He was a man who would certainly never have drawn to him so much power in the commonwealth, or possessed it so long, had he not teemed with great gifts, both natural and acquired. For he wondrously strengthened, governed, and increased the Roman empire; he adorned the city with sundry buildings such as had not before been seen, making this boast:—'I found a city of brick, and leave it of marble.' In like manner, thou, if thou meetly extend the borders of thy kingdom, rule it in peace, and adorn it with new laws and new buildings, thou shalt not, for such misdeeds, lose the name of a good king, or the favour of the nation. And, as Octavian sang, of old, boasting of his Rome, thou mayst sing of thy kingdom,—'I lately found Scotland without laws, barren in crops, and herds of cattle; I now leave it in peace, and fruitful in all good things.'"

CHAPTER IV.

Malcolm tries him a second time, by asserting himself to be a Thief—Macduff answers by laying down the Remedy for this Vice.

"ALL thou tellest me is true," said Malcolm, "but my spirit is always so eagerly prone to this vice, that sometimes it can scarcely be curbed by reason. But there is yet a besetting sin which stands in my way, one much more disgraceful than this;—and I should not speak of it, for very shame. However, I will not hide it from thee, my friend, though I must tell it in secret. I am a paltry thief, and a robber. For as the loadstone naturally attracts iron, so does my wretched heart, attracted by everything fair and delightful and pleasant to the eyes, strongly yearn for it; and, luring on the other members of my body, by some force they cannot resist, unceasingly prompts them to steal. Thou mayst be sure of this: that it seems to me quite impossible for me not to steal. Therefore it would be much pleasanter and more endurable to go a needy beggar, from door to door, or to die at last, than that through me, when set upon the pinnacle of the kingship, the kingly majesty should be wronged by such shameful misdeeds. The higher a man is, the greater the scandal of his fall into vice, compared with that of the backsliding of a man in a lower station." "That is, no doubt, true," rejoined Macduff, "for, the higher the rank, the more grievous the fall. In sooth, the higher a man is raised on the ladder of honour, the more ought he to be distinguished for his virtues; and the higher he climbs up the steep of virtue, the greater shame to him if he fall into the depths of vice. A prince, likewise, is doubly a wrong-doer if he stray from the path of virtue. For, first, he entangles himself in vice, and, next, he affords the humbler classes an example of wrong-doing. For

'The fickle rabble changes with the chief.'

But, to return: what thou sayest—that it seems to thee that thou canst not help stealing, and, as thou saidst above, committing adultery—is incompatible with God's law, which He wrote with His own hand. For He has written,—'Thou shalt not commit adultery,' 'Thou shalt not steal;' and we must believe that, in His precepts for the observance of His law, God wrote things not impossible, but possible for us. Furthermore, no one is tried beyond his powers: for there is no doubt that, with regard to all vices and virtues, it depends on our free will whether we eschew them or yield to them. We can certainly keep all God's precepts, whether in doing right, or in taking heed not to do wrong, if we bring meet and willing earnestness to bear. So neither this nor the foregoing excuse is a valid one. Every one is aware that the crime of theft comes of want; while, on the other hand, it is always one of the conditions of kingly majesty to be wealthy, and continually full of all manner of riches, lacking nothing. What man, then, of sound mind, will not leave off stealing, when he can boast of wealth of all kinds, to overflowing? Never, when thou art king, wilt thou lack gold, or silver, or precious stones, or jewels; or whatever, in short, shall be welcome and pleasant to thy heart. Be brave in spirit, therefore. Do thy best to seize the wealthy office of king, and refuse not to cast away far from thee those heinous sins, that of stinking sensuality, to wit, and that needy fault, avarice, which leads to theft.

CHAPTER V.

Malcolm tries him a third time, by confessing that he is most false and cunning—Macduff can find no remedy for this fault, and retires in sorrow.

BUT Malcolm, wishing to probe to the core the heart of his friend Macduff, who had not yet been fully tested, answered by propounding the following problem:—"Grateful and useful to me are the antidotes thou boldest out for screening the two faults I have mentioned; but there remains yet untouched the wound of a third blemish,—that of unfaithfulness, and the sin of cunning, lurking within me. I must indeed confess that I am false, though I hide it; ingenious in contriving cunning devices; keeping with few the faith I have plighted; yet making feigned promises to keep it with all. There is always, in my inmost spirit, this wickedness, that, if ever an opportunity presents itself, I would rather cheat a man by the hidden artfulness of smooth feigning, than openly trust my cause to be settled by the doubtful chances of fortune. Now, help thou me in this sin also, as thou didst in the foregoing ones; and palliate it, I pray thee, with some cloak from thy shrewd mind, and whatever the tenor of thy proposal may require, I am ready to fulfil it with all my might." When Macduff heard this, he was beyond measure astonished; and, after being silent for some time, he sighed, and said,—"Oh wretched men that we are! the most wretched of wretches! Alas for us! for us, I say, who have struggled to follow only such as thou, a silly, inglorious man, steeped in vice, and lacking all virtue! Alas for us! Why were we born? How unhappy may we be called! What a misfortune has befallen us! for are we not confounded by a threefold chance against us? Of three accursed evils, we must incur at least one: that is to say, we must either lose our wives and children, and all our earthly goods, and, as wanderers, undergo perpetual banishment; or serve a tyrant king, who, by rights, ought not to be set over us or the state, and to whom it belongs, as is usual with all tyrants, to exercise his insatiable avarice, and cruel despotism, among the people; or be subject unto thee, our liege king, by law;—far be it from us! for the tenor of thine own confession asserts thee to be unworthy of being king, chief, or private person. Thou confessest thyself to be lustful, and a thief, and, what is worse—nay, the meanest of all sins,— false, cunning, and faithless, and an artful deceiver. Lo! what other kind of badness seems to be left, but that thou shouldst call thyself a traitor? But it follows, as a matter of course; for when such faults are hidden in the depths of the heart, treachery is, without fail, found lurking therein in their company. So, forasmuch as all the kindled torches of unrighteousness are gathered together within thee, and a burning and craving covetousness, and a haughty and unbearable cruelty reign in the breast of thine adversary, neither of you shall ever lord it over me; I will rather choose banishment for ever." With these words, unable to contain himself any longer, he burst into tears, which furrowed his cheeks; and wringing his hands, and groaning deeply, and weeping and moaning, he looked mournfully northwards, and said: " Scotland, farewell for ever!"

CHAPTER VI.

Malcolm, now assured of his good faith, promises to return to the Kingdom with him.

MACDUFF, then, was going away; when Malcolm, finding to the full that he detested perfidy above all things, and feeling now assured of his good faith, quickly followed him, and asked him to stop and speak with him, saying,—"Dearest of all my friends, beloved above all living, hitherto I have been only troubled as to whether thou art faithful or faithless; lest thou, like some froward ones sometime, as thou art aware, should have been urging my return, with feigned quibbles, as they did, that I might be betrayed to my rivals. Therefore did I wish to find thee out by these several tests. And since thou hast been tried, and I know that thou loathest the brand of guile and treachery, I hold thee, and always shall hold thee, faithful, far more fully than thou deemest. I am not sensual, or a thief, or faithless; but it was to try thee that I pretended I was given to such faults. Far be it from me that these filthy sins and the like, which are loathed by all men, should have dominion over me more than over the rest of mankind. Come, then, my dear friend. Henceforth fear not! Thou shalt not be an exile from thy fatherland and thy children,—nay, thou shalt be the first in the kingdom, after the king. From now, take comfort, and be strong. Thou shalt bring me back into my land, the land the Lord gave our fathers to dwell in." On hearing this, Macduff fell on his face to the ground; and, as he had been before all bathed in tears through anguish, mourning with dismal sobs, so was he now through joy and exultation; and, clasping Malcolm's feet and kissing them, he said: "If what thou sayest be true, thou bringest me back from death to life. Hasten, my lord, hasten, I beseech thee, and delay not to free thy people, which yearns for thee above all things.

> If thou would keep good men, and true, from harm,
> Men who have fought without one helping arm,
> Men on whose necks foes, for three lustres, trod.
> Help them, in pity, for the love of God.
> Stay not to think, but up, and fell the foe;
> Lighten the burden of thy people's woe.
> Gird on thy sword, thy trusty weapons take;
> For strong thy limbs, and firm thy sturdy make.
> A Scot, the heir of a long royal race.
> Good hap advance thee to thy father's place.
> Thou shalt, I swear, possess the kingly throne;
> All rights are thine, nought does thy rival own.
> Be ever bold to battle for thy right;
> Yet think not rashness e'er can speed the fight.
> If fate allow, tempt not the headlong fray;
> For, unprepared, the best but blindly stray.
> Let not the foe forestall thee in the field;
> Beware thou lest the vantage-ground thou yield."

CHAPTER VII.

Malcolm's return to Scotland—Machabeus falls in battle.

WHEN the discussion of these points was over, and all doubt and ambiguity were removed, Malcolm sent this Macduff back into Scotland, with a secret message to his friends, that they should be carefully prepared, and without doubt expect his return shortly. Then, after Macduff was gone, Malcolm at once presented himself before King Edward, and humbly besought him that he would graciously deign to let some of the English lords, who were willing freely to do so, set out with him to Scotland and recover his kingdom. The mild king at once assented to his prayer, and granted free leave to all who wished it; and graciously promised, moreover, that he himself also would back him up with a powerful army. Malcolm, thereupon, returned thanks beyond measure to that holy king most mild, who was the compassionate adviser and ready helper of all who were unjustly afflicted; and, departing from him, as soon as he was ready, he took with him, of the English lords, only Siward, Earl of Northumberland, and set out to gain possession of Scotland. But he had not yet reached the borders of the kingdom, when he heard that the people of the country was stirred by feuds, and divided into parties between Machabeus and Macduff, by reason of the report spread by the latter, who had preceded him, and had not been cautious enough in adhering to his plans in the matter. So Malcolm hastened on speedily with his soldiery, and rested not until he had, by combining bands of men from all sides, organized a large army. Many of these, who had formerly been following Machabeus, had fallen away from him, and cleaved to Malcolm with their whole strength. Thereupon Machabeus, seeing that his own forces were daily diminishing, while Malcolm's were increasing, hurriedly left the southern districts, and made his way north, where he hoped to keep himself in safety among the narrow passes of the country and the thickets in the woods. Malcolm, however, unexpectedly followed after him, at a quick pace, across the hills, and even as far as Lunfanan; and, engaging there suddenly in a slight battle with him, he slew him, with a few who stood their ground, on the 5th of December 1056. For the people whom Machabeus had led forth to the battle knew full well that Malcolm was their true lord; so, refusing to withstand him in battle, they forsook the field, and fled at the first trumpet-blast. *William*, in describing the aforesaid battle, says:—Siward, Earl of Northumbria, at King Edward's command, engaged Machabeus, king of the Scots, despoiled him of his life and his kingdom, and there set up Malcolm, the son of the king of Cumbria, as king. This is how *William*, ascribing none of the praise for the victory in this battle to Malcolm, assigned it all to Siward; while the truth is, that the victory was entirely owing to the former alone, with his men and his standard-bearer. This at least I am pretty sure of,—that had Malcolm not been there, this people would not have fled from the battle, even if King Edward, and his men to boot, had been present with Siward.

CHAPTER VIII.

The author makes allowance for the people of any kingdom deserting an unlawful King in battle—Lulath is raised to the throne—His death.

NOW, allowance might be made for the flight of this faithful people, who, long weighed down by tyranny, either could not, or durst not, rise up against it, yet, in their hearts, kept restlessly brooding over their king's cruel death, and the rightful heir's unlawful banishment for so long a time; so that, not deigning to submit any longer to this uneasy subjection of theirs under a man of their own class, they took this opportunity of giving the rightful heir, by their flight, an opening for surely recovering the kingdom. For, truly, it seems, I think, that the faithful native-born people of any country, when its head, that is to say, its king, has been taken away by violence, or is suffering any humiliation, certainly suffers with him, and grieves for his reproach, as if sorrowing for its own;—as it is said in the proverb:—"When the head aches, the other members droop." Now, this is true of healthy members, which suffer with the aching of the head; not of rotten or cankered members, which feel not faintness when the head is aching. For it often happens that, from the touch of such members, certain members fall into an incurable distemper; and thus sometimes the head also is infected by them with such a distemper, so that the whole body may be made a monstrosity. May not, indeed, any body whatsoever deserve to be called a monstrosity, whereof the foot,—the lowest member I mean,—festering with a fiery distemper, and not allayed in time by the hands, with cautery, overrides the more worthy members, and infects its own head with poison, tearing it off, and unnaturally putting itself, instead of the head, upon the neck and shoulders? Now, at the same time and year as the battle of Lumfanan, Griffin, king of Wales, routed Radulph, Earl of Hereford, in battle; and, having slain Levegar, bishop of that town, and Eglenoth, the Sheriff, with many others, he burnt up with fire the town and the whole county, together with the bishop. But Siward, as soon as he had received news of this from his king, by sure hand, hastily came home again, as he was bidden, never more to go back to Malcolm's assistance. For, on the death of Machabeus, some of his kinsfolk, who were just the men for such a piece of iniquity, came together, and bringing his cousin Lulath, surnamed *the Simple*, to Scone, set him on the royal seat and appointed him king—for they hoped that the people would willingly obey him as king; but no one would yield him obedience, or become a party to anything that had been or was to be done. On hearing this, Malcolm sent forth his earls hither and thither after him. But their efforts were fruitlessly spun out through four months; until, searching in the higher districts, they found him at a place called Essy, in the district of Strathbolgy, and slew him with his followers; or, as some relate, Malcolm came across him there, by chance, and put him to death, in the year 1057, on the 3d of April, in Easter week, on a Thursday. They also relate that both these kings, Machabeus and Lulath, were buried in the island of Iona.

CHAPTER IX.

Accession of King Malcolm to the kingdom—He fights with a Traitor.

WHEN all his enemies had been everywhere laid low, or were made to submit to him, this aforesaid Malcolm was set on the king's throne, at Scone, in the presence of the chiefs of the kingdom, and crowned, to the honour and glory of all the Scots, in that same month of April, on Saint Mark's day, in that same year—1057, to wit, the first year of the emperor Henry IV., who reigned fifty years. The king reigned thirty-six years and six months. He was a king very humble in heart, bold in spirit, exceeding strong in bodily strength, daring, though not rash, and endowed with many other good qualities, as will appear in the sequel. During the first nine years of his reign, until the arrival of William the Bastard, he maintained security of peace and fellowship with the English. In the thirteenth year of the said King Edward, his brother the late King Edmund Ironside's son, whose name was Edward, came to

England from Hungary, bringing with him his wife Agatha, his son Edgar, and two daughters—Margaret, afterwards queen of the Scots, and Christina, a holy nun; and he was received with great rejoicings by his uncle the king, and the whole English people. We shall speak of these at greater length later, in their proper place. Of Malcolm, the high-souled king of the Scots, says *Turgot*, we instance this as worthy of mention, to the end that this one of his doings, here set down, may show forth to those who read of it how kind was his heart, and how great his soul. Once upon a time it was reported to him that one of his greatest nobles had agreed with his enemies to slay him. The king commanded the man who had brought him this news to hold his peace; and himself awaited in silence the arrival of the traitor, who happened then to be away. So when the traitor came to court with a great train to set a trap for the king, the latter, putting on as pleasant a countenance as usual towards him and his followers, pretended that he had heard nothing, and knew nothing, of what he was brooding over in his mind and deep down in his heart. To make a long story short, the king bade all his huntsmen meet at daybreak, with their dogs. Dawn, then, had just chased away the night, when the king, having called unto him all the nobles and knights, hastened to go out hunting, for an airing. After a time, he came to a certain broad plain, begirt by a very thick wood, in the manner of a crown; in the midst whereof a hillock seemed to swell out as it were, enamelled with the motley beauty of flowers of divers hues, and afforded a welcome lounge to the knights whenever they were tired out with hunting. The king then halted upon this hillock, above the others, and, according to a law of hunting, which the people call *tristra*, told them all off, severally, with their dogs and mates, to their several places; so that the quarry, hemmed in on every side, should find death and destruction awaiting it at whatever outlet it might choose. But the king himself went off apart from the others, alone with one other, retaining his betrayer with him; and they were side by side.

CHAPTER X.

The fight—The Traitor is worsted.

NOW, when they were out of sight and hearing of all, the king stopped, and, with a stern look that meant strife, broke out into these words:—"Here we are," said he, "thou and I, man to man, with like weapons to protect us. There is none to stand by me—king though I be—and none to help thee; nor can any see or hear. So now, if thou can, if thou dare, if thy heart fail thee not, fulfil by the deed what thou hast conceived in thy heart, and redeem thy promise to my foes. If thou think to slay me, when better, when more safely, when more freely, when, in short, couldst thou do so in a more manly way? Hast thou poison ready for me? Who knows not that is only what a girl would do? Wouldst thou entrap me in my bed? An adulteress could do so too. Hast thou a dagger concealed to strike me unawares? None but would say that is a murderer's, not a knight's part. Act rather like a knight, not like a traitor. Act like a man, not like a woman. Meet me as man to man, that thy treachery may seem to be free at least from meanness; for, disloyalty it can never be free from!" All this time, the wretched man could hardly bear up under this; but soon, struck by his words as by the weight of a thunderbolt, with all speed he alighted from the horse he was riding, and, throwing away his weapons, fell, in tears, at the king's feet; and, with a trembling heart, thus spake:—"My lord the king, let thy kingly might overlook this unrighteous purpose of mine for this once; and whatever my evil heart may have lately plotted, touching such a betrayal of thy body, shall henceforth be blotted out. For I promise before God and his mother that, for the future, I shall be most faithful to thee against all men." "Fear not, my friend," rejoined the king, "fear not. Thou shalt suffer no evil through me or from me, on account of this. I bid thee, however, name me hostages in pledge, and bring them to me." The hostages were named, and soon after brought to the king; who thereupon said,—"I say unto thee, on the word of a king, that the matter shall stand as I promised thee before." When, therefore, that traitor had, in due time, satisfied the king's wishes in the above particulars, they returned to their companions, and spoke to no man of what they had done, or said.

CHAPTER XI.

Death of Edward, King of the English—The nobles would have made the blessed Margaret's brother, Edward, King, had the Clergy consented—Vision of Saint Edward.

King Edward, says *William*, bowed with age, and having no children himself, while he saw Godwin's sons growing in power, sent to the king of the Huns (but *Turgot* says, to the emperor) to send him over Edward, the son of his brother Edmund Ironside, and all his family;—for that either he was to succeed to the kingdom of England by hereditary right, or his sons should do so; because his own childlessness ought to be made good by the help of his kindred. Edward accordingly arrived, but immediately paid the debt of nature at St. Paul's in London, leaving his son Edgar, with his afore-named sisters, surviving him. This Edgar, the king recommended to the nobles, as being by blood the next for the kingship. The king, at length, when he had not fully completed his twenty-fourth year on the throne, died on the Eve of Epiphany; and the next day, while the grief for the king's death was still fresh, Harold, the son of Godwin, extorted fealty from the chiefs—though, according to others, these consented—and seized the diadem of the kingship, which he held scarcely nine months; for he was slain in battle by William the Bastard. After him the nobles would, but for the bishops, who would not support them, have chosen Edgar king—and he was so chosen by some, as the king had commanded. So speaks *William*. But it seems to me that they did wrong in this, both before God and the people: before God, because one whom He had preferred for the kingship, by his birth, from so many kings, his forebears, begotten, as he was, in the rightful line of descent, it was not lawful for them to reject, nor unjustly to rob him of his patrimony—guiltless, as he was—with their tongues sharper than any sword; for they knew that a king's boyhood, or old age, or even his weak-mindedness, stands firm upon the fealty and submissiveness of his subjects;—and before the people, inasmuch as, to their own confusion, and to the eternal reproach and scandal of all the inhabitants of the kingdom, they set up over themselves, not according to the justice of law, but following their heart's desires, a man without the least right to reign. Harold, son of Godwin, son of Edric (of whom, not the fame, but the infamy is noticed in various writings), appointing that useless member king over them, in the stead of the rightful head. Whence it came to pass that, shortly after, they wandered in wretchedness and sorrow through strange countries, having been driven out of their own homes, and having nowhere to lay their heads; as says the prophet:— They that do evil shall be driven out of their borders; but they that abide the Lord shall inherit the land. So the Lord himself, for a happy omen to the Scots, freely joined to their royal line that holy royal line which was thus kept up by them, though not forsaken by Him. For He wished that they should inherit the land and reign together; and from them, by His providence, from that time even until now, have sprung forth, and shall spring forth as long as they shall please Him, kings sitting on the kingly throne. From the following vision, which was revealed to Saint Edward, when in the agonies of death, it is evident that the clergy did wrong in the above matter. After he had lain, says *William*, two days speechless, in a deep sleep, his speech was loosed, and, "I saw," said he, "two monks standing beside me, who, I knew, lived religiously in Normandy, and died happily. They began by saying that they were the messengers of God, and then spake as follows:— 'Since the chiefs of England, leaders, bishops, and abbots, are not the ministers of God, but of the devil, God hath delivered this kingdom, after thy death, into the hands of the enemy, for a year and a day; and devils shall wander over all this land.'" And when the king said that he would show these things unto the people, so that, like the Ninevites of old, they might repent, "Neither of these two things," said they, "shall come to pass: for neither shall they repent, nor shall God have mercy on them"—and so forth. *William* also says:—Thus the English—who, had they been united in one mind, could have retrieved the ruin of their country—would have no one of their own people, and so brought in the stranger.

CHAPTER XII.

How William the Bastard's coming to England was brought about—Saint Paternus, the Scot.

BUT William the Bastard, count of Normandy, hearing that Harold had usurped the kingdom of his cousin Edward, was goaded on by various causes to come to England. First, because of the breach of the treaty which they had contracted between them by oath: for Harold had pledged himself to give William the castle of Dover at that time, and the kingdom of England after Edward's death; while William had promised that Harold should wed his daughter, who was still under age. Next, because Harold's father, Godwin, had treacherously put to death his cousin Alfred, together with many Englishmen and Normans at Ely— all his comrades except every tenth man, being beheaded. Also, because this Godwin had banished out of England the archbishop Robert and Earl Odo, together with all the French. Being therefore irritated on account of these and other matters, he gathered his forces together from all sides, and sailed over into England; and, on the 14th of October 1066—the tenth year of the emperor Henry and king Malcolm—he deprived this same Harold of his kingdom and his life together, in a slight and ill-contested battle at Hastings. In the second year of this emperor, Padbrunna (Paderborn), a city of Germany, was burnt down, together with its cathedral. In a monastery of monks in that same city, there was a certain Scot, Paternus by name, who had long been a recluse, and had oftentimes foretold this fire. In a certain Teutonic city, says *Peter Damianus*, there was a servant of God, named Paternus, living shut up in a little cell hard by a monastery. To him it was revealed that unless the people made haste to appease God by repentance, the whole city would perish by fire within thirty days! The vision was noised abroad, but they would not be converted. He, however, bade them take away all the valuables of the monastery, that they might be saved; and at length a fire burst out suddenly in seven parts of the city, and burnt the whole city and the monastery to ashes. But when the fire had reached the little cell of the man of God, and he was asked to come forth, he would not; but intrusting all to the judgment of God, he and his little cell were burnt up. In the year of William the Bastard's arrival in England, a comet was seen; whence a rhymer says:—

"In the year one thousand and six and sixty more,
A comet's tresses streamed o'er England's shore."

CHAPTER XIII.

Wretched and treacherous lives led by the English before William's arrival.

William has sorrowfully stated, in his Chronicle, the cause of the sad slaughter of the battle of Hastings, wherein, through that cause, the English lost their kingdom; and it has been thought proper to put it in also into this chronicle, that our chieftains may take example therefrom, and learn to take heed lest, at any time, they be burdened by besetting sins of such kind and so great—far be it from them!—that they be, like him, unable to withstand their foes in battle. That was a fatal day to England, says *William*, a mournful downfall of our dear country, in passing over to its new lords. For it had before been used to the manners of the Angles, which had altered a good deal, according to the times. In the first years of their arrival, they were savage in look and manner, of warlike habits, heathen in their customs; but afterwards, when they had embraced Christ's faith, little by little, as time went on, in proportion to the ease in which they lived, did they put the use of arms in the second place, and turned their thoughts entirely to religion. To say nothing of the poor—even kings, who from the greatness of their power could over-freely indulge in pleasures, took to the frock, some of them in their own country, some of them at Rome, and won a heavenly kingdom, and gained a life of bliss. What shall I say of so many bishops, hermits, and abbots? Does not the whole island blaze with so many relics of natives, that you can scarcely pass a village of any consequence but you hear the name of some new saint? Nevertheless, afterwards, in course of time, for a good many years before the arrival of the Normans, the upper classes, given up to gluttony and wantonness, went not to church in the morning after the manner of Christians, but, in their chambers, and in the arms of their wives, barely listened to a priest who hurried through the rites of matins or the mass. The commonalty, left unprotected in their midst, became the prey of the most powerful—who amassed heaps of treasure, by either swallowing up their substance, or selling their persons into far off lands. There was one custom of theirs repugnant to nature: many of them, when their maid-servants were with child by them, and had glutted their lust, were wont to sell them either to some common brothel, or to service abroad. The clergy, contented with a smattering of letters, could scarcely stammer out the words of the sacraments; and one who knew grammar was an object of wonder and astonishment to the rest. The monks made a mockery of the rule of their order by fine clothes and every kind of food without distinction. Drinking-bouts were indulged in by all, who continued nights as well as days in that occupation. They eat till they brought on surfeiting, and drank till they were sick; whence there followed the vices which wait on drunkenness, and unman the minds of men. So it came to pass that, when they engaged William with more rashness and headlong fury than military skill, they themselves and their country sank into slavery by one, and that by no means a hard-fought, battle. For nothing is more bootless than rashness; and what is begun with a rush, soon ends, or is checked. But as God, in His mildness, often cherishes the bad with the good in quietness, so does He in His sternness, sometimes fetter the good with the bad in bondage.

CHAPTER XIV.

Happily for the Scots, Edgar Atheling and his sister Margaret, afterwards Queen of the Scots, land in Scotland.

So Edgar Atheling, says *Turgot*, seeing that everywhere matters went not smoothly with the English, went on board ship, with his mother and sisters, and tried to get back to the country where he was born. But the Sovereign Ruler, who rules the winds and waves, troubled the sea, and the billows thereof were upheaved by the breath of the gale; so, while the storm was raging, they all, losing all hope of life, commended themselves to God, and left the vessel to the guidance of the waves. Accordingly, after many dangers and huge toils, God took pity on His forlorn children, for when no help from man seems to be forthcoming, we must needs have recourse to God's help—and at length, tossed in the countless dangers of the deep, they were forced to bring up in Scotland. So that holy family brought up in a certain spot which was thenceforth called Saint Margaret's Bay by the inhabitants. We believe that this did not come about by chance, but that they arrived there through the providence of God Most High. While, then, the aforesaid family tarried in that bay, and were all awaiting in fear the upshot of the matter, news of their arrival was brought to King Malcolm, who at that time was, with his men, staying not far from that spot; so he sent off messengers to the ship, to inquire into the truth of the matter. When the messengers came there, they were astonished at the unusual size of the ship, and hurried back to the king as fast as they could, to state what they had seen. On hearing these things, the king sent off thither, from among his highest lords, a larger embassy of men more experienced than the former. So these, being welcomed as ambassadors from the king's majesty, carefully noted, not without admiration, the lordliness of the men, the beauty of the women, and the good-breeding of the whole family; and they had pleasant talk thereon among themselves. To be brief—the ambassadors chosen for this duty plied them with questions, in sweet words and dulcet eloquence, as to how the thing began, went on, and ended; while they, on the other hand, as guests newly come, humbly and eloquently unfolded to them, in simple words, the cause and manner of their arrival. So the ambassadors returned; and when they had informed their king of the stateliness of the older men, and the good sense of the younger, the ripe womanhood of the matrons, and the loveliness of the young girls, one of them went on to say:—"We saw a lady there—whom, by the bye, from the matchless beauty of her person, and the ready flow of her pleasant eloquence, teeming, moreover, as she did, with all other qualities, I declare to thee, O king, that I suspect, in my opinion, to be the mistress of that family—whose admirable loveliness and gentleness one must admire, as I deem, rather than describe." And no wonder they believed her to be the mistress; for she was not only the mistress of that family, but also the heiress of the whole of England, after her brother; and God's providence had predestined her to be Malcolm's future queen, and the sharer of his throne. But the king, hearing that they were English, and were there present, went in person to see them and talk with them; and made fuller inquiries whence they had come, and whither they were going. For he had learnt the English and Roman tongues fully as well as his own, when, after his father's death, he had remained fifteen years in England; where, from his knowledge of this holy family, he may happen to have heard somewhat to make him deal more gently, and behave more kindly, towards them.

CHAPTER XV.

King Malcolm weds Saint Margaret—He gladly welcomes all English fugitives.

THE king, therefore, says *Turgot* again, when he had seen Margaret, and learnt that she was begotten of royal, and even imperial, seed, sought to have her to wife, and got her: for Edgar Atheling, her brother, gave her away to him, rather through the wish of his friends than his own—nay, by God's behest. For as Hester of old was, through God's providence, for the salvation of her fellow-countrymen, joined in wedlock to King Ahasuerus, even so was this princess joined to the most illustrious King Malcolm. Nor was she, however, in bondage; but she had abundant riches, which her uncle, the king of England, had formerly given to her father, Edward, as being his heir (whom also the Roman emperor, Henry, himself, had sent to England, as we stated a little ago, graced with no small gifts), and a very large share thereof the holy queen brought over with her to Scotland. She brought, besides, many relics of saints, more precious than any stone or gold. Among these was that holy Cross, which they call *the black*, no less feared than loved by all Scottish men, through veneration for its holiness. The wedding took place in the year 1070, and was held, with great magnificence, not far from the bay where she brought up, at a place called Dunfermline, which was then the king's town. For that place was of itself most strongly fortified by nature, being begirt by very thick woods, and protected by steep crags. In the midst thereof was a fair plain, likewise protected by crags and streams; so that one might think that was the spot whereof it was said:—"Scarce man or beast may tread its pathless wilds." Malcolm, says *William*, gladly welcomed all the English fugitives, affording to each such protection as was in his power—to Edgar, to Stigand, Archbishop of Canterbury, and to Aldred of York—but especially to Edgar, whose sister he made his consort, out of regard for her old and noble descent. On his behalf, Malcolm harried the border provinces of England with fire and rapine. This king Malcolm, with his men, and Edgar, Marcher and Waldeof, with the English and Danes, often brooded over that nest of oppression, York, the only stronghold of rebellion; and there they often killed William's leaders, whose deaths I should, perhaps, not be doing too much were I to recount one by one. These two, Stigand and Aldred, the chiefs of the clergy, had been in London when this Edgar, the son of Edward, son of Edmund Ironside, would, after King Edward's death, and likewise after William's victory, have been raised to the throne by all the others, had they themselves not wickedly withstood them. Of them—and of all the rest, I think—was it said by the prophet—"Judge ye justly, O children of men!" And seeing they judged unjustly, God justly brought again the same judgment upon their heads; so that, being straightway ousted from all their property, they sought a place of refuge under the wings of him they had unjustly spurned from them; and they secretly arrived in Scotland.

CHAPTER XVI.

The Sons and Daughters he begat of Margaret—Ravages he commits in England.

MARGARET, says *Turgot*, was, as already stated, joined in wedlock to this most illustrious man, Malcolm, king of the Scots, in the year 1070, the fourteenth year of his reign. Some, however, have written that it was in the year 1067. Her sister Christina, for her part, is blessed as the bride of Christ. Malcolm begat, of Margaret, six sons: namely, Edward, Edmund, Ethelred, Edgar, Alexander, and that most vigorous and courteous of kings, David; and two daughters, Matilda, afterwards queen of England, and surnamed *the good*, and Mary, countess of Boulogne—of each of whom we shall speak presently, in the proper place. Of how great worthiness was this blessed Queen Margaret in the eyes of God and man, her praiseworthy life, death, and miracles, a book written thereon will show forth to those who read it. So writes *Turgot*. Many a time, however, did the king, from the earliest days of *William* the Bastard's reign even until after his death, march into the northern provinces of England, with a strong hand, wasting and destroying all things round about; taking away, in a hostile manner, by spoiling and plunder, all that had breath; and consuming with fire and sword, from off the face of the earth, all he did not take away for the use of man. He likewise carried off countless crowds of people; so that there was hardly a house or cottage in his kingdom that did not shelter some prisoner of the male or female sex. But who can unfold and tell how many of these the blessed queen, the king's consort, ransomed, and restored to freedom—these whom the violence of their foes had carried off from among the English folk, and reduced to slavery? But the king kept continually coming into England, destroying and spoiling; and laid Northumbria waste beyond the river Tees. At length he came to an understanding with the nobles of the whole of Northumbria, after having slain Walcherius, bishop of Durham, and many others, at Gateshead. The whole country, except some castles, surrendered to him, and all the inhabitants submitted and swore fealty to him. Now, though Malcolm was bound to do homage to William the Bastard for twelve towns situated in England, he threw off his allegiance on some provocation from certain Normans, and, in his fearful raids, heaped upon them these unbearable disasters which they well deserved. About the twelfth year of Henry IV., says *Vincentius*, the Scots kept making inroads upon England on one side, and the French on the other; and the English were wasted by famine to such a degree, that some fed on human flesh, and many on horse-flesh.

CHAPTER XVII.

The Northumbrians give hostages to King Malcolm, and cleave to him—He routs William's brother, Odo.

At that time King William, after he had got the kingdom, and arranged everything to his satisfaction, besieged the castle of Dol, in the parts beyond the sea, and was forced to raise the siege by the strong hand of the French king, Philip. Robert Curthose, also, his eldest son, made war upon his father in aid of King Philip; for William would not give him Normandy, as he had promised him in that king's presence. A few days afterwards, however, peace was established, and William and his son were reconciled. Now while William was still in Normandy, news reached him that some of the dwellers in his borders—the inhabitants of Northumbria, to wit—had gone over from him to King Malcolm; so, to get them back, he sent against them, with a large force, his brother, Odo, bishop of Bayeux, whom he had made earl of Kent. The Northumbrians, however, having already given hostages to King Malcolm, held fast to the Scots; and, after wasting their country, Odo went back to the south. Malcolm pursued the retreating Odo, inflicting some loss on his troops; and, pouring his host about the banks of the river Humber, he destroyed the lands of the Normans and English round about, with incredible slaughter, and returned to his native land with booty and spoils without end. But King William, unable to brook the never-tiring inroads of this outbreak, sent his son Robert to Scotland, to make war upon King Malcolm. Robert, however, achieved nothing; and, on his return, built Newcastle-upon-Tyne. For long after William had invaded England, many Northumbrian and southern lords, being supported by the help of the Scots, for many years held the city of York and the whole country, and made frequent inroads and most cruel outbreaks against the Normans across the river Humber. Now Earl Waldeof, Siward's son, whom King Malcolm always held his most faithful friend, and whom King William feared above all the English who had withstood him, was craftily entrapped by the latter, by a marriage with his niece Judith, and taken; and after he had long kept him in chains, William bade him be beheaded. His dead body was brought down to Croyland, and buried there. And God there showed that it is a true opinion which asserts that his death was wrongful; for, in His mercy. He works numberless miracles through him. Waldeof, singly, to use *William's* own words, had cut down many of the Normans, at the battle of York—cutting off their heads, as they marched in one by one through the gate. He had sinewy arms, a brawny chest, and was tall and sturdy in his whole body; and they surnamed him *Digera*, a Danish word which means *strong*. But King William, coming back from his expeditions across the sea, in the fifteenth year of his reign, laid the whole of Northumbria waste.

CHAPTER XVIII.

Virtuous and Charitable works of King Malcolm and the Queen.

I WILL here shortly repeat somewhat of the virtuous works and almsgiving of that high-minded King Malcolm, as *Turgot* bears witness in his Legend of the Life of the blessed queen. For, as David the prophet sang in the Psalm, "with the holy shalt thou be holy," even so did the king himself learn, from the exhortations of the holy queen, to rejoice in holy works, and to keep his heart from iniquity. Doubtless he was afraid in any way to shock that queen, so estimable in her life, when he saw that Christ dwelt in her heart; and would rather hasten with all speed to obey her wishes and wise advice. Whatever, also, she eschewed he was wont to eschew; and in his love, to love whatever she loved; and he learnt, by her example, oftentimes to pass the watches of the night in prayer, and most devoutly to pray to God with groans and tears from the heart. I confess, says *Turgot*, I confess I wondered at that great miracle of God's mercy, when I sometimes saw the king's great earnestness in prayer, and such great compunction in praying in the breast of a layman. In Lent, and the days of Advent, before Christmas, the king, unless prevented by great press of secular business, was wont, after he had gone through matins, and the celebration of the mass at daybreak, to come back into his chamber, where he and the queen would wash the feet of six beggars, and lay out something to comfort their poverty. Meanwhile, as the poor became more numerous, it became customary that they should be brought into the king's court; and while they sat round in a row, the king and queen would walk in, and the gates be shut by the servants. Thus, except the chaplains, some monks, and a few servants, no one was allowed to be present at their almsgiving. Then the king on the one side, and the queen on the other, served Christ in the poor, with great devoutness handing them meat and drink specially prepared for that purpose. Indeed the king and queen were both equal in works of charity—both remarkable for their godly behaviour. After this, the king was wont to busy himself anxiously with things of this world, and affairs of state; while the queen would go to church, and there, with long-drawn prayers, and tearful sobs, heartily offer herself a sacrifice unto God. So far *Turgot*.

CHAPTER XIX.

Death of William the Bastard—He could not go to his grave without challenge—Good understanding come to between William Rufus, son of William, and Malcolm—Virtues of Malcolm and his queen.

IN the thirty-first year of King Malcolm, William the Bastard, king of England, died at Rouen; and his body was taken down the Seine to Caen. Thence, says *William*, might be seen the wretchedness of earthly vicissitude;—that man, formerly the glory of all Europe, and more powerful than any of his predecessors, could not, without challenge, find a place of everlasting rest. For a certain knight, to whose patrimony that place belonged, loudly protested against the robbery, and forbade the burial: saying that the ground was his own, by right of his forebears; and that the king ought not to rest in any place which he had seized by force. Whereupon, at the desire of Henry, the only one of his sons who was there, a hundred pounds of silver were paid to this brawler, and set his audacious challenge at rest. In the same year of our

Lord—namely, 1087—his son William Rufus succeeded to the English throne, and reigned 'thirteen years. In the fifth year of his reign, he and his brother Robert combined against their younger brother Henry, and during the whole of Lent, laid siege to Mount St. Michael, across the sea; but without success. At length peace was made between them; and William, coming back with his two brothers, encountered King Malcolm, who was laying Northumbria waste. Peace was then made between them, by Earl Robert, on these terms: that the king of Scotland should obey King William; that William should restore to Malcolm the twelve towns the latter had held under William's father; and that Malcolm also should give twelve golden merks a year. This King William, when about to fight against his brother in Normandy, put an end to the war, says *William*, without achieving what he had aimed at; and as the turbulence of the Scots and Welsh called him away, he betook himself to his kingdom, with both his brothers. He then at once set on foot an expedition, first, against the Welsh, and then, against the Scots; but he did nothing striking or worthy of his greatness, and lost many of his knights, both killed and taken prisoners. At that time, however, through the efforts of Earl Robert, who had long since gained the good graces of the Scots, a good understanding was brought about between Malcolm and William. Nevertheless there were many disputes on both sides, and justice wavered by reason of the fierce enmity of the two nations. This same Malcolm fell, the second year after, rather through guile than force, by the hand of the men of the Northumbrian earl Robert Mowbray. Now when his wife, Margaret, a woman remarkable for her almsgiving and her modesty, got news of his death, she was sick of lingering in this life, and prayerfully besought God for death. They were both remarkable for their godly behaviour—but she especially. For during the whole of her lifetime, wherever she might be, she had twenty-four beggars whom she supplied with food and clothing. In Lent, forestalling the chanting of the priests, she used to watch all night in church, herself assisting at triple matins—of the Trinity, of the Cross, and of St. Mary; and afterwards repeating the Psalter, with tears bedewing her raiment and upheaving her breast. Then she would walk out of church, and feed the poor—first three, then nine, then twenty-four, at last three hundred—herself standing by with the king, and pouring water on their hands. So far *William*.

CHAPTER XX.

Foundation of the Church of Durham by Malcolm—Siege of the Castle of Murealden by the same—He and his Son slain there.

THIS King Malcolm, practising these and the like works of piety, as we read in *Turgot*, began to found and to build the new church of Durham—this same King Malcolm, William, bishop of that church, and Turgot, the prior, laying the first stones in the foundation. He had likewise, long before, founded the church of the Holy Trinity at Dunfermline, and endowed it with many offerings and revenues. But when he had, in his wonted manner, many a time carried off much plunder out of England, beyond the river Tees—from Cleveland, Richmond, and elsewhere—and besieged the Castle of Alnwick (or Murealden, which is the same thing), smiting sore those of the besieged who made head against him, those who had been shut in, being shut out from all help of man, and acknowledging that they had not strength to cope with so mighty and impetuous an army, held a council, and brought to bear a novel device of treachery, on this wise:—One, more experienced than the rest, mighty in strength, and bold in deed, offered to risk death, so as either to deliver himself unto death, or free his comrades from death. So he warily approached the king's army, and courteously asked where the king was, and which was he. But when they questioned him as to the motive of his inquiries, he said that he would betray the castle to the king; and, as a proof of good faith, he canied on his lance, in the sight of all, the keys thereof, which he was going to hand over. On hearing this, the king, who knew no guile, incautiously sprang out of his tent unarmed, and came unawares upon the traitor. The latter, who had looked for this opportunity, being armed himself, ran the unarmed king through, and hastily plunged into the cover of a neighbouring wood. And thus died that vigorous king, in the year 1093, on the 13th of November, to wit—Saint Brice's day. The army was thus thrown into confusion. And grief was heaped upon grief: for Edward, the king's firstborn, was mortally wounded, and met his fate on the 15th of November, in the year above noted—the third day after his father—at Edwardisle, in the forest of Jedwart. He was buried beside his father, before the altar of the Holy Cross, in the Church of the Holy Trinity, at Dunfermline. King Malcolm, after he was killed, says *William*, for many years lay buried at Tynemouth; and he was afterwards conveyed to Scotland, to Dunfermline, by his son Alexander.

CHAPTER XXI.

Death of Saint Margaret—Siege of the Castle of Maidens by Donald, the King's brother, who invades the Kingdom—Flight of the King's Sons out of the Kingdom.

WHEN the queen, who had before been racked with many infirmities, almost unto death, heard this—or, rather, foreknew it through the Holy Ghost—she shrived, and devoutly took the Communion in church; and, commending herself unto God in prayer, she gave back her saintly soul to heaven, in the Castle of Maidens (Edinburgh), on the 16th of November, the fourth day after the king. Whereupon, while the holy queen's body was still in the castle where her happy soul had passed away to Christ, whom she had always loved, Donald the Red, or Donald Bane, the king's brother, having heard of her death, invaded the kingdom, at the head of a numerous band, and in hostilewise besieged the aforesaid castle, where he knew the king's rightful and lawful heirs were. But, forasmuch as that spot is in itself strongly fortified by nature, he thought that the gates only should be guarded, because it was not easy to see any other entrance or outlet. When those who were within understood this, being taught of God, through the merits, we believe, of the holy queen, they brought down her holy body by a postern on the western side. Some, indeed, tell us that, during the whole of that journey, a cloudy mist was round about all this family, and miraculously sheltered them from the gaze of any of their foes, so that nothing hindered them as they journeyed by land or by sea; but they brought her away, as she had herself before bidden them, and prosperously reached the place they wished—namely, the church of Dunfermline, where she now rests in Christ. And thus did Donald come by the kingdom, having ousted the true heirs. Meanwhile Edgar Atheling, brother to the just mentioned queen, fearing that it might be with his nephews as the common saying is, "Trust not the sharer of thy throne," thought it, therefore, safer to take them away for a time, than to intrust them to their uncle, that they might reign with him;—for every one seeks a partner in sin, but no one does so in the kingship. Wherefore he gathered together the sons and daughters of the king and of the queen, his sister, and, secretly bringing them over with him into England, sent them to be brought up by his kinsmen and acquaintances, not openly, but in hiding, as it were. For he feared lest the Normans—who had, at that time, seized England—should try to bring evil upon him and his, seeing that the throne of England was their due by hereditary right; and, though he had stayed there in secret, as it were, for a short time, yet it was told the king that he was mixed up in treason against him. And thus what he dreaded befell him on this wise.

CHAPTER XXII.

An Englishman, Orgar by name, challenges Edgar Atheling to single combat for treason against King William II.

AT that time, while *William* II. was reigning, a certain recreant English knight, Orgar by name, wishing to curry favour with the king, came forward and challenged this Edgar Clito, that is, of *glorious birth*—for so they called him—for treason against the aforesaid King William. Thereupon the cause was brought before the king, for Edgar was begotten of the kingly stock, and was, by rights, the nearest to the English throne. So the king, thinking that he had good reason to beware, upheld the plaintiff with his kingly might and protection; nor could there have been any doubt as to Edgar's sentence, if the offence he was charged with could have been proved. This made Edgar anxious;

and he began busily to inquire whether any one would dare to take up his cause either by word or counsel. But, though he promised a reward, fear of the king stood in his way: because the nobility believed they could not, with impunity, side with him; for they would have incurred the king's hatred by defending him. While he was in suspense, therefore, and downcast with deep anxiety, a knight of Winton, named Godwin, an Englishman by birth, and of no mean blood, being not unmindful of Edgar's ancient parentage, engaged to lend him his help in this awkward matter. Now the day fixed for the settlement of this cause was already at hand. There, straightway, stood the plaintiff, with his supercilious bearing—who, because he seemed to excel in bodily strength, and by reason of his skill in war, in which he was well versed, deemed that no one was his match in battle. Moreover, the king's favour heightened this conceit; and he was thereby so puffed up that he believed he could easily prove whatever he chose to lay to another's charge. Since, therefore, he had thus challenged him, Edgar was forced to defend himself in single combat, or to get another to fight in his stead; for, by getting a judgment in this way, he hoped to establish the truth of the matter. Godwin, therefore, having taken up Edgar's cause, by means of an oath on either side, as is customary, stood forth as Edgar's champion. Soon there was much warlike arraying on either side, and they came together to battle. Orgar, puffed up with the king's favour, and hedged about with the king's hangers-on, marched onwards glittering with arms showily bedight. Godwin, on the other hand, entered the lists with a no less confident heart, though he was not, like his opponent, backed up by the leaders who sided with the king. Now Godwin, though he dreaded the king's wrath for upholding the opposite side, nevertheless rightly deemed that he owed it to nature to take up the cause of one who, as he knew, ought naturally and rightly to have dominion over him and the rest, as their leader. And hence he upbraided the challenger with just reproof: inasmuch as the latter, being an Englishman by birth, seemed to fight against nature; for that he ought to reverence Edgar as his lord, as being, by right of birth, one to whom he owed himself and all he had. But when a herald had imposed silence on all, the judge threw within the lists the wagers of battle of both, and appealed to God, from Whom nothing is hid, to show forth the truth in this cause. So the matter was, in the end, referred to arms, and the cause to the Supreme Judge.

CHAPTER XXIII.

Duel—The Challenger is slain by Godwin of Winton.

THEY each went at the other, without loss of time,—the plaintiff and the defendant. Soon stroke followed stroke on either side. Orgar charged, and while the other received the blow upon his shield, tore off a good piece of the shield. Nor was Godwin idle, for his wrath was kindled by that heavy stroke; and, while the other incautiously bent down his shield, he rose to the stroke, and dealt him a blow between the head and shoulder, hewing through the knots of his corslet, and that bone which joins the left shoulder to the neck. But by this blow the sword-hilt was loosened, and cheated the striker's hand; so the sword slipped out of the hand that held it. When his foe perceived this, though he was badly wounded, and his left hand was disabled, yet he plied his adversary more sorely, and thought to have disabled him the more easily that the latter lacked the aid of that wherewith especially he was to have fought. But that hope beguiled its lord; for Godwin, though his adversary withstood him with his whole might, thrust forward his shield, and between the dreadful blows of the striker, picked up from the ground the sword that had just slipped from his grasp. But, as he could not grip it tight because of the thinness of the hilt, he grasped the edge of the sword with the first and second fingers; and though he could not, in striking, hurt his adversary without hurting himself, yet he seemed not behind his adversary in thrusting and showering deadly strokes. For he neither gave way before the attacks of his foe, nor left off his blows. With one stroke, indeed, he put out his adversary's eye, and cut his head open; and, with a second, he wounded so sore the remaining part of his false foe's body, and brought it to nought, that

Orgar no longer tried to keep his feet, but fell grovelling on the ground, almost dead. And now, with great clattering of armour, Godwin nimbly set his foot upon his prostrate foe, and all at once the enemy's treachery and cunning now came out, and were laid bare, and he was openly found guilty of perjury: for, he drew out a knife, which was hidden in his boot, and strove to stab Godwin; whereas, before the conflict was begun, he had sworn that he would carry no weapons in this duel but such as became a knight. But he soon paid the penalty of his perjury. So, when the dagger was wrested from him, and hope forsook the guilty man, he straightway confessed his crime. This confession, however, was of no use to him in prolonging his life; for he was stabbed all over, wound after wound, until the violent pain and deep wounds drove out his ungodly soul. When the chances, therefore, of this battle were thus at an end, all wondered and were praising the righteous judgment of God,—seeing that, while the challenger was overthrown, he who was the defender of truth and innocence did not get a single wound from his assailant. And thenceforth, by reason of his signal display of valour, he became a great favourite with both king and leaders; and the king even granted him the lands and property of his worsted foe in possession by hereditary right. But Edgar Atheling, also, being thus proved most faithful to the king, became, moreover, his great friend; and the latter, furthermore, endowed him with many gifts and honours.

CHAPTER XXIV.

Duncan, Malcolm's illegitimate son, wrests the kingdom from his uncle Donald—His death—Donald recovers the kingdom—At this time the King of Norway takes possession of our Isles.

NOW when the throne of Scotland had been usurped by Donald, King Malcolm's lawful heirs—that is to say, Edgar, Alexander, and David, who, though the least in years, was nevertheless endowed with the greatest virtue—tarried in England through fear of him. For, as stated below, the king's three other older sons were not then living. Edward, as was said, was slain with his father. About Ethelred I find nothing certain, in any writings, as to where he died or was buried; except that, as some assert, he lies buried in Saint Andrew's Church at Kilremont. Edmund, a vigorous man, and devout in God's service, after his death was buried at Montacute, in England. *William*, however, has written that Edmund's death happened otherwise, as will be seen afterwards in the sequel. Meanwhile Duncan, King Malcolm's illegitimate son, when he was with King William Rufus, in England, as a hostage, was by him dubbed knight; and, backed up by his help, he arrived in Scotland, put his uncle Donald to flight, and was set up as king. But when he had reigned a year and six months, he fell slain at Monthechin by the Earl of Mernys, by name Malpetri, in Scottish, Malpedir, through the wiles of his uncle Donald, whom he had often vanquished in battle; and he was buried in the island of Iona. After his death, Donald again usurped the kingship, and held it for three years; while he had reigned for six months before Duncan. And thus after King Malcolm's death, so sad for the Scots, these two—Donald and Duncan, to wit—reigned five years between them. Now *William*, writing about the aforesaid Edmund, says:—Of the sons of the king and Margaret, Edmund was the only one who fell away from goodness. Partaking of his uncle Donald's wickedness, he was privy to his brother Duncan's death, having, forsooth, bargained with his uncle for half the kingdom. But being taken, and kept in fetters for ever, he sincerely repented; and, when at death's door, he bade them bury him in his chains, confessing that he was worthily punished for the crime of fratricide. While these, then—namely, Donald, Duncan, and Edgar, too—were struggling for the kingdom in this wise, the king of the Noricans (Northmen), Magnus, the son of King Olave, son of King Harold surnamed Harfager, sweeping the gulfs of the sea with a host of seamen, subdued the Orkneys to his dominion, and the Mevanian islands, both of Scotland and England (Man and the Western Isles), which, indeed, for the most part, used to belong to Scotland by ancient right. For the Scots continued, without any break, to hold these same islands from the time of Ethdacus Rothay, Simon Brek's great-grandson, who was the first of all the Scots to dwell in the islands—about five hundred years before the Scottish king Fergus, son of Feradach, entered the soil of Albion—even until now, for a space of nearly two thousand years.

CHAPTER XXV.

Return of Malcolm's sons from England—Flight of Donald from battle.

MEANWHILE, when Edgar Clito saw that Donald had wickedly usurped the throne of Scotland, which, by right, belonged to his nephews, and that he would not restore it, though more than once besought thereto by ambassadors, by a friendly intervention, he was stirred to wrath. So he gathered together from all sides a vast number of his friends, and being strengthened by the aforesaid King William's help, set out against Donald in order to drive him out, and appoint, as king of Scotland, his nephew, Edgar, a younger son of King Malcolm and his sister Margaret. While, therefore, young Edgar was hastening towards his native soil, and was in fear of the turbulence of his foes, Saint Cuthbert stood before him, in the stillness of night, and said:— "Fear not, my son; for God has been pleased to give thee the kingdom. And this shall be a token unto thee: When thou shalt have taken my standard with thee from the monastery of Durham, and set it up against thine adversaries, I shall up and help thee; and thy foes shall be scattered, and those that hate thee shall flee before thy face!" When the young man awoke, he reported the matter to his uncle Edgar; and, committing himself and all his friends to God and to the patronage of Saint Cuthbert, he carried out, with a stout heart, what the saint had encouragingly bidden him do. When, afterwards, the armies met, and Saint Cuthbert's standard was raised aloft, a certain knight of English birth, named Robert, the son of the aforesaid Godwin, and the heir and rival of his father's prowess, being accompanied by only two knights, charged the enemy, and slew their mightiest, who stood out, like champions, in front of the line of battle. So, before the armies had neared one another, Donald and his men were put to flight; and thus, by the favour of God and the merits of Saint Cuthbert, Edgar happily achieved a bloodless victory. See how a faithful home-born people is afraid to withstand its true and liege lord—and so forth, as already shown in Chapter VIII. Let, therefore, the lawless usurpers of kingdoms beware, and shrink from leading a faithful people to war against their lawful and liege lord, or his heir, any more than a good son against his father. But Edgar, being now in better heart, revived the manly courage of his men—though, indeed, that was not needed—and marched into the kingdom of his fathers, which rightfully belonged to him; and, as he marched in, the kingdom was joyfully offered him by the inhabitants, with none to hinder or gainsay; and he accepted it, and governed it gloriously ever after.

CHAPTER XXVI.

Accession of King Edgar, Malcolm's son, to the Throne—Donations made to Saint Cuthbert

IN the year 1098, therefore—the forty-second of the Emperor Henry,—Edgar, son of King Malcolm and Margaret, succeeded his uncle Donald, and reigned nine years and some months. Donald himself, indeed, was by him taken prisoner, blinded, and doomed to perpetual imprisonment. Now, when Edgar had been peacefully raised to the throne, and had undertaken to order all things according to his will, he remembered that saying of Solomon's, "In the days of prosperity be not unmindful of adversity." So he was not unmindful of his leader, Saint Cuthbert; and gave, granted, and confirmed to the monks of Durham, in perpetuity, his estate of Coldingham, with all the pertinents thereof. This princely man and bountiful king likewise heaped gift on gift; for he gave and confirmed in possession to the bishop of Durham and his successors, the noble village of Berwick, with its appurtenances. This great gift of the king's the whole bishopric thankfully received, and held it in happy peace; until Ranulf, the bishop, proved himself unworthy of it—and justly so—on this wise. While King Edgar was on his way to William II., king of England, that Robert, son of Godwin, of whom mention was made above, tarried, with the king's leave, on an estate the king had given him, in Laudonia (Lothian); and while he was seeking to build a castle there, he was at last, all of a sudden, beset and taken by the countrymen and barons of Durham—and that same Bishop Ranulf was at the bottom of it. In being thus taken, however, he left a signal remembrance of his bravery among the dwellers in the whole country. Now when Edgar, on his return, heard of this, he brought Robert, who had been set free by order of the king of England, back with him to Scotland, in great honour; and whatever he had previously given the bishop, he took back to himself—being thoroughly well advised therein. In the eleventh year of King William II., says *William*, Magnus, king of the Noricans (Norwegians), who has been spoken of above, subdued by his arms the Orkney Islands, the Mevanian, and whatever other islands lie in the sea; and while he was steadily making his way to England, by Anglesea, he was met by Hugh Earl of Chester, and Hugh Earl of Shrewsbury, and driven out by their arms. Hugh of Shrewsbury fell there.

CHAPTER XXVII.

Marriage of Edgar's sisters, Matilda to Henry King of England, and Mary to Eustace Count of Boulogne—Their sons and daughters—Edgar's death.

Now this King Edgar was a sweet and amiable man, like his kinsman, the holy King Edward, in every way; using no harshness, no tyrannical or bitter treatment towards his subjects; but ruling and correcting them with the greatest charity, goodness, and loving-kindness. In the fourth year of his reign, on the 2d of August, *William Rufus*, king of England, having gone out hunting in the New Forest, was unknowingly, and without malice aforethought, slain by Walter Tirel, a knight from over the sea, while the latter was letting fly a shaft at some wild beast. The king fell without uttering a word afterwards, thus in one short hour atoning for many misdeeds. He was at once deserted by all his train; and being carried away on a cart by some countrymen, he was buried under the tower at Winchester. He was succeeded in the kingship by his younger brother Henry, surnamed *Beauclerk*, to whom this King Edgar, the same year, gave his sister Matilda to wife. She was anointed and consecrated queen the following Martinmas, by Archbishop Anselm. But Mary, his younger sister, Edgar gave in marriage to Eustace the younger, Count of Bouillon. The characters of these sisters, and their good deeds, will be afterwards, in this little book, in some wise shown forth to whoever would know somewhat thereof. But this same Henry, king of England, begat, of Queen Matilda, a son named William; who, when seventeen years of age, together with his illegitimate brother Richard, his sister and niece, Richard, Earl of Chester, and many nobles, both men and women, as well as 140 knights and 50 seamen, was drowned in the sea at Barbefloth, while coming back to England from Normandy with his father. The king barely escaped with a few followers. The king likewise begat, of Matilda, a daughter named Matilda; who, worthy of an empire by her wisdom, beauty, and wealth, wedded Henry, the Roman emperor. To this Matilda, Henry, king of England, her father, made all the English lords swear fealty, before he crossed the sea a second time; for he had no heir to the throne but her. Then the aforesaid Eustace, Count of Boulogne, begat of the aforesaid Mary, Queen Matilda's sister, a daughter, likewise named Matilda, who married a man of great vigour, begotten of a stock equally of kings and of consuls, Stephen, Count of Mauritania (Moriton), King Henry's nephew, and afterwards king of England. Though I pass over the daughters, I hold up the mothers as a pattern to all living. For, while beset by the pomps of this world, they were rich in holy virtues—a thing rarely found; tended the poor of both sexes, of whatever condition they might be, as though they were Christ's members; and most tenderly cherished men of religious orders, clerics, priests, and monks, with singleness of love, as their patrons, and men who with Christ were to be their judges. But after Edgar had reigned nine years and three months in happy peace, as was said above, he ended his life at Dundee on the 8th of January, and was entombed in the church of Dunfermline, before the great altar.

CHAPTER XXVIII.

Accession of his brother Alexander, surnamed Fers—His character.

HE was succeeded by his brother Alexander, surnamed Fers (fierce), in the year 1107—the first of the emperor Henry V., who wedded Matilda, this Alexander's niece, and daughter of Henry, king of England, and the good Queen Matilda. Henry held the empire twenty years; and King Alexander reigned seventeen. Now the king was a lettered and godly man; very humble and amiable towards the clerics and regulars, but terrible beyond measure to the rest of his subjects; a man of large heart, exerting himself in all things beyond his strength. He was most zealous in building churches, in searching for relics of saints, in providing and arranging priestly vestments and sacred books; most open-handed, even beyond his means, to all new comers; and so devoted to the poor, that he seemed to delight in nothing so much as in supporting them, washing, nourishing, and clothing them. For, following in his mother's footsteps, he vied with her in pious acts so much, that, with regard to three churches—Saint Andrew's church at Kilremont, to wit, and the churches of Dunfermline and Scone, one of them founded by his father and mother, and the other founded and erected by himself at Scone, the chief seat of government, in honour of the Holy Trinity and the Archangel Saint Michael—he endowed them with offerings so many and so great, that his descendants rather impoverished them than added unto them; save that his illustrious successor and brother David kept them in good condition, and by his gifts raised Dunfermline especially—where he himself also rests—and enlarged it by fresh buildings. (Alexander also founded the monastery of Canons of the island of Emonia (Inchcolm), by Inverkeithing.) He it was who bestowed the Boar's Chase upon the blessed Andrew. He it was, likewise, who gave so many privileges to the aforesaid church of the Holy Trinity, at Scone. He had founded and built it on the spot where both the Scottish and Pictish kings had whilom established the chief seat of government; and, when constructed with a framework of stone, according to the custom of that time, he had had it dedicated—to which dedication, by strict order of the king, nearly the whole kingdom flocked. That church, indeed, with all its pertinents, he freely made over, God so ordering it, to the governance of canons-regular called from the church of Saint Oswald at Nostle (Nastlay, near Pontefract), and of the others after them who should serve God, until the end of the world.

CHAPTER XXIX.

Death of his sisters, namely, Queen Matilda and the Countess Mary—Their holy acts—Their burial.

IN the eleventh year of this Alexander's reign, his sister Matilda, surnamed the Good, queen of England, died on the 1st of May, and was buried with honour in the church of the Apostle Saint Peter, at Westminster, in London, in the chapel behind the great altar. In the midst thereof, on the top of a tomb tastefully and cunningly fashioned, with costly workmanship, are enshrined the remains of the holy King Edward; and, round about the tomb, kings are buried in state. On this queen's virtues some one has written these lines:—

> "Weal brought no joys to her, no sorrow woe;
> She smiled at woe; 'twas weal she dreaded so.
> Beauty no frailty brought, nor sceptre pride;
> Meekness her might, shame did her beauty hide.
> May's opening day, when night enthralled us here,
> Took her away to Day's eternal sphere."

I also, some time ago, read another epitaph of hers, hung upon that same tomb, and written in letters of gold, thus:—"Here lies Matilda, the good queen of England, whilom wife of King Henry I., and daughter of Malcolm, king of Scotland, and his wife. Saint Margaret. She died in the year 1117. A day would not suffice to tell of all her goodness and uprightness of character." *William* says:—Matilda, King Henry's wife, daughter of Malcolm, king of the Scots, was descended from an old and illustrious stock of kings. She was, from a tender age, remarkable for holiness; rivalling her mother in godliness; never allowing anything wrong in her manners, as far as she herself was concerned; and, but for the king's bed, of unblemished chastity, and unscathed even by suspicion. Wrapped in hair-cloth under her regal dress, she used, in Lent, to wear out the thresholds of the churches with her bare feet; nor did she shrink from washing the feet of the sick, or touching with her hands their sores dripping with matter, and, finally, lingering over them with long kisses, and laying their table; and her one pleasure was listening to divine service. Amid all this, she was snatched away, to the great loss of her country's people—but not to her own. Her body was nobly cared for, entering into its rest at Westminster; while her spirit showed, by no trifling tokens, that it dwells in heaven. She died, willingly leaving the throne after seventeen years and six months. Thus far *William*. But her sister Mary, Countess of Bouillon, departed this life in the third year before her sister's death, and rests in peace at Saint Saviour's monastery in Bermondsey, on the other side of London. Though she had not royal rank, she was no less upright than the queen, her sister. Her marble tomb, having the images of kings and queens engraved upon it, shows forth the descent of her who rests there. On the surface of that tomb, an inscription, written in letters of gold, thus briefly sums up her life and extraction:—

"Here the good Countess Mary lies entombed;
Whose acts with charity and kindness bloomed.
Royal her blood, she grew in virtue's might;
Kind to the poor, dwell she in heaven's height."

These two sisters, Matilda and Mary, daughters of King Malcolm and Margaret, fitly adorned their high birth by their marriage, their gentle demeanour, their great piety, and their free-handed dispensing of their worldly goods to the poor and to churches.

CHAPTER XXX.

Praise of the virtues of that Queen Matilda; of one good work especially, told by her hr other, King David, to the Abbot Baldred.

WHOSOEVER would write about the wondrous glory of the good queen Matilda, sister of the said kings, Edgar, Alexander, and David (whom I shall tell you about), of her virtuous mind, how zealous and devout she was in divine service and sacred vigils, how lowly, moreover, with all her power—whosoever would do this, will show forth to us another Hester in our times. We have forborne to do this, both on account of the magnitude of the subject, and because our knowledge of these things is, as yet, too little. I will, however, relate one thing she did, which I heard from the mouth of David, a king renowned and never to be forgotten, and whereby, in my opinion, how she behaved to Christ's poor will be clearly enough brought out. When, says he, I was still a youth serving at the king's court, one night while I was in my lodging with my fellows, doing I know not what, I was called by the queen herself to her chamber, and went there accordingly; and lo! a house full of lepers, and, standing in the midst, the queen, who, having laid aside her cloak, and girded herself with a linen cloth, put water into a basin, and began to wash and dry their feet, pressing them, when dry, between her hands, and kissing them most devoutly. "What doest thou, madam?" said I to her. "Surely, if the king knew of such a thing, he would never deign to touch, with his lips, thy mouth defiled by such rottenness." She then, smiling, said:—"Who knows not that the feet of the everlasting King are to be preferred to the lips of a king who must die? Of a truth, therefor called I thee, that thou might, by my example, learn to do such works." Then, taking up the basin, "Do," said she, "what thou didst behold me doing." At these words, I was sore afraid, and answered that I could on no account undergo that. For as yet I knew not the Lord, and His Spirit had not been revealed unto me. She, however, went on persisting; so I laughed out, "Have mercy on me!" and hied me back to my fellows. Now King Alexander, than whom no man was more devoted to the clergy, more bountiful to strangers, or more unbending towards his own people, paid the debt of nature at Strivelin (Stirling), in full health of body and faculties, on the 24th of April 1124, and, being taken away from this life, gave up the ghost to heaven, and his body to the ground. He was buried in state at Dunfermline on the day of Saint Mark the Evangelist, near his father, in front of the great altar, after having completed seventeen years and twenty-one days on the throne.

CHAPTER XXXI.

Accession of the Messed King David—Praise of him and his brothers—He weds Matilda, daughter and heiress of Waldeof, Earl of Huntingdon.

DAVID, the youngest of the sons of Malcolm and Margaret, and the pride of his race, succeeded his brother Alexander in the year above mentioned—the eighteenth of the emperor Henry V.—and reigned twenty-nine years, two months, and three days.

He was pious and God-fearing; bountiful in almsgiving; vigorous towards his people; sagacious in the task he was intent upon, of enlarging the kingdom by fair means; and, in short, he shone forth in the beauty of every virtue—whence he always abounded in the ripe fruit of good works. How very powerful this king was, how many conquests he made, above all other kings, by fair means, and how many abbeys and houses of God he founded, *Baldred*, in bewailing his death, will show forth truly to the reader, as will be seen below. He, indeed, betrayed no pride in his manners, no cruelty in his words, nothing unseemly in what he said or did. There was no king like him among the kings of the earth in his day; for he was godly, wise, lowly, modest, sober, and chaste, etc. Never, says *William*, have we been told among the events of history, of three kings,—and at the same time brothers,—who were of holiness so great, and savoured so much of the nectar of their mother's godliness. For, besides their feeding sparingly, their plentiful almsgiving, their zeal in prayer, they so thoroughly subdued the vice that haunts king's houses, that never was it said that any but their lawful wives came to their bed, or that any one of them had shocked modesty by wenching. Before this King David was raised to the throne, the king of the English, his sister the good Queen Matilda's husband, gave him to wife Matilda, the daughter and heiress of Waldeof, Earl of Huntingdon, and Judith, who was the niece of the first King William; and, of this Matilda, David had a son named Henry, a meek and godly man, and of a gracious spirit, in all things worthy to have been born of such a father. Meanwhile the empress Matilda, on her husband the emperor's death without children, came back to her father Henry, king of England; and the latter afterwards gave her to wife to Geofiroy, Count of Anjou, who begat of her a son, Henry, the future king of England. On the death of the aforesaid Henry, king of England, Stephen, Count of Boulogne, and his nephew, through his sister, seized the throne, in violation of his oath—for he had, during the said king's lifetime, consented by oath that the kingdom should go to the king's daughter, the empress Matilda. Count Geoffroy was indignant at this, but did him little, if any, hurt.

CHAPTER XXXII.

War waged by King David against Stephen, King of England—Conquest of Northumbria and Cumbria by a Battle fought at Allerton.

WHEN David, king of Scots, and uncle of that empress, heard this, he at once rose up against Stephen, and began to lay waste the northern regions of England—namely, Northumbria and Cumbria. And when he had repeatedly invaded now this, now that, region, and plundered them, the nobles of both provinces, at the head of a large force, beset him at Allerton (Northallerton), on the 21st of August, and there a battle was fought, and many fell on either side. At length, when a great multitude of the English had been slain, the others fled, and many of the nobles were carried off prisoners. They all, however, went back about the Feast of All Saints, being freed by ransom; while Cumbria, as well as Northumbria, and their pertinents, were surrendered to King David. But King David and King Stephen were straightway set at peace on this wise: to wit, that Northumbria should go back to King Stephen, while Cumbria was freely left with King David. This peace, however, which was entered into between them, lasted only a short time; for King David made ready for war with the Northumbrians. Wherefore Turstan, archbishop of York, came to the castle of Marchmont—that is, Roxburgh—and meanwhile obtained from the king that he should not, for the time, lay the country waste. But not long after, when the truce came to an end, the country was all sadly laid waste, forasmuch as King

Stephen would not give it to David's son Henry, whom he had begotten of the aforesaid Countess Matilda. So the following year—that is, in 1138—on Ash-Wednesday, King Stephen came with a large army to Roxburgh; and being there struck with a sudden panic, he straightway returned in shame. Then, again, the following year, this King Stephen came to Durham, where he tarried fifteen days, to treat for peace; while King David was at Newcastle. They had a solemn interview on the subject of peace; and, at the instance of Queen Matilda,—Stephen's wife, and King David's niece through his sister Mary,—they came to an understanding to this effect: namely, that King David's son, Henry, should do homage to King Stephen for the earldom of Huntingdon, and freely hold the earldom of Northumberland. For Matilda, this Henry's mother, was the daughter and heiress of Waldeof, Earl of Huntingdon, who was the son and heir of Siward, Earl of Northumberland. Now, when King David returned from Newcastle, he came to Carlisle, in which town he had a very strong keep built, and made the city walls a great deal higher. To him, moreover, repaired Henry, his niece, the Empress Matilda's son, and future king of England, having been sent by his mother; and he there received the knightly belt from King David, having first given a pledge that his heirs would at no time lop off any part of the lands which had then, through this feud with England, passed under the dominion of the Scots.

CHAPTER XXXIII.

David's son Henry weds Ada, daughter of William Earl of Warenne—Their Sons and Daughters, and to whom the latter were wedded—Henry's death.

KING David's son, Henry, Earl of Northumberland and Huntingdon, took Ada to wife, the daughter of the elder, and sister of the younger, *William*, Earl of Warenne, and sister of Robert, Earl of Leicester, and of Waleran, Count of Melent (Melun). Her mother was the sister of Radulf, Count of Peronne, and cousin to Louis, king of France. By her he had three sons; namely, Malcolm, the future king of Scotland; David, who was afterwards Earl of Huntingdon and Garviach; and William, who was also to be afterwards king—and as many daughters. One, Ada, was given in marriage to Florence, Count of Holland. The second, Margaret, wedded Conan, Duke of Brittany and Earl of Richmond, and bore him a daughter, named Constance, who was given in marriage to Geoffroy, brother of Richard, king of England. Of her this Geoffroy begat a son, named Arthur, who was afterwards drowned at sea, a daughter named Alice, who conceived of Peter Mauclerk, and bore a son, named John, afterwards Duke of Brittany, and another daughter, named Eleanor, who perished at sea, with her brother Arthur. Earl Henry's third daughter, Matilda, moreover, departed this life in the same year as her father. Now this Henry, the king's only son, Earl of Northumberland and Huntingdon, a youth of comely mien, with his father's virtues budding within him, was taken away from this life on the 12th of June 1152, before he had completed the years of the first bloom of youth. He was a most handsome lad, amiable to all men, the expected successor to the throne, a prince of most unassuming spirit, a well-disciplined and pious man, devout towards God, and a most compassionate guardian of the poor; in short—to recount all his good qualities—he was in all things like his father, save that he was a little more fair-spoken. Leaving the three sons above mentioned, and two daughters surviving him, he was, amid very deep mourning and wailing on the part of both Scots and English, buried near Roxburgh, at the Monastery of Calkhow (Kelso), which his father had reared from its very foundations, and endowed with ample possessions and great honours. In the fourth year of King David, Lothaire was elected to succeed the emperor Henry V., and was eleven years emperor. In the seventh year of this same David, his wife. Queen Matilda, died, and was buried at Scone. The same year, Angus, earl of Moray, was, with his men, slain at Strucathrow. In the fifteenth year, Conrad III. succeeded the emperor Lothaire, and was fifteen years emperor. The same year died John de Temporibus, in the three hundred and sixty-first year of his age; for he was a squire of Charles the Great. At this time, likewise, flourished the great teacher, Richard of Saint Victor, the Scot. In the eighteenth year was born to Henry, the king's son aforesaid, a son named Malcolm, who was to be king; in the nineteenth, David, afterwards earl; and in the twentieth William, who was, likewise, to be king.

CHAPTER XXXIV.

King David bids his grandson Malcolm, Henry's son, he taken about through the kingdom, and proclaimed as the future King—David's death to be bewailed, not on his own account, but for the Scots.

KING DAVID, disguising his sorrow at the death of his only son, straightway took Malcolm, his aforesaid son's firstborn, and giving him Duncan, Earl of Fife, as governor, bade him be taken about, with a large army, through the country, in Scotland, and proclaimed heir to the throne. Taking likewise the younger brother William, the king came to Newcastle; and having there taken hostages from the Northumbrian chiefs, he made them all subject to the dominion of that boy. What was done then with the third grandson David, or where he was, I have not found in any writings. But the king came back, and left nothing in disorder, nothing unsettled, in all the ends of the kingdom. Then, the following year, after Easter, he went to Carlisle, that he might settle the affairs of the west of the kingdom also, as of the east; when, all of a sudden, that godly and religious king was smitten with a grievous sickness, and, on the 22d of May, the Sunday before Ascension-day, in the year 1153, after he had ruled the kingdom gloriously for twenty-nine years and one month, he died happily, putting off his manhood, and surrendering his body to the earth, and his soul to the fellowship of angels in heaven. He was buried in state in the pavement before the high altar of the church of the Holy Trinity at Dunfermline, which, first founded by his father and mother, had been added to in property and buildings by his brother Alexander, while he himself also had loaded and endowed it with more ample gifts and honours; and he was laid there, at a good old age, beside his parents and brothers. His memory is blessed through all generations; for there never, from time immemorial, arose a prince like him. He was so devout in divine service, that he never missed saying and hearing, day by day, all the canonical hours, and even the vigils for the dead. And this also was praiseworthy in him—that, in a spirit of prudence and firmness, he wisely toned down the fierceness of his nation; and that he was most constant in washing the feet of the poor, and merciful in feeding and clothing them. He, moreover, behaved with lowliness and homeliness towards strangers, pilgrims, and regular and secular clergy; and most lavishly gave them gifts of his bounty. For he was a glorious king, fed and clad with everyday thrift; and, in holiness and integrity of life and in disciplined behaviour, he showed himself on a level even with votaries of religion. And, in sooth, his life, worthy to be praised—nay, to be wondered at—by all, was followed by a precious death. Therefore, whosoever aims at dying a happy death, let him read the life of this king so dear to God, and the following lament on his death; and, by the example of his most happy death, let him learn how to die.

CHAPTER XXXV.

Preface to the Abbot Baldred's Lament on King David's death—Praise of Henry, king of England, forasmuch as King David sprang from his family, and was knighted by him.

HERE follows the Preface to the Lament of the Abbot Baldred of Rivaulx, on King David's death; which he wrote in sorrow and wailing, and sent to the son of that David's niece, the empress—namely, Henry, who was to be king of England—that he might, by his example, learn the way to live aright, as well as to die blessed:—

To the most illustrious Henry, Duke of Normandy, and Count of Aquitaine and Anjou, brother Baldred, by some called Ethelred, the servant of Christ's servants who are at Rivaulx—greeting and prayers.—So much is virtue in accordance with nature, and vice opposed to her, that even the vicious will praise and think well of virtue; nor will even the vicious palliate vice, if it follow upon the judgment of man's reason. For Vice, blushing herself, as it were, at the foulness inborn in her, always seeks a lurking-place, and longs for secrecy; while Virtue, on the other hand, alive to her own comeliness and grace, is at all times dancing and tripping it, only from her lowliness avoiding the common gaze, and shrinking from the witness of man. Since, therefore, the love of virtue and the hatred of vice dwell by nature in a reasoning soul, whoever strives after virtue and good behaviour easily draws and turns unto him the love of all men. Hence is it, most illustrious sir, that the fame of thy virtue has sunk deep into the minds of many who have not seen thee with their eyes; for it is a wonder, no less than a delight, to all to find, at such an age, so much wisdom; amid such allurements, so much self-restraint; in matters so great, so much foresight; in so lofty a station, such austerity; in such austerity, such kindliness. For who is not amazed that a youth, who is struggling for the throne should eschew rapine, forbear from slaughter, keep from setting on fire, bring no hardships upon the poor, preserve peace and respect towards priests and churches? Whence thou art not unworthily proclaimed by all the glory of Anjou, the bulwark of Normandy, the hope of England, and the pride of Aquitaine. This alone is left—that thou should acknowledge Christ Jesus as the bounteous Dispenser of these gifts, and long for Him as thy Keeper. But I, indeed, bethinking myself of whose seed thou art sprung from, give thanks unto the Lord my God for that, in such fathers' stead, such a son has shone, like a fresh flood of light, upon us. And though all thine ancestors' virtues have met in thee, yet I rejoice, above all, that the spirit of David, the most Christian king of Scots, rests within thee. For I deem that it was through God's Providence it came to pass that King David's pure hands girded thee with the knightly belt, that, through them, the grace of Christ might pour into thee the virtue of that king's chastity, lowliness, and godliness. And as, sorrowing for his recent death, I have shortly, less as a historian than as a mourner, summed up his life and character, according as my feelings wavered between love and fear, hope and grief, I am anxious to address this lament unto thee, taking thee, in my inmost heart's love, as the heir of his godliness. And when thou have read therein his praiseworthy life and precious death, imitate thou the former, that thou may be worthy to rival the latter.

CHAPTER XXXVI.

Beginning of the Lament, for all his people had reason to bewail him.

THE God-fearing and pious King David has passed away from this world. Though he has found a place worthy of his soul, yet his death bespeaks our wailing. For who, but he who grudges peace and prosperity to mankind, would not mourn that a man the world stands so much in need of, should have been withdrawn from human affairs? Young men and maidens, old men and children, put on sackcloth, and sprinkle yourselves with ashes; let your crying be heard on high, and your wailing in the heavens. O priests of the Lord, and ministers of your God,—weep ye between the sacristy and the altar; for he has departed from you, who was wont to cheer you, to clothe you twice over, to endow you with gifts, and exalt you with honours. Nevertheless, weep ye not over him, but weep ye over yourselves and your sons. Indeed, even now the Spirit tells me he is resting from his troubles: for his works follow him. Therefore no evil has befallen that best of men; if any has befallen, it has befallen us. But how can I say—"If any has befallen"? Alas! it is beyond belief how great an evil has befallen us; for we have lost a man who lived not for himself but for all men, cared for all men, and looked to the wellbeing of all men; the guide of manners, the chider of wickedness, the encourager of virtue; whose life was the mould of lowliness, the mirror of righteousness, and the pattern of chastity. He was a meek king, a righteous king, a chaste king, a lowly king. Who would find it easy to say how profitable he was unto the life of man—he whom meekness had made loveable, righteousness terrible, chasteness calm, and lowliness affable? And if all these things are deemed most worthy of praise in any private person, how much more so in a king, to whom power gives freely what is unlawful, whose faults his underlings eagerly ape and fawningly applaud—while impunity gives boldness, and lust sharpens and kindles wantonness? For the sinner is praised by sinners for the desires of his heart; the unrighteous speak well of him who worketh unrighteousness. Who, then, is this, that we may praise him? For he has done wonders who could transgress in his life, and transgressed not. Who is like unto thee among the kings of the earth, O best of kings; who didst show thyself poor amidst gold, lowly on a throne, chaste among pleasures, mild in arms?—who didst behave to the people with moderation, to knights as an equal, to priests as an inferior, becoming all things to all men, that thou might counsel all men to virtue.

CHAPTER XXXVII.

Lament continued—He was beloved by God and man, and undertook the Sovereignty rather because of others' need than through lust of power.

JUSTLY, therefore, is the remembrance of thy name sweet to our hearts, soothing to our feelings, celebrated in our discourse; for that title fits thee well—"beloved of God and man;" and thy memory is blessed. David was truly beloved of God, Who directs the meek in judgment. Who teaches the mild His ways. That mild and lowly-hearted God loved, forsooth, the meek and godly king, rewarding his uprightness at a great price even in this life, not sparing the misdeeds of his life, now punishing, now recompensing; but always giving heed to the object of his wishes, and thus always hearkening unto him to his well-being. So didst Thou, Lord, hearken unto him—so, God, didst Thou bestead him, even though taking vengeance on all his devices. For in him was surely fulfilled, to the very letter, what is written in the Psalm, "The meek shall inherit the earth, and delight in fulness of peace." Now, we know that he sought not the kingship, but shrank from it; and that he rather undertook it because of others' need, than greedily seized and entered upon it through lust of power. Hence he so shrank from those services which, after the manner of their fathers, are rendered by Scottish men on a king being newly raised to the throne, that it was with difficulty that the bishops could get him to receive them. But, on his elevation to the kingship, he betrayed no pride in his behaviour, no cruelty in words, no unseemliness in deeds. Hence, all the savageness of that nation became meekness, and was soon overlaid with so much kindliness and lowliness, that, forgetting their inborn fierceness, they bowed their necks under the laws which the king's meekness laid down, and thankfully welcomed a peace until then unknown to them. Nor did that meekness seem slack or slothful; for, in punishing the wicked, it yielded in all things to justice, so that the king should not seem to bear the sword in vain; and he kept his meekness in his heart, lest he should seem not to wreak judgment, but rather to humour his impulses. I believe that he never, without a heart sore bruised, wreaked vengeance even on those who had been guilty of treason towards him. We have often seen him beat his breast, and shed tears, in punishing robbers and traitors; so as to make it manifest that, in punishing the guilty, he, as the administrator of the laws, obeyed justice, but gave not way to fierceness. Therefore he, as being meek, not unjustly inherited the earth—more of it than any of his ancestors were masters of, in our day; and he delighted in fulness of peace between savage nations, which were set against each other by differences of tongue and manners, and were most unfriendly one to the other, because of the slaughter and wounds each had dealt to the other—a peace which he settled with so much tact, and kept with so strong a will, that we have hardly ever seen such a treaty preserved for so long a time even between kindred nations, and men of the same blood and tongue.

CHAPTER XXXVIII.

Lament continued—Bishoprics and Monasteries founded and endowed by him.

He excelled in this, it seems to me—that he so kept within bounds on either side that, for all the strictness of his justice, he was beloved by all, and for all the mildness and mercy of his justice, he was feared by all; although he always longed rather to be loved than feared. Hence he seemed not undeservedly beloved by God and man. He was plainly beloved by God; for at the very outset of his reign, he diligently practised the things of God, in building churches and founding monasteries, to which, also, he gave increase of property and wealth, as each had need. For, whereas he had found only three or four bishops in the whole kingdom of the Scots, while the other churches tottered on without a chief pastor, with both morals and substance going to wrack and ruin, at his death he left twelve bishoprics, what with the old ones he restored, and the new he reared. He also established and left monasteries of divers orders—the Cluniac, the Cistercian, the Tyronensian, the Arovenian, the Præmonstratensian, the Belvacian—namely, those of Calkhow (Kelso), Melrose, Jedwart (Jedburgh), Newbotill (Newbattle), Holmcultrane, Dundrennan, the monastery of Holyrood at Edinburgh, those of Cambuskenneth and Kinloss, and a monastery of holy nuns close to Berwick, as well as many others full of friars. Among these he was even as one of themselves; praising goodness, and well-pleasing, and perfect;—and if haply anything less worthy of praise cropped up, he would be ashamed, and would disguise it; submissive to all men, caring for all men; lavishing much, and exacting nothing. Oh! sweet soul, whither art thou gone away, whither fled? Our eyes seek thee, and cannot find thee; our ears are listening to hear the voice of thy mirth, the voice of lowliness, the voice of shriving, the voice of comforting—and lo, it is hushed. Where is that most gentle look which beamed so mildly on the poor, so meekly on the holy, so mirthfully on thy companions? Where are those eyes so full of godliness and grace, wherewith thou wast wont to rejoice with the joyful, and to weep with those that wept? What do ye, O my eyes, what do ye? Why do ye not unfeignedly bring forth that wherewithal ye are in labour, and give vent to that ye hide within you? Shed ye tears day and night, and spare not; for this shall be my delight in remembering my sweetest lord and friend. Nor do I mourn alone. I know there are, mourning with me, priests and clerics, whom he revered as fathers. There are holy nuns mourning,—and monks, whom he took to his bosom as brothers. There are, mourning, knights, whose comrade—and not their lord—he acknowledged himself. There are, mourning, widows, whom he shielded; the fatherless, whom he cheered; the poor, whom he sustained; the wretched, whom he cherished.

CHAPTER XXXIX.

Lament continued—He was the comforter of the sorrowing and the father of the fatherless.

He was, indeed, the comforter of the sorrowing, the father of the fatherless, and the ready judge of the widow. For while he intrusted the other business of the country to other judges, he always kept for himself what concerned the poor and the widows. He heard, he defended, he judged them. Nor was any poor man, widow, or orphan, who wanted to lay any grievance before him, forbidden to walk into his presence; but as soon as they were shown in by the usher,—even though the king were engaged in the most important and urgent matters or deliberations, with any persons, great or small,—he would break off everything to hear them. I have even seen him, with my own eyes, sometimes, when ready to go out hunting, and, with his foot in the stirrup, on the point of mounting his horse, withdraw his foot, at the voice of a poor man begging that a hearing should be given him, leave his horse, and walk back into court, giving up all thoughts of returning to his design for that day; and surpassing, or at least rivalling, the judgments of Trajan—that most courteous and princely chief—kindly and patiently hear the cause on which he had been appealed to. He was, moreover, wont to sit at the gate of the king's court, and hear carefully the causes of poor old women, who, on certain days, were called up from any part of the country they came to; and he would give satisfaction to each, often after much trouble. For they would often wrangle with him, and he with them, when he would not admit the person of a poor man to judgment, in violation of justice, and they would not listen to reason, as he put it to them. I will say nothing of how he won upon the feelings of all men by the wondrous courtesy and sweetness of his manner, how he suited himself to the ways of all men, so that he was neither thought soft by the harsh, nor hard by the soft. In short, if it fell out that priest, or knight, or monk, rich or poor, citizen or pilgrim, tradesman or peasant, talked with him, he conversed with each on his business or duties in so seemly and unassuming a tone, that each in turn thought the king had his affairs only at heart; and thus he sent them all away merry and edified. For he did his utmost to draw on that rough and boorish people towards quiet and chastened manners; so much so that he looked after not only the great affairs of State, but all things, down to the very least—such as gardens, buildings, or orchards—in order that he might, by his example, stir his people up to do likewise.

CHAPTER XL.

Lament continued—He was always anxious to bring hack to peace and concord those at variance, especially wrangling Clergy.

BUT, above all things, he was anxious that priests of the Lord, especially, and men of religious orders, should be free from feuds, as well at home among themselves as with those outside. So whensoever strife arose among them—such is man's wretchedness!—his spirit had no rest, nor had his flesh repose, until he had by prayers and coaxing—nay, sometimes by tears, but seldom by threats, made them be at peace again, as of yore. Nor, in such a cause, was he too proud, humbly, with holy words, to bow that kingly head to the knees of such an one as haply seemed too unbending on this side; so that he who could not be overcome by kindliness might be overcome by shame. Moreover, there is truly no need to praise the chastity that was in him: for, after he had once entered into wedlock, he was true to his wife's bed; so that not only did he never know another, but he never even looked at another unbecomingly; and, as in flesh, so was he pure in mind, hand, thought, behaviour, eyes, and speech. For his life was so public, his doings so open and above-board, that he was never even singed by ever so light a suspicion on this score. Nought about him was hidden but his counsels: and his chamber was open to all, at his sitting or lying down, or at his retiring. Hence—wonderful to say!—with so much grace was he endowed by God's power, that, after the death of his wife, whom he outlived twenty-three years, he never, even in sleep, suffered the wrong of fleshly taint. Why tremblest thou, O my soul? Why art thou afraid to bring forward such things as are unpleasing—since we must not only praise the righteousness of good men, but also commend their repentance, after any shortcoming? We have read that Aaron, the first high priest under the law, vouchsafed consent unto the people, who asked that an idol be made unto them. Moses himself was pronounced, by the judgment of heaven, to have done wrong at the waters of strife. The Scripture bears witness that Miriam, the prophetess, was smitten with leprosy, for murmuring against Moses. After numberless gifts of spiritual graces, holy David, as though forgetful of God's goodness, first committed adultery with the wife of his faithful servant, whom he afterwards slew through marvellous treachery. I own it—our David also sinned. He sinned, not by defiling himself with any wickedness, but by ministering more than behoved him to others' cruelty by his might. For when, after the death of his sister's son Henry, king of England, he had led an army into England, these wild men, bitter foes to the English, raged, beyond the wont of man, against the Church, against priests, against either sex, against all ages, and wreaked cruel judgments upon them. Now, though these things were done against his will—nay, though he forbade them—still, as it was in his power not to have brought them, not to have brought them again when he had once put them to the test, or perhaps to have better kept them under, we own with tears that he also sinned. Let others make allowances for him by pleading his zeal for justice, by bethinking themselves of the oath which he had taken, by asserting loudly that it beseemed his kingly virtue, because he kept his word; because he broke not his oath; because he bore arms against men forsworn; because he tried to bring back to the rightful heirs a kingdom which their father had made over to them, which the clergy and people had confirmed to them by a sworn pledge. Haply, the record of this plea had some place in thy pity, good Jesus; but I, knowing that it is good to confess unto Thee, have chosen to beg, not to plead—seeking mercy, not challenging judgment.

CHAPTER XLI.

Lament continued—He would have resigned the Throne, and betaken himself to the spot where Our Lord suffered, had he not been turned back by the advice of Churchmen, the tears of the Poor, the groans of the Widow, the desolation of the People, and the crying and wailing of the whole Country.

THEREFORE I say, Enter not into judgment with thy servant, O Lord; for in thy sight is no man justified, unless forgiveness of all his sins is vouchsafed him by Thee. For the king himself would rather accuse than excuse himself—would rather beat his breast than thrust it forth. We know also that he so loathed this sin, and sighed after virtue most zealously, that he would have resigned his throne, laid down his sceptre, and betaken himself to holy warfare on the spot where Our Lord suffered and rose again, had he not been turned back by the advice of priests and abbots, the tears of the poor, the groans of the widow, the desolation of the people, and the crying and wailing of his whole kingdom; and though he was kept back in body, he was not in mind and wishes. He trusted altogether to the advice of monks; and keeping beside him some good brethren, renowned in warfare for the temple of Jerusalem, he made them the guardians of his morals by day and night. I pass over his almsgiving, his frequency in prayer, at mass, and in psalmody; for he had been the wonder of all, from childhood itself, for his observance of these things. Now this is what cheers me in my sorrow, good Jesus—not to be able to say that he sinned not, but that he repented, that he wept, that he confessed; that he followed the advice of Daniel, who said to Nebuchadnezzar, "Ransom thy sins with alms, and thine iniquities with mercy to the poor." Moreover, O Spring of goodness, and Source of pity, didst Thou not bestead him when Thou didst take vengeance on all his devices? Thou didst chide him, O Lord, Thou didst chide him as a father chideth his son; yet in mercy, for in Thy wrath Thou didst not withhold Thy mercy. For Thou gavest him the affection of a son amid scourgings, so that he should not murmur nor backslide,—nay, should give thanks amid scourgings, saying, with the Prophet, "All Thou hast done unto us, O Lord, in righteous judgment hast Thou done it." These were his words, these his feelings, when his host was scattered abroad, when he was driven by his own knights to yield to the force of circumstances. These were his words when God sent as a foe against him a certain mock bishop, who lied and said he was the Earl of Moray's son; wherein was clearly enough seen the power of God, in whose hand are all the laws of kingdoms, by whose nod all things are regulated—the Lord Himself, who maketh peace, and createth evil. Let not the wise, therefore, boast of his wisdom, nor the strong of his strength; for the steps of man are guided by the Lord, who scourged with the lies of a certain monk that invincible king, who had subdued unto himself so many barbarous nations, and had, without great trouble, triumphed over the men of Moray and of the Islands. Yet, though that monk straightway reaped a reward worthy of his works, this most Christian king acknowledged the hand of the Lord in all these things.

CHAPTER XLII.

Lament continued—God scourged him in his Son's death—His God and Lord found him watching.

LASTLY, O God of vengeance, that his patience might be made known unto all, Thou didst pour upon him Thy wrath, and all the wrath of Thy fury, chastening him with sore chastisement, when Thou didst take from him his only son. And such a son! For he was a most comely lad, amiable and sweet towards all men, beloved by all who saw him, and inclined to all goodness. O Lord my God, with what stripes of sorrow didst Thou grieve his heart, when he himself bore to the grave his only-begotten, whom he had found most loving and like himself, and who, he hoped, would have done such a service unto him. Nevertheless, while the rest were weeping and wailing, this man, in whom nothing was wanting for virtue, bore with so much patience the rod of his Father Most High, that he both refrained from tears, and, forgetful of himself, took his meals with his household, that day, after his royal custom. Far be it from us, therefore, to lay this sin at his door; seeing that God's justice punished it in this life—that he himself condemned it by the confession of his own mouth—that he washed it with his tears—that he atoned for it by his alms—that he cleansed it by daily contrition of heart; himself his own accuser, himself judge against himself, himself his own executioner. "For if we judged our own selves," says Paul, "verily we should not be judged." Lay down, then, O my soul, lay aside thy sadness for a while, and muse in gladness of mind on the spirit of the end of his life, which he spent so religiously—the spirit wherein, being turned unto God with his whole heart, and watching with loins girded and lamps burning, he awaited the coming of the Lord. He watched—a man who took upon himself to judge nothing, to decree nothing, to appoint nothing, without the advice of monks and men most upright. He watched—a man who gave praise to the Lord seven times a day, and rose at midnight to shrive himself unto Him. He watched—a man who, with his own hands, this year, daily laid out upon the poor quite twice his wonted alms, after the sacred solemnities of the mass, and of prayers; and thus, lingering, the rest of the day-time, among clerks and religious brethren, listened, with lowly ear, to such things as were unto edification. He watched—a man who most wisely made his will a year before he departed this life; and, handing over what treasure he had into the hands of monks, intrusted it to their good faith to mete out as he himself had prescribed. He watched—a man who, every Lord's day, shrived himself of his sins, and partook of Christ's body and blood; and thus, with ears ever listening for the voice of the bridegroom calling, anxiously looked for his coming.

CHAPTER XLIII.

Lament continued—His Time was all taken up with Prayer, Alms, or some seemly task

IN short, when, on account of something our house needed, I came into his presence in these holy days of Lent, I own I found, in the king, a monk—in the court, a cloister—in a palace, the discipline of a monastery. For, certain hours he spent in religious duties, intent on psalms and prayers; and a certain time, likewise, he set apart for ministering to the poor. And that nothing might be wanting in him for a seemly life, he even, at a meet hour, busied himself in some seemly task, such as planting herbs, or grafting upon another stock slips cut off from their own roots. Finally, after he had taken his meal at the right hour, he unbent his mind a little in some sort of religious ease, with religious brethren, and a few of the more distinguished men; and thus, after he had, while the sun was still up, gone through the usual service for the dead, when the hour of dusk was over, he sought his chaste bed without a word, and spoke no more to any one until sunrise. Oh! happy soul, which the Lord, when He came, found thus watching; and which, therefore, thus prepared, happily entered into wedlock with Him. But lo! the thought of our unhappiness breaks in upon the exultation of my spirit, and the fruit of tears, which sympathy brings forth, furrows with renewed grief a face which Christian faith and piety had dried. What, therefore, shalt thou do, O desolate Scotland! Who shall cheer thee? Who shall take pity on thee? Thy harp is turned into mourning; and thy pipes into the voice of weeping. Thy lamp is quenched; thy heart fainteth; thy manhood droopeth; the brightness of thy glory waneth—for he is no more who shed his light upon thee, and, of an untilled and barren land, made thee pleasant and plenteous. Thou once, a beggar among lands, wast wont, with thy hard sod, to bring hunger upon thine indwellers; but now, softer and more fruitful, thou dost, of thy fulness, relieve the wants of neighbouring lands. He it is that has decked thee with castles and towns, and with lofty towers. He it is that has enriched thy harbours with outlandish wares, and gathered together the wealth of other countries for thine enjoyment. He it is that has turned thy hairy cloaks into costly garments, and has covered thy nakedness of old with purple and fine linen. He it is that has quelled thy savage ways by Christian piety. He it is that has enjoined thee wedded chastity, which thou scarcely knewest—nay, even wouldst not keep inviolate when once entered upon; and has given a more seemly life unto thy priests. He it is that, by word as well as example, has prevailed upon thee to go often to church, and to be present at the divine sacrifices; and has made it known that due offerings and tithes should be paid to the priests. What then shalt thou bestow in return for all he has bestowed upon thee? Thou hast, in sooth, some in whom thou mayest requite him. Thou hast some to whom thou mayest give thanks for the good he did—to whom thou mayest pay the good turn which he earned. Thou hast them in his grandsons—from whom, haply, God's providence withdrew their grandfather's help so soon for nothing else but that thy loyalty might be put to the proof, and thy gratitude tested. They are, indeed, under age; but the king's age is reckoned according to the loyalty of his knights. Pay ye to the sons what ye owe to the father; let them find you thankful for the benefits ye have received.

CHAPTER XLIV.

Lament continued—The trials of the English taught the Scots to be faithful to their kings, and preserve mutual harmony among themselves.

MOREOVER, let the trials of the English teach you to be faithful to kings, and preserve mutual harmony amongst you; lest strangers eat up your country before your eyes, and the land be made desolate as by the ravages of the foe. For, as we read in Holy Writ, Joash was seven years old when he began to reign in Jerusalem, having been raised to the throne by the high priest Jehoiada, with the consent of the priesthood and people; and he reigned better during his more helpless years, under the advice of the high priest and the lords, than in his more stalwart age, in his own wisdom and power. Even as every kingdom divided against itself shall be made desolate, so a good understanding between the chiefs is the kingdom's stay. The king indeed is dead; but have ye, in the king's stead, the love he earned from you. Let that love dictate laws to you, fill up your concord to the brim, and constrain you to keep loyalty towards his boys, and friendship towards his allies: else heaven and earth will be witnesses against you;—the angels who were guardians of his chastity will be witnesses against you;—the saints ye gave as hostages of your fealty, by swearing on their relics, will be witnesses against you;—the king himself, who, through love for the boys, looks from that bright tract of heaven upon this earthly region, and is worthy of the loyalty and constancy of each, he himself will be a witness against you. But thou. Lord, King of Sabaoth, who judgest righteously and triest the reins and the heart, remember David and all his meekness, remember him in the boys he has left behind; for they are bequeathed unto Thee fatherless, and Thou shalt be the Helper of the orphans. And thou, sweetest king, be turned again unto thy rest; for the Lord hath dealt well with thee, seeing that he snatched thy soul from death, thine eyes from tears, and thy feet from slipping. This we take for granted from thy pity, good Jesus—of whom it was given him both to believe aright, and to live godly, and to die holily. For, as will be shown in what follows, a precious death closed his praiseworthy life, which, by Thy grace working in him, was moulded by the Christian faith.

CHAPTER XLV.

Lament continued—On Wednesday the 20th of May, he perceived that his dissolution was at hand; and having taken the Sacrament of the Lord's Body, he bade them bring forward the Lord's Cross.

BUT when smitten with the sickness whereby he was to be released from the flesh, on Wednesday, the 20th of May, perceiving that his dissolution was at hand, he called his attendants, and without hesitation explained to them what he felt was the matter with him. But they, in the way men do, fell to comforting the sick man, and went as far as to promise him life and health. This most wise king, however, taking no comfort at all in the promise of a longer life, begged that such things, rather, should be told and advised him, as the exigency of this last hour called for. And, as this hour came not upon him while he was unprepared, he renewed the will which he had made a year before; correcting certain things that had to be corrected, and by the advice of the monks, setting in order, in a few words, such state matters as seemed to need setting in order. Then turning to himself with his whole heart, he kept earnestly commending his last hours to God. And though all his limbs were heavy with the weight of illness, nevertheless he walked into the oratory, as he was wont, both for mass and for the canonical hours. But when, on Friday, his malady began to grow worse, and the violence of the disease had robbed him of the power of standing as of walking, he summoned the clerks and monks, and asked that the sacrament of the Lord's body should be given him; and on their making ready to bring him what he had ordered, he forbade them, saying that he would partake of those most holy mysteries before the most holy altar. When, therefore, he had been carried down into the oratory by the hands of the clerks and knights, and the mass had been celebrated, he begged that a cross he reverenced, which they call *the black cross*, should be brought forward for him to worship. Now that cross is an hand's breadth in length, wrought out of purest gold with marvellous workmanship, and opens and shuts like a case. Within it is seen a piece of the Lord's Cross (as has often been proved by the evidence of many miracles), with Our Saviour's likeness upon it, most handsomely carved out of ivory, and wondrously decked with golden ornaments. This cross, the pious Queen Margaret, this king's mother, who was sprung from the seed of the emperors and kings of Hungary and England, had brought to Scotland, and handed down as an heirloom to her sons. So when the king had most devoutly worshipped this cross, which was no less feared than loved by all Scottish folk, and had first, with many tears, shrived himself of his sins, he fortified himself for his departure by partaking of the heavenly mysteries.

CHAPTER XLVI.

Lament continued—His Extreme Unction—He threw himself off the bed upon the ground, and took that Sacrament with great devoutness.

AT last he was brought back into his chamber; and when the priests came to go through the sacrament of Holy Unction, he rose up, as best he could, and throwing himself off the pallet upon the ground, he received that healing rite with so much devoutness that, whenever the clerks chanted a little too hurriedly, he checked them by both hand and word, and himself followed every single word, and responded to every single prayer. When, therefore, everything had been duly fulfilled, he awaited the last day with the greatest quietness of body and mind, earnestly entreating his attendants to publish his death unto all as soon as he should be gone. "The sooner," said he, "my death becomes known, the sooner will God's pity hold out some comfort to me, through the good offices of my friends." Thus, from that time forth, rapt in God's praises, he subdued his drooping limbs to his spirit, which he was, all that day, by psalms and prayers, preparing for its departure. But on the Saturday—that is, the day before he departed this life—when he was reading over the one hundred and eighteenth Psalm, with great contrition of heart, and had, in the course of his psalmsinging, reached the sixteenth chapter of this Psalm, he groaned aloud, as the force of those words sank deep into his soul; and after repeating that chapter seven times, he cried out with inward emotion, "I have done judgment and justice; give me not over unto mine accusers." For he felt, through the teaching of the Spirit, if I mistake not, how he might most safely answer the accuser who treads close upon our heel (that is to say, our end), what prayers he might offer up to the Judge in his own defence; so he said, "I have done judgment,"—and so forth. In sooth, he who fulfils the judge's duty against himself, softens the stern judge's sentence; and he who, before death, does judgment in truth, fearlessly awaits God's judgment after death: wherefore he cried out devoutly, "I have done judgment," and so forth. The old accuser came unto Our Saviour; but finding nothing of his own in Him, who has done no sin, he departed abashed. What, therefore, shall he do, in whom the accuser, when he comes unto him, recognises something of his own—that is to say, a sin? Why, let him, of course, cry unto Him in whom the accuser shall find nothing, and say, "I have done judgment," and so forth. For there is a judgment of the heart, and there is a judgment of the lips, and there is a judgment in deed. That most Christian king did judgment in his heart, when his conscience pricked him inwardly for his shortcomings. He did it with his lips, when he confessed his sins against himself. He did it also in deed, when he punished himself with self-imposed smart. He has done judgment therefore, by accusing himself; and he has done justice by pitying the woes of others.

CHAPTER XLVII.

Lament continued—In his very sickness, when his life was at stake, he remembered the poor, and asked the Cleric, his secretary, whether he had dispensed the usual Alms that day.

FOR what is more just than that he who asks for mercy himself, should show mercy unto the needy? Now, how lavish that man was in showing mercy and lending to the poor, was clearly enough shown on that very day, wherein, though he had shut out from his breast all worldly anxiety, all cares of state, even all feeling for his sons, yet he laid not aside, in such a pass, that care which he was wont to take of the poor. In fact, in the middle of his psalm-singing, looking round at his cleric Nicholas, whom he had found most faithful in keeping his treasure and bestowing alms, he stretched forth his arm, and put it round the neck of the latter, so that he leant over the pallet; then the king asked him whether the alms he himself was wont to give out daily, with his own hands, among Christ's poor, had been dispensed that day. And when the latter had told him that everything had been done in the usual way, he gave thanks unto God, and repeated the psalm he had interrupted. Since, therefore, he has done judgment by punishing himself for his shortcomings, and has done justice by pitying others, trusting in the hope of God's mercy cried he out, "I have done judgment and justice; give me not over unto mine accusers;" and as the remaining verses of this chapter agree with this opening, no wonder he dwelt upon these with the most willingness and delight. And when he came to the one hundred and nineteenth psalm, feeling a something of sweetness and healthfulness therein, he repeated that also, like the former, seven times. Calling to mind, it may be, what distress he had endured, a little before, in the recollection of his sins—what comfort he had found in the hope of Christ's mercy, when he thought over the judgment and justice which he had done, he cried out, in great devoutness of mind, "In my distress I cried unto the Lord, and he heard me." But lest that cunning accuser should again trump up some guileful tale against him, he added what that psalm goes on to say:—"Deliver my soul, O Lord, from unrighteous lips, and from a deceitful tongue." But what shall be given thee, O Christian soul, or what shall be added unto thee, against a deceitful tongue? What but the sharp arrows of the Mighty One, and coals to spread desolation! Therefore cry thou:—"Take hold, O Lord, of weapons and shield; and stand up for my help."

CHAPTER XLVIII.

Lament continued—He went on praying while singing Psalms.

LET God himself hurl back against the enemy his sharp arrows,—the spear and the nails wherewith he was pierced upon the cross, and stabbed with five wounds, as it were by sharp arrows,— wounds whereby He, of His freely-vouchsafed goodness, healed our wounds, which the enemy had inflicted upon us by the gratification of our five senses. What, then, will the deceitful tongue of the wily serpent cast in my teeth, seeing that He who did no sin has borne the penalty of my sin, being wounded for our iniquities, and bruised for our misdeeds? If, therefore, to the sharp arrows (that is, faith in Thy suffering, good Jesus) be added the coals (that is, the fire of Thy love), the accusing enemy is quickly driven back, as is the blight of the sin clean swept away.—Then, with a lighter heart, and with many a sigh for things above, loathing this earthly estate through contemplation of the heavenly, he went on to say: "Woe is me, that my sojourn is prolonged! I have dwelt with the dwellers in Cedar; my soul hath long dwelt there." But I consider that what follows is also very appropriate to him:—"With those that hate peace, I am for peace; when I spake unto them, they fought against me without a cause,"—inasmuch as he so often spared those who betrayed him, and often denied a hearing to such as would pledge themselves to prove, by the ordeal of battle, others guilty of treason; and when his friends would say unto him, "If thou send these away thus, others will attempt a like misdeed against thee more fearlessly," he would answer that his life was not at the mercy of man, but rather was in God's power. Accordingly they often returned him evil for good; and while his care was for such things as would bring them peace, they would fight against him,—yea, without a cause. Moreover, from his repeating these verses seven times—which number, as we read, is hallowed by the Holy Ghost—we are plainly given to understand that Christ's Spirit itself was there, and poured into him the mood of those verses, fostering his drooping soul with its power. When, therefore, he was, by those who were there, besought to give his spirit rest from the labour of singing psalms, "Let me rather," said he, "muse on those things which are God's; that my spirit, about to set out homewards from this banishment, may be refreshed by a travelling-store of God's Word. For when I shall have been brought up for God's judgment, and shall stand trembling, none of you will answer for me, none of you will watch over me, nor is there any one who can pluck me out of His hand." In such devoutness did he reach the close of the day; and until the night which followed it did he linger in great tranquillity.

CHAPTER XLIX.

Lament continued—On Sunday the 24th of May, when the sun had dispelled the darkness, the King, taking leave of the darkness of the body, passed into the joys of the true light.

NOW, on the Sunday which preceded Christ's Ascension—that is to say, on the 24th of May—at daybreak, while the sun was, with the rays of his light, dispelling the darkness of night, the king, emerging from the darkness of the body, passed into the joys of the true light, with tranquillity so great that he seemed not to have died, and with devoutness so great that he was found to have raised towards heaven his two hands joined together upon his breast. Come ye and help him, ye saints of God! Come ye and meet him, ye angels of the Lord! Take ye up his soul, worthy of fellowship, with you, and lay it in Abraham's bosom, with Lazarus, whom he despised not, but cherished—with the holy apostles and martyrs, whose remembrance he furthered and upheld—with Christ's priests and confessors, whom he reverenced in their successors and their churches—with the holy virgins, with whom he vied in purity—with despisers of the world, of whom he made unto himself friends, of the mammon of unrighteousness, and to whom, in

Christ's name, he humbled himself in all lowliness. Let the mother of mercies stand by him—she whose pity is of the most avail to him, even as she is more powerful than the rest. But I, though a sinner, and unworthy, yet remembering the benefits, my sweetest lord and friend, which thou hast lavished upon me from my earliest years—remembering the favour wherein thou didst now, at the last, receive me—remembering the kindliness wherewith thou didst hearken unto all my petitions—remembering the munificence thou hast shown towards me—remembering the embraces and kisses wherewith, not without tears, thou didst send me away, while those who stood by marvelled—for thee do I shed my tears, give loose to my feelings, and pour out all my soul. This sacrifice do I offer for thee, thus do I requite thy kindness; and since this is too little, my mind shall, from its inmost marrow, always think of thee in that place where the Son is daily offered up to the Father, for the salvation of all men—the Son, who with the same God the Father and the Holy Ghost liveth and reigneth God, ever world without end. Amen.

CHAPTER L.

His Pedigree traced on the Father's side up to Japhet, son of Noah.

I THINK it meet in these writings to bring in this glorious King David's pedigree on the father's side, which I got long ago from the Lord Cardinal of Scotland, the noble Doctor Walter of Wardlaw, Bishop of Glasgow; that it may be known unto you, kings of these days, and to all readers, of how old, how noble, how strong and invincible a stock of kings he came (whereof ye also are come)— kings who have, until now, through the blessed King Most High, been keeping the kingly dignity unspotted for a longer time, with freer service, and, what is more glorious, with a stronger hold of the Catholic faith than all other kings, save only a few, if any. For that blessed King David was the son of the most noble Malcolm, king of Scots, the husband of the blessed Queen Margaret, and

Son of Duncan,

Son of Beatrice,
Daughter of Malcolm the Most Victorious,
Son of Kenneth,
Son of Malcolm,
Son of Dovenald,
Son of Constantine,
Son of Kenneth, the first sole sovereign; from whom, as was seen in Book IV., Chapter VIII., the royal line is traced to that most vigorous king, Fergus son of Erth, who nobly wrested the kingdom from the Romans and Picts, after these had usurped it, and held it three-and-forty years.

And that Erth was the son of Euchadius, brother to King Eugenius, who was slain by the Romans and Picts.

Eugenius was the son of Angusafith,
Son of Fechelmech,
Son of Angusa,
Son of Fechelmech Romach,
Son of Sencormach,
Son of Crucluith,
Son of Findach,
Son of Akirkirre,
Son of Echadius,
Son of Fechrach,
Son of Euchodius Reid,
Son of Conere,
Son of Mogal,
Son of Lugtach,
Son of Corbre,
Son of Dordremore,
Son of Corbrefynmore,
Son of Coneremore,
Son of Etherskeol,
Son of Ewin,

Son of Ellela,
Son of Iaire,
Son of Detach,
Son of Syn,
Son of Rosyn,
Son of Ther,
Son of Rether,
Son of Rwen,
Son of Arindil,
Son of Manre,
Son of Fergus, who brought the Scots out of Ireland, and first reigned over them in British Scotia; and the chain of whose royal lineage stretches up, as was seen above in Book I., Chapter XXVI., as far as Simon Brek, who brought over with him to Ireland, from Spain, the Coronation stone of the kings.

This Simon Brek was the son of Fonduf,
Son of Etheon,
Son of Glathus,
Son of Nothachus,
Son of Elchatha,
Son of Syrne,
Son of Deyne,
Son of Demal,
Son of Rothach, the first who dwelt in the Scottish islands. He was the son of Ogmayn,
Son of Anegus,
Son of Fiathath,
Son of Smyrnay,
Son of Synretha,
Son of Embatha,
Son of Thyema,
Son of Faleng,
Son of Etheor,

Son of Jair,
Son of Ermon,
Son of Michael Espayn,
Son of Bile,
Son of Neande,
Son of Bregayn,
Son of Bratha,
Son of Deatlia,
Son of Erchatha,
Son of Aldoch,
Son of Node,
Son of Nonael,
Son of Iber Scot,
Son of King Gaythelos and Scota, first king and queen of the Scottish nation. Whence this line:—

"Iber, their son, first bore the name of Scot."

This Gaythelos was the son of Neolos, king of Athens,
Son of Fenyas,
Son of Ewan,
Son of Glonyn,
Son of Lamy,
Son of Etheor,
Son of Achnemane,
Son of Choe,
Son of Boib,
Son of Jeyn,
Son of Mayr,
Son of Hethech,
Son of Abyur,
Son of Arthech,
Son of Aroth,
Son of Jara,

Son of Esralb,
Son of Richaith,
Son of Scot,
Son of Gomer,
Son of Japhet,
Son of Noah.

CHAPTER LI.

Prologue to his Pedigree on his Mother's side.

SINCE, says *Baldred*, we have, in this lament, given a short description of the excellent character of David, the pious king of Scots, I have thought it worth while to subjoin, briefly and truthfully, his pedigree on the mother's side; so that, when ye have seen, successors of his, how great was the prowess of your forebears of the same lineage, how in them manhood glowed and godliness shone forth, ye may even acknowledge that it is but natural for you to abound in wealth, to blossom with virtues, to be famous for your victories, and,—what is more than all this,—to shine with Christian piety and the prerogative of justice. For it is the greatest spur towards keeping one's character at its best, to know that one has gotten nobility of blood from such as were all of the best of men; as a noble mind is always ashamed to be found degenerate in a glorious race, and it is against nature that bad fruit should grow from a good root. Let me, then, starting from King David himself, the most renowned of men, and, even as was written above of his father's pedigree, ascending, through his most glorious mother, to Adam, the father of all mortals, show you the line of our English kinship, as I have been able to find it in the truest and oldest histories or chronicles; so that afterwards, passing over the oldest kings of England, whose history sheer length of time has swept away, we may, on our way back, take the more prominent kings, and succinctly touch upon their more lofty deeds. And, when ye have seen that their great glory has passed away through death and time, while they, through the merits of their lives, have earned the heavenly guerdon, which could not perish, ye shall learn always to set justice above wealth and worldly glory, that after the life which lasts for a time ye may reach the life everlasting.

CHAPTER LII.

His Pedigree on the Mother's side traced, according to Baldred, as far as Shem, son of Noah; and from him to Seth, the son of Adam, who is the father of all.

THIS most excellent King David, therefore, was the son of Margaret, the glorious queen of Scots, who enhanced the splendour of her name by the holiness of her character.

Her father was Edward,
Who was the son of the invincible King Edmund Ironside,
Whose father was Ethelred,
Whose father was Edgar the Peaceful,
Whose father was Edmund,
Whose father was Edward the Elder,
Whose father was the noble Alfred,
Who was the son of King Ethelwlf.
Who was the son of King Egbert,
Whose father was Alchmund,
Whose father was Eaffa,
Whose father was Aeppa,
Whose father was Ingels,
Whose brother was a most famous king, named Ine,
Whose father was Ceonred,
Who was the son of Ceowald,
Son of Cutha,
Son of Cuthwine,
Son of Ceaulin,
Son of Chinrik,
Son of Creodda,
Son of Ceordik. This king, after the lapse of forty-six years from the first coming of the Saxons into Britain, won a kingdom in Wessex; and,

in course of time, his successors conquered the other kingdoms of the English.

Ceordik was the son of Elesa,
Son of Eda,
Son of Gewise,
Whose father was Wige,
Whose father was Freawine,
Whose father was Freodegare,
Whose father was Brand,
Whose father was Baldege,

Whose father was Woden, among some called Mercury. He had so much weight among his people that they dedicated to his name the fourth day of the week, and called it Woden's day. This custom is, to this day, still kept up among the English; for they call that day Wednesday. The Roman heathens, indeed, used to call it Mercury's day.

This pedigree of Baldred's differs in some wise, though little, from that which William has given in his Chronicle. Now, as the above passage will do for my purpose, I forbear to follow up the matter any further; for I have read none but the books of these writers upon this genealogy. If, indeed, I had seen a third, I should have wished to leave out the odd one, and, in the end, follow the two which agreed.

ANNALS.

I.

Coronation of King Malcolm the younger Prince Henry's son, called "the Maiden."

NOW all the people took Malcolm, a boy of thirteen—a son of Henry, earl of Northumberland and Huntingdon, who was the son of King David himself—and made him king at Scone, in the room of his grandfather David; of whom it may truly be said: "Prosperity abideth with their seed; their grandchildren are an holy heritage." His brother William had the earldom of Northumberland in possession, while the earldom of Huntingdon was subject unto his youngest brother David, as will be seen below. No unworthy successor of David, king of Scots, was Malcolm, the eldest of his grandsons. For, treading in that king's steps in many good points, and even gloriously outdoing him in some, he shone like a heavenly star in the midst of his people. In the first year of his reign, Sumerled, kinglet of Argyll, and his nephews—the sons of Malcolm Macbeth, to wit—being joined by a great many, rose against their king, Malcolm, and disturbed and troubled great part of Scotland. Now that Malcolm was the son of Macbeth; but he lied and said he was the son of Angus, earl of Moray, who, in the time of King David of happy memory, was, with all his men, slain by the Scots at Strucathroch (Strickathrow in Forfar), while he was plundering the country. Upon his death, this Malcolm Macbeth rose against King David, as it were a son who would avenge his father's death; and while plundering and spoiling the surrounding districts of Scotland, he was at length taken, and thrust, by that same King David, into close confinement in the keep of Marchmont Castle. So Sumerled kept up the civil war; but his nephew, Donald, one of Malcolm Macheth's sons, was taken prisoner, at Withterne (Whithorn), by some of King Malcolm's friends, and imprisoned in that same keep of Marchmont, with his father. The year after this Donald was taken, his father Malcolm made peace with the king, while Sumerled still wickedly wrought his wickedness among the people.

II.

ON the death of the English king, Stephen, Henry, duke of Normandy, and son of the empress, was anointed king, in the second year of Malcolm, king of Scotland. As soon as he was raised to the throne, unmindful of his promise and oath, which he had formerly sealed with a vow to King David, his mother's uncle, he laid claim to Northumberland and Cumberland, which had now many years yielded obedience to the king of Scots, and was making great ado about invading them; and he also declared that the earldom of Huntingdon was his own property. A peace, though a hollow one, was, however, made for a time, between those kings; and, in the meantime. King Malcolm came to King Henry at Chester—at whose instigation I know not—and did homage to him, without prejudice, however, to all his dignities, in the same way as his grandfather. King David, had been the old King Henry's man; hoping, some suppose, by so doing, to be left in peaceful possession of his property. At that place, however, accursed covetousness gained over some of his councillors, who were bribed, it is said, by English money; and the king was soon so far misled by their clever trickery as, in that same year, to surrender Northumberland and Cumberland to the king of England, after having consulted with only a few of his lords. The king of England, however, restored to him the earldom of Huntingdon. Now, on account of this, the estates (*communitas*) of all Scotland were, with one accord, roused to stifled murmuring, and hatred against their lord the king, and his councillors. Meanwhile, these same kings met together, the following year, at Carlisle, on some business; but they took leave of each other without having come to a good understanding, as most men; could see. Afterwards, however, when a few years had slipped: by—that is, in the seventh year of the reign of the king of Scots—King Henry led a strong army against Toulouse; but as Louis, king of France, defended the town,

Henry was baffled in the chief aim he was striving after, and retraced his steps; and thus, out of the most profound peace sprang up the most deep-rooted feud. King Malcolm, though against the will of many of his great men, was with Henry in this expedition; and, on their way back thence, was by him girded with the sword of knighthood, in the city of Tours.

III.

AT length the Scottish lords, seeing their king's too great intimacy and friendship with Henry, king of England, were sore troubled, and all Scotland with them. For they feared this intimacy had shame and disgrace in store for them; and they strove in all earnestness to guard against this. So they sent an embassy after him, saying (or, rather, they thought and said within themselves):—"We will not have this man reign over us." Thereupon, he returned from the army at Toulouse, and came to Scotland, on account of divers pressing matters; and by his authority as king, he bade the prelates and nobles meet together at his borough of Perth. Meanwhile the chief men of the country were roused. Six earls—Ferchard, earl of Stratherne, to wit, and five other earls—being stirred up against the king, not to compass any selfish end, or through treason, but rather to guard the common weal, sought to take him, and laid siege to the keep of that town. God so ordering it, however, their undertaking was brought to naught for the nonce; and after not many days had rolled by, he was, by the advice of the clergy, brought back to a good understanding with his nobles. He then, thrice in the same year, mustered an army, and marched into Galloway against the rebels. At last, when he had vanquished these, made them his allies, and subdued them, he hied him back in peace, without loss to his men; and afterwards, when he had thus subdued them, he pressed them so sore, that their chieftain, who was called Fergus, gave up the calling of arms, and sending off his son and heir, Vithred, to the king, as a hostage, donned the canonical garb at the monastery of Holyrood, in Edinburgh. Meanwhile the king, by the help and advice of his friends, gave his sister Margaret in marriage to Conan, duke of Brittany, and his sister Ada to Florence, count of Holland. Peace, also, was restored between the kings of France and England; and the English king Henry's son, Henry, not yet six years old, took to wife the French king Louis's daughter, not yet two.

IV.

AT this time, the rebel nation of the Moravienses, whose former lord, namely, the Earl Angus, had been killed by the Scots, would, for neither prayers nor bribes, neither treaties nor oaths, leave off their disloyal ways, or their ravages among their fellow-countrymen. So having gathered together a large army, the king removed them all from the land of their birth, as of old Nebuchadnezzar, king of Babylon, had dealt with the Jews, and scattered them throughout the other districts of Scotland, both beyond the hills and this side thereof, so that not even one native of that land abode there; and he installed therein his own peaceful people. Sumerled, likewise, king of Argyll, of whom we have spoken above, impiously fought, for twelve years, against King Malcolm, his lord. At length, bent on plunder, he brought up at Renfrew with a strong army and very large fleet, which he had levied out of Ireland and sundry other places, but, through God's vengeance, he was, with his son Gellicolan, and a countless multitude of traitors, slain there by a few countrymen. Now, when this King Malcolm grew up, and reached the years of youth, he refused to marry, although besought to do so by the earls and all the people of his kingdom, with all manner of entreaties, and, as far as respect for the king's rank would allow, urged to do so; and, before God, he vowed chastity, abiding his whole time in the spotless purity of maidenhood. For though, on the strength of his kingly rank, he could often have transgressed, yet he never did transgress. He harmed none, but wished men well; was pleasant to all, and displeased none; and was very devout towards God: for with the whole straining of his mind, and all the longing of his inmost heart, did he yearn to reign with Christ for ever. Nevertheless, he had many trials and reproaches to bear at the hands of the dwellers in his kingdom, according to that saying of Solomon's: "Son, when thou undertakest God's service, stand in righteousness and fear, and make ready thy soul to the trial." He, indeed, having conceived the warmth of the love of God, had set his heart upon heavenly things; so that, looking down upon all earthly things, he quite neglected the care, as well as governance, of his kingdom. Wherefore he was so hated by all the common people that William, the elder of his brothers—who had always been on bad terms with the English, and their lasting foe, forasmuch as they had taken away his patrimony, the earldom of Northumberland, to wit—was by them appointed warden of the whole kingdom, against the king's will; while his younger brother, Earl David of Huntingdon, abode in England.

V.

In the year 1165, the thirteenth of King Malcolm's reign, at the end of the month of August, two comets appeared—one to the south, and the other to the north—which, according to some, foreboded the king's death. A comet is a star which appears, not at all times, but chiefly against a king's death, or a country's downfall. When it appears with a shining diadem of hair, it heralds a king's death; but if with scattered tresses glowing red, it forebodes a country's downfall. And sometimes it betokens storms or wars, as in these lines:—

> "There is a star bodes storm or war.
>   On high when it has crept;
> And if thou seek its name to speak,
>   Boëtes 'tis yclept."

Now Malcolm, being guided by God in the blessings of sweetness, so that his heart was kindled with the love of the Most High, wherewith he was upheld, all his life excelled in brightness of chastity, in the glory of lowliness and innocence, in purity of conscience, and holiness, as well as staidness of character; so that, among laymen, with whom he had nothing in common but his dress, he was as a monk; and among men, whom he ruled, he seemed, indeed, an angel upon earth. He founded the monastery of Cupar, to the praise of God. But when he had completed twelve years, seven months, and three days, on the throne, Christ called him away on Thursday the 9th of December; so he put off manhood for the fellowship of angels, and lost not, but exchanged, his kingdom. And thus this man of angelic holiness among men, and like some angel upon earth, of whom the world was not worthy, was snatched away from the world by the heavenly angels, in the bloom of his lily-youth,—the twenty-sixth year of his age.

VI.

This is the vision of a certain cleric, devout towards God, and formerly a familiar friend of the king's, about the glory of this same King Malcolm, of holy memory. While this cleric was devoutly watching at the king's grave, sleep stole upon him amid his psalm-singing; and the king seemed to him to be standing by, clad in snow-white robes, with a glad but speechless countenance, and not sorrowful; and ever as he asked him, in verse, with one half of each couplet, somewhat of his plight, the king would answer each question in verse, with the other half of every couplet, to the following effect:—

Cleric. A king thou wast; what art thou now?
  King. A servant once, lo! now I reign.
C. Why lingers still thy flesh below?
  K. My spirit seeks the heavenly plain.
C. Art thou in torment, or content?
  K. Nay, not in pain. I rest in peace.
C. Then what hath been thy punishment?
  K. A bitter lot ere my decease.
C. Where art thou, friend? Where dwells thy sprite?
  K. In paradise that knows not woe.
C. Why does thy raiment gleam so white?
  K. A maid I to my grave did go.
C. Why answerest so shortly, friend?

  K. My life is eloquent for me.
 C. Thy days thou didst in sickness spend,
  K. But now from sickness am I free!
 C. Why lost we thee? Why did we part?
  K. That I might find the saints on high.
 C. What was it grieved thy gentle heart?
  K. This wicked world is all a lie.
 C. Tell me, when shalt thou come again?
  K. When the great Judge shall judge at last.
 C. Will Scotia for thy loss complain?
  K. Not now, but when this time is past.
 C. Wilt leave me now? What dost thou fear?
  K. The burden of the life I bore.
 C. Hast thou no word thy friends to cheer?
  K. Bid them farewell for evermore.

  This most godly King Malcolm fell asleep in the Lord at Jedworth (Jedburgh); and his body was brought, by nearly all the prominent persons of the kingdom, in great state, to Dunfermline, a famous burial-place of the Scottish kings;—where are entombed Malcolm the Great and his consort the blessed Margaret (his great-grandfather and great-grandmother), and their holy offspring. It rests interred in the middle of the floor, in front of the high altar, on the right of his grandfather David.

VII.

Coronation of King William.

  To proceed—after King Malcolm's death, the prelates and all the lords of Scotland met at Scone, at the command of his brother William, then warden of the kingdom, and there, with one accord, set up the latter as king. So, on Christmas Eve, that is, the fifteenth day after the king's death, this William, the friend of God, the lion of justice, the prince of peace, was consecrated king by Richard, bishop of Saint

Andrews, with other bishops to help him, and raised to the king's throne. In the autumn before the king's death, King Henry had led a large army into Wales, which had rebelled against him; but meeting with no success, he put out the eyes of King Richard's sons, who had previously been put into his hands as hostages, and lopped off the noses and ears of his daughters. For he had formerly—eight years before—made himself master of that country, as it was thought; seeing that he had then, with great slaughter of his own men, taken hostages of the king and the barons. When, however, he had returned thence, seeing himself threatened by grievous wars there and everywhere, he bethought him of making sure of the steady friendship of the Scottish nation; so he sent word to his Wardens of the Marches to bespeak peace rather than war from the Scots, and to sound them as to a peaceful understanding. Finally, at this juncture, Matthew, count of Bouillon, the consort of King Stephen's daughter, gathering together a fleet from all sides, made ready—it was rumoured—six hundred vessels, to man with Flemings, and lead to the invasion of England the following year. Therefore there was a great stir made throughout England, and everywhere an earnest endeavour to secure friends.

VIII.

Now at this time, and even from the time Northumberland was given back to King Henry, there reigned between the kingdoms no steady peace, but rather some frail truce, many a time broken, and many a time patched up again; whereby the borders of the countries, where they touched each other, were sadly crippled. Wherefore, on these and other grounds, an agreement was drawn up by commissioners from either country, and confirmed by the warrant of each king and of all the lords, that, in order to get back Northumberland, and to secure an indissoluble bond of everlasting peace, William, king of Scots, should go to his cousin, King Henry, then at Windsor, awaiting his coming thither. This was, accordingly, done. So, on his arrival at Windsor, William was welcomed with great rejoicings. But just as the kings were talking over their affairs, all of a sudden, untoward news from parts beyond the sea burst upon King Henry's ears; and when he had got a connected account thereof, he put all business aside, and crossed the sea at the head of a huge army. William, king of Scots, however, could, by no contrivance of his nobles who were with him, or of any one else, be restrained from setting out with him, against the will of all, so that he might witness the shock of brave warriors; and in those parts he distinguished himself with splendid knightly renown, giving to all men hope of uncommon prowess. And thus, having first ratified the truce, he came back to his own kingdom with honour, while the treaty of peace which was to have been arranged was put off to an appointed time of fitting leisure. Afterwards, war broke out again between the kings of France and England, about the city of Toulouse, and for sundry reasons on both sides; so that, besides many other evils, the earldom of Anjou and the district of the Vexin were fearfully ravaged by fire and pillage, while the French king, with his army, tarried four days in the Vexin. The second year after this, however, peace was again made between them, when both kings had undergone many a risk. As a pledge of this peace, the French king's other daughter, begotten of the daughter of the king of Spain, was given to Richard, a son of the king of England. Richard, moreover, got the dukedom of Aquitaine from the king of France; and did him homage, and swore faithful allegiance to him for the honour of the duchy. Henry, also, the firstborn of the king of England, got from the king of France, the lordship of Brittany, together with the districts of Anjou and Cenoman (Maine)—doing homage for these, as he had already done for the duchy of Normandy.

IX.

THE following year, having done what he had to do across the water, this king came back from Normandy; and, in this voyage back, many perished by shipwreck, while he himself barely escaped. King William, however, in order to settle that same matter they had before been engaged in—namely, to come to an understanding about arranging a peace—came to him at Windsor, on Easter Eve, the day appointed by their agents, and was welcomed by him with great honours. After the feast, they were closeted together; and when they came to talk the matter over, William asked that Northumberland should be restored to him upon the same terms as the king of England had promised it him upon, in their former negotiation. But, seeing that, as already said, the latter had yielded this through fear of wars assailing him, now that these were smothered and quieted he felt safer, and refused to give it back. Wherefore King William went off unappeased, with none of his business settled; and, by hurried and unbroken stages, safely came home to Scotland. In that same year, namely, 1170, that king had his son Henry, then twenty years old, crowned, and consecrated king at Westminster; overlooking the advice of Solomon, who says:—"Lest thou give thine honour unto others, and thy years unto the cruel; lest haply strangers be filled with thy strength, and thou mourn at the last." Now his crowning was the occasion of many afterwards losing their earthly lives. For, after an interval of three years, an accursed feud sprang up between them. When invested with the royal diadem of his father, who was now of his own accord deposed from the height of kingship, this new king Henry brooked ill any governance or sovereignty of the kingdom above himself; since, as was being said by some, he ought rightfully to reign alone, as though, when the son was crowned, the father's reign had ended. So, on these and other grounds, he swelled with indignation against his father. Then, accompanied by his two brothers, Geoffroy and Richard, he went to his father-in-law, Louis, king of France, to brew troubles for his father. And soon, by the advice of Louis, he was trying everywhere, like a second Absalom, to bring evil upon his father, and, with the most idle promises, kept urging William, king of Scots, Philip, count of Flanders, and many other powerful men, both in these parts and across the sea, to fall away, little by little, from the father to the son, and by every means make ready for warlike operations. English and Norman noblemen followed them, and, with right hands clasped, pledged themselves to do battle.

X.

THE younger King Henry, as already said, trusting in the advice, and upheld by the support, of the French, and with Philip, count of Flanders, for his ally and companion, led his army into Normandy, against his father, and took a castle, called Albemarle,, and the Earl of Albemarle himself, as well as Earl Simon, whom the elder King Henry had sent to help him; and these earls he kept in a dungeon. He also took a great many other towns by storm. In this army, Matthew, count of Boulogne, received a deadly wound, and died. King William, also, putting faith in the pledges of that new king, who promised him Northumberland and Cumberland, levied an army for the war, and besieged Wark Castle for some time; but with no success. So he set out thence, and, with the highland Scots, whom they call *bruti*, and the Gallwegians, who knew not how to spare either place or person, but raged after the manner of beasts, he laid Northumberland waste, and stripped, in part, the land this side of the river Humber, slaughtering the inhabitants in more than one spot. He then bent his steps towards Carlisle, and made every effort to take the city by storm. It so happened, however, that at this time Robert earl of Leicester, having summoned a great many knights, and no small number of Flemish foot, was, with his consort also in mail, sent into England by the younger King Henry. But when, on the 16th of October, he encountered the English host, who were hastening to meet him, a good many of his foot were slain, and the rest put to flight; while he himself was taken, and consigned to bonds at Porchester. Upon hearing this, the king of Scots, who had settled down to the siege, raised it, and led his troops back to his own kingdom. At the beginning of this year, there was seen a meteor of a very deep red, flashing with wondrous brightness in a sky clear and free from any overshadowing clouds; so that those who saw it were aghast, for it was deemed by some to have foreboded bloodshed.

XI.

King William taken.

THE second year after—that is, in 1174—King William led an array into England, and besieged and took Appleby and Wayniland. Thereupon the Northumbrians, for a sum of money, obtained peace until the eighth day after Whitsunday; and William, having thus made his raid successfully, went back without loss. Meanwhile, when he had returned to Scotland from Appleby, he rested not; but, again mustering his army, he led it into England, and took Borough-under-Moor. So, after having wasted Cumberland, as he was going back through Northumberland, ravaging and plundering, he came before Alnwick; and, when at watch there, with a few knights he had kept beside him, while all his army was scattered about pillaging the country, lo! he was taken by the enemy, who, passing themselves off for Scotsmen, suddenly came upon him unawares; and he was carried off, with hardly any of his men knowing anything about it. Nor was this done without the deliberate will of God, Who, in His loving-kindness, bethought him of William's fierceness, and contrived, in his foresight, both that the king himself might be rescued from the perpetration of evils so great, and that, by a bridle being put into his jaws, the British realms might be restored to peace, as Merlin foretold;—and not only that this country's turmoil might be lulled, but also that peace might be renewed in all the parts of France beyond the sea. On the 13th of July, therefore, having been taken prisoner—or rather, by the ordering of God's loving-kindness, rescued from the shedding of Christian blood, he was brought to the king of England, the elder Henry, Matilda's son, who commanded that he should be at once taken across to Normandy, and kept in custody in the castle of Falaise. When this became known. King William's brother, David, speedily left Leicester, for which he fought, and betook himself over to Scotland as fast as he could. At this time, also, the Scots and men of Galloway, on their king being taken, wickedly and ruthlessly slew their French and English neighbours, in frequent invasions, with mutual slaughter; and there was then a most woeful and exceeding great persecution of the English, both in Scotland and Galloway, so that neither sex was spared; but in most places, and wherever they could be caught, all ransom was scouted, and they were cruelly slain.

XII.

MEANWHILE Rouen was besieged by Henry's son, the young King Henry, Louis, king of France, and Philip, count of Flanders. But when the old King Henry found this out, seeing that the whole English kingdom was tranquillized to his heart's content, and was fast under his sovereignty again, by a most binding treaty of peace, he hastened to the sea, and crossed over without delay, to his people's support; and, that he might be the more sure of being upheld by the obedience of his men, and strike the greater terror and dismay into his foes, he dragged the Scottish king from the keep of Falaise, brought him with him, and put him under arrest, locked up in Caen. When, however, the Scottish king, as already said, had been betrayed into the hands of his foes, all the old king's enemies—those, even, who had been the chief instigators of the quarrel—began, frightened and humbled, to treat for peace; and, at the instance of some good men, the father and son came to an understanding, while peace was wholly restored and renewed in the parts beyond, as well as this side of, the water. King Henry, the father, likewise, at the intercession of the king of France, unconditionally released all the prisoners but the king of Scotland, and gave them back, when released, their honours and goods. Lo how they loved him! May he not say with the prophet:—"All my friends have forsaken me"—allies who, at any rate, feigned true friendship for him—to wit, that they would be partakers with him in the subsequent events of the war, and be in fast fellowship with him in peace? Hence they had, although with clashing aims, promised that the war and peace of one should hold good with another and with all; and though they were bound by the straitest treaty, yet the noising abroad of his capture damped the courage of all these friends of his. All the Philistines, likewise, fled away together when Goliath was slain. But he justly suffered this for holding out help to an undutiful son, who, under colour of right, but without zeal for it, was carrying on an unrighteous war against his father. He did, moreover, forego a most righteous ground for war, as the chiefship and crown of all England ought, by acknowledged right, to have been his. Indeed, if he were cunningly doing this for his own sake, to weaken his enemies, he craftily tricked such as were knit in fellowship with him, and thus waged a righteous war unrighteously. For, not only from an unrighteous deed or cause, but many a time from an unrighteous aim, has it chanced that a combatant who has carried on a righteous war unrighteously has been worsted or slain.

XIII.

UNLIKE Octavianus Augustus Cæsar are those princes who are easily roused to war. Of this successful warrior, *Eutropius* relates that he so loathed war, strife, and uproar, that he never, without just cause, declared war against any nation. He used to say that it showed a boastful and shallow disposition to hurry the safety of the citizens into danger from the uncertain upshot of a struggle, for the burning love of triumphing, and for a laurel crown—fruitless leaves; that nothing befitted a good prince less than rashness; that whatever could be brought forth by fair means would be done soon enough, and that one should by no means take up arms, save with the hope of something to gain; that a victory won with heavy loss, for slight reward, was like fishing with a golden hook, the loss whereof, when broken off and gone, no profit of catching can make up for. So far *Eutropius*. When, however, the other magnates were released, as already stated, Richard, bishop of Saint Andrews, and Richard, bishop of Dunkeld, and many of the prelates, earls, and barons of the kingdom of Scotland, went across the sea to King Henry, in Normandy, about setting their king free. He was accordingly set free, and allowed to go home, about the next Purification of the Blessed Virgin after he was taken; and he was thus restored to the governance of his kingdom. But William, king of Scots, gave up his castles of Roxburgh, Berwick, and the Castle of Maidens (Edinburgh) to wardens appointed thereto, under the sovereignty of the English king, and was given hostages by the king of England, for the maintenance of peace; and so there was made between them a covenant which should last unshaken. Then, on the 15th of August, all the bishops and prelates of Scotland, at their lord the king's command, met together at York, and were fast bound to Henry, king of England, under the sanction of an oath, and the plighting of their troth. To whom all the earls and barons of that kingdom, their lord the king so bidding them, even as it then behoved him to do, submitted by the tie of homage, and were bound to him by an oath of fealty.

XIV.

BUT while this was going on, the Gallwegians, led by Gilbert, son of Fergus, treacherously made a conspiracy, just after their king's capture; and, separating themselves from the kingdom of Scotland, that same year, they disturbed the adjacent lands. Ochtred, moreover, son of Fergus, who was a true Scot, and could not be shaken, was taken prisoner by his brother Gilbert, on the 22d of September, and given over unto bonds; and, at length, his tongue was cut off and his eyes were torn out, and he was ruthlessly murdered. Upon learning this, the king, now released, led an army against them, into Galloway; but when these came to meet him, some Scottish bishops and earls stepped in between them, and, through their mediation, they were reconciled, by a money settlement, and by giving hostages. The winter after this, on the 29th of January, the king of England held a general council at Northampton, whereat the king of Scotland was present; and, at the command of both kings, all the bishops and prelates of the kingdom of Scotland were there met together. These were warned, on one side, under the threat of banishment, and, on the other, it was hinted to them, in wrong-headed exhortations, under the pretext of advice, that they should submit to the metropolitan bishop They all, however, strove hard to avert the threatened danger; and, better counsels prevailing, the proposal was unanimously, rejected by them—by having, however, had recourse to delays. Thereupon, through their efforts, the olden dignity of their Church was secured by apostolic authority, and its liberty strengthened, by Pope Alexander, with the protection of privileges. Before the aforesaid council, also, Vivian, cardinal priest of Saint Stephen in Mount Cælius, came to Scotland as legate, armed with the warrant of great authority, crushing and trampling upon everything he came across, ready to clutch, and not slow to snatch. Thence he crossed over to Ireland to fulfil his errand; and, after holding a council there, he came back to the Scots country, and, on the 1st of August, held a solemn council at the monastery of Holyrood, at the Castle of Maidens (Edinburgh), renewing, upon apostolic authority, many decrees of the ancients, and establishing some new ordinances.

XV.

Now, in that aforesaid council at Northampton, whereat were present Richard, archbishop of Canterbury, and Roger, archbishop of York, together with the clergy of both kingdoms, a certain Scottish cleric, named Gilbert, perceiving their attempt to enthral the Scottish Church, was almost maddened; and, when warned by the archbishops to say out whatever he liked, he lifted up his voice, though against the will of all his own prelates and clergy, and, glowing like red-hot iron, poured forth these or such like passionate words: "Ye would indeed," said he, "men of England, have been noble—yea, nobler than the men of well-nigh any country—had ye not craftily changed the might of your nobleness, and the strength of your dreaded courage, into the insolence of tyranny; and your enlightened wisdom and knowledge into the wily quibbles of sophistry. For ye trust not yourselves to order your actions aright under the guidance of reason; but, both puffed up by your teeming hosts of knights, and trusting in the delights of wealth and all manner of substance, ye, through some wrongful lust or greed of mastery, aim at subduing to your sway all the bordering provinces and nations; nations nobler than you—I will not say in numbers, or in might—but in blood, and in antiquity; nations whom, if ye look into the writings of old, ye ought rather humbly to obey, or, at least, quenching the touchwood of all ill-will, hereafter maintain brotherly love with, and reign with, for aye. And now, moreover, priding yourselves in all the wickedness ye have wrought, ye are striving, without putting forward any plea of right, but by brute force, to crush the Scottish Catholic Church, your mother, which was free from the beginning, and which, while ye were wandering through the pathless wilds of heathendom, set you upon the bulwark of faith, and brought you into the way of truth and life—Christ, the home of everlasting rest; washed your kings and princes, and their peoples, with the water of holy baptism; taught and instructed you in the precepts of God; and gladly welcoming many of your nobles and common folk, who took delight in giving themselves up to reading, saw that their daily food was given them free of cost, as well as books to read, and masters, for nothing. She likewise consecrated, appointed, and ordained your bishops and priests; and Bede bears witness that, for the space of thirty years or more, she held the primacy and chief episcopal dignity north of the river Thames. What return, pray, are ye making to a Church which has lavished so many benefits upon you? Is it not bondage, or such like,—giving evil for good, as the Jews with Christ? I, indeed, look not for anything else, should your wish be followed by deeds, than that ye should bring down to the utmost wretchedness of bondage Her whom it beseems you to treat with all worship and reverence." At these words, some of the English praised him highly, in that he had fearlessly, for his country's sake, vented the feelings of his heart, truckling to none, and undaunted by the sternness of his hearers; others, again, because he had put forward what went against their wishes, of course thought him a vapouring and fiery Scot. But Roger, archbishop of York, broke up the council; and, rising with a smile on his face, patted Gilbert on the head with his hand, and said to the bystanders:

" 'Twas not from his own quiver came that shaft."

XVI.

AFTER this, in the year 1179, William, king of Scotland, with his brother Earl David, and a large army, advanced into Ross against Macwilliam, whose real name was Donald Bane, and fortified two castles there—namely, Dunschath and Ederdone; and when he had fortified these, he hied him back to the southern tracts of his kingdom. But after seven years were overpast, seeing that this man went on in his wonted wickedness, the king, with a numerous army, and in very strong force, set out for Moray against this same enemy of his, Donald Bane, who said he was sprung of royal seed, and was the son of William, son of Duncan the Bastard, who was the son of the great Malcolm, king of Scotland, called Canmore. This man, relying upon the treachery of some disloyal men, had first, indeed, wrested from his king the whole of Ross, by his tyrannous insolence; and then, having for no little time held the whole of Moray, he had seized upon the greater part of the kingdom, with fire and slaughter, and aimed at the whole thereof. Now, while the king was making some stay, with his army, at the town of Inverness, and had been harassing Donald Bane and his adherents by daily plundering and spoiling, it fell out, one day, that some of his men, whom he had as usual sent out, to the number of two thousand, throughout the woods and country to plunder and to reconnoitre, lo! all of a sudden, stumbled unawares upon Macwilliam and his troops lurking in a moor which is called Macgarvy, near Moray. Macwilliam, seeing that those of the king's army were few in comparison with his own men, engaged them at once, and charged them. But they manfully and fearlessly withstood him with all their might, and, by God's help, slew him, with five hundred of his men, and routed the rest, on Friday the 31st of July—thus giving him the meet reward he had earned. They then brought away his head to the king, as a gazing-stock for the whole army.

XVII.

BUT, for the whole time from the king of Scots being taken until the time he regained his former liberty, the dwellers in the southern and northern belts of the country were at odds, and were engaged in civil war with each other, with fiendish slaughter. At that time, also, in the year 1185, died that lover and wager of civil war, Gilbert, son of Fergus, and lord of Galloway—he who had wickedly killed his brother Ochtred, after he had cut out his tongue and put out his eyes. Now this was sure to happen, by the will of God, who, in His loving-kindness, hearkeneth unto the constant crying of the poor and needy, and gladly snatcheth them from the hands of the stronger. Upon his death, Ochtred's son, Rotholand, upheld by the king's help, gathered his army together, and, on Thursday the 4th of July, fought a battle with Gilpatrick, and Henry Kennedy, and Samuel, and a great many other Gallwegians, who, in Gilbert's time, had been the instigators and whole cause of all the hostile feeling and war. In this struggle, the aforesaid fosterers of wickedness, with their abettors, and others not a few, perished by the avenger's sword; and the Lord requited them worthily after their deserts. That same year, this Rotholand, at the king's command, hunted down a certain Gillicolin, a tyrant and robber chief, and drew up his army in battle array against him, on the 30th of September. This Gillicolin had been infesting all Lothian, by frequent spoiling and giving way to robbery, and many nobles had he bereft of life and property; and, at length, making a hostile attack upon Galloway, was tyrannously usurping to himself the lands of Gilbert—though there was no great injustice in this—and the sovereignty of those parts of Galloway. But, on their coming to blows, Gillicolin perished, with many of his men; and thus his tyranny came to a' shameful end. In this struggle, Rotholand's brother, and a few of those who sided with him, fell slain.

XVIII.

HENRY, king of England, was very bitter against Rotholand, for the death of the Galloway traitors, whom, in defending himself and his rights, the latter had, the year before, overthrown in battle; and, through the promptings of certain evil-minded persons, feeling a deep hatred towards him, he levied an army against him, from all parts of England, and advanced as far as Carlisle. Rotholand, however, at the bidding and advice of his lord the king of Scotland, came thither to him, and they arrived at an honourable understanding. King William afterwards, on account of this Rotholand's faithfulness, and the many times he had so well bestead both him and the kingdom, gave him the whole land of Galloway—that is to say, Gilbert's lands, besides the lands he had himself formerly held by right of inheritance. He also restored peace and harmony between Rotholand and Gilbert's son. To this son of Gilbert's, likewise, who did forego his father's lands, and quietly agreed that Rotholand should enjoy them for ever, the king granted the whole of Carrick in possession for all time. In the aforesaid year—that is, 1186—on the 21st of April, about the first hour of day, the sun looked the colour of fire, so red that the whole face of the earth, when touched by his rays, seemed to beholders to be drenched with blood. This, some declared, was a partial eclipse. It had, indeed, been preceded, that same month, on the 6th of April, at night, about dusk, by a total eclipse of the moon, which many had beheld. But the astrologers had foretold that these two tokens should be of those very kinds, and at those very times, hours, and moments; and had publicly foreshown that they boded bloodshed, disasters, and storms, and disturbance of kingdoms in many parts of the world. And this, in fact, came true the following year. For Saladin, prince of Babylon and Damascus, with a numberless multitude of his men, marched into the borders of the land of Jerusalem, and, at the outset, killed the Master of the Hospital of Jerusalem, together with nearly two hundred Templars and other knights. Then he so smote the whole Christian host, that but a small number escaped. In this deadly fight, two thousand Christian knights were slain, and thirty thousand foot; while the Turks and other heathen triumphed over them to their heart's content—woe worth the day! Now this pitiful defeat of the Christians who dwelt at Jerusalem took place on the 4th day of the month of July, through the sufferance of God, who now, because they wronged His divine Majesty, enthralled the Christian people to strangers, stirred up at His nod; even as, under the old law, He had, as we read, dealt with the people of the Jews. They fiercely invaded every city, town, and castle; and then, at length, besieged, took, defiled, and fortified the workshop of our salvation—to wit, the holy Jerusalem and our Lord's sepulchre.

XIX.

THE empress's son, Henry, king of England, fleeing before his son Richard's pursuit, came by the end of his life and reign at the town of Chinon, in the year 1189, the thirty-fifth of his reign; and was buried at Fonteurault. It came to pass that while this king was being taken to be buried, clad in kingly apparel, with a golden crown on his head, gilt gloves and a ring on his hands, and with shoes embroidered with gold; begirt with a sword; lying upon the bier with uncovered face; and holding a golden rod in his hand, his son Richard Rufus, Count of Poitou, suddenly came to meet him, and do obeisance to his corpse. As soon as he was thus come, blood trickled from the dead king's nostrils, as if he were deeply indignant at his son's arrival. Weeping and wailing, however, Richard went with his father's body to the burial-ground; and it was there consigned to earth with solemn obsequies worthy of a kingly corpse. So Richard succeeded him in the kingship, by the wish of all alike; and, by the consent equally of the clergy and of the people, he was raised to the throne, and invested with the king's diadem at Westminster;—Baldwin, archbishop of Canterbury, with the rest of the bishops and prelates of England, placing the crown upon his head, on the 3d of September. For his brother Henry, the young king—of whom we spoke above—had departed this life six years before the death of his father, the aforesaid Henry, and in the thirteenth year after his own crowning. And thus the hopes of all those who had fought for him, which had nearly been blighted by his death, suddenly began to live anew in the crowning of his brother Richard, who had been a partaker with his brother, as long as he had lived, in the whole of the quarrel with their father, and, after his death, had unweariedly carried on the war in like manner.

XX.

King William released from fealty to England.

As soon, therefore, as his coronation was over, he, by a general decree, in full Parliament constituted by the advice of his prelates and lords, freed and released all his friends and allies, both English and French, who had cleaved to him and to his brother Henry, formerly the young king, at the time of the war against their father (which we have already gone into), and from whom his father had, for that reason, wrung any taxes, bonds, or bargains whatsoever. He also freely gave back, with usury, the lands, property, and ransoms, and all other goods whatsoever, that had been taken from them. To William, king of Scots, he restored his castles of Roxburgh and Berwick. The Castle of Maidens (Edinburgh), likewise, had been given back to him before, by King Henry, the father. Richard also released the king and kingdom of Scots from all thraldom and bond of allegiance, oaths and pledge of fealty, and even from the terms of the old covenant—whereto the aforesaid king had, that his body might be set free, bound himself and his kingdom to the king and kingdom of England. He, likewise, freed and sent back to the Scottish kingdom the hostages whom William had given King Henry, for the keeping unshaken the covenant made between them. He also, on receiving from William ten thousand merks, granted that the Scots kingdom should be for ever free, quit, and exempt, from the jurisdiction and dominion of the English kingdom. The writs and charters, moreover, wherein those old covenants and extorted bonds had been set out, were cancelled and annulled, and given back to King William; while Richard drew up writs and charters wherein were contained that immunity and the recovered freedom and exemption of the Scots; and having given them force, by signatures of witnesses and the warrant of their seals, handed them over to the keeping of the king and kingdom of Scots for ever, in witness and warrant of the exemption made and their recovered freedom. The purport of one of these is in the following words:—

"Richard, by the grace of God, king of England, duke of Normandy and Aquitaine, earl of Anjou and Poitou; to the archbishops, bishops, abbots, priors, earls, barons, justiciaries, sheriffs, and all his ministers and lieges of the whole of England—Greeting: Know ye that we have given back to our cousin William, by the grace of God, king of Scots, his castles of Berwick and Roxburgh, with all their pertinents, as his by right of inheritance, and to be held for ever by him and his heirs in the said kingdom. Furthermore, we have remitted Tinto him all customs and bargains which our father Henry, king of England, of happy memory, extorted by fresh escheats, through his capture. Provided, of course, that the said king do wholly and fully unto us, for his lands in England, what his brother Malcolm, king of Scots, did unto Our ancestors, as he was bound by law to do. And we shall do unto him and his successors, whatever Our ancestors were bound by law to do: to wit, in safe-conduct in coming to court, and returning from court, and, while tarrying at court, in procurations, and dignities, and honours, and all the privileges of the same, due, by law, from old time (according as it shall be ascertained by four of our lords, elected by the said King William, and four lords of the kingdom of Scotland, elected by us), after William the Bastard, the conqueror of the said kingdom of England, and his heirs, obtained the said kingdom of England. But if any of Our men, after William, king of Scotland, was taken by Our father, has seized the borders or marches of the kingdom of Scotland, and has unlawfully retained them without a judgment. We will that they be wholly restored, and brought back to the former state in which they were before his capture. Furthermore, touching his lands, which he has in England, whether demesnes, or fees—in the earldom of Huntingdon, to wit, and in all other places—he and his heirs for ever may hold them with that freedom and fulness wherewith his brother Malcolm, king of Scotland, held them, and was entitled to hold them by right of inheritance; unless the aforesaid King Malcolm has feued any of the said lands to any one: Provided, however, that if any land was afterwards feued, the services of these feus belong to him and his heirs. And whatever Our father gave to the aforesaid Malcolm or the aforesaid William, we hold it valid, and for Us and Our heirs confirm it for ever, and will hold it fast. We also give back to the same William, king of Scotland, the allegiance of his men, and all the charters which Our said father had of him, by reason of his capture. And if any others are by chance kept back through forgetfulness, or shall hereafter be found, We command that they be of none effect whatsoever. But this William has become Our liegeman for all his lands in England (for which his ancestors were the liegemen of Our ancestors), and has sworn fealty unto Us. Witness myself, in the year of Our Lord one thousand one hundred and ninety, and the first year of Our reign."

XXI.

NOW the prelates and rectors of churches, the earls, also, and lords of the whole kingdom of Scotland, assembled at Holyrood Church at Edinburgh, and undertook to pay off the sum of money which the king had agreed upon, for his honours and the freedom of his kingdom, with the king of England. And having shared the payment among them—though this was done not without loss and damage to their substance—they cheerfully paid it, at regular terms and times, settled beforehand, to Richard, king of England, about to set out to the rescue of the Holy Land. But King Richard, before starting, gave his chancellorship to William of Longchamp, bishop of Ely; and he also set him over the whole of England as judge and justice, and intrusted to him the guardianship of the whole kingdom. Afterwards, King Richard, having carried out the vow he had laid himself under, was minded to come back secretly through Germany; but, being caught by some who lay in wait for him, and sent to the emperor Henry, he was by him kept in close ward. Meanwhile John, called "Lackland," King Richard's brother, hankering after the throne of England, fortified the castles he could get in any way whatever throughout England, and handed them over to his men to guard, thus unsettling the whole country. At length King Richard, having stated a sum for his ransom, and left hostages with the emperor, brought up at Sandwich in England, on the 13th of March, in the fourth year after his setting out. But William, king of Scotland, on hearing from messengers of his cousin King Richard's arrival, straightway came to him with no mean force; and in a short time, by his advice as well as help, Richard tranquillized the kingdom, well-nigh split up. So they were together until the 15th of May,—that is, Whitsunday. Now an aid was imposed on England for the king's ransom, such that one penny in thirteen was levied; and silver chalices, also, were taken from the churches for that purpose. William, king of Scotland, of his own accord, freely sent two thousand merks from Scotland, out of the king's treasury. Moreover, there was thenceforth, for the whole of the time of King Richard, so hearty a union between the countries, and so great a friendship of real affection knit the kings together, like David and Jonathan, that the one in all things faithfully carried out what the other wished; and even the two peoples were reckoned as one and the same. The English could roam scathless through Scotland as they pleased, on foot or on horseback, this side of the hills and beyond them; and the Scots could do so throughout England, though laden with gold or any wares whatever.

XXII.

IN the year 1196 there was so grievous a famine that men were starving everywhere. That same year King William led an army into Caithness. Crossing the river Oikel, he killed some of the disturbers of the peace, and bowed to his will both provinces of the Caithness men, routing Harald, the earl thereof, until then a good and trusty man—but at that time, goaded on by his wife, the daughter of Mached, he had basely deceived his lord the king, and risen against him. Then, leaving there a garrison for the country, the king hurried back into Scotland. The following year, again, a battle was fought in Moray, hard by the castle of Inverness, between the king's men and Rodoric and Torphin, Earl Harald's son; but the king's enemies were put to flight. Rodoric, also, with many others, fell slain. When the king heard of this, he was highly indignant against Harald, and led an army into Moray; and, scouring all those highland districts—namely, Sutherland, Caithness, and Ross—he at last was so lucky as to get hold of Harald, whom he brought across the Scottish sea as far as Roxburgh Castle, and threw him into a dungeon there until peace should be made. At length, however, Harald made his peace with his lord the king, and, leaving there his son as a hostage, went back to his own land. But, not long after, on account of the father's bad faith, and because the peace established between him and the king was afterwards wickedly broken through, the son was deprived of his eyes and genitals, and died in the aforesaid dungeon.

XXIII.

Now this most fortunate king of Scotland, William, had, nearly twelve years ago, with great splendour and rejoicings, taken to wife Ermyngarde, daughter of the Viscount of Beaumont, who was the son of the daughter of William the Bastard's eldest son, Robert Curthose. By her he had a son, named Alexander,—to the great gladness of his people, and the refreshment of the whole kingdom of the Scots, as the after course of these annals will show forth. He was born at Haddington, on Saint Bartholomew's Day, in the year 1198. In every place in the whole country, the common folk used to forsake their menial work on this day, wherein they first heard tidings of his birth, and spend it in joy; while priests and churchmen donned the alb, and walked in procession, with loud voice glorifying God in hymns and canticles, and humbly praising Him. The following year, Richard, that noble king of England, so friendly to the Scots, was, while storming a castle named Chaluz, situated in Poitou, mortally hit by a shot from a crossbow, under the shield of Marchederius, prince of the Brabanters, on the 12th of April; and he died at Longtronc, on the 16th of April,—

that is, Friday before Palm Sunday. He was succeeded by his brother John, who was crowned at Westminster on Ascension Day; and, crossing the sea some time afterwards, John made, by terms unmeet and unseemly for him and his kingdom, some sort of shameful peace with Louis's son, Philip, king of France. On King John's return. King William, under his safe-conduct and that of the nobles of England, came to meet him in England, about the Feast of Saint Martin; and, at a great council which was brought together at Lincoln, did homage (without prejudice to all his dignities) for all his lands and honours, which he had a right to in England, and which his predecessors had formerly held.

XXIV.

SUNDRY ambassadors went and came between William, king of Scotland, and John, king of England, who had made his way like a wildcat into Northumberland as far as the Tweed, and thence as far as Carlisle, levying a tax of fifteen merks of forest dues from the barons. But in Lent, having done nothing in the matter of the king of Scotland, and putting him off with lying promises, John sailed across into Normandy, because of a serious war which had broken out, over the water, between himself and Philip, king of France; and he remained there the whole of the following year, in unsuccessful warfare, returning thence only when he had lost his lands and all his castles beyond the sea. But William, king of Scotland, about the Feast of Saint Simon and Saint Jude, made all the nobles of the whole country, at a general council at Musselburgh, swear fealty to his own son Alexander, then three years old. Civil wars, however, were not over at this time; indeed, at the utmost bounds of Scotland, they were carried on even more habitually. For the Earl of Orkney, the oft-mentioned Harald, had formerly sailed on a secret voyage to Caithness; and, on the plea that John, bishop of that province, was an informer, and the instigator of the misunderstanding between him and the lord king, he had, as he thought, the bishop's eyes put out and his tongue lopped off; but it turned out otherwise, for the use of his tongue and of one eye was, in some measure, left him. Now when these tidings reached the king, he lost no time, and, before that very Christmas, he sent an army into Caithness, against Harald. This army, however, met with little or no success, and returned; for Harald had retreated to the furthest coast, returning as soon as the army had gone back. The following spring, therefore—that is, in 1202—as the lord king was getting ready to sail towards the Orkneys against the said Harald, the latter, under the safe-conduct of Roger, bishop of Saint Andrews, met him at Perth; and there, by the intercession of that bishop and other good men, came to a good understanding with the king, and swore that he would in all things abide by the judgment of the Church. And thus he was restored to his earldom, on payment of two thousand pounds of silver to the lord king.

XXV.

ON his recovery from a serious illness, whereby he had been kept back at Traquair, King William set out to meet John, king of England, who was coming to Norham; and there they had an interview. But the king of England was not pacified; and, brooking ill the Scottish king's views, went off to the southern parts of his kingdom. Now the cause of the quarrel was this:—The king of England had begun to strengthen a castle at Tweedmouth, in order to destroy the village of Berwick. The king of Scotland would not stand this; so he twice pulled it down to the very ground, after having taken, routed, and put to the sword all its founders, workmen, and guards. Thereupon King John, being stirred up in his heart against the king of Scots, encamped, with a strong and numerous force, about the river Tweed, near Norham, for the purpose of provoking the before-mentioned king to battle. The latter, having mustered his army and fortified his castles, marched forward as far as Roxburgh, with no less a force to back him. Many and sundry messengers, therefore, hurried backwards and forwards between the kings, and many and sundry were the things commanded and demanded by the king of England of the king of Scotland,—things out of keeping with his kingship and freedom. When all these things had been flatly refused, they at length hit it off in this decision: to wit, that the Scottish king's daughters, Margaret and Isabella, should be handed over to the king of England, to be given in marriage, after nine years next following were over, to his sons, Henry and Richard, who were infants as yet. Provided, indeed, that one of the former were betrothed to the one of the latter to whom the heirship of the throne might fall. This was sworn by King John. Moreover, the castle which was being reared at Tweedmouth, for the destruction of Berwick, was broken down; and at no time hereafter shall it be reared. All his old honours shall be left entire to the king of Scotland. And, for all this to be wholly and fully observed, 15,000 merks must be paid to John, king of England, within two years, at four terms.

XXVI.

IT was, likewise, settled and agreed between them, in these days, that the king of Scotland should absolutely and unconditionally resign to the king of England all the lands and possessions he himself had held of him; and that the said king of England should give them back to Alexander, the son and heir of the Scottish king, who was to hold them of the king of England. This was done, the same year, at Alnwick: where Alexander swore fealty and did homage to King John for the whole of his said lands, possessions, and honours—with as much freedom, to wit, as either his father, or such of his predecessors as had formerly done so with the most freedom to themselves, and honour to John, or to any English king. It was also agreed that, thenceforth, not the king, but the heir to the Scottish throne for the time being, should swear fealty and do homage to the king of England for the aforesaid lands, honours, and possessions. Now when these things had been secured by writings and indentures, the dwellers in both kingdoms began to treat together for an everlasting peace. So, the third year after—that is, in 1212—the aforesaid kings, each having sent the other word thereof by messenger, had an interview at Durham, on Candlemas Day, and afterwards came to Norham. There, in the presence of many of the nobles of either king, and also of the worshipful lady, the queen of Scotland, the form of peace and love, to be cherished for ever between the kingdoms and kings, was renewed, and secured by charters drawn up on either side. And, for the knitting of a stronger bond of love, Alexander, the son of the king of Scotland, was sent with the greatest pomp and state, by his father, to the king of England, by whom he, together with some noble and highborn boys of the kingdom, was girded with the sword of knighthood, in London, on the middle Sunday of Lent—that is, "The Lætare, Jerusalem"—the 8th of March, in the fourteenth year of his age. Then the king of England sent him away with gifts, and he went back to his father about Easter.

XXVII.

At this time Alan, lord of Galloway, and constable of the king of Scotland, did homage to John, king of England, at Norham, by his lord the king's will and leave, for some broad lands which the latter had bestowed upon him. Now this is how he came to be constable. On the death of William of Morville, long ago, as he had no sons, he was succeeded by Alan's father, Rotholand, lord of Galloway, as heir, through a marriage formerly contracted between the latter and the said William's sister; and Rotholand gave King William 700 merks of silver, for the heirship and the honour of the constableship aforesaid. Then Gothred, the son of Macwilliam, being seized and fettered through his own men's treachery, was brought before the king's son, the lord Alexander, at the king's manor and castle of Kincardine, and was there beheaded, and hung up by the feet. Now this Gothred, son of Macwilliam, had come, the year before, about the Lord's Epiphany—by the advice, it was said, of the thanes of Ross—out of Ireland into those parts, trampling under foot everything he came across, and infesting the greater part of the kingdom of Scotland. But the king's army was suddenly sent against him, so as either to kill him, or to drive him out of the country; and King William himself went after him, and in that same following summer built two towns in those parts. After the king's decease, the garrison of one of these towns surrendered of their own free will; and it was burnt down by Gothred and his men. The king of England, also, came as far as Norham, to have an interview with the king of Scotland; but as this king was at that time lying sick at Haddington, the interview did not come off. Nor was the Lord Alexander, the king's son—although the king of England had asked this very urgently—allowed to go to him; for they feared his wiles.

XXVIII.

IN the autumn, moreover, about the Feast of St. Peter, which is called *ad vincula*, in the year 1214, King William set out for Moray, where he made some stay; and having made a treaty of peace with the Earl of Caithness, and taken his daughter as a hostage, he came back from Moray into Scotland. From Scotland, however, he went to Lothian; and on his way back thence, he came, by short stages, and in great bodily weakness, to Striveline (Stirling). He there lingered for some time, failing in strength from day to day; and after his son had been accepted as the future king, by the bishops earls, and barons, William departed this life, full of goodly days, and at a good old age, charging his familiar friends and officers about paying back all debts and services in full, as became a good prince. And fully armed with thorough devoutness, a clear shrift, true charity, the viaticum of Christ's body, and the rest of the sacraments, while his kingdom abode in the deepest peace, breathed he out his last breath, in a blissful end, and flitted to Christ's presence, we trust, about the third hour of the night, on Thursday, the 4th of December, in the aforesaid year—the forty-ninth of his reign, and the seventy-fourth of his age. How great was that distinguished king's worthiness in God's sight, may be gathered from a certain miracle, which was on the following wise. Upon one occasion— namely, in 1206—between Candlemas and the 1st of March, this king went, under the safe-conduct of some English nobles, to John, king of England, at York; and after a stay of four days there, when his business was over, he sped safely back. At that time, at York, in the presence of many nobles of England and Scotland, a boy was, by his touch and blessing, healed of a grievous sickness, which was upon him; while all wondered and stood aghast. But that he was beloved by worthy men, even as he was by God, is shown in this case, for instance. Once Jocelin, bishop of Glasgow, and Arnald and Osbert, abbots of Melrose and Kelso, with other men of mark, went off to Rome, on the business of their king and country; and when they had skilfully transacted it, they came home again, in good health and spirits. Pope Lucius, however, hearing of the fame of King William—that he was zealous for God, and took great pains in maintaining the laws of his kingdom—sent over, by them, to his best beloved son, with his fatherly blessing, a golden rose, set upon a wand, also of gold. Besides, Pope Innocent and Pope Celestinus had, before this, written to him about the freedom of the Scottish Church.

XXIX.

Coronation of King Alexander II. at Scone.

The next day after the king's death, very early in the morning, while Walter, bishop of Glasgow—Robert, elect of Ross—the queen—William of Boscho, the chancellor—and a good many of his household, abode with the deceased king's body, the Earls of Fife, Stratherne, Atholl, Angus, Menteith, Buchan, and Lothian, together with William, bishop of St. Andrews, took the king's son, Alexander, a lad of sixteen years and a half; and, bringing him as far as Scone, they raised him to the throne, in honour and peace, with the approval of God and man, and with more grandeur and glory than any one until then; while all wished him joy, and none gainsaid him. So King Alexander, as was meet, held his feast in state, at Scone, on that day (that is to say, Friday), and the Saturday following (namely, the Feast of St. Nicholas), as well as the next Sunday. On the Monday, at the bridge of Perth, he met his father's body, which was being taken down, in great state, to Abirbroth (Arbroath), to be buried, as the king himself, before his death, had directed. And thus, followed by all the nobility of the whole kingdom, save a few of the nobles who guarded the uttermost parts of the kingdom, William, the kindly king of Scots, and to be had in kindly remembrance for everlasting, was buried on Wednesday, the 10th of December, in front of the high altar, in the church of the monastery of Abirbrothoc (Arbroath), which he had himself caused to be built up from the very foundations, to the honour of God and Saint Thomas the Martyr, Archbishop of Canterbury; and which he had, after endowing it with many estates and possessions, committed to the monks of Kalkhow (Kelso). May God be gracious unto his soul! Amen.

XXX.

EARL DAVID, likewise, though neither lively in mind nor vigorous in body, came as quickly as he could to his nephew, King Alexander, and kept the aforesaid feast with the king at Scone, for two days. Thence, however, he set off, with the long, to meet the body of the king, his brother, at the head of Perth bridge; and, getting off his horse, he took upon his shoulder one handle of the bier, and, with the rest of the earls who were there, devoutly carried the body as far as the boundary, where a cross was ordered to be set up; and afterwards, at the king's burial, he stood by as chief mourner, as became a brother. To this David, the late King William, his brother, after he had been released, and had come back from England, had given the earldom of Huntingdon, to be held of him—likewise the earldom of Garviach, the town of Dundee, the town of Inverbervie, and the lordship of Lanforgonde, together with many other lands. David had, moreover, taken to wife a most noble damsel, Matilda, daughter of Hugh, the late glorious Earl of Chester, that most renowned son of Ranulph, that most renowned earl thereof; and by her he had a son, who, also, was called Henry. That same noble Earl David had, also by her, had a son before, named Robert, who—woe worth the day!—being overtaken by an untimely death, paid the debt of nature, and found a burial-place at the abbey of Lindores, which his father had newly founded. Wherefore many in Scotland, as well as in England and other countries, were filled with tears and grief.

XXXI.

THAT same Earl David likewise begat, of his said wife Matilda, one son, named John, who afterwards succeeded him—and three daughters: Margaret, Isabella, and Ada. Margaret he gave in wedlock to Alan of Galloway, Rotholand's son, who of her begat a daughter named Darworgilla; his second daughter, Isabella, he gave to Robert of Bruce, who of her begat a son named Robert; and his third daughter, Ada, he joined in matrimony to Henry of Hastings—and by her this same Henry had a son named Henry. Now Earl David, after having lain sick a long time, at length went the way of all flesh, at Jerdelay, in England, and breathed his last on Monday, Saint Botulph's Day, in the year 1219. And though it had been his will, when he was alive, that his body should be taken down to his own monastery of Lindores, yet, by the advice of some, it was taken down to the abbey of Sautreia, and there interred in state, the day after Saint Botulph's Day—that is on Tuesday. He was a man of pious memory, and worthy to be always had in remembrance, God be gracious unto his soul! Amen. He was succeeded by his son, who was, by the English, called "John the Scot," and whom, together with many other nobles, both of England and Scotland, King Alexander afterwards invested with the arms of knighthood, at Roxburgh, at his royal feast on Whitsunday. Afterwards, nearly thirteen years after Earl David's death, Ranulph, earl of Chester, died childless, and was succeeded by John the Scot, Earl David's son and his own nephew, who also died without children.

XXXII.

THE five years' interdict came to an end, throughout all England, about the 1st of July, in the year King William died. But, for this release from the interdict, John, king of England, put the kingdom of

England, as also himself, under subjection to our lord the Pope for ever; and, in witness of this subjection, he himself, and the magnates of his territory, promised, with their hands on a shrine, that he and all his heirs would furnish to God, and to the sovereign pontiff and all his successors, an annual rent—of one thousand merks of silver, to wit—from his own treasury; and he gave his golden charter thereto. Now, the year before, a certain English ploughman, named Peter, who—through what spirit I know not—foretold things to come, had been, from day to day, rebuking the very king of England, John himself, for his cruelty towards the Church; and for ever shouting out fearlessly before his face that he would shortly lose the honour of the throne and the name of king, and that he would reign but for a year. The following year, however, the king, seeing he had escaped the day appointed for him by Peter, as stated above, had this Peter hanged upon a gallows-tree. But Peter asserted that he was unjustly being put to death; for that he had foretold the truth, as he maintained that the king was already not reigning, since he had put under another's sway the sovereignty of the kingdom. The following year, the king of Scotland's enemies—namely, Dovenald Bane, son of Macwilliam, Kennach MacAth, and the son of a certain king of Ireland—entered Moray, with a numerous crowd of miscreants. These foes of the king's were attacked by Makentagart and mightily overthrown; and the latter, having cut off their heads, presented them as new gifts to the new king, Alexander, and was therefor graced, by the king, with the honour of knighthood.

XXXIII.

AFTER the Christmas of the year 1215, which he had kept merrily at Forfar, Alexander, king of Scots, with our lady the queen, his mother, and many noblemen of the kingdom, was at Striveline (Stirling), at the Epiphany; and thence he went on to Lothian, and held a parliament at

Edinburgh, whereat he gave back the chancellorship to William of Boscho, the constableship to Alan of Galloway, and the chamberlainship to Philip of Walloniis—just as it had been before, in his father's lifetime; and as for the rest, he gave to each his rights, as their feus required. Soon after, however, some kind of council was held, by a few persons, at Haddington; and some, who had been contented before, withdrew from Court discontented. The king then came thence into Scotland, and met the queen, his mother, at Forfar; whereupon they set out together for Abbirbrothoc (Arbroath), to see the grave of King William, of pious memory. At this time, moreover, the barons and nobles of England, who would not brook the burdens and wrongful customs which King John daily laid upon them, bound themselves by a common oath to insist, with one mind, upon the king's granting them the ancient liberties and free customs granted of old, to the Church and kingdom of England, by Henry, son of William the Bastard, according to the terms of his charter;—for that otherwise they would withdraw themselves from his sway. But when this king had put them off with false promises and repeated wrongs, at length their hearts were stirred up, and they would wait no longer; but, shunning even an interview, they set about dealing with the matter by arms. Alexander, king of Scotland, too, and Llewellyn, king of Wales, being beset with prayers and promises, allied themselves to the barons of England; although the king of Wales had taken king John's daughter to wife.

XXXIV.

As soon as the king of Scotland had gathered his forces together, he set off into England, and besieged Norham Castle; but shortly, by the advice of his friends, he granted a truce to the besieged, and led his host into Northumberland, which he brought under his yoke, and received the submission of its people. When John, king of England, heard of this, taking with him some freebooters and other hangers-on of his, he went his way towards Scotland, took Berwick Castle, and then, going across by the sea-coast, stormed Dunbar. Thence he marched on into Lothian, wasting and burning everything he could get at within the kingdom of Scotland. But inasmuch as God was pleased to withstand him, and, in his loving-kindness, to forbear from the shedding of blood, John did not push on beyond Haddington. Retracing his steps, he burnt down Berwick Castle, together with the town; and, breaking down the bridge after his army, he went back as far as Dover, bringing under his sway all the country he had passed through, near Berwick. Now King Alexander, having gathered together the strength of the whole kingdom all about, longed to come to blows with the English, and pitched his tents on the river Esk, near Pentland. But when he saw that the king of England had retreated, he hastily followed after him; and burning up Northumberland, he marched through the bishopric of Durham, and got as far as Richmond. Then, bending his steps towards the western parts of Westmoreland, he ravaged almost all those lands, and went home again across the Solway water, hard by Carlisle, with plunder without, end.

XXXV.

MEANWHILE the lord Louis, the first-born of the king of France, to the end that he might restore the liberties of the kingdom and the Church, sided with the barons of England, and took from them hostages for their fealty and homage; and having marshalled his forces, he, at the head of a countless soldiery, sailed over in a fleet laden with meat and engines of war. He brought up in England, in the year 1216; while King John, with his army, tarried at Sandwich—the nearest port, as he thought; but, not daring to come to blows, the latter betook himself to a safer spot. Louis, however, came to London; and, to the unspeakable joy of the barons and of his own followers, was welcomed, with great honour, on Whitsunday,—for, during the course of that time, the barons were tarrying in London. But Alexander, king of Scots, having got his army together again, made his way into England, about the 5th of August, everywhere sparing the churches, and church property, and the lands of the barons, but wasting the king's lands and those of his hangers-on, until he came to Louis at Dover. He was welcomed, with honour, by Louis; and, having made a stay there of fifteen days or upwards, after treating of, and secretly winding up, sundry matters with him, he at length made ready to cross over to his own country. But on his way back to Scotland, after their interview and negotiations, his road was barred by John, king of England, who had caused the bridges and boats of the river Trent to be broken down and upset, and the fords to be cut through, and was besetting all the roads, both by sea and land, whereby Alexander could get across. But, God so ordering it, he ended his misdeeds and plottings with his life, and died on the day of Saint Luke the Evangelist, at Newark, a town lying hard by the river Trent; while the king of Scotland sacked his scattered army's camp, and sped safely back to Scotland, without loss, and with great glory.

XXXVI.

As soon, then, as the king of Scotland had returned from England, he called upon all those who were with him to make haste and give their horses a little rest after the long journey, and by every means get ready to return to England,—which they did. Accordingly, having gathered his forces together, he marched back, with a huge force, into England, carrying off everything at will; until at length he wheeled off to besiege Carlisle, and strongly blockaded it with his whole force. The besieged, on the other hand, having constant onslaughts made upon them, and having lost all hope of being relieved, surrendered the city and castle to the king, on promise that life and limb would be spared. That same year, moreover,—in the foregoing summer, to wit—a certain cardinal, named Gualo, was, by Pope Innocent, sent as legate to England to succour John, king of England; for, on the strength of the payment of the yearly tribute, and the subjection of England, the Pope was now most friendly towards John. Upon that king's death, however, as above related, this legate got together the army which had marched under the king, and set his first-born son Henry, now in his ninth year, to reign in his father's stead. So Henry was crowned at Winchester. Hearing, likewise, of the troubles, oppression, and unbearable evils which were wrought in England by the king of Scotland, Gualo laid an interdict upon that king, his army, and the whole kingdom of the Scots. Thereupon there arose very great distress in the Scottish Church. For, at the instance of Gualo, the legate in England, a rescript was sent by Pope Honorius to the priors of Durham, Gysburn, and Tynemouth, who declared all the prelates of Scotland excommunicated, forasmuch as they had given the Communion to the king of Scotland and his army, who had fallen under the ban pronounced at the Lateran Council, wherein were excommunicated all King John's enemies, and their abettors: because the king of Scotland had sided with Louis, the first-born of the king of France; because he had fought against John, king of England, breaking down the castle of Tweedmouth, which had been rebuilt by John, in spite of his oath, over against Berwick; and especially because he had not yielded to the request of Gualo, the legate, that he should surrender Carlisle to King Henry.

XXXVII.

FINALLY, at that time, the castle of the city of Lincoln was besieged by the barons of England, and the strong army of Louis, the first-born of the king of France. But on being set upon by Gualo, the legate, with the army of Henry, king of England, they raised the siege; and, in the course of one hour, all the barons and nobles of England who followed Louis were taken, and a certain French earl, who had come to the aforesaid siege with the English army, was slain. Thus were the mighty of England led away captive, while their castles and estates fell under King Henry's dominion. But the lord Louis, who had, all this while, been tarrying in London, seeing that luck had turned, and that it threatened to go hard with him in the result of the war, thought better of it, and made peace with the king of England, after having received a pledge from him that all who had risen against him would be restored to the plight they had been in before the war had broken out. Thereupon Louis went home across the water, under a safe-conduct, in the year 1217, about Michaelmas. But Gualo, the legate, sent messengers to Alexander, king of Scotland, to promise him absolution; and began to treat for a perpetual treaty of peace, the surrender of Carlisle, and indemnity for losses—all which he got. And although Master Walter of Wisebeth (Wisbeach) came by our lord the Pope's authority, to take off the interdict in Scotland, nevertheless Gualo, in his wiliness, craftily made him put off that absolution, until peace should have been made between the kings—or, according to some, until he should, in the meanwhile, have slaked the thirst of his moneybag with draughts of money.

XXXVIII.

So our lord Alexander, king of Scotland, and all the laymen who followed him, got absolution, at Berwick, from the archbishop of York, and the bishop of Durham. Thence he went on to Northampton, under the safe-conduct of the king and barons of England; and he there did homage for his lands and honours in England, as had been the English king's right from old time. And, having surrendered Carlisle, which he had taken, and secured peace, he went back to his own kingdom; though he could not obtain from the said Gualo that the prelates and clergy of his land might be included in the terms of that peace. But, by the advice of some, led by I know not what spirit, a general interdict was proclaimed throughout Scotland, about the Feast of Saint Nicholas, and all the clergy, both regular and secular, found themselves, as it were, excommunicated—except William, lord bishop of Saint Andrews, who, on his way back, a little before, from France, where he had tarried during the time of warfare, had barely managed to get the benefit of absolution from Gualo, the legate aforesaid,—having first, however, sworn upon the Body that he had not lent advice, help, or favour to the adversaries of John, king of England.

XXXIX.

ABOUT Candlemas, the prior of Durham and the archdeacon of York, being sent by the legate of England, came to Scotland, and gave absolution to the clergy of Scotland, in this form: They made all the clergy, both regular and secular, come together before them, at some borough or city, and took a sworn pledge from them that they would abide by the legate's commands, and would make a true and clean shrift on such matters as they might ask them about; whereupon they gave them absolution, the latter naked and barefoot before the doors of the churches where they had come together, or before the abbeys where the former were baiting. And in this fashion they went about through Scotland, from Berwick even unto Abirbrothoc (Arbroath), baiting at place after place, as they thought fit, and, by the advice of some who wished to please them, getting everywhere costly procurations, and money without end, and many offerings. But the bishops of the kingdom, the king's household clergy, and all the beneficed clergy of the whole country, who had either taken part in the war, or had in any way ministered unto the combatants, these kept back for Gualo, the English legate, to absolve; while the abbots and certain other prelates to whom they had given absolution, they kept suspended from their office, until they should have more fully earned the favour of the legate himself. Therefore, about the festival of Easter, nearly all the prelates of Scotland went to Alnertone (Northallerton), to meet the legate of England, who sent some of them to Rome to get absolution, while to others he gave absolution there, having been appeased with large sums of money. Some, again, he utterly deprived of their benefices, or suspended until his grasping covetousness had been fully glutted. Thus it happened, by God's righteous judgment, that since, in their trouble, they would not follow sound counsel, but, fearing for their frock more than for their conscience, made their judge one who was not their judge, they felt this man's tyranny, and learnt thenceforth to struggle willingly to guard their privileges, and the liberties of the kingdom. But King

Alexander sent messengers to the court of Rome, and renewed the privileges whilom granted to his predecessors.

XL.

AFTERWARDS, in the year 1220, Alexander, king of Scotland, went, with some of the chief men of the kingdom, under a safe-conduct, to meet Henry, king of England, at York, about the Feast of the Holy Trinity. There negotiations were busily carried on between them. The king of Scotland bound himself to wed the eldest sister of the king of England, while the latter bound himself to see that the Scottish king's sisters—whom his own father had formerly taken, as already said, to get them married—were worthily mated; and they both took an oath on the Body to that effect, before a certain Pandulph, the English legate, and a good many other lords of either kingdom. Thus a peace was established, which was to last time without end; and they returned home in peace. But, the following year, after Whitsunday, Alexander, king of Scotland, in great state, and with a great bevy of knights, proceeded, again under a safe-conduct, to York, as had been agreed between those kings the year before; and, on the Friday before the Nativity of Saint John the Baptist, he was, to the great joy of both sides, betrothed to the English king's eldest sister, named Joan, as yet a girl of very tender age. And so our lord the king went safely home again with his betrothed, who, when she grew up, turned out very handsome, and comely, and beautiful. That same year, having raised an army out of Lothian and Galloway, and other outlying provinces, the king sailed for Argyll. But a storm arose; and being obliged to put back, he brought up at Glasgow, in safety, though not without danger. The following year, also, after Whitsunday, he led back the army into Argyll, for he was displeased with the natives for many reasons. The men of Argyll were frightened: some gave hostages and a great deal of money, and were taken back in peace; while others, who had more deeply offended against the king's will, forsook their estates and possessions, and fled. But our lord the king bestowed both the land and the goods of these men upon his own followers, at will; and thus returned in peace with his men.

XLI.

NOW, the same year—namely, in 1222—forasmuch as Adam, bishop of Caithness, and sometime abbot of Melrose, claimed tithes and other church rights from his subjects, these were kindled with fury; and, on Sunday, within eight days after the Blessed Mary's Nativity, being gathered together in a body of over three hundred men, they took him, beat, bound, wounded, and stripped him; and, throwing him down into his own kitchen, which had been set on fire, burnt him, after they had killed a monk of his, and one of his servants. But John, earl of Caithness, although he was dwelling close by, and had seen the people, armed, pouring in from all sides, upon being moreover, asked by some of that bishop's servants to bring help, dissembled and said: "If the bishop is afraid, let him come to me." Whence, also, it was believed by many that he was privy to that crime. But our lord the King Alexander, when he was on the point of starting for England, on the business of his realm, and had halted at Jed worth (Jedburgh), was brought news of this crime, by trustworthy messengers. So he put that business aside; and, raising an army, as became a Catholic man, he went forth even unto Caithness. The aforesaid earl, however, though he proved, by the witness of good men, that he was guiltless, and had given no countenance or advice to those ruffians, yet, because he had not straightway sought to take meet vengeance upon them, had to give up great part of his lands, and a large sum of money, to the king, in order to win his favour. He, likewise, handed over for punishment many of those who had wrought this deed; and the king had them mangled in limb, and racked with many a torture.

XLII.

AFTER Gilbert, archdeacon of Moray, had been there chosen bishop of Caithness, in presence of our lord the king and the chief men of his host, the king and his men returned home safe and sound, by God's vouchsafing, although there was at that time a very great storm, with floods of rain. Now while this was going on, the prelates of Scotland, fearing that, if news of so great an atrocity reached our lord the Pope, he would, perhaps, send a legate or an envoy to make inquiries as to what had happened, made known to that sovereign pontiff, by messengers of their own, both the truth of the matter, and the king's zeal in avenging the crime. Thereupon the Pope highly commended both their diligence and the king's task. But, the very next year, while King Alexander was keeping his birthday at Forfar, the Earl of Caithness met him there, and, by giving him money, got back that land which the king had, the year before, claimed as a quittance for the aforesaid bishop Adam's death. There were indeed a great many, at that time, who, within themselves, did not think well of this proceeding, and suspected that our lord the king had been overreached in this matter by evil advisers. Later, however, the earl did not escape punishment for that crime. For, afterwards, when seven years had gone by, that same earl was hemmed in by his foes, and killed and burnt in his own house. And he had richly earned such a death as he had, without a cause, made the venerable bishop Adam undergo. During this same time, some unrighteous men of the race of Macwilliam—namely, Gillespie, and his sons, and Rodoric—started up in the uttermost bounds of Scotland. But when they strove to overwhelm the kingdom by force, God gave them over, with their abettors, into King Alexander's hand; and thus the land was no longer troubled by their lawlessness.

XLIII.

IN the year 1235, Alexander, king of Scotland, mustered an army and entered Galloway, to quiet the land, and revenge himself upon the rebels. When the natives found this out, they unexpectedly started out of the hills and woods, and assailed the king and his army, who were resting in their tents—for that spot, full as it was of marshes, and goodly with gi-ass, as far as the eye could reach, gave them no little confidence. But Makintagart, who had then been made Earl of Ross, burst with furious might upon the rear of the natives, and swept down many, and many he forced to flee. The illegitimate son of Alan, lord of Galloway, however—Thomas, who had erst, in his father's lifetime, been betrothed to the daughter of the king of Man, and who was the leader of this heinous attempt, went back to Ireland, with Gilroth, an abettor of his. Next day, all the Gallwegians came with ropes round their necks, and begged for peace and the king's favour; so the king kindly accepted their submission. But this same Thomas, Alan's bastard son, came back to Galloway from Ireland, together with a king's son and many others; and, as soon as he got there, he broke up his ships, lest the Irish should think of fleeing. Soon after, however, seeing that his own men could not withstand the king's majesty, he, by the advice of the bishop of Whitehern, as well as of Patrick earl of Dunbar, and the abbot of Melrose, humbly besought the king for peace; so the king kept him, a little while, in the Castle of Maidens (Edinburgh), and then let him go. But the rest of the Irish, who would not fly the country, were slain in an attack by the citizens of Glasgow. Two of the chiefs, however, the king ordered to be torn asunder by horses, at Edinburgh. At that time, also, even the Scots of the king's army, when he had gone back, despoiled the lands and churches of Galloway with unheard-of cruelty—so much so that a monk at Glenluce, who was at the last gasp, was left naked but for his hair-shirt; and, at Tongueland, the prior and sacristan were slain in the church.

XLIV.

ON the day of Saint Maurice, in the year 1237, Alexander, king of Scots, and Henry, king of England, with the queens, their wives, and the lords of either kingdom, met at York; where, for fifteen days, they talked over the knotty business of the kingdoms, in presence of Otho, the legate of our lord the Pope. When their negotiations were over, the king of Scotland went home again in safety. But the queen of Scotland went with the queen of England, to Canterbury, for the purpose of praying; and the following year—the year 1237, to wit—on the 4th of

March, she died near London, in the arms of her brothers, Henry, king of England, and Richard, duke of Cornwall, who had her body buried in state in the church of the convent of Tarent. As, therefore, the king had begotten of her neither son nor daughter, he, on Whitsunday, the 15th of May 1239, by the advice of his lords, took to wife, at Roxburgh, the daughter of a nobleman, Ingram of Coucy. This lady was named Mary; and of her the king begat a son on whom the father's name was bestowed. So Alexander, the first-born of the king of Scotland, was born at Roxburgh, on the day of St. Cuthbert's translation, Wednesday, the 4th of September, when his father was beginning the forty-fourth year of his age, and was well-nigh at the end of the twenty-seventh of his reign.

XLV.

HAVING got together a numerous army, Henry, king of England, came to Newcastle-upon-Tyne, to wage war against Alexander, king of Scotland, forasmuch as a certain castle, which is called Hermitage (at Castleton), had been reared by the Scots, in the marches between Scotland and England, in Liddesdale. So King Alexander, with his army well equipped, went to meet him, as far as Caldwell, where all the chiefs renewed their fealty to our lord the king; and thus, all of one mind, they marched on as far as Pentland, ready to come to blows with the king of England, if he should enter Lothian. But, at the instance of the archbishop of York, and other great men, peace was restored between the kings; and the king of Scotland sped safely home again. The king of England, however, wheeled off towards Wales; because the Welsh were in rebellion against their English-born masters, and neither could, nor would, bear their thraldom any longer. The Welsh, therefore, the remains of the Britons, who, from the days of Brutus, their first prince, had had a king and prince of their own nation, were, during this time, so utterly subdued, that it is in London, the chief English city, that they try their causes—according to Merlin's prophecy:—The red dragon (that is, the Britons) shall pine away at the very end of the pool (that is, the very end of the island), quelled by the white dragon (whereby the English are meant).

XLVI.

Death of this King Alexander II.

THAT renowned king of Scots, Alexander II., while he was on his way to restore peace to the land of Argyll, was overtaken by grievous sickness, and carried across to an island which is called Kerneray (Kerrera); and there, in the year 1249, after he had partaken of the sacraments of eternal salvation, his blissful soul was snatched away from this life, and joined—as we believe—all the saints in the heavens. But his body was brought down to the church of Melrose, as he himself had willed in his lifetime; and after the obsequies due had been solemnly celebrated, after the manner of kings, it was there committed to the bosom of the earth, on Thursday, the 8th of July, about the ninth hour, in the fiftyfirst year of his age, and the thirty-fifth of his reign—for he was sixteen years and a half old when he was made king. While he lived, he was a most gentle prince towards his people, a father to the monks, the comforter of the needy, the helper of the fatherless, the pitiful hearer and most righteous judge of the widow and all who had a grievance, and, towards the church of Christ, a second Peter. These lines have been written on him:—In him

> "The church a buckler had, the people peace.
> The wretch a leader—second of his name;
> While thrice ten years and five his reign enclose.
> Kerrera's Isle beheld his soul's release,
> Blest fellowship with saints on high to claim;
> His earthly bones lie buried at Melrose."

He, also, together with his mother Ermengarde, founded and endowed the abbey of Saint Edward of Balmurinath (Balmerino), whither was sent the brotherhood of Melrose, with the Lord Alan, the abbot thereof, on the day of Saint Lucy the Virgin, in the year 1229; and there, four years afterwards, was buried that same noble queen Ermengarde, his mother—to wit, in the year 1323, the forty-seventh after her betrothal.

XLVII.

ALEXANDER, son of the aforesaid King Alexander, a boy of eight years of age, came to Scone on the following Tuesday, the 13th of July, with a number of earls, barons, and knights. There were, likewise, there, the venerable fathers, David of Bernham, bishop of Saint Andrews, and Galfrid, bishop of Dunkeld, a man in great favour with both clergy and people, zealous in temporal and spiritual things, who endeared himself with both great and poor, but was a terror to evil-doers. The abbot of the monastery of Scone itself was also there. But lo! as soon as they were gathered together, there arose a dispute among the nobles. For some of them would have made not a king, but a knight, on that day, saying that it was an Egyptian day. Now this was said not because of the Egyptian day, but because the lord Alan Dorwart, then justiciary of the whole of Scotland, wished to gird Alexander with the sword of knighthood on that day. While they were arguing, the lord Walter Comyn, Earl of Menteith, a man of foresight and shrewdness in counsel, answered and said that he had seen a king consecrated who was not yet a knight, and had many a time heard of kings being consecrated who were not knights; and he went on to say that a country without a king was, beyond a doubt, like a ship amid the waves of the sea, without rower or steersman. For he had always loved King Alexander, of pious memory, now deceased—and this boy also for his father's sake. So he moved that this boy be raised to the throne as quickly as possible,—for it is always hurtful to put off what may be done at once; and, by his advice, the said bishops and abbot, as well as the nobles, and the whole clergy and people, with one voice, gave their consent and assent to his being set up as king.

XLVIII.
Coronation of King Alexander III. at Scone.

AND it came to pass that when this same earl, Walter Comyn, and all the clergy, heard this, they joined unto them some earls—namely, the lord Malcolm, Earl of Fife, and the lord Malise, Earl of Stratherne—and a great many other nobles, and led Alexander, soon to be their king, up to the cross which stands in the graveyard, at the east end of the church. There they set him on the royal throne, which was decked with silken cloths inwoven with gold; and the bishop of Saint Andrews, assisted by the rest, consecrated him king, as was meet. So the king sat down upon the royal throne—that is, the stone—while the earls and other nobles, on bended knee, strewed their garments under his feet, before the stone. Now, this stone is reverently kept in that same monastery, for the consecration of the kings of Albania; and no king was ever wont to reign in Scotland, unless he had first, on receiving the name of king, sat upon this stone at Scone, which, by the kings of old, had been appointed the capital of Albania. But lo! when all was over, a highland Scot suddenly fell on his knees before the throne, and, bowing his head, hailed the king in his mother tongue, saying these words in Scottish;—"Benach de Re Albanne Alexander, MacAlexander, MacVleyham, MacHenri, MacDavid,"—and, reciting it thus, he read off, even unto the end, the pedigree of the kings of Scots. This means, in English:—"Hail, king of the Albanians, Alexander, son of Alexander, son of William, son of Henry, son of David, son of Malcolm, son of Duncan, son of Beatrice, daughter of Malcolm, son of Kenath, son of Malcolm, son of Donald, son of Constantine, son of Kenath, son of Alpine, son of Ethach, son of Ethafind, son of Echdach, son of Donald Brek, son of Echa Vuid, son of Edaim, son of Cobram, son of Donengard, son of Fergus the Great, son of Erth, son of Etehac Munremor, son of Engusafich, son of Fechelmech as Lingich, son of Enegussa Buchin, son of Fechelmech Romaith, son of Sencormach, son of Crinchlinth, son of Findachai, son of Akirkirre, son of Ecchach Andoch, son of Fiachrach Catmall, son of Ecddach Ried, son of Conor, son of Mogalama, son of

Lugthag Etholach, son of Corbre Crumgring, son of Darediomore, son of Corbre Findinor, son of Coneremore, son of Ederskeol, son of Ewein, son of Eliela, son of Jair, son of Dethach, son of Sin, son of Rosin, son of There, son of Rether, son of Rowen, son of Arindil, son of Mane, son of Fergus, first king of Scots in Albania." This Fergus also was the son of Feredach, although he is, by some, called the son of Ferechere; but these differ little in sound. This discrepancy is perhaps due to a blunder of the writer, from the word being hard to utter. Then the said Scot, going on with the said pedigree, from man to man, read through until he came to the first Scot—namely, Iber Scot. This Iber was the son of Gaithel Glas, son of Neoilus, whilom king of Athens; and was begotten of Scota, daughter of the Pharaoh Chenthres, king of Egypt.

XLIX.

AGAIN, in the second year of King Alexander III., on the 19th of June 1250, this king, and the queen his mother, with bishops and abbots, earls and barons, and other good men, both clerics and laymen, in great numbers, met at Dunfermline, and took up, in great state, the bones of the blessed Margaret, sometime queen of Scots, out of the stone monument where they had lain through a long course of years; and these they laid, with the deepest devoutness, in a shrine of deal, set with gold and precious stones. Meanwhile, the magnates of Scotland saw the danger in the country being under the governance of a boy king, and that his councillors, who were perhaps the greatest men of the whole kingdom, were swayed by the advantages each one had to gain. So, in order to avoid these and other threatening dangers, they, by the advice of the clergy, despatched a solemn embassy to Henry, king of England, to the end that the treaty of peace formerly made between him and the late king Alexander might be renewed, and most firmly secured by an alliance through a marriage to be contracted between the young king Alexander and this same King Henry's daughter. So, when this embassy came to London, the king of England granted all their demands to their hearts' content; and he also sent back with them to the king of Scotland, an embassy of his own, to ask him to come with his advisers and magnates, under the king's safe-conduct, sealed with the seals of the lords of England, and meet him and his councillors at York, on the following Christmas, in order to settle the aforesaid business. Accordingly, Alexander, king of Scotland, and Henry, king of England, with the chiefs of either kingdom, met there, and all things were happily settled, even as they had before been arranged; while the kings and the lords of both kingdoms swore, with their hands upon the most holy Gospels, that they should thenceforth be faithfully kept. Never did any of the English or British kings, in any past time, keep his pledges towards the Scots more faithfully or more steadfastly than this Henry; for, nearly the whole time of his reign, he was looked upon by the kings of Scotland, father and son, as their most faithful neighbour and adviser;—a thing which never, or seldom, had happened, save in the days—alas! so few—of Richard Cœur de Lion.

L.

ALEXANDER, king of Scotland, therefore, a boy of nine, there received the honour of knighthood at the hands of Henry, king of England, on Christmas Day, amid the greatest joy and good wishes of the lords of either kingdom; and, on the morrow—that is, on Saint Stephen's Day—the king of England gave his first-born daughter, named Margaret, in marriage to the king of Scotland. Meanwhile, some persons there were being accused before the king, by Walter Comyn, Earl of Menteith, and William, Earl of Mar, of treason towards him. By reason whereof some were afraid, and went home again stealthily, like cowards. The king of Scotland, however, having, by the advice of the king and magnates of England, arranged and regulated everything with moderation, went home again with his consort, and, disguising his intentions, awaited better times for correcting excesses of this kind. Robert, abbot of Dunfermline, likewise, the king's chancellor, was accused of intending to legitimate, by the great seal, the king's illegitimate sister (namely, the wife of Alan, the Hostiary), so that she might become the king's heiress in the succession to the throne. But as soon as he came back to Scotland, he gave up the seal to the king and his magnates, and it was straightway broken up in the people's sight; while a smaller seal was given to Gamelin, who became the king's chancellor, and who, the third year after, was chosen bishop of Saint Andrews. Meanwhile, all the king's first councillors were dismissed, and fresh ones created: namely, Walter Comyn, Earl of Menteith; Alexander Comyn, of Buchan; William Earl of Mar; and Robert of Ross, the king's cousin. But these councillors were so many kings. For he who saw the poor crushed down in those days, the nobles ousted from their inheritance, the drudgery forced upon citizens, the violence done to churches, might with good reason say, "Woe unto the kingdom where the king is a boy!"

LI.

WHEN, therefore, judgment and righteousness in the kingdom of Scotland were slumbering, Henry, king of England, of the goodwill he bore his son the king, and the lords, on being besought of them, came, like a leal father, to Wark Castle. There the kings and their advisers set busily to work to talk over the state of the kingdom of Scotland. All the Scottish king's councillors were forthwith dismissed from their offices; and Richard bishop of Dunkeld was appointed his chancellor—David of Lyndsay, chamberlain—and Alan Durward, high justiciary, for seven years. But when that peaceful King Henry had returned with his train, a great feud arose among the magnates of Scotland, by reason of the king's new councillors demanding from his former councillors an account of the king's squandered goods, and calling upon them, by letters obligatory, to answer for their deeds. On his way back, the king of England slew many Jews at Lincoln, because they had ruthlessly killed a boy, named Hugh, and made a holy martyr of him. For this he hanged some on the gallows, and others he caused to be hunted down by horses through the streets; for they had hung the said child upon a cross, and put him to death there.

LII.

WALTER COMYN, Earl of Menteith, and his accomplices, were more than once summoned before the king and his councillors, upon many grave charges; but they did not appear. But as they durst not await their trial according to the statutes of the kingdom, they took counsel together, and, with one accord, seized the king, by night, while he was asleep in bed at Kinross, and, before dawn, carried him off with them to Strivilyn (Stirling), the day after that of Saint Simon and Saint Jude, in the year 1257. They also took away by force the great seal, which was held by Master Robert Stutewill, dean of Dunkeld, and vice-chancellor to Richard, bishop of Dunkeld. The ringleaders in this kidnapping were Walter Comyn, Earl of Menteith—Alexander Comyn, Earl of Buchan—William Earl of Mar, a man of great shrewdness in evil deeds—John Comyn, a man prone to robbery and rashness—Hugh of Abernethy—David of Lochore—Hugh of Barclay—and a great many other hangers-on of these disaffected men, who did all as they pleased and naught as was lawful, and reigned over the people, right or wrong. And thus the last going astray was worse than the first. Thenceforth there arose much persecution and distress among the Scots lords; because the king's later advisers strove to pay back to the former ones the evils and losses they themselves had erst undergone. Whereupon there followed such grinding of the poor and robbing of churches, as have not been seen in Scotland in our day.

LIII.

BUT Walter Comyn, the oft-mentioned Earl of Menteith, who was the leader of those who had seized the king, died a sudden death—poisoned, it is said, by his wife. Upon his death, the countess, his wife, disdaining the noble lords who wished to wed her, married a low-born English knight, named John Russel. The magnates of Scotland took this in high dudgeon, and charged her with the death of the earl, her former husband; so both John himself and the countess were loaded with chains. Then Walter Bullock, on his wife's behalf, boldly claimed the earldom of Menteith, and got the magnates to side with him. The countess, however, unable to make head against the attacks of so many adversaries, took a sum of money, and, with her husband, set off out of Scotland in disgrace. Then she sent messengers to the court of Rome, to complain of the violence done her, and of having been despoiled of her inheritance; and, at her request, an envoy, named Pontius, was afterwards sent from our lord the Pope Urban, into England, and came to York, to make inquiry, at our lord the Pope's special command, into the wrongs and annoyances unjustly inflicted upon that countess. So Pontius had this Walter Bullock, the holder of the said earldom, summoned, as well as well-nigh all the bishops, abbots, and lords of Scotland, to bear witness to the truth in this matter. Now this was against the privileges of the king and kingdom of Scotland—that any one should be called to account by any one outside his own borders. So the king, considering that not only were he himself, and his kingdom, and his people, aggrieved by this summons, but also his ancient privileges were, in this respect, done away with, since he himself was ready to decide this cause according to the laws of his kingdom, brooked not that he and his country should be any longer unduly put upon, and appealed to the supreme pontiff against the said Pontius. And so this suit is still pending under discussion.

LIV.

ON the 9th of May 1261, in the thirteenth year of King Alexander, a stately and venerable cross was found at Peebles, in the presence of good men, priests, clerics, and burgesses. But it is quite unknown in what year and by what persons it was hidden there. It is, however, believed that it was hidden by some of the faithful, about the year of Our Lord 296, while Maximian's persecution was raging in Britain. Not long after this, a stone urn was discovered there, about three or four paces from the spot where that glorious cross had been found. It contained the ashes and bones of a man's body—torn limb from limb, as it were. Whose relics these are, no one knows as yet. Some, however, think they are the relics of him whose name was found written in the very stone wherein that holy cross was lying. Now there was carved in that stone, outside, "Tomb of the Bishop Saint Nicholas." Moreover, in the very spot where the cross was found, many a miracle was, and is, wrought by that cross; and the people poured, and still pour, thither in crowds, devoutly bringing their offerings and vows to God. Wherefore the king, by the advice of the bishop of Glasgow, had a handsome church made there, to the honour of God and the Holy Cross. That same year—on the last day of February, to wit—was born the king's first-born daughter, named Margaret, who was afterwards betrothed to the king of Norway.

LV.

ABOUT the Feast of the blessed Peter, which is called *ad vincula*, in the year 1263, Hako, king of Norway, came to the new castle of Ayr, with eight score war-ships, having on board 20,000 fighting men: for he said that all the Scottish islands lying between Ireland and Scotland were his by right of inheritance. So he took the castles of Bothe (Bute) and Man, and sacked the churches along the sea-board. Whereupon, at God's command, on the very day that both the kings had appointed for battle, there arose, at sea, a very violent storm, which dashed the ships together; and a great part of the fleet dragged their anchors, and were roughly cast on shore, whether they would or not. Then the king's army came against them, and swept down many, both nobles and serfs; and a Norican (Norwegian), King Hako's nephew, a man of great might and vigour, was killed. On account of this, the king of the Noricans (Norwegians) himself, sorrowing deeply, hurried back, in no little dismay, to Orkney; and while wintering there, awaiting a stronger force to fight it out with the Scots, he died. These rhymes have been made about him:—

"Hako, that bold and mighty lord.
Of lamblike gentleness,
Holds o'er the unjust his threat'ning sword.

But does the just caress."

He was succeeded by his son, named Magnus, a man of great wisdom and good sense, and renowned for his love of letters. The following was made up about him in like manner:—

"I rule the Noric coast;
Magnus the name I boast."

LVI.

ON the 21st of December 1264—the day of St. Agnes the Virgin—there was born unto King Alexander, at Jedworth (Jedburgh), a son, called by his father's name—to wit, Alexander. Therefore God's praises rang throughout all the ends of Scotland, for a twofold cause: namely, that in one and the same day the king got news, by one messenger, of the death of the king of the Norwegians, who troubled the king and kingdom; and, by another, of the birth of his young son. But as soon as the death of Hako, king of the Norwegians, was made known to the king of Scotland, the latter hastily got a strong army together, and made ready to set out, with a fleet, towards the Isle of Man. The king of Man, however, hearing of this, and being panic-stricken, despatched his ambassadors to the king to beg that a truce might be granted him, so that he might present himself before the king in Scotland. But the king was prudent enough not to swerve from his purpose, or turn back; but, after sending the king of Man a safe-conduct, he quickly mustered his troops, and, at their head, made for the Isle of Man. When the king of Scotland had reached the town of Dumfries, that petty king met him, and became his man, doing homage unto him for his petty kingdom, which he was to hold of him for ever;—upon this condition, however: that if the king of the Norwegians, for the time being, undertook to molest him, he should have safe shelter for him and his in Scotland, for all time to come; while, on the other hand, the petty king of Man should furnish to his lord, the king of Scotland, as often as the latter had need of them, ten war galleys—five twenty-four-oared, and five more twelve-oared. When this business was settled, Alexander Earl of Buchan,

William Earl of Mar, and Alan the Hostiary, took with them, with due haste, by the king's instructions, no mean band of knights and natives, and went to the Western Isles of Scotland, where they slew those traitors who had, the year before, encouraged the king of Norway to bring up in Scotland. Some of these they put to flight; and, having hanged some of the chiefs, they brought with them thence exceeding great plunder.

LVII.

THE following year, Hako's son, Magnus, king of Norway, sent his chancellor, Gilbert, bishop of Hamere, to Alexander, king of Scotland, at Perth, to offer him the islands of Bute and Aranch (Arran), to be had in peaceful possession for ever, provided, however, that he himself might hold in peace all the other islands which his father Hako had demanded. The king scouted the very idea of this; so the bishop, having heard the answer to his message, went off to his own country, and pointed out to his king that his trouble had been thrown away. He advised the king, however, to treat with the Scots. The next following year, therefore—that is, in 1266—this same Norican king, Magnus, sent his chancellor and others of his magnates into Scotland, to bestow upon Alexander, king of Scots, on behalf of their lord the king of Norway, by letters embodying his resolution, all the islands between Scotland and Ireland, which his father Hako had declared to be his; and they also gave back to the said king of Scots all right or claim which King Magnus himself, or any of his predecessors, had ever had on the said islands: Provided, however, that, on his side, the king of Scots paid to the said king of Norway 4000 merks of silver within two years, and afterwards 100 merks a year to him and his heirs. Now, though this covenant gave satisfaction to some, yet to more it was distasteful. For, through a long course of time, long before the Scots had come to Britain, having been first brought in by Eugenius Rothay, a leader of theirs, had they been dwelling in the aforesaid islands; and thereafter, until that deadly time of the struggle of the sons of Malcolm Canmore, king of

Scotland, against their uncle Donald—when the kingdom was wholly split up, and the Norican king Magnus, son of Olave, attacked the islands in great force, and brought them under his sovereignty—the Scots had possessed the same continually, without any break or hindrance.

LVIII.

THE year before, a great feud had arisen between Henry, king of England, and his son Edward, on the one hand, and Simon de Montfort, Earl of Leicester, and the magnates of England, on the other. These magnates cast out of England, in dismay, Eleanor, queen of England, and all of French birth. But the king and his son gathered a strong army together from all sides, and fought a battle against the said magnates at Lewes. At length, after no little slaughter of lords and people had been made on either side, the king and his son Edward were taken, as well as John Comyn, and some others from Scotland, who, at the Scots king's bidding, had come to King Henry's rescue, and were taken and thrust into prison in London. Afterwards, however, the English king's son, Edward, who had been kept in the closest custody, escaped by unheard-of cleverness, through the management of Gilbert Earl of Gloucester. Thereupon a large army was assembled from all sides, and a desperate battle was fought at Evesham, between the said Edward and Simon de Montfort. In this struggle, Simon himself and his first-born, Henry, were killed; and it is said that eighty-seven lords and three hundred nobles, besides serfs and foot, fell in this battle. Now King Alexander had, of his own free will, levied three men from every hyde of land, to despatch them to the assistance of the king of England and his son Edward, in this war; but, hearing of the overthrow of Simon and his confederates, the Scots people were spared this trouble. All who had stood out with Simon in the war were disinherited, and outlawed from England; so that, within a week, the king bestowed, it said, the lands of 17,560 nobles upon aliens. There were, however, deadly plots at that time between the king and the rest of the barons. Villages were burnt down, towns razed to the ground, churches sacked; and there was never any peace or security. The king's son Edward, at length, wishing to bring under his yoke all those who had rebelled against him, took John de Vesci, and some others, by stealth, at Alnwick Castle, and sent them over to London; then he took up his quarters at Roxburgh, in order to have an interview with the king of Scotland. He was met by the king of Scotland and Queen Margaret, sister to the said Edward, and nearly all the nobility of Scotland; and after many rejoicings and compliments made by each to the other, they returned home in joy.

LIX.

MEANWHILE Ottobonus, legate of the Roman See, came to England to restore peace between the king and the barons, and took up his abode in Loudon. Considering, however, that he was labouring in vain, he wrote to the bishpps of Scotland to send him four merks from every parish church, and six merks from every cathedral church, by way of procuration. But King Alexander of Scotland, having received this money—2000 merks—from the clergy, utterly forbade that this should be done; and, moreover, appealed to the Apostolic See about it. Then, in the year 1268, all the bishops of Scotland were summoned by this same legate, Ottobonus, to compear before him, wherever he might be, in the fortnight after Easter, to hold his council. In like manner he commanded the clergy of Scotland to send either two abbots, or two priors, for the whole kingdom of Scotland. The bishops, in a general council, deputed Richard, bishop of Dunkeld, and Robert, bishop of Dunblane, on their behalf, so that nothing which could damage or aggrieve them might be enacted in their absence. But the rest of the clergy sent, on their behalf, the abbot of Dunfermline and the prior of Lindores. So the legate enacted some new statutes—chiefly about the secular and regular priests of the Scots—which the bishops of Scotland utterly refused to abide by. That same year, many, in all lands, took the badge of the cross against the Saracens. Louis, the most Christian king of France, with a great swarm of his lords, took the badge of the cross.

So did Edward and Edmund, sons of the king of England, and a great crowd of Englishmen with them. For the expenses of these, Pope Clement, by the advice of Ottobomis, and at the instance of the king of England, wrote to the clergy of Scotland to pay to the king of England every tenth penny of all the income of their Church. The king and clergy, however, with one voice and with one heart, scorned to do this. But, the following year, Henry, king of England, again sent his ambassadors into Scotland, to ask the clergy for one penny in ten; and the clergy, as before, protested, appealed to our lord the Pope, and sent clerks to his court.

LX.

IN the year 1271, Louis, king of France, after he had won from the discomfited Saracens a certain very large island named Barbary, met his doom; as did his first-born son Louis, and much people of the Christians with them—among others, David Earl of Athol, and Adam Earl of Carrick, and a great many other Scottish and English nobles. Now Adam Earl of Carrick left an only daughter, named Martha, as his heiress; and she succeeded him in his domain and earldom. After she had, therefore, become mistress of her father's domain, as she was, one day, going out hunting at random, with her esquires and handmaidens, she met a gallant knight riding across the same country—a most seemly youth, named Robert of Bruce, son of Robert, surnamed the Bruce, the noble lord of Annandale in Scotland, and of Cleveland, in England. When greetings and kisses had been given on each side, as is the wont of courtiers, she besought him to stay and hunt, and walk about; and seeing that he was rather unwilling to do so, she by force, so to speak, with her own hand, made him pull up, and brought the knight, although very loath, to her castle of Turnberry with her. After dallying there, with his followers, for the space of fifteen days or more, he clandestinely took the countess to wife; while the friends and well-wishers of both knew nothing about it, nor had the king's consent been got at all in the matter. Therefore the common belief of the whole country was that she had seized—by force, as it were—this youth for her husband. But when this came to King Alexander's ears, he took the castle of Turnberry, and made all her other lands and possessions be acknowledged as in his hands; because she had wedded with Robert of Bruce without having consulted his royal majesty. By means of the prayers of friends, however, and by a certain sum of money agreed upon, this Robert gained the king's goodwill, and the whole domain. Of Martha, by God's providence, he begat a son, who was to be the saviour, champion, and king, of the bruised Scottish people, as the course of the history will show forth; and his father's name Robert, was given him.

"In twelve seven four since Christ our manhood wore,
And at the feast when Benedict deceased.
That noble knight, King Robert, saw the light.
Called from the womb by Heaven's almighty doom."

LXI.
WHEN a very old man, Henry, that most peaceable king of England, after having governed his kingdom in the greatest peace and righteousness for fifty-six years, flitted to Christ, on the 20th of November 1273, the twenty-fourth year of the reign of Alexander, king of Scots; and he was buried at Westminster, in London. He was succeeded on the throne of England by his son, Edward, called Longshanks, who was then in the Holy Land; and all the magnates, clergy, and people of England swore fealty to Edward while he still kept on in the wars with the barbarians. When Edward afterwards came back, the king of Scotland, with his queen and children, made every effort to be present at his coronation, which took place in London, on the day of the Assumption of the blessed Virgin Mary, in the year 1274. The king of Scotland was there, with great pomp; as were also the queen, and many lords and nobles. That same year, however, on the 26th of February, the said queen of Scotland, Margaret, King Henry's daughter, and this King Edward's sister, died at the castle of Cupar, and was entombed beside King David, at Dunfermline. The third year after.

King Alexander went on a pilgrimage, to Saint Thomas, in England; and there, without prejudice to all his dignities, did homage to Edward, king of England, as he had formerly done to Edward's father also, for his lands in England: namely, for the lands and lordship of Penrith, and sundry others, which King Henry had given him of old, as a marriage portion with his daughter Margaret, queen of Scotland, now deceased; also for the other lands and ancient honours formerly possessed by his predecessors the kings of Scotland, except the earldom of Huntingdon—for which domain Simon, abbot of Dunfermline, and William Earl of Mar, had erst been sent by the aforesaid Alexander, king of Scotland, to that same King Henry, almost in his last days; but Henry would on no account give it up, and kept the whole earldom for himself, though the king of Scotland had, through his forefathers, been holding the honours thereof from days of yore, and possessed them wholly at the time of the peace.

LXII.

MASTER BAIAMUND was sent by our lord the Pope, and came to Scotland, to levy and put by the tithes, as an aid for the Holy Land. On the day after the Feast of the king and martyr, Saint Oswald, in the year 1275, he held his council at Perth and, at a sitting there, together with the bishops and clergy, he decreed that all the beneficed clergy, without excepting any—not even the privileged—should, under stress of an oath and of excommunication, pay tithes of all the goods and income of the Church, not after the old taxation, but according to their real worth. Moreover, this Baiamund, at the request of the bishops and abbots, went back to court, to beg our lord the Pope, on behalf of the clergy of Scotland, to take the old taxations of all their goods, whereby seven years were reckoned as only six. But he came back to Scotland without having sped well. Meanwhile, through the bishop of Durham, there sprung up a dispute between Alexander, king of Scotland, and Edward, king of England, about the boundaries and marches of the two kingdoms. To settle this dispute, three bishops of Scotland—those of

Saint Andrews, Glasgow, and Dunblane—with a great many earls and other nobles, met, on behalf of the king of Scotland, at Berwick-on-Tweed, in the middle of Lent, in the year 1278; while, on behalf of the king of England, there met, at Tweedmouth, the bishops of Norwich and Durham, the Sheriff of Newcastle, and a great many other knights and clergy, to treat of the aforesaid boundaries and marches. But they went away without having settled the business.

LXIII.

ON the Sunday next after Martinmas, in the winter of the year 1282, the lord Alexander, son of Alexander, king of Scotland, took to wife, at Roxburgh, the daughter of the lord count of Flanders, in the presence of many Flemish knights and ladies, amid unbounded joy and compliments. A great many Scottish bishops, abbots, earls, barons, knights, and the other nobles, also, were there met together; and after remaining there for the space of fifteen days, when the wedding had been solemnized in great state, they at length hied them home again. But, alas! this great joy was, within a short time, followed by deep mourning. For this Alexander, this gallant youth, who, it was hoped, would have been the heir to the Scots throne, died, the next year, at Lindores, in the twentieth year of his age, and was buried at Dunfermline, amid the boundless grief of the whole people, the tears and groans of all the clergy, and the endless sobs of the king and the magnates. He died in the year 1283. His younger brother, David, moreover, had departed this life before him, at Strivelyn (Stirling) Castle, at the end of the month of June 1281, amid the deep wailing of all the Scots, and the still deeper wailing of the king; and he lies buried in the monastery of Dunfermline. His death was the beginning of Scotland's sorrows to come. Alas! woe worth the day, Scotland! for, even though thou had known that so many days of mourning and tears were in store for thee, evils so great are hastening upon thee without fail,

"That, if thou knew, thou ne'er could think to bear them."

But after the death of the aforesaid Alexander, the king's firstborn, four knights, sent by the count of Flanders, came to our lord the king of Scotland, in order to bring to her father, the aforesaid count, his daughter, the widow of Alexander, the king's son lately deceased. Our lord the king and his councillors were long in treaty on this matter, and, at length, agreed that the aforesaid lady should go back to her father, without plighting her troth to our lord king for her dowry. This was done accordingly; and they were sent away with gifts, and hied them home.

LXIV.

MARGARET, likewise, the king's only daughter, was, before her brother Alexander died, betrothed to Hangow, king of Norway, and, about the beginning of the month of August, she crossed the water with a noble train—with Earl Walter and the countess of Menteith, the abbot of Balmurinach (Balmerino), Barnard of Monteält, and many other knights and nobles. Of these, while on their way back, after the solemn celebration of the nuptials, the said abbot, and Barnard, and many others, were drowned. But Earl Walter and his wife sped back safely to Scotland from Norway. This lady Margaret, however, queen of the Norwegians, after she had lived a year and a half with the king, her husband, paid the debt of nature on the 9th of April, the beginning of the same year her brother Alexander died. Of her, the Norican king begat only one daughter, also named Margaret, who likewise departed this life—as will be told below—as soon as she was grown up. The king of Norway, however, after the death of the queen, his spouse, and daughter of the king of Scotland, sent a solemn embassy to the latter king, to ask and recover, for the use of his own daughter aforesaid—the Scottish king's granddaughter, to wit—a rent of seven hundred merks on certain lands, according to covenants entered upon between those kings, and supported by writs. The king welcomed these ambassadors kindly, and, despatching, by the advice of his lords, an embassy of his own to the Norwegian king, sent them back in honour, with vast and sundry gifts.

LXV.

Now, in these days—namely, in the year 1281—the English king Edward, with a countless host, made his way into Wales, where he overcame Llewellyn, the prince of the British nation; and, after much people had been killed on either side, at length the prince himself was ruthlessly and seditiously murdered. So King Edward, by fierce warfare, made himself lord of the whole of Wales, and superior of the remains of the Britons. Therefore, to show his great gladness, and on account of the wished-for victory gained over the Welsh, he held a round table in Wales, at the foot of Snowdon. This king, also, carried off by force the whole of the papal tithes collected in his kingdom for six years, according to the real worth of all the income of the Church, in aid of the Holy Land, and put by in sundry monasteries and cathedral churches of his kingdom—the journey to the Holy Land being thus thwarted. With this countless sum of money, therefore, it is said, he got Wales, he fortified the strongholds, castles, and town walls thereof, and, at the cost of that money, he allayed a most grievous war which he shortly afterwards waged against the Scots. Meanwhile David, brother to this Llewellyn, prince of Wales, had this judgment passed upon him, in London, by that same tyrant king: that he should be drawn by horses as a traitor, hanged as a robber, beheaded as a freebooter, that his bowels should be burnt, and his body quartered, one part of his body being sent to each of the four parts of the kingdom. Moreover, he issued there this edict, which was cried by the voice of heralds throughout all England and Wales: that no one of British birth, of whatever condition he might be, should spend a night within walled towns, castles, strongholds, or any fortresses whatever, on pain of loss of life and limb. This chapter is shortly introduced there, lest any foreign nation which may read the said history should, unchastened by the example of the Welsh, unwarily fall under the dominion of most wretched thraldom to the English.

LXVI.

IN the tenth year after the queen's death—namely, in 1284—King Alexander, by the advice of his liegemen, took steps to send his ambassadors—to wit, his chancellor, Thomas of Charteris, Patrick of Græme, William of St. Clair, and John of Soulis, knights—to look him out a spouse sprung of a noble stock. So, without delay or tarrying at all, they went off to France, after the Feast of Candlemas.

LXVII.

Betrothal of Yolande, Daughter of the Count of Dreux, in France, to Alexander III., King of Scots—This King's Death.

THE Lord Alexander III., king of Scotland, was, on the day of Saint Calixtus, betrothed to Yolande, daughter of the count of Dreux; and a great many nobles, both of France and Scotland, with a countless throng of both sexes, solemnly met together to celebrate their nuptials royally. When these were over, the French, except a few who abode with the queen, hied back in gladness, laden with various gifts. The same year, on the 19th of March, this Alexander of goodly memory, the illustrious king of Scotland, died at Kinghorn, and was buried in state at Dunfermline. How worthy of tears, and how hurtful, his death was to the kingdom of Scotland, is plainly shown forth by the evils of after times. This king reigned thirty-six years. All the days of the life of this king, the Church of Christ flourished, her priests were honoured with due worship, vice was withered, craft there was none, wrong came to an end, truth was strong, and righteousness reigned. Moreover, rightly, and by reason of the merits of his uprightness, was he called king: seeing that he ruled himself and his people aright, allowing unto each his rights; and if, at any time, any of his people rebelled, he curbed their madness with discipline so unbending, that they would put a rope round their necks, ready for hanging, were that his will and pleasure, and bow themselves under his rule. By reason whereof he was looked upon with equal fear and love, both far and near, not only by his friends, but also by his adversaries,—and especially by the English. And all the time he lived upon earth security reigned in steadfastness of peace and quiet, and gleeful freedom. Scotland, truly unhappy, when bereft of so great a leader and pilot; while—greater unhappiness still!—he left no lawful offspring to succeed him. Thou hast an everlasting spring of mourning and sorrow in the death of one whose praiseworthy life bestowed, on thee especially, such increase of welfare.

LXVIII.

Beginning of the government of the Guardians after King Alexander's death.

WHEN, however, the aforesaid noble prince was dead, as well as all the children begotten of his body, and all his lawful heirs and kinsmen, in any way, either lineally or collaterally, descended from his grandfather King William—except one little girl, named Margaret, the daughter of Margaret, queen of Norway, late daughter of the aforesaid King Alexander—the kingdom of Scotland was six years and nine months without the governance of a king—as was said in the old prophecy:—

"While twice three years, and moons thrice three roll by,
Under no prince the widow'd land shall lie."

So it was governed by six guardians: namely, William Fraser, lord bishop of Saint Andrews—Duncan, Earl of Fife—and John Comyn, Earl of Buchan, deputed from the northern part, this side of the Forth; and Robert, bishop of Glasgow—the lord John Comyn—and James, steward of Scotland, appointed from the southern side of the water of Forth. Duncan of Fife, however, shortly afterwards put off this mortal coil, as will be seen further on. But, while the aforesaid number of years still lasted, Edward I., king of England, a noble prince, seeing that the aforesaid girl, named Margaret (daughter of the king of Norway, as well as daughter of his own sister's daughter), was the true and lawful heiress of the kingdom of Scotland, and aiming, with all zeal and earnestness, at joining and uniting the aforesaid kingdom of Scotland to his own kingdom, ordained and appointed, in the year 1289, six special commissioners and envoys extraordinary, to arrange, plan, and treat, between himself and the aforesaid guardians of Scotland, as well as the other bishops and the whole of the clergy, and the nobles—earls and barons—and the whole Estates of the realm, for contracting a marriage between Edward, his own son and heir, and the aforesaid Margaret, then the true heiress of Scotland.

LXIX.

Now when the ambassadors had told their business, and were duly carrying on negotiations with the nobles of the aforesaid Estates, the before-mentioned guardians, by the advice of the others of the kingdom, determined that they would agree to the request of those ambassadors: provided, however, that, with respect to the rights and customs, both lay and ecclesiastical, theretofore used and kept, the kingdom of Scotland were as free and quit of all thraldom and subjection, as ever it had been, at its best and freest, during the lifetime of Alexander III., the illustrious king thereof;—according to what appears in a certain instrument drawn up by them, a copy whereof is more fully contained in the book of the pleading of Baldred. And in case the aforesaid marriage did not hold good, or either of the contracting parties deceased without issue, while the other survived,—in any case or event, the aforesaid kingdom was to be freely, entirely, and absolutely, without any subjection, restored and returned to the next heirs. So, in order that the said matter might be carried through to the end wished for, the nobles of Scotland solemnly despatched to the king of Norway, two knights, distinguished for their knowledge and character—Michael of Wemyss and Michael Scot—to perform the marriage, and bring the girl to the kingdom. But, woe worth the day! before the thing was consummated, the said maiden departed this life, in the year 1291. Upon her death, a dispute straightway arose between John of Balliol and Robert of Bruce the elder (for there were three then alive, called by the same name: to wit, Robert, this elder noble—his son—and his grandson, who, afterwards, was king of the kingdom of Scotland, by right and inheritance). This dispute was, in time, settled in the following way.

LXX.

Discussion of the rights of Robert of Bruce and of John of Balliol.

THE nobles of the before-mentioned kingdom, with its aforenamed guardians, oftentimes discussed among themselves the question as to who should be made their king; but they did not make bold to utter what they felt about the right of succession, partly because it was a hard and knotty matter; partly because different people felt differently about those rights, and wavered a good deal; partly because they justly feared the power of the parties, which was great, and greatly to be feared; and partly because they had no superior who could, by his unbending power, carry their award into execution, or make the parties abide by their decision. When they had earnestly thought over this, they, at length, with one consent, decided among themselves to send special messengers to Edward, king of England, that he might become supreme judge in this matter, and declare the right of each; and, by his might, duly coerce, according to the requirements of the law, that party against whom he might pronounce his award. Therefore they sent the lord bishop of Saint Andrews, W. Eraser, in conjunction with some others, to fetch him, while he was looking after his own business in distant parts. Edward came, on being asked, and fixed a day for all the nobles of the kingdom of Scotland, of whatever standing or condition they might be, to meet together before him at Berwick; and he commanded that the parties between whom the controversy was, as well as all the others who claimed a right to the said kingdom, should be called: provided, however, that such summons or compearing should beget no prejudice to the kingdom of Scotland, and also that no right or superiority of dominion should thereby accrue to Edward; as he was called thereto, not as lord paramount, or judge by right, but as a friendly umpire, and the strongest neighbour, to settle a quarrel, equally by his wisdom and his might, after the manner of a friendly peacemaker, and for the sake of reciprocity. Against this they guarded in set terms, by letters-patent from him, before the day and opening of the lawsuit.

LXXI.

ALL the freeholders of the kingdom of Scotland, therefore, who should, or could, be there, met together before him at Berwick, and swore an oath that they would steadfastly abide by his award, to be issued as a judgment, so far as it declared the right of succession to the throne; and all the bishops and others of the clergy, as well as the aforesaid wardens, earls, and barons, and the other estates, both of burgesses and freeholders, bound themselves by an authentic instrument, supported by the seals of all the above-mentioned, that they would, all and sundry, obey, as rightful and actual king, and overlord, that one of the two competitors that Edward declared should reign. When, therefore, this had been arranged, this oft-mentioned king chose men distinguished by their knowledge and years, for their character and trustiness, and the most discreet in each station or degree, to the number of eighty, according to some—but, according to others, forty—and according to the opinion of certain men, four-and-twenty, twelve of whom were from England and twelve from Scotland. These, when they had taken a solemn oath to speak the truth, he commissioned to bar all the rest who claimed a right to the throne—for they were very many; and, by what they owed to the oath they had sworn, and at the peril of their souls, to search faithfully and determine between the aforesaid—namely, John and Robert; and, having determined between them, to make known unto him which of them had the better and clearer right to the throne of Scotland, so as to succeed the foresaid King Alexander, by right of near kinship, according to the approved custom of the kingdom. The assize, having been arranged as stated above, was removed to a spot away from the haunts of the people, and closely guarded; and the king alone was wont to go in, when and as often as he would, unaccompanied, to those of the assize, and would oftentimes ask how the thing would go. At length, from their hints, he gathered that, according to law and approved custom, the right of Robert the Bruce was the stronger.

LXXII.

THEREUPON he strengthened the guard of the assize, and withdrew; and having privily called his own people, he announced to them the determination of the assize, and, with their counsel, debated as to what was to be done in the above matter. But Anthony Bek, bishop of Durham, put this question to him:—"If Robert of Bruce were king of Scotland, where would Edward, king of England, be? For this Robert is of the noblest stock of all England, and, with him, the kingdom of Scotland is very strong in itself; and, in times gone by, a great deal of mischief has been wrought to the kings of England by those of Scotland." At this, the king, patting him on the head—as it were—answered in the French tongue, saying:—"Par le sank Dieu, vous aves bun chante;" which is to say, "By Christ's blood! thou hast sung well. Things shall go otherwise than I had arranged at first." In like manner, all of his council, now stealthily, now openly, suggested unto him that he should never give judgment without receiving their subjection—for that a fit time was at hand, when he could fulfil the desire he had so long brooded over. When this had been thus well weighed, he sent for the elder Robert of Bruce, and asked him whether he would hold the aforesaid kingdom of him in chief, so that he—Edward—might make and appoint him king thereof. Robert answered straightforwardly, and said:—"If I can get the aforesaid kingdom by means of my right and a faithful assize, well and good; but if not, I shall never, in gaining that kingdom for myself, reduce it to thraldom—a kingdom which all the kings thereof have hitherto, with great toil and trouble, kept free from thraldom, in security of peace." When he heard this, and Robert had moved away, Edward called John of Balliol, and plied him in like manner with the same question as before; but Balliol, after having quickly deliberated with his council, which had been quite bought over, fell in with the aforesaid king's wishes, that he should hold the kingdom of Scotland of him, and do him homage for the same. Thereupon, the parties were, soon after, called up; and, in presence of the nobles of Scotland and England, Edward pronounced John Balliol to be the lawful heir in the succession to the throne, and by his award decided that he had the stronger right. After the judgment was given, however, the Earl of Gloucester, holding Robert of Bruce by the hand, in the sight of all, spoke thus unto the king:—"Recollect, O king, what kind of judgment thou hast given to-day; and know that thou must be judged at the last." And straightway, at that earl's bidding, the aforesaid Robert Bruce withdrew; nor did he ever tender homage or fealty to John of Balliol.

LXXIII.
Account, or Pedigree, of the Kings of Scotland.

THAT the right of John of Balliol and Robert of Bruce, however, might be brought out more clearly, there is here brought in, abridged, the line of descent of the kings of Scotland, coming down from King Malcolm and his spouse. Saint Margaret, to the death of Margaret, daughter of the king of Norway and Margaret, queen of that kingdom—the daughter, to wit, of King Alexander III., at whose death all issue descending either lineally or collaterally from King William, was utterly extinct and wiped out. When this has been seen, the right of the aforesaid, who long wrangled for the throne of Scotland, will be more easily and clearly evident.

LXXIV.

IN the year 1067, Malcolm, king of Scotland, took to wife Margaret, of whom he begat six renowned sons,—namely, Edward, Edmund, Ethelred, Edgar, Alexander, and David; and two daughters—Matilda, and Mary. Of these six sons, three reigned successively—namely, Edgar, Alexander, and David. But all the sons, except David, died childless; and he begat only one son, named Henry, Earl of Huntingdon. This Henry begat three sons—Malcolm, William, and David—and died before his father. Upon King David's death, his grandson Malcolm, then twelve years old, reigned eight years, and died. He was succeeded by his brother William, who reigned fifty-two years, and died, and was buried in the monastery of Abirbrothoc (Arbroath), which he had himself founded. This King William begat Alexander II., who succeeded him, and reigned thirty-six years. He died at Curlay (Kerrera), and was buried at Melrose. This Alexander begat Alexander III., who succeeded his father, and reigned thirty-six years. He died at Kinghorn, in the thirty-seventh year of his reign, and was buried at Dunfermline. This Alexander III. begat, of Margaret, queen of Scotland, and sister of King Edward I. of England (she lies entombed at Dunfermline), two sons— Alexander, and David; but they both died childless before their father. He also begat, of that same queen, one only daughter, named Margaret. This daughter was betrothed to Eric, king of Norway, who had, by her, one only daughter, named Margaret, who died in girlhood;—and thus ended the whole offspring of King William of Scotland, and his successors, and was utterly extinguished and ended. Therefore it is fitting and needful to go back to David, the aforesaid King William's younger brother.

LXXV.

King William's brother David, Earl of Huntingdon.

DURING the reign of King Malcolm and King William, their younger brother David became Earl of Huntingdon, through the Countess thereof, whom he had taken to wife, and of whom he begat three daughters. The first was called Margaret, and wedded Alan of Galloway. Of her, Alan begat two daughters, the first of whom, named Darvorgilla, wedded John of Balliol, who begat, of her, one son, named John, afterwards king of Scotland; and this John begat Edward of Balliol. In this Edward, the male line of Balliol came to an end; for he had neither son nor daughter by Darvorgilla. The aforesaid John of Balliol, moreover, begat one daughter, named Marjory—the sister, to wit, of the aforesaid King John. This Marjory wedded John Comyn, who, of her, begat one son, named John, whom Robert of Bruce, afterwards king, killed at Dumfries. This John Comyn begat one only daughter, who wedded David, Earl of Athol. Of her, this David begat many sons, the first and eldest of whom, named David, took to wife the daughter of Henry of Beaumont. This lady was begotten by the said Henry of the first-born daughter, and one of the heirs, of John Earl of Buchan; and, of her, that David begat one son, named David. The sister of that Darvorgilla, daughter of the aforesaid Alan of Galloway and Margaret, his bride, was wedded to Roger de Quincy. Of her, this Roger begat three daughters, who were united to three nobles—namely, John of Ferrers; Alexander, Earl of Buchan (whose first-born daughter the aforesaid Henry of Beaumont took to wife); and Lord de la Zouche. From them sprang a countless offspring; but it would be no less difficult than long to run over their descent.

LXXVI.

Earl David's daughter Isabella, who wedded Robert of Bruce.

THE second daughter of the aforesaid Earl David, brother of the above-named King William, was named Isabella, and was taken to wife by the lord Robert of Bruce. This Robert begat one son, named Robert; who begat Robert, Earl of Carrick; who begat Robert, king of Scotland, and many other sons and their uterine brothers; but all these—except Robert, afterwards king—died without lawful issue. He had, also, many daughters, one of whom—the eldest—wedded Gartnay, Earl of Mar. This Earl Gartnay begat Donald (called Bane), Earl of Mar, who died at the battle of Duplin, shortly after having been appointed warden of Scotland. This Donald Bane begat Thomas, Earl of Mar, who was betrothed to the heiress of Menteith; but afterwards, egged on by the devil, he, by trumping up colourable pretexts, and untrue pleas, got a divorce, without there being any offspring between them. Another daughter wedded Hugh, Earl of Ross, who, of her, begat Earl William.

LXXVII.

Issue of King Robert Bruce by his first wife.

NOW King Robert, when he was Earl of Carrick, took to wife Isabella, sister of the aforesaid Gartnay, Earl of Mar; and, of her, he begat an only daughter, named Marjory, who wedded Walter, Steward of Scotland, and of whom this Walter begat an only son, named Robert Stewart, afterwards king. This Robert took to his bed one of the daughters of Adam More, knight; and of her he begat sons and daughters, out of wedlock. But he afterwards—in the year 1349, to wit—bespoke and got the dispensation of the Apostolic See, and espoused her regularly, according to the forms of the Church.

LXXVIII.
That King's Issue by his second Wife.

UPON the death of the aforesaid Isabella, Robert, while still earl, took to wife Elizabeth, daughter of Haymer de Burc, Earl of Ulster. Of her, this Robert, then king, begat two daughters—Matilda and Margaret. The said Margaret wedded the Earl of Sutherland, who, of her, begat an only son, named John. This John was, with his father, a hostage in England for the release of David II., king of Scotland. But his mother departed this life just after she had given him birth. I will say nothing at all about her sister, Matilda; for she did nothing worth remembering. The aforesaid King Robert likewise begat, in the seventeenth year of his reign, an only son, named David, who succeeded him on the throne.

LXXIX.
Death of John of Balliol.

YE must know, likewise, that John of Balliol, the husband of the aforesaid Darvorgilla, died before the death of the aforesaid King Alexander III.; while she, however, outlived him. As for Earl David's third daughter, named Ada, who wedded Henry of Hastings, let those whom it concerns, or who wish to know, trace and follow up her issue. Now, after having seen this, let skilled men seek and trace which of the suitors had the stronger right; for this is a true history, and a correct account of the degrees of kinship, and of the descent, of all the aforesaid.

LXXX.

Daughters of King Malcolm and Saint Margaret; and degree of kinship between David and Edward, the kings of Scotland and of England.

OF the above-mentioned Saint Margaret, also, the aforesaid Malcolm begat two daughters—Matilda, and Mary. Matilda wedded Henry the Clerk, son of William the Bastard, conqueror of England. Of her, this Henry begat the empress Matilda, who wedded the emperor Henry, and lived twenty years with him. The emperor died without issue; and, after his death, the empress returned to her still surviving kinsfolk. She afterwards, by their advice, wedded the Count of Anjou and Poitou—Geoffroy, by name—who begat, of her, one son, named Henry. This Henry afterwards succeeded to the kingdom of England and the dukedom of Normandy through his mother, and to the dukedom of Anjou and Poitou through his father; and under him suffered Saint Thomas, Archbishop of Canterbury. He had four sons: namely, Henry, his first-born, who was crowned king in his father's lifetime, and died before his father, childless; the second, named Richard, who succeeded his father on the throne; the third, named Geoffroy, Earl of Brittany; and the fourth son, named John, who succeeded his brother, the said Richard, on the throne. This John begat Henry the peaceful; Henry begat Edward the tyrant; Edward begat Edward II.; Edward II. begat Edward III.; Edward III. begat Edward, Prince of Wales, who predeceased his father; Prince Edward begat Richard, who now is. Now, having shortly run through all this, we must go back to the Annals.

LXXXI.

Guardians of the kingdom chosen, after the death of King Alexander III.

WHEN the body of Alexander III., of renowned memory, the aforesaid illustrious king of Scotland, had been handed over for burial by the Church, in the year 1286, six guardians—of whom enough was said a little further back—were chosen by the clergy and estates of the whole kingdom of Scotland, in a parliament held at Scone on the 2d day of April, And the kingdom was six years and nine months without the governance of a king, according to the words of the prophecy, "While twice three years," etc.

LXXXII.

Slaughter of Duncan, Earl of Fife.

ON the 7th of April 1288, Duncan, Earl of Fife, son of Colban, son of Malcolm, was slain at Petpolloch (Pittelloch), by Patrick of Abernethy and Walter of Percy, knights, with the advice and consent of William of Abernethy, knight, who, as had been forecasted between them, secretly lay in wait, with many men, on another road, for the passing of the said earl; so that the latter could nowise escape them alive. When they had perpetrated this wickedness, Andrew of Moray followed after them, seeking them, in their wretched flight with their men, through sundry places, this side of the Scottish sea, and beyond it. Two of them—namely, Walter, and William—he manfully caught in a village which is called Colbanston, in Clydesdale; and he there straightway punished Walter and two squires with sentence of death, and committed William to prison for life, at Douglas Castle, in the keeping of the lord William of Douglas. Patrick, however, fled to France, and there ended his days.

LXXXIII.

Marriage to be contracted between the son of the King of England, and Margaret, daughter of the King of Norway.

IN the year 1290, six ambassadors-extraordinary—namely, two bishops, those of Durham and Carlisle; two earls, those of Lincoln and Warenne; one knight, named William de Vesci; and Henry dean of York—and special commissioners of Edward I., king of England, were sent to treat with the guardians, nobles, and estates of the kingdom of Scotland, about contracting a marriage between Edward, his son and heir, and Margaret, the daughter of the king of Norway, then the true heiress of Scotland: as is more fully shown in a letter drawn up by these ambassadors, and handed to the said guardians. Of this letter, moreover, we have spoken above. The same year, the Jews were cast out of England.

LXXXIV.

Dispute which arose between Robert Bruce and John of Balliol.

IN the year 1291 died Margaret, daughter of Eric, king of Norway. She was the lawful heiress of Scotland. That same year, the lawsuit was begun, and the dispute, or controversy, arose between two men—John of Balliol, and Robert of Bruce—about the right to reign and succeed to the throne of Scotland. At length, however, at the instance of the magnates of Scotland, Edward I., king of England, on being asked, came to Berwick; and sentence was there given, by that king, in favour of John of Balliol, in the manner and form above stated.

LXXXV.

John of Balliol created King of Scotland.

ON the last day of November 1292, this John of Balliol was made king at Scone; and having been there set on the royal throne, as is the custom, he was promoted in due manner. That same year, on the 26th day of December, though against the will of the first men of the kingdom, of all but a few, this John did homage to Edward I., king of England, for the kingdom of Scotland, as he had before promised in his ear, submitting to thraldom unto him for ever.

LXXXVI.

Steps which led to the Deprivation of the same.

I MUST mention that, at the time of this John, king of Scotland, some who sought to deprive Macduff—brother of Duncan, the lately murdered Earl of Fife—of his lands and property of Kilconquhar, dragged him to court before the above-named King John, in full parliament. But because the king, as it seemed to the aforesaid Macduff, showed too much favour to the other side, he appealed from his sentence and court to the king of England to hear him; and, following up his appeal as actively as he could, he managed to get the aforesaid John, king of Scotland, summoned to the English king's parliament, held in London. John accordingly appeared in person; and, in spite of the English king and his party, he determined, after talking the thing over with his council, that he would answer by proxy. When, therefore, the king was called, and appeared in court by proxy, the king of England, sitting upon the judgment-seat, would nowise listen to the aforesaid king's proxy, until the king of Scotland, who was then sitting beside the king of England, should rise from his place, and, standing in court before him, impart his answers to his proxy with his own lips. John fulfilled these commands; and, having undergone from all numberless insults and slights, against his kingly rank and dignity, he at length imparted his answers to his proxy. And thus, after taking leave, he returned home very greatly crestfallen. So he straightway appointed a parliament, and called together the chiefs of the kingdom—both of the clergy and of the people; and, having openly set forth the insults, slights, contempt, and shame, which he had endured he strove, by all means in his small measure of power, to find some offset against the aforesaid king's wickedness. At length, it was there determined that King John should utterly recall the homage and fealty he had tendered to the king of England, as wrung from him by force and fear; and that he could no longer obey his commands at all, to the injury of his kingdom's freedom. So he despatched to the aforesaid king of England, by Henry, abbot of Abirbrothoc (Arbroath), letters-patent to this effect, stamped with his seal, claiming back and recalling his homage and fealty. When these letters were presented, the king answered, in the French tongue: "A ce foil, felim tel foli fet;" and he straightway added: "Sul ne voit venir a nous, nous vendrum aly." When this answer had been given, the aforesaid abbot—who had been sent thither out of spite, forasmuch as, owing to his knavery, he was hateful to many of the lords and others of his country—was unable to get from the king of England any longer letters of safe-conduct; so, owing to the shortness of the time which was left before his safe-conduct ran out, he barely escaped alive.

LXXXVII.

The King of England has the King of Scotland cited to the Marches, etc.

THE often-mentioned king of England more than once sent for the king of Scotland to compear at the marches and borders of the kingdom, and had him summoned before him to stand his trial for his disobedience and rebellion. But he would not deign to come when peremptorily summoned; so, because of his manifold contumacy, as well as because of his misconduct in breaking through his oath of fealty and homage, Edward passed against him a sentence of deprivation and deposition from the kingdom, as also from all other lands and possessions which John held of him; so that him whom he had, in spite of the law, promoted to the kingship, he, by the law, deprived, both by a sentence and in deed, of all the honours bestowed upon him.

LXXXVIII.

The King of England beguiles the first Robert of Bruce with smooth words.

MEANWHILE the king of England made ready for coming to blows; and, calling the lord Robert of Bruce, the grandfather, he acknowledged that he had given an unrighteous sentence. So he recalled the same, and promised and pledged himself faithfully to the aforesaid Robert to promote him to the throne, as having the better and stronger right; while the other should be utterly set aside and deprived for ever. By this promise, so full of smooth words and all manner of falsehood, he led him on to write a letter himself to all his friends dwelling in Scotland, and advise them to surrender and deliver up to him all castles and fortified strongholds: for that the whole aim of the king of England was directed to this—that he might constitute and appoint him king.

Accordingly, Robert wrote what the other suggested. When, however, Edward got what he wished, he nowise kept his pledges.

LXXXIX.
The Nobles of Fife sent to guard the town of Berwick—Their Death.

WHILE this was going on, John, king of Scotland, by the advice of the magnates who cleaved to him, marshalled and sent off all the nobles and freeholders, as well as the rest of the good men, of the county of Fife (which was then without a head, and bereft of its lawful pilot), despatching them to guard and defend the town of Berwick, where the greatest danger was then threatening. There the king of England brought up with a strong fleet collected from the Cinque Ports, and laden with a great throng of men; and when these made a great onslaught on the side facing the sea, the garrison of the town, who were active under arms, stout in body, and fierce in spirit, drove them back by force, and burnt with fire eighteen ships laden with armed men, all of whom they slew. In what year, month, or day, these things above related happened, the writer of this chronicle did not know for certain. This, however, may be taken as beyond a doubt,—that all the aforesaid events took place, in the order in which they are set down, in the years 1293, 1294, and 1295.

XC.
Taking of the town of Berwick by Edward I., King of England.

ON the 30th of March 1296, the king of England, being strongly stirred up by the causes stated above, marched in person, with a large force, upon the town of Berwick; and as he could not take it by force, he thought to outwit the garrison by sleight and cunning. So he pretended he was going to withdraw; and, striking his tents, he made a feint of going far away. But on the 30th of March, bearing aloft the craftily counterfeited banners and war-ensigns of the Scottish army, he neared the gates of the town. When the garrison of the town saw this, they became right glad and merry, because they had got news that their king would soon be there to rescue and help them; and being thus unhappily deceived through that promise, they trustfully opened their gates, like true men that knew no guile. But as soon as the trick was found out, and they became aware of the truth, they strove to withstand the foe. Being, however, hemmed in by the enemy, and assaulted on every side, they were wretchedly borne down by a sudden charge. On this wise, therefore, was the town taken, and all were swept down; and, sparing neither sex nor age, the aforesaid king of England, in his tyrannous rage, bade them put to the sword 7500 souls of both sexes; so that, for two days, streams flowed from the bodies of the slain. There were the nobles of Fife utterly destroyed.

XCI.

Expulsion of the English from the Kingdom of Scotland.

THE same year, on the 20th of April, owing to most unmistakeable grounds for mistrust, and strong proofs of villanous plotting against the king and state, all the beneficed English in the bishopric of Saint Andrews were formally deprived of their benefices by William of Kinghorn and Patrick of Campania, surrogates of William Eraser, bishop of Saint Andrews, who was abroad. In like manner, every single other Englishman, both clerk and layman, was cast out of the kingdom of Scotland for plotting.

XCII.

Battle of Dunbar.

ON the 27th of April, in the same year, was fought the battle of Dunbar, where Patrick of Graham and many nobles fell wounded; while a great many other knights and barons, in the hope of saving their lives, fled to Dunbar Castle, and were there readily welcomed. But they were all—to the number of seventy knights, besides famous squires, together with William, Earl of Ross—made over, like sheep offered to the slaughter, by Richard Seward, warden of the said castle, to the king of England.

XCIII.

Abettors of John of Balliol and Robert Bruce.

It should be noted, moreover, that from the first mooting of the matter of the feud between those noble men—Bruce, and Balliol—about the right of succeeding to the kingdom of Scotland, that kingdom was rent in twain. For all the Comyns and their whole abettors stood by Balliol; while the Earls of Mar and Athol, with the whole strength of their power, cleaved, in the firm league of kinship, to the side of Robert of Bruce, who was steadfastly tended in the indissoluble bond of love by Robert, bishop of Glasgow. It was for this reason—according to the general opinion—that the aforesaid earls with their troops, through good-will and love for Bruce, fled scathless from the field, on the day the aforesaid battle was fought; and thus the adverse party was exposed to utter ruin, and the foe of both gained so gladsome and welcome a victory. And, even as afterwards, while King Robert of Bruce was making war, all Balliol's followers were looked upon with mistrust in that king's wars, so also, in this Balliol's war, the aforesaid bishop and earls, with all the abettors of Bruce's party, were generally considered traitors to their king and country. But, alas! through this quarrel, the harmless rabble, exposed to the ravenous biting of these wolves, lay mangled far and wide over the land.

XCIV.

Answer given by the King of England to the first Robert Bruce.

So, after the victory gained over the Scots at Dunbar, the elder Robert of Bruce came up to the king of England, and besought him to faithfully fulfil what he had long ago promised him, as to his getting the kingdom. But that old framer of wiles, in no little indignation, answered thus, in the French tongue: "Ne avonis ren autres chose a fer, que avous reamys ganere?" that is to say: "Have We nothing else to do but to win kingdoms for thee?" So that noble man, perceiving, from such an answer, the crafty king's falsehood, withdrew to his lands in England, and was no more seen in Scotland.

XCV.
John of Balliol and Ms son Edward taken.

THE aforesaid king then marched on, and the castles of Dunbar, Edinburgh, and Strivelyn (Stirling), were given up to him; and he followed after the aforesaid John, king of Scotland, as far as the castle of Forfar. He was there met by John of Comyn, lord of Strabolgi, who made his submission unto him. According to the account given by some, this Comyn immediately afterwards brought back the aforesaid King John and his son Edward, from Aberdeen to the castle of Montrose; and, upon the king of England coming to the aforesaid castle of Montrose, King John, stripped of his kingly ornaments, and holding a white wand in his hand, surrendered up, with staff and baton, and resigned into the hands of the king of England, all right which he himself had, or might have, to the kingdom of Scotland. After a few days' time, the king of England had him and his son Edward taken down to London by sea; and there he had them both kept, a good while, closely guarded. But, in course of time, while the son was kept back, the father was set free—having, however, first sworn a most solemn oath that he would never claim the right of reigning in the aforesaid kingdom of Scotland. So, being thus reinstated in his lands of Balliol (Ballieule) in France, he there ended his days. Afterwards, moreover, his son Edward, when he had duly sworn the above oath, was given back to him; and, after his father's death, Edward abode there until he set about his own war, which was set on foot and begun at the battle of Duplin. Thus ended the reign of King John of Balliol, who reigned three years and a half.

XCVI.
The Estates of Scotland do homage to the King of England.

THAT same year, after the seizure of the king of Scotland, the Estates of Scotland did homage and swore fealty to the king of England, surrendering unto him their castles and fortified towns. He, however, made no change at all—except in a few cases—in any of the wardens of castles, the bailies of towns, and the king's ministers, who had been wont to minister unto the kings of Scotland, either by ancient custom, or by hereditary right; but, having taken from them an oath of fealty, he allowed them all, except the wardens of the castles of the chief boroughs, to stay in the same position and offices they had formerly served in. And thus he hastened home.

XCVII.
The Magnates of Scotland meet together to guard the Kingdom.

THE same year, not long after the king of England had withdrawn, the magnates of Scotland summoned a parliament of their own, at Scone; and twelve peers or guardians were there appointed to guard and defend the freedom of the kingdom, and of the Estates thereof. And, in order that this appointment might be the more strongly secured, they swore one to another to afford each other countenance, advice, and help, in all time to come. After this, they built castles, repaired those which were in ruins, set trusty garrisons in the strongest positions, and made ready to withstand bravely the lawless usurpation of that most wicked king of England. That same year, in order to humble and lessen that king's fell power, John Comyn, Earl of Buchan, with a great army, ravaged the northern parts of England with fire and sword, and laid siege to the town of Carlisle; but he withdrew thence without having compassed his end.

XCVIII.
Rise and First Start of William Wallace.

THE same year, William Wallace lifted up his head from his den—as it were—and slew the English sheriff of Lanark, a doughty and powerful man, in the town of Lanark. From that time, therefore, there flocked to him all who were in bitterness of spirit, and weighed down beneath the burden of bondage under the unbearable domination of English despotism; and he became their leader. He was wondrously brave and bold of goodly mien, and boundless liberality; and, though, among the earls and lords of the kingdom, he was looked upon as lowborn, yet his fathers rejoiced in the honour of knighthood. His elder brother, also, was girded with the knightly belt, and inherited a landed estate which was large enough for his station, and which he bequeathed, as a holding, to his descendants. So Wallace overthrew the English on all sides; and gaining strength daily, he, in a short time, by force, and by dint of his prowess, brought all the magnates of Scotland under his sway, whether they would or not. Such of the magnates, moreover, as did not thankfully obey his commands, he took and browbeat, and handed over to custody, until they should utterly submit to his good pleasure. And when all had thus been subdued, he manfully betook himself to the storming of the castles and fortified towns in which the English ruled; for he aimed at quickly and thoroughly freeing his country and overthrowing the enemy.

XCIX.
Battle of Stirling Bridge.

IN the year 1297, the fame of William Wallace was spread all abroad, and, at length, reached the ears of the king of England; for the loss brought upon his people was crying out. As the king, however, was intent upon many troublesome matters elsewhere, he sent his treasurer, named Hugh of Clissingham, with a large force to repress this William's boldness, and to bring the kingdom of Scotland under his sway. When, therefore, he heard of this man's arrival, the aforesaid

William, then busy besieging the English who were in Dundee Castle, straightway intrusted the care and charge of the siege of the castle to the burgesses of that town, on pain of loss of life and limb, and, with his army, marched on, with all haste, towards Strivelyn (Stirling), to meet this Hugh. A battle was then fought, on the 11th of September, near Strivelyn (Stirling), at the bridge over the Forth. Hugh of Clissingham was killed, and all his army put to flight: some of them were slain with the sword, others taken, others drowned in the waters. But, through God, they were all overcome; and the aforesaid William gained a happy victory, with no little praise. Of the nobles, on his side, the noble Andrew of Moray alone, the father of Andrew, fell wounded.

C.

William Wallace winters in England.

THE same year, William Wallace, with his army, wintered in England, from Hallowmas to Christmas; and after having burnt up the whole land of Allerdale, and carried off some plunder, he and his men went back safe and sound. The same year, moreover, on the 20th of August, all the English—regular and beneficed clergy, as well as laymen—were, by this same William, again cast out from the kingdom of Scotland. And, the same year, William of Lamberton was chosen bishop of Saint Andrews.

CI.

Battle of Falkirk.

IN the year 1298, the aforesaid king of England, taking it ill that he and his should be put to so much loss and driven to such straits by William Wallace, gathered together a large army, and, having with him, in his company, some of the nobles of Scotland to help him, invaded Scotland. He was met by the aforesaid William, with the rest of the magnates of that kingdom; and a desperate battle was fought near Falkirk, on the 22d of July. William was put to flight, not without serious loss both to the lords and to the common people of the Scottish nation. For, on account of the ill-will, begotten of the spring of envy, which the Comyns had conceived towards the said William, they, with their accomplices, forsook the field, and escaped unhurt. On learning their spiteful deed, the aforesaid William, wishing to save himself and his, hastened to flee by another road. But alas! through the pride and burning envy of both, the noble Estates (*communitas*) of Scotland lay wretchedly overthrown throughout hill and dale, mountain and plain. Among these, of the nobles, John Stewart, with his Brendans; Macduff, of Fife; and the inhabitants thereof, were utterly cut off. But it is commonly said that Robert of Bruce,—who was afterwards king of Scotland, but then fought on the side of the king of England—was the means of bringing about this victory. For, while the Scots stood invincible in their ranks, and could not be broken by either force or stratagem, this Robert of Bruce went with one line, under Anthony of Bek, by a long road round a hill, and attacked the Scots in the rear; and thus these, who had stood invincible and impenetrable in front, were craftily overcome in the rear. And it is remarkable that we seldom, if ever, read of the Scots being overcome by the English, unless through the envy of lords, or the treachery and deceit of the natives, taking them over to the other side.

CII.

William Wallace resigns the office of Guardian.

BUT after the aforesaid victory, which was vouchsafed to the enemy through the treachery of Scots, the aforesaid William Wallace, perceiving, by these and other strong proofs, the glaring wickedness of the Corny ns and their abettors, chose rather to serve with the crowd, than to be set over them, to their ruin, and the grievous wasting of the people. So, not long after the battle of Falkirk, at the water of Forth, he, of his own accord, resigned the office and charge which he held, of guardian.

CIII.
John Comyn becomes Guardian of Scotland.

THE same year, John Comyn, the son, became guardian of Scotland; and remained in that office until the time when he submitted to the king of England—to wit, the next year after the struggle at Roslyn. But, within that same time, John of Soulis was associated with him, by John of Balliol, who had then been set free from prison, and was dwelling on his lands of Balliol. Soulis did not long keep his charge and governance; but as he was simple-minded, and not firm enough, bearing many a rebuff, he was looked down upon; so he left Scotland, and withdrew to France, where he died.

CIV.
Truce granted, at the instance of the King of France, to the Estates of the Kingdom of Scotland.

IN the year 1300, Philip, king of France, sent a cleric, named Pierre de Muncy, and one knight, Jean de Barres, to Edward, king of England, to obtain a truce between Edward himself and the Estates of Scotland. At his instance, the king of England granted a truce to the kingdom of Scotland, from Hallowmas, in the above-mentioned year, to the next following Whitsunday. And it was at the instance of the king of France, not as in any way the ally of the kingdom of Scotland, but as his cousin and particular friend, and the friendly peacemaker between the two sides, that he granted this truce. This, moreover, he forced the aforesaid ambassadors to own before he granted the truce.

CV.
John of Soulis.

THE same year, John of Soulis, one of the guardians of Scotland, without mentioning the other guardian, with the advice of the prelates, earls, barons, and other nobles of the Estates of the kingdom of Scotland, despatched the lord William, archdeacon of Lothian, Master Baldred Bisset, and William of Eglisham, as commissioners and special envoys to Boniface VIII., then sovereign Pontiff, to break and lay bare unto him the sundry and manifold hardships brought upon the kingdom of Scotland by the enmity of the said king of England; and to get meet relief against his harassing outrages—as is more fully contained in the commission of those ambassadors, a copy whereof, together with that Baldred's pleading against the king of England, and many letters bearing on that lawsuit, is in a pamphlet written by Alan of Montrose.

CVI.

The King of England summoned to the Court of Rome.

NOW the king of England, having been summoned by the Pope, in the year 1301, sent two proofs patent to that same sovereign Pontiff, in order to give him a clear insight into the right which he averred was vested in him, from days of old, to the throne of Scotland. But Baldred, in a lucid discourse, shortly answered all his arguments, plainly showing, by strong proofs and very clear evidence, that they were utterly devoid of truth—as may be seen in his pleading. The same year, a castle, viz., the Pel de Lithcu (Peel of Linlithgow), was built by the king of England.

CVII.

Conflict of Roslyn.

ON the 27th of July 1302, took place the great and famous engagement between the Scots and English, at Roslyn, where the English were defeated, though with great difficulty. From the beginning of the first war which ever broke out between the Scots and English, it is said, there never was so desperate a struggle, or one in which the stoutness of knightly prowess shone forth so brightly. The commander and leader in this struggle was John Comyn, the son. Now this was how this struggle came about, and the manner thereof. After the battle fought at Falkirk, the king of England came not in person, for the nonce, this side of the water of Forth; but sent a good large force, which plundered the whole land of Fife, with all the lands lying near the town of Perth, after having killed a great many of the dwellers in those lands. On the return of this force, with countless spoils, that king hied him home again with his host. Now this was brought about, doubtless, by God's agency: for had he made a lengthened stay then, or after the battle of Dunbar and the seizure of King John, he would either have subjugated the whole land of Scotland, and the dwellers therein, to his sway, or made it a waste with naught but floods and stones. But the goodness of God, Who alone tends and heals after wounds, so governed the actions and time of that king, that, being stirred up to battle, and engrossed with sundry wars, he could not put off all other matters, and give himself up to subduing this kingdom. So that king of England went back with his men, having first appointed the officers of the sheriffdoms, and the wardens of the castles, in the districts beyond the water of Forth, which were then fully and wholly subject unto his sway- —with the exception of a few outlaws (or, indeed, robbers), of Scottish birth, who were lurking in the woods, and could not, because of their misdeeds, submit to the laws. But John Comyn, then guardian of Scotland, and Simon Eraser, with their followers, day and night did their best to harass and annoy, by their great prowess, the aforesaid king's officers and bailiffs; and from the time of that king's departure, for four years and more, the English and the Anglicized Scots were harried by them, in manifold ways, by mutual slaughter and carnage, according to the issue of various wars.

CVIII.

WHEN the aforesaid king had got news of this, he sent off a certain nobleman, Ralph Confrere, his treasurer (Ralph de Manton, the Cofferer), a man stout in battle, and of tried judgment and wisdom, with a certain body of chosen knights, thoroughly well-armed, to seek out, in every hole and corner, those who troubled and disturbed the king's peace, and not to forbear punishing them with the penalty of death. So they entered Scotland, and went about ranging through the land, until they, at Roslyn, pitched their tents, split up into three lines apart, for want of free camping room. But the aforesaid John Comyn and Simon, with their abettors, hearing of their arrival, and wishing to steal a march rather than have one stolen upon them, came briskly through from Biggar to Roslyn, in one night, with some chosen men, who chose rather death before unworthy subjection to the English nation; and, all of a sudden, they fearlessly fell upon the enemy. But having been, a little before, roused by the sentries, all those of the first line seized their weapons, and manfully withstood the attacking foe. At length, however, the former were overcome. Some were taken, and some slain; while some, again, fled to the other line. But, while the Scots were sharing the booty, another line straightway appeared, in battle-array; so the Scots, on seeing it, slaughtered their prisoners, and armed their own vassals with the spoils of the slain; then, putting away their jaded horses, and taking stronger ones, they fearlessly hastened to the fray. When this second line had been, at length, overcome, though with difficulty, and the Scots thought they had ended their task, there appeared a third, mightier than the former, and more choice in their harness. The Scots were thunderstruck at the sight of them; and being both fagged out in manifold ways,—by the fatigues of travelling, watching, and want of food—and also sore distressed by the endless toil of fighting, began to be weary, and to quail in spirit, beyond belief. But, when the people were thus thrown into bewilderment, the aforesaid John and Simon, with , hearts undismayed, took up, with their weapons, the office of preachers; and, comforting them with their words, cheering them with their promises, and, moreover, reminding them of the nobleness of freedom, and the baseness of thraldom, and of the unwearied toil which their ancestors had willingly undertaken for the deliverance of their country, they, with healthful warnings, heartened them to the fray. So, being greatly emboldened by these and such-like words, the Scots laid aside all cowardice, and got back their strength. Then they slaughtered their prisoners, with whose horses and arms they were again—as it were—renewed; and, putting their trust in God, they and their armed vassals marched forward most bravely and dashingly to battle. The shock was so mighty and fierce, that many were run through, and bereft of life; and some of either host, after awful spear-thrusts, savage flail-strokes, and hard cudgelling, withdrew from the ranks, by hundreds, forties, and twenties, to the hills, time after time, fagged out and dazed by the day's fighting. There they would throw back their helmets, and let the winds blow upon them; and after having been thus cooled by the breeze, they would put away their wounded horses, and, mounting other fresh ones, would thus be made stronger against the onslaughts of the foe. So, after this manifold ordeal and awful struggle, the Scots, who, if one looked at the opposite side, were very few in number—as it were a handful of corn or flour compared with the multitude of the sea-sand—by the power, not of man, but of God, subdued their foes, and gained a happy and gladsome victory.

CIX.

The King of England scours the plains and hills, and brings the Kingdom of Scotland under peaceful subjection to himself

IN revenge for the foregoing outrages, the king of England, with a very large force, both by sea and by land, entered Scotland, in the year 1303, with the deliberate design of once for all fully bringing it, and the dwellers therein, under his yoke; or, of sweeping out the inhabitants altogether, and reducing the land itself to an utter and irreclaimable wilderness. Having, therefore, scoured the hills and plains, both on this side of the hills and beyond them, he, in person, reached Lochindorb; and, after making some stay there, he received the submission of the northern districts, and appointed officers of his in all the castles and fortified towns surrendered to him. Returning thence leisurely, he received the submission of all the communities, as well as fortresses and castles they passed through, with none to withstand or attack him; and, after much winding about through the land, he got to Dunfermline, where he lingered a long time, wintering there until Candlemas. The same year, his son and heir, Edward of Carnarvon, Prince of Wales, made a long stay in the town of Perth. Food was in such plenty there, for the whole of the aforesaid time, that a laggen, Scottish measure, of good wine sold for fourpence.

CX.

The Estates of Scotland make their submission to the King of England.

THE same year, after the whole Estates of Scotland had made their submission to the king of England, John Comyn, then guardian, and all the magnates but William Wallace, little by little, one after another, made their submission unto him; and all their castles and towns—except Strivelyn (Stirling) Castle, and the warden thereof—were surrendered unto him. That year, the king kept Lent at Saint Andrews, where he called together all the great men of the kingdom, and held his parliament; and he made such decrees as he would, according to the state of the country—which, as he thought, had been gotten and won for him and his successors for ever—as well as about the dwellers therein.

CXI.

Stirling Castle besieged by the King of England.

JUST after Easter, in the year 1304, that same king besieged Strivelyn (Stirling) Castle for three months without a break. For this siege, he commanded all the lead of the refectory of Saint Andrews to be pulled down, and had it taken away for the use of his engines. At last, the aforesaid castle was surrendered and delivered unto him on certain conditions, drawn up in writing, and sealed with his seal. But when he had got the castle, the king belied his troth, and broke through the conditions: for William Oliphant, the warden thereof, he threw bound into prison in London, and kept him a long time in thrall. The same year, when both great and small in the kingdom of Scotland (except William Wallace alone) had made their submission unto him; when the surrendered castles and fortified towns, which had formerly been broken down and knocked to pieces, had been all rebuilt, and he had appointed wardens of his own therein; and after all and sundry of Scottish birth had tendered him homage, the king, with the Prince of

Wales, and his whole army, returned to England. He left, however, the chief warden as his lieutenant, to amend and control the lawlessness of all the rest, both Scots and English. He did not show his face in Scotland after this.

CXII.
Rise of Robert of Bruce, King of Scotland.

AFTER the withdrawal of the king of England, the English nation lorded it in all parts of the kingdom of Scotland, ruthlessly harrying the Scots in sundry and manifold ways, by insults, stripes, and slaughter, under the awful yoke of slavery. But God, in His mercy, as is the wont of His fatherly goodness, had compassion on the woes, the ceaseless crying and sorrow, of the Scots; so He raised up a saviour and champion unto them—one of their own fellows, to wit, named Robert of Bruce. This man, seeing them stretched in the slough of woe, and reft of all hope of salvation and help, was inwardly touched with sorrow of heart; and, putting forth his hand unto force, underwent the countless and unbearable toils of the heat of day, of cold and hunger, by land and sea, gladly welcoming weariness, fasting, dangers, and the snares not only of foes, but also of false friends, for the sake of freeing his brethren.

CXIII.
League of King Robert with John Comyn.

SO, in order that he might actually give effect to what he had gladly set his heart upon, for the good of the commonwealth, he humbly approached a certain noble, named John Comyn (who was then the most powerful man in the country), and faithfully laid before him the unworthy thraldom of the country, the cruel and endless tormenting of the people, and his own kind-hearted plan for giving them relief. Though, by right, and according to the laws and customs of the country, the honour of the kingly office and the succession to the governance of the kingdom were known to belong to him before any one else, yet, setting the public advantage before his own, Robert, in all purity and sincerity of purpose, gave John the choice of one of two courses: either that the latter should reign, and wholly take unto himself the kingdom, with its pertinents and royal honours, for ever, granting to the former all his own lands and possessions; or that all Robert's lands and possessions should come into the possession of John and his for ever, while the kingdom and the kingly honour were left to Robert. Thus, by their mutual advice as well as help, was to be brought to maturity the deliverance of the Scottish nation from the house of bondage and unworthy thraldom; and an indissoluble treaty of friendship and peace was to last between them. John was perfectly satisfied with the latter of the aforesaid courses; and thereupon a covenant was made between them, and guaranteed by means of sworn pledges, and by their indentures with their seals attached thereto. But John broke his word; and, heedless of the sacredness of his oath, kept accusing Robert before the king of England, through his ambassadors and private letters, and wickedly revealing that Robert's secrets. Although, however, Robert was more than once sounded thereupon by the aforesaid king, who even showed him the letters of his adversary who accused him, yet, inspired by God, he always returned an answer such that he over and over again softened the king's rage by his pleasant sayings and skilful words. The king, however, both because he was himself very wily and shrewd, and knew full well how to feign a sham friendship, and also because Robert was the true heir of the kingdom of Scotland, looked upon the latter with mistrust,—the more so because of John's accusations. So, because of his aforesaid grounds for mistrust, Edward bade Robert stay always at court; and he delayed putting him to death—or, at least, in prison—only until he could get the rest of this Robert's brothers together, and punish them and him at once, in one day, with sentence of death.

CXIV.

King Robert accused before the King of England, by John Comyn.

AS the said John's accusations were repeated, at length, one night, while the wine glittered in the bowl, and that king was hastening to sit down with his secretaries, he talked over Robert's death in earnest,—and shortly determined that he would deprive him of life on the morrow. But when the Earl of Gloucester, who was Robert's true and tried friend in his utmost need, heard of this, he hastily, that same night, sent the aforesaid Robert, by his keeper of the wardrobe, twelve pence and a pair of spurs. So the keeper of the wardrobe, who guessed his lord's wishes, presented these things to Robert, from his lord, and added these words: "My lord sends these to you, in return for what he, on his side, got from you yesterday." Robert understood, from the tokens offered him, that he was threatened by the danger of death; so he discreetly gave the pence to the keeper of the wardrobe, and forthwith sent him back to the Earl with greeting in answer, and with thanks. Then, when twilight came on, that night, after having ostentatiously ordered his servants to meet him at Carlisle, with his trappings, on the evening of the following day, he straightway hastened towards Scotland, without delay, and never stopped travelling, day or night, until he was safe from the aforesaid king's spite. For he was under the guidance of One of whom it is written:—"There is no wisdom, no foresight, no understanding against the Lord, who knoweth how to snatch the good from trial, and mercifully to deliver from danger those that trust in Him."

CXV.

Death of John Comyn's messenger.

Now, when Robert was nearing the borders of the marches, there met him a messenger whom, when he sighted him afar off, he suspected, both from the fellow's gait and from his dress, to be a Scot. So, when he got nearer, he asked him whence he came and whither he was making his way. The messenger began to pour forth excuses for his sins; but Robert ordered his vassals to search him. Letters, sealed with Robert's seal about the covenant entered into between him and John Comyn, were found addressed to the king of England through this messenger, and were forthwith pulled out. The messenger's head was thereupon struck off, and God very much be praised for His guidance in this prosperous journey.

CXVI.

Death of William Wallace.

IN the year 1305, William Wallace was craftily and treacherously taken by John of Menteith, who handed him over to the king of England; and he was, in London, torn limb from limb, and, as a reproach to the Scots, his limbs were hung on towers in sundry places throughout England and Scotland.

CXVII.

John Comyn's death.

THE same year, after the aforesaid Robert had left the king of England and returned home, no less miraculously than by God's grace, a day is appointed for him and the aforesaid John to meet together at Dumfries; and both sides repair to the above-named place. John Comyn is twitted with his treachery and belied troth. The lie is at once given. The evil-speaker is stabbed, and wounded unto death, in the church of the Friars; and the wounded man is, by the friars, laid behind the altar. On being asked by those around whether he could live, straightway his answer is:—"I can." His foes, hearing this, give him another wound;—and thus was he taken away from this world on the 10th of February.

CXVIII.

Coronation of King Robert Bruce.

NOW, when a few days had rolled on, after the said John's death, this Robert of Bruce, taking with him as many men as he could get, hastened to Scone; and, being set on the royal throne, was there crowned, on the 27th of March 1306, in the manner wherein the kings of Scotland were wont to be invested;—and great was the task he then undertook, and unbearable were the burdens he took upon his shoulders. For, not only did he lift his hand against the king of England, and all partakers with him, but he also launched out into a struggle with all and sundry of the kingdom of Scotland, except a very few well-wishers of his, who, if one looked at the hosts of those pitted against them, were as one drop of water compared with the waves of the sea, or a single grain of any seed with the multitudinous sand. His mishaps, flights, and dangers; hardships, and weariness; hunger, and thirst; watchings, and fastings; nakedness, and cold; snares, and banishment; the seizing, imprisoning, slaughter, and downfall of his near ones, and—even more—dear ones (for all this had he to undergo, when overcome and routed in the beginning of his war)—no one, now living, I think, recollects, or is equal to rehearsing, all this. Indeed, he is reported to have said to his knights, one day, when worn out by such numberless and ceaseless hardships and dangers:—

"Were I not stirred by Scotland's olden bliss.
Not for earth's empire would I bear all this."

Moreover, with all the ill-luck and numberless straits he went through with a glad and dauntless heart, were any one able to rehearse his own struggles, and triumphs single-handed—the victories and battles wherein, by the Lord's help, by his own strength, and by his human manhood, he fearlessly cut his way into the columns of the enemy, now mightily bearing these down, and now mightily warding off and escaping the pains of death—he would, I deem, prove that, in the art of fighting, and in vigour of body, Robert had not his match in his time, in any clime. I will, therefore, forbear to describe his own individual deeds, both because they would take up many leaves, and because, though they are undoubtedly true, the time and place wherein they happened, and were wrought, are known to few in these days. But his well-known battles and public exploits will be found set down below, in the years wherein they took place.

CXIX.

Battle of Methven.

The same year, on the 19th day of June, King Robert was overcome and put to flight, at Methven, by Odomar of Valence, who was then warden of Scotland on behalf of the king of England, and was staying at the then well-walled town of Perth, with a great force of both English and Scots who owed fealty and submission to the king of England. Now, though the foresaid king did not lose many of his men in this struggle, yet, because of the bad beginning, which is often crowned by an unhappy ending, his men began to be disheartened, and the victorious side to be much emboldened by their victory. Then, all the wives of those who had followed the king were ordered to be outlawed by the voice of a herald, so that they might follow their husbands; by reason whereof, many women, both single and married, lurked with their people in the woods, and cleaved to the king, abiding with him, under shelter.

CXX.

Conflict at Dairy, in the borders of Argyll.

THE same year, while this king was fleeing from his foes, and lurking, with his men, in the borders of Athol and Argyll, he was again beaten and put to flight, on the 11th of August, at a place called Dairy. But there, also, he did not lose many of his men. Nevertheless, they were all filled with fear, and were dispersed and scattered throughout various places. But the queen fled to Saint Duthac in Ross, where she was taken by William Earl of Ross, and brought to the king of England; and she was kept a prisoner in close custody, until the battle of Bannockburn. Nigel of Bruce, however, one of the king's brothers, fled, with many ladies and damsels, to Kyndrumie (Kildrummie) Castle, and was there welcomed, with his companions. But, the same year, that castle was made over to the English through treachery, and Nigel, and other nobles of both sexes, were taken prisoners, brought to Berwick, and suffered capital punishment. The same year, Thomas and Alexander of Bruce, brothers of the aforesaid king, while hastening towards Carrick by another road, were taken at Loch Ryan, and beheaded at Carlisle—and, thus, all who had gone away and left the king, were, in that same year, either bereft of life, or taken and thrown into prison.

CXXI.

Sundry troubles which fell upon King Robert

THE Earl of Lennox and Gilbert of Haya, alone among the nobles, followed the aforesaid king, and became his inseparable companions in all his troubles. And though sometimes, when hard pressed by the pursuing foe, they were parted from him in body, yet they never departed from fealty and love towards him. But, soon after this, it came to pass that the aforesaid king was cut off from his men, and underwent endless woes, and was tossed in dangers untold, being attended at times by three followers, at times by two; and more often he was left alone, utterly without help. Now passing a whole fortnight without food of any kind to live upon, but raw herbs and water; now walking barefoot, when his shoes became old and worn out; now left alone in the islands; now alone, fleeing before his enemies; now slighted by his servants; he abode in utter loneliness. An outcast among the nobles, he was forsaken; and the English bade him be sought for through the churches like a lost or stolen thing. And thus he became a byword and a laughing-stock for all, both far and near, to hiss at. But when he had borne these things for nearly a year alone, God, at length, took pity on him; and, aided by the help and power of a certain noble lady, Christiana of the Isles, who wished him well, he, after endless toils, smart, and distress, got back, by a round-about way, to the earldom of Carrick. As soon as he had reached that place, he sought out one of his castles, slew the inmates thereof, destroyed the castle, and shared the arms and other spoils among his men. Then, being greatly gladdened by such a beginning after his long spell of ill-luck, he got together his men, who had been scattered far and wide; and, crossing the hills with them in a body, he got as far as Inverness, took the castle thereof with a strong hand, slew its garrison, and levelled it with the ground. In this very way dealt he with the rest of the castles and strongholds established in the north, as well as with their inmates, until he got, with his army, as far as Slenach (Slaines).

CXXII.

Rout at Slenach (Slaines).

IN the year 1307, John Comyn, Earl of Buchan, with many nobles, both English and Scots, hearing that Robert, king of Scotland, was, with his army, at Slenach (Slaines), marched forward to meet him and give him battle. But when they saw the king, with his men, over against them, ready for the fray, they halted; and, on Christmas Day, overwhelmed with shame and confusion, they went back, and asked for a truce, which the king kindly granted. After the truce had been granted, the king abode there, without fear, for eight days; and he there fell into a sickness so severe, that he was borne on a pallet whithersoever he had occasion to be moved.

CXXIII.

Death of King Edward I., King of England.

THE same year died Edward I., king of England, on the 5th of April, at Burgh-upon-Sands. This king stirred up war as soon as he had become a knight, and lashed the English with awful scourgings; he troubled the whole world by his wickedness, and roused it by his cruelty; by his wiles, he hindered the passage to the Holy Land; he invaded Wales; he treacherously subdued unto him the Scots and their kingdom; John of Balliol, the king thereof, and his son, he cast into prison; he overthrew churches, fettered prelates, and to some he put an end in filthy dungeons; he slew the people, and committed other misdeeds without end. He was succeeded by his son Edward II., who was betrothed to Elizabeth, daughter of Philip, king of France.

CXXIV.
Bout at Inverury.

In the year 1308, John Comyn and Philip of Mowbray, with a great many Scots and English, were again gathered together, at Inverury, But when King Robert heard of this, though he had not yet got rid of his grievous sickness, he arose from his pallet, whereon he was always carried about, and commanded his men to arm him and set him on horseback. When this had been done, he too, with a cheerful countenance, hastened with his army against the enemy, to the battle-ground—although, by reason of his great weakness, he could not go upright, but with the help of two men to prop him up. But when the opposing party saw him and his ready for battle, at the mere sight of him they were all sore afraid and put to flight; and they were pursued as far as Fivy, twelve leagues off. So when the rout was over, and the enemy were overthrown and scattered, King Robert ravaged the earldom of Buchan with fire; and, of the people, he killed whom he would, and, to those whom he would have live, he granted life and peace. Moreover, even as, from the beginning of his warfare until the day of this struggle, he had been most unlucky in the upshot of every battle, so, afterwards, there could not have been found a man more fortunate in his fights. And, from that day, the king gained ground, and became ever more hale himself; while the adverse party was daily growing less.

CXXV.
Victory over the Gallwegians, at the River Dee.

THE same year, at the Feast of Saint Peter and Saint Paul, Donald of the Isles gathered together an imposing host of foot, and marched up to the river Dee. He was met by Edward of Bruce, who overcame the said Donald and all the Gallwegians. In this struggle, Edward slew a certain knight named Poland, with many of the nobles of Galloway; and arrested their leader, the said Donald, who had taken to flight. After this, he burnt up the island.

CXXVI.
Conflict of King Robert with the men of Argyll.

THE same year, within a week after the Assumption of the blessed Virgin Mary, the king overcame the men of Argyll, in the middle of Argyll, and subdued the whole land unto himself. Their leader, named Alexander of Argyll, fled to Dunstafinch (Dunstaffnage) Castle, where he was, for some time, besieged by the king. On giving up the castle to the king, he refused to do him homage. So a safe-conduct was given to him, and to all who wished to withdraw with him; and he fled to England, where he paid the debt of nature.

CXXVII.

IN the year 1310, so great was the famine and dearth of provisions in the kingdom of Scotland, that, in most places, many were driven, by the pinch of hunger, to feed on the flesh of horses and other unclean cattle.

CXXVIII.

IN the year 1311, the aforesaid King Robert, having put his enemies to flight at every place he came to, and having taken their fortresses, and levelled them with the ground, twice entered England, and wasted it, carrying off untold booty, and making huge havoc with fire and sword. Thus, by the power of God, the faithless English nation, which had unrighteously racked many a man, was now, by God's righteous judgment, made to undergo awful scourgings; and, whereas it had once been victorious, now it sank vanquished and groaning.

CXXIX.
The town of Perth taken by King Robert.

On the 8th of January 1312, the town of Perth was taken with the strong hand by that same King Robert; and the disloyal people, both Scots and English, were taken, dragged, and slain with the sword; and thus,—

"Fordone, they drained the gall themselves had brewed."

The king, in his clemency, spared the rabble, and granted forgiveness to those that asked it; but he destroyed the walls and ditches, and consumed everything else with fire. The same year, the castles of Buth, Dumfries, and Dalswinton, with many other strongholds, were taken with the strong hand and levelled with the ground. The same year, the town of Durham was, in great part, burnt down by the Scots; Piers de Gaveston was killed by the Earl of Lancaster; and Edward, the first-born of the king of England, was born at Windsor.

CXXX.

Roxburgh Castle taken by James of Douglas.

On Fasten's Even, in the year 1313, Roxburgh Castle was happily taken by the Lord James of Douglas, and, on the 14th of March, Edinburgh Castle, by the Lord Thomas Randolph, Earl of Moray; and their foes were overcome. The same year, the king entered the Isle of Man, took the castles thereof, and victoriously brought the land under his sway.

CXXXI.

Conflict at Bannockburn.

Edward II., king of England, hearing of these glorious doings of King Robert's, and seeing the countless losses and endless evils brought upon him and his by that king, gathered together, in revenge for the foregoing, a very strong army both of wellarmed horsemen and of foot— crossbow-men and archers, well skilled in war-craft. At the head of this body of men, and trusting in the glory of man's might, he entered Scotland in hostile wise; and, laying it waste on every side, he got as far as Bannockburn. But King Robert, putting his trust, not in a host of people, but in the Lord God, came, with a few men, against the aforesaid king of England, on the blessed John the Baptist's day, in the year 1314, and fought against him, and put him and his to flight, through the help of Him to whom it belongeth to give the victory. There, the Earl of Gloucester and a great many other nobles were killed; a great many were drowned in the waters, and slaughtered in pitfalls; a great many, of divers ranks, were cut off by divers kinds of death; and many—a great many—nobles were taken, for whose ransom not only were the queen and other Scottish prisoners released from their dungeons, but even the Scots themselves were, all and sundry, enriched very much. Among these was also taken John of Brittany, for whom the queen and Robert, bishop of Glasgow, were exchanged. From that day forward, moreover, the whole land of Scotland not only always rejoiced in victory over the English, but also overflowed with boundless wealth.

CXXXII.

Edward crosses into Ireland.

EDWARD of Bruce, King Robert's brother, entered Ireland, with a mighty hand, in the year 1315; and, having been set up as king there, he destroyed the whole of Ulster, and committed countless murders. This, however, some little time after, brought him no good. In the year 1316, King Robert went to Ireland, to the southern parts thereof, to afford his brother succour and help. But, in this march, many died of hunger, and the rest lived on horse-flesh. The king, however, at once returned, and left his brother there. In the year 1317, the cardinals were plundered, in England, by Robert of Middleton, who was, soon after, taken, and drawn by horses, in London.

CXXXIII.

The town of Berwick taken.

IN the year 1318, Thomas Randolph, Earl of Moray, destroyed the northern parts of England; and, on the 28th of March of the same year, the Scots took the town of Berwick, which had been, for twenty years, in the hands of the English. On the 14th of October of the same year was fought the battle of Dundalk, in Ireland, in which fell the lord Edward of Bruce, and a good many Scottish nobles with him. The cause of this war was this: Edward was a very mettlesome and high-spirited man, and would not dwell together with his brother in peace, unless he had half the kingdom to himself; and for this reason was stirred up, in Ireland, this war, wherein, as already stated, he ended his life.

CXXXIV.

Berwick besieged by the King of England.

IN the year 1319, on the day of the finding of the Holy Cross, Edward, king of England, besieged the town of Berwick; but, meeting with no success, he quickly retreated in great disorder. The same year, the Earl of Moray burnt up the northern parts of England, as far as Wetherby; and, at the end of the month of August, he pitched his tents at Boroughbridge.

CXXXV.

Treachery of John of Soulis and his adherents.

IN the beginning of the month of August 1320, Robert, king of Scotland, held his parliament at Scone. There, the lord William of Sowlis and the Countess of Stratherne were convicted of the crime of high treason, by conspiring against the aforesaid king; and sentence of perpetual imprisonment was passed upon them. The lords David of Brechin, Gilbert of Malerb, John of Logic, knights, and Richard Broune, esquire, having been convicted of the aforesaid conspiracy, were first drawn by horses, and, in the end, underwent capital punishment. The lords Eustace of Maxwell, Walter of Barclay, sheriff of Aberdeen, and Patrick of Graham, knights, Hamelin of Troupe, and Eustace of Retreve (Rattray), esquires, were accused of the same crime, but were not found guilty in any way. It so happened, also, at the same time, that when Roger of Mowbray had been released from the trammels of the flesh, his body was taken down thither, and convicted of conspiracy; whereupon it was condemned to be drawn by horses, hanged on the gallows, and beheaded. But the king had ruth, and was stirred with pity: so he yielded him up to God's judgment, and commanded that the body of the deceased should be handed over for burial by the Church, without having been put to any shame. The same year, on the 17th of March, our lord the Pope's legates came to the king of Scotland, at Berwick.

CXXXVI.

IN the year 1321, there was a very hard winter, which distressed men, and killed nearly all animals. The same year, the Earl of Moray destroyed the northern parts of England, and the bishopric of Durham, with famine, fire, and sword.

CXXXVII.

The King of Scotland crosses into England, and the King of England into Scotland.

ON the 1st of July 1322, Robert, king of Scotland, entered England, with a strong hand, and laid it waste for the most part, as far as Stanemore, together with the county of Lancaster. The same year, on the 12th of August, Edward II., king of England, entered Scotland with a great army of horse and foot, and a large number of ships, and got as far as the town of Edinburgh; for he sought to have a struggle and come to blows with the aforesaid king. But the king of Scotland, wisely shunning an encounter for the nonce, skilfully drew away from his army all animals fit for food. So, after fifteen days, Edward, being sore pressed by hunger and starvation, went home again dismayed, having first sacked and plundered the monasteries of Holyrood in Edinburgh, and of Melrose, and brought them to great desolation. For, in the said monastery of Melrose, on his way back from Edinburgh, the lord William of Peebles, prior of that same monastery, one monk who was then sick, and two lay-brethren, were killed in the dormitory by the English, and a great many monks were wounded unto death. The Lord's Body was cast forth upon the high altar, and the pyx wherein it was kept was taken away. The monastery of Dryburgh was utterly consumed with fire, and reduced to dust; and a great many other holy places did the fiery flames consume, at the hands of the aforesaid king's forces. But God rewarded them therefor, and it brought them no good. For, the same year, on the 1st of October, King Robert marched into England in hostile wise, and utterly laid it waste, as far as York, sacking the monasteries, and setting fire to a great many cities and towns. But Edward II., king of England, came against him at Biland, with a great force, both of paid soldiers from France, and others hired from a great many places, and of natives of the kingdom itself; but he was put to flight at the above-named place, in the heart of his own kingdom, not without great slaughter of his men, and in no little disorder. Out of his army, John of Brittany, Henry of Stibly (Sully), and other nobles, not a few, fled to the monastery of Rivaulx, and were there taken; and they were afterwards ransomed for sums untold. Thus, the king of Scotland, having gained a gladsome victory, went home again, with his men, in great joy and honour. The same year, on the 1st of October, Andrew of Barclay was taken, and, having been convicted of treachery, undenvent capital punishment.

CXXXVIII.

Ambassadors sent by the King of Scotland to the Pope and the King of France.

IN the year 1325, ambassadors were sent by Robert, king of Scotland, to treat for a renewal of the friendship and alliance formerly struck up between the kings of France and Scotland, and to restore them in force for ever, that they might last for all time imto them and their successors; and also that he might be at one, and come to a good understanding, with the holy Roman Church, which had, through the insinuations of enemies, been somewhat irritated against the king and kingdom. So when all this business had been happily despatched, these messengers sped safely home again. In that year—on Monday the 5th of March, to wit, in the first week of Lent—David, King Robert's son, and the heir of Scotland, who succeeded his father in the kingdom, was born in the monastery of Dunfermline, after complines.

CXXXIX.

The Queen of England brings hired soldiers into England.

IN the year 1326, the lady Elizabeth, queen of England, brought a great many hired soldiers from sundry parts of the world; and, after having taken her husband. King Edward, and thrown him into prison, she bade Hugh de Spensa (Despenser), and his father, be hanged on the gallows, and be torn limb from limb. Because of this outbreak, a bishop was beheaded in London; and a great many earls, barons, and nobles were everywhere condemned to a most shameful death. The same year, Edward III., then fifteen years old, on his father being thrown into prison, was, though unwilling, crowned king of England, at Candlemas. That year, moreover, was, all over the earth, beyond the memory of living man, fruitful and plentiful in all things to overflowing. The same year, the whole Scottish clergy, the earls and barons, and all the nobles, were gathered together, with the people, at Cambuskenneth, and, in presence of King Robert himself, took the oaths to David, King Robert's son and heir,—and to Robert Stewart, the aforesaid king's grandson, in case that same David died childless. There, also, Andrew of Moray took to wife the lady Christina, that king's sister.

CXL.

Messengers sent to the King of Scotland by the English.

IN the year 1327, the English sent messengers to the king of Scotland, under a show of wishing to treat for a secure peace. But though they met together more than once, they made no way. At length their double-dealing was laid bare, and the Scots entered the northern parts of England, with a strong hand, on the 15th of June, and wasted it with fire and sword. The same year, in the month of August, the Earl of Moray and James of Douglas, with many Scottish nobles, invaded England, with arms in their hands, and, after having brought great loss upon the English, pitched their tents in a certain narrow place named Weardale; while, over against them, and at the outlet of the road, as it were, over 100,000 English troops were posted round the Scots. There the armies lay, for eight days, in sight of each other, and daily harassed one another with mutual slaughter; but they shunned a hand-to-hand battle. At length, however, the Scots, like wary warriors, sought an opportunity of saving themselves; and, having struck down in death many of the foe, and taken a great many English and Hainaulters, they returned home safe and sound, by a round-about road, by night.

CXLI.

THE same year, a few days after their retreat, the king of Scotland besieged Norham Castle, and, soon after, Alnwick Castle, one after the other; and, in that siege of Norham, William of Montealt, knight, John of Clapham, and Robert of Dobery, were killed through their own want of skill. The same year, on the 17th of March, ambassadors were sent by the king of England to the king of Scotland, at Edinburgh, to arrange and treat for a firm and lasting peace, which should abide for all time. So, after sundry negotiations, and the many and various risks of war incurred by both kingdoms, the aforesaid kings there came to an understanding together about an indissoluble peace; and the chiefs and worthies of either kingdom tendered their oaths thereto, which were to last unshaken for all time, swearing upon the soul of each king faithfully to keep all and sundry things, as they are more fully contained under certain articles of the instruments thereof, drawn up on either side as to the form of the peace. And, that it might be a true peace, which should go on without end between them and between their respective successors, the king of Scotland, of his own free and unbiassed will, gave and granted 30,000 merks in cash to the king of England, for the losses he himself had brought upon the latter and his kingdom; and the said king of England gave his sister, named Joan, to King Robert's son and heir, David, to wife, for the greater security of peace, and the steady fostering of the constancy of love.

CXLII.

Espousal of King David—Death of William of Lamberton, Bishop of Saint Andrews.

ON the 17th of July 1328, David, King Robert's son and heir, was, to the unspeakable joy of the people of either kingdom, married to Joan, sister of Edward III., king of England, at Berwick, in presence of

Elizabeth, the girl's mother, then queen of England. The same year died William of Lamberton, bishop of Saint Andrews.

CXLIII.

Death of King Robert of Bruce.

ON the 7th of June 1329, died Robert of Bruce, of goodly memory, the illustrious king of Scots, at Cardross, in the twenty-fourth year of his reign. He was, beyond all living men of his day, a valiant knight.

CXLIV.

Death of James of Douglas.

ON the 26th of August 1330, James of Douglas and the king of Spain gathered together the hosts which were flocking from different parts of the world, in aid of the Holy Land, and warred down the Sultan, and numberless Saracens with him; and when these had been overcome and put to flight, after a great many of them had been killed, and the booty had been shared, the said king went back safely, with his army. But the aforesaid James, alas! kept a very few with him, as his army; and as this was by no means hidden from another sultan, who was lurking in ambush, the latter, with his men, started out from his hiding-place, and challenged James to battle. No sooner had the said James recognised his army and banners afar off, than, in his fearlessness, he dashingly charged them with his men. A great many Saracens were there slain; and James himself ended his days there in bliss, while he and his were struggling for Christ's sake. With him, a certain William of St. Clair, and Robert Logan, knights, and a great many others, lost their lives. This James was, in his day, a brave hammerer of the English; and the Lord bestowed so much grace upon him in his life, that he everywhere triumphed over the English.

CXLV.

Coronation of King David.

ON the 24th of November 1331, David, son and heir of King Robert, was anointed king of Scots, and crowned at Scone, by the lord James Ben, bishop of Saint Andrews, specially appointed thereunto by a Bull of the most holy father John XXII., then sovereign Pontiff. We do not read that any of the kings of Scotland, before this David, were anointed, or with such solemnity crowned. The same day, John Stewart, Earl of Angus—Thomas Randolph, son and heir of Thomas Earl of Moray—and other nobles of the kingdom of Scotland, received the order of knighthood.

CXLVI.

Battle of Duplin.

ON the 20th of July 1332, died Thomas Randolph, Earl of Moray, and warden of Scotland. After his death, all the magnates, both churchmen and laymen, were gathered together at Perth, on the 2d of August; and, after a great deal of wrangling and sundry disputes, they, with one voice, chose Donald, Earl of Mar, as guardian of the kingdom. On that very day, news was brought to the said guardian, and to the rest of the lords of the kingdom, that Edward of Balliol had brought up, in the water of Forth, with a great throng of ships, on the 31st of July; and on the 6th of August, Balliol landed at Kinghorn. The same day Alexander of Seton, with a few men, withstood him in front, and fell, with three or four others. The said Edward, however, marched on thence, with his men; and, after calling at the monastery of Dunfermline, reached Duplin Moor on the 11th of the aforesaid month. Here a desperate battle was fought, from the dawn of day until the ninth hour; Edward was victorious; and great ruin loomed up before the Scottish nation. On that day, the said guardian, with the two Earls of Moray and Menteith, the lords Robert Bruce, Alexander Eraser, and other valiant nobles, barons, knights, and squires, and men of lower condition and rank without number, perished in this no less astounding than unhappy massacre, struck down, not by the strength of man, but by the vengeance of God. For, from the bruising of their bodies squeezing against one another, more fell, though unwounded, than were slain by shaft or sword. Moreover, Duncan Earl of Fife (under whose banner 360 men-at-arms had been killed), and many others, were taken.

CXLVII.

Edward of Balliol made King at Scone.

THE same year, on the 24th of September, the aforesaid Edward of Balliol was made king, at Scone, by Duncan, Earl of Fife, and William of St. Clair, bishop of Dunkeld, who had beforehand submitted to this Edward; and there were gathered together there the abbots, priors, and Estates (communitas) of Fife and Fothreve, Stratherne, and Gowry, whose submission had already been received by the above-mentioned Edward. The names of the magnates who came with this Edward, in order to get their own lands in the kingdom of Scotland, are these:— Henry of Beaumont; David, Earl of Athol; Henry of Ferrers, with his two brothers; Alexander of Arnot (Moubray); Richard Talbot; Walter Comyn; and many others. Now these, when they marched forward to battle, were 600 in all; while the Scottish army was 30,000 strong. The slain are put at 3000.

CXLVIII.

The town of Perth taken—Battle of Annan.

THE same year, on the 7th of October, was taken the town of Perth; wherein was taken Duncan, Earl of Fife (warden of that town on behalf of the aforesaid Edward of Balliol) together with his wife's daughter, and many other kinsfolk of his. Among others, Andrew of Tulibardine was taken, and convicted of being a traitor towards the king; so he suffered the death of the body. The same year, on the 16th of December, John Randolph, Earl of Moray, Archibald of Douglas, and Simon Eraser, with a few other nobles, were gathered together in the town of Moffat, and came, by night, to the town of Annan. There they soon came suddenly to blows with Edward of Balliol, and Edward was put to flight. In this struggle, John of Mowbray, Henry of Balliol, Walter Comyn, and many others, were slain; and Edward himself barely escaped, with a few followers. Alexander of Bruce was there taken by the Earl of Moray, but snatched from death.

CXLIX.

Conflict at Halidon.

ON the 31st of March 1333, the town of Berwick was besieged by Edward III., king of England. Having broken the bonds of peace and alliance, he, with all the strength of Wales, Gascony, and England—having been, moreover, joined by the many Scots who sided with Edward of Balliol—steadily kept up the said siege until the 19th of July. On that day was fought the rueful battle of Halidon, where (according to meaning of its name aforesaid) the Scots were overcome, and almost utterly swept away—especially those who abetted, and had tenderly at heart the cause of king David. The names of those killed on king David's side are these:—Archibald of Douglas, then guardian of Scotland; Hugh, Earl of Boss; Kenneth, Earl of Sutherland; Alexander of Bruce, Earl of Carrick; Andrew Eraser, and his brother Simon; James Eraser; and a great many other nobles, whose names it would be more sad than profitable to repeat one by one. In the town of Berwick, at that time, were Patrick Earl of March, and the warden of the aforesaid town—Alexander of Seton, the father, whose son, named Thomas, had been given to the king of England, as a hostage for the surrender of the aforesaid town on or before a day beforehand fixed upon therefor. But when the time had run out, forasmuch as the aforesaid Alexander was still awaiting succour, and would not give up the town on the day fixed upon, this Thomas was hanged on the gallows, before his father's face; while his brother, named William, had, on account of the defence of the town, been, a little before, drowned among the English ships, while the father looked on. But after the battle had been fought, straightway all hope of rescue and help was quenched, and the town was surrendered and given up to the king of England, all the dwellers therein being saved harmless in life, limb, and property.

CL.

Dispute between Edward of Balliol, and Henry of Beaumont, and David, Earl of Athol.

ABOUT the end of the month of August 1334, a misunderstanding arose at Perth between Edward of Balliol, who stood up for Alexander of Mowbray, and the Lords Henry of Beaumont, David Earl of Athol, and Richard Talbot, who were striving to oust the said Alexander from his inheritance, and to bring in his brother's daughters before him, by right of succession. So, being at odds upon this matter, they withdrew from one another. Edward took the road towards Berwick; Henry of Beaumont, towards Dundrage (Dundarg); the Earl of Athol, towards Lochindorb. Richard Talbot made for England; and, while on his way through Lothian, he and his followers were there taken prisoners, on the 8th of September. The Lord Alexander of Mowbray, however, fearing the strength of the opposite side, cast in his lot altogether with Andrew of Moray, who had, a little before, on payment of his ransom, been set free from prison. So, with their united forces, they together besieged Henry of Beaumont, for some time, in Dundrage Castle. But Henry of Beaumont, despairing of being relieved, taking into account, moreover, the want of provisions, and reflecting that he could not defend the castle, yielded and gave up the aforesaid castle to the above-mentioned Andrew and Alexander, on the 23d of December, on condition of being saved harmless in life, limb, and all his goods, and being granted, besides, a safe and sure conduct to cross into England, with his wife, children, and whole family; and he promised faithfully, and duly swore, to exert himself for the restoration of peace. After not many days had rolled by, he and his went on board ship at Dundee, and betook themselves to England without delay. John of Randolph, Earl of Moray, however, who, after the struggle at Annan, had straightway gone to the king of France, came home again, then, all of a sudden, and doggedly pursued the Earl of Athol, through rough ways and smooth; so the latter, seeing that he could in no wise escape, was forced, by the violent pursuit of the Earl of Moray, to submit to King David, on the 27th of September, tendering him fealty and homage, which he confirmed by oath.

CLI.

Messengers of the King of France.

THE same year, on the 4th of March, there came to Perth messengers, sent by the king of France to treat for peace between the kings of Scotland and England. This step was taken with the consent, as well as by the directions, of the supreme Pontiff, Benedict XII., who addressed letters-patent severally to the kings of Scotland and England. The king of England, however, would not deign to hear, or even see, them. Other messengers, again, from the kings of France and Scotland, were sent; but he utterly rejected peace and concord.

CLII.

The King of England comes to Perth, with Edward of Balliol.

IN the month of April 1335, Robert Stewart, and the Earl of Moray, then guardian of Scotland, held their parliament at Dervesy (Dairsy); and there appeared there the Earl of March, Andrew of Moray, Alexander of Mowbray, and William of Douglas, on the one hand—who behaved discreetly and quietly,—and David Earl of Athol, with a great force, on the other; but, by reason of the latter's insolence, nothing was there done worthy of aught but scorn. This man cleaved to Stewart (who was then not governed by much wisdom), and, looking down upon the Earl of Moray, became very troublesome to all who were there; but the wary tact of the first-named nobles skilfully parried his wild fierceness. The same year, by direction of the guardians, all the inhabitants dwelling in the plains fled, in crowds, to the hills and fastnesses, with their movable goods and all their beasts; and, on the 6th of July, the fleet of the king of England brought up in the water of Forth. Then the king of England, and Edward of Balliol, who had with them 90,000 horsemen and nine score ships, pitched their tents at Perth; and, tarrying there until the arrival of the Earl of Athol, they plundered all the country round.

CLIII.

John Earl of Moray taken.

THE same year, on the 30th of July, the Count of Gellere (Guelders), who had come over from parts beyond the sea to bring help to the king of England, on this same pending matter, came to blows, at Edinburgh, with the united forces of the Earl of March, and the Earl of Moray (who kept away from the northern districts, because of the tyrannousness of the Earl of Athol); but he was beaten, and had to yield. The Earl of Moray, however, who was beyond measure courteous and soft-hearted towards his foes, feeling sure that he would thereby give great pleasure to the king of France, from whom he had lately parted, let the aforesaid Count of Gellere and his men go back free and scathless, without ransom or any other burden, and restored the booty which had been taken from him;—and all for love of the king of France. And, the better to show his good-will, he accompanied him in person to the marches; but he was overtaken unawares by the onslaught of the garrison of a castle, taken by those churls, and thrown into prison. The same year, when not many days were overpast, the Earl of Athol made his submission to the king of England and to Edward of Balliol, and swore fealty to them, at Perth, faithfully promising them that he would, before long, bring back under their sway all the Scottish magnates. On the strength of this promise, he was made warden of Scotland on behalf of those kings. After these things, those who had fled came back, the castles were fortified, the kingdom was tranquillized, and the king of England returned, with his forces; but the great tjrranny and cruelty this Earl practised among the people words cannot bring within the mind's grasp: some he disinherited, others he murdered; and, in the end, he cast in his mind how he might wipe all the freeholders from off the face of the earth.

CLIV.

Death of the Earl of Athol, at Kilblen.

THERE were, at that time, three magnates of Scotland,—to wit, Andrew of Moray, who was, the same year, about the Feast of St. Matthew, made guardian of Scotland on behalf of King David, at Dunbretane (Dumbarton); the Earl of March; and William of Douglas— who had not yet made their submission to the English, or to Edward of Balliol, but had, through the respect and forbearance, in some wise, of the king and magnates of England, been lurking in hiding, now here, now there, looking with gaping mouth, as it were, for better times. Now, when the aforesaid imdrew learnt, from hearsay, that his castle, with his wife, was besieged by the aforesaid Earl, he asked and got leave from the lord William of Montagu (then a chief councillor of the king of England), and, with the help of the aforesaid Earl of March and William of Douglas, made ready, with all haste, to relieve his castle. So these three, with their abettors, heartily sympathizing with their sorrowing countrymen in their awful sufferings, chose rather to die in battle than see the woes of their nation. So, with one consent, and with a lusty heart, they gave themselves to danger as a ransom for their thraldom; and, raging like bears or lions robbed of their cubs, they hastened to battle. They came to blows on the 30th of November, in the forest of Kilblen, where they slaughtered the Earl himself, as well as five knights and the rest of his partisans, under an oak; and when they had got the victory, they mercifully spared the rabble who were with him against their will. After this struggle, the said Andrew and the others came to the castle of Cupar, and besieged it. Therein were a great many Scots who had gone over to the English; but, on receipt of letters from the kings of France and Scotland, he granted the garrison of the castle a truce up to a certain time. In the meantime he called the chiefs of the kingdom together at Dunfermline, and was there, by all, approved as guardian of Scotland. He then went off beyond the hills, and tarried long in the north.

CLV.

The King of England and Edward of Balliol arrive at Perth.

In the year 1336, the king of England and Edward of Balliol came to Perth, with a great force both by sea and by land; and, taking with him some chosen men, the aforesaid king hastened straight to Lochindorb, whence he brought away the wife and the heir of David Earl of Athol. Then, consuming the whole of Moray with fire, he reached Elgin; and, marching on thence—leaving, moreover, the churches and canonical buildings of Elgin untouched—he, by the all-devouring flames, levelled with the ground the town of Aberdeen; and thus he came back to the town of Perth, after having strengthened the strongholds of Dunottar, Kynnef, and Lauriston. Then, after talking matters over earnestly, he, by the advice, especially, of the aforesaid men of the kingdom of Scotland, ordered that the town of Perth should, with all haste, be strengthened in its walls and moats, towers and gates; and he singled out six monasteries—viz., Dunfermline, Saint Andrews, Lindores, Balmurinach (Balmerino), Abberbrothoc (Arbroath), and Coupar-Angus—to build up, of hewn stone, at their own charges and expense, the three greater sides, with as many towers. By the impost for these works, the said monasteries were greatly impoverished. At the same time, the castles of Saint Andrews and of Lochris (Leuchars), were rebuilt by Henry of Beaumont and Henry of Ferrers. The same year, while the king of England tarried at the town of Perth, his brother, John of Eltham, making his way through the western districts of Scotland, consumed with fire and sword the lands which had lately submitted to the king, his brother; and a great many souls who fled to the churches, were, with the churches themselves, destroyed and clean swept away by being set on fire. The king, however, at Perth, took him to task for all this,—as he was bound to do; and when he answered the king in angry mood, he was suddenly smitten by his brother's sword, and shuffled off this mortal coil. But the king soon after went back to England, and left Edward of Balliol, with a strong force, in the town of Perth. At this time, Henry of Beaumont, whenever he of himself, or through others, could catch any who had taken part in the struggle at Kilblene, ordered them all, in revenge for the death of his son-inlaw, to be racked with divers tortures, and put to death without mercy. Among these, much guiltless blood was shed. The same year, Strivelyn (Stirling) Castle was strengthened by Sir William of Montagu, who set Sir Thomas of Rokeby therein; Edinburgh Castle, by Sir John of Strivelyn (Stirling); and Roxburgh Castle, by Sir William of Felton, knights.

CLVI.

Andrew of Moray.

THE same year, in the month of October, Andrew of Moray, then guardian of Scotland, mustered an army, and besieging the strongholds of Dunnottar, Kynneff, and Lauriston, took them, and levelled them with the ground. Then he tarried the whole winter in the forest of Platen, and other very safe places in Angus, being often waylaid by the English, and braving their dangerous attacks. So, through the ceaseless marauding of both sides, the whole land of Gowrie, Angus, and Mearns was, for the most part, almost reduced to a hopeless wilderness, and to utter want. The same year, in the month of February, shortly after the stronghold of Kinclevin had been broken down to the very foundation, this same guardian combined with the Earls of March and of Fife, William of Douglas, and many other nobles of Scotland, and marched into Fife, where he levelled with the ground the tower of Falkland, plundered the land everywhere around, took the inhabitants prisoners, and put them up for ransom. Thus he got to Saint Andrews, and, with his engines, mightily besieged the castle thereof for three weeks. On the last day of February, this castle was surrendered unto him, on condition of the inmates thereof being saved harmless in life, limb, and all their goods. Luchris (Leuchars) Castle had, a little while before, been dealt with in like manner in all respects. Afterwards, shifting his camp thence on the 6th of March, he got to the tower of Bothwell in the following Lent, took it by storm after some little time, and levelled it with the ground;—not without loss to his men, however, for Stephen Wisman fell there.

CLVII.
Andrew of Moray besieges Strivelyn (Stirling) Castle.

IN the months of April and May 1337, Strivelyn (Stirling) Castle was besieged by this guardian. But, upon the king of England coming with a large army, the guardian saw that they were too many for him to withstand in battle. So he and his withdrew therefrom, safe and sound, after William of Keith had been, no less unhappily than strangely, killed with his own lance. The same year Edinburgh Castle was besieged by him, and the Estates (*communitas*) of Lothian submitted unto him. But, by means of the falsehood and deceit of certain Scotsmen, he was, by the English forces, made to withdraw from the siege thereof, after he had appointed Lawrence of Preston sheriff of Lothian. Thereupon followed, on the part both of Scots and English, the wholesale destruction of Lothian. The same year, on the 13th of January, Dunbar Castle was besieged by William of Montagu, Earl of Salisbury, and the Earl of Arundel, the leaders of the English king's army. This siege was kept up with the strong hand, with many huge engines, balisters, and all the contrivances of war-craft, for twenty-two weeks; and, on the 16th of June next following, they were called back by letters preceptory from the king of England, leaving their task undone. The same year, happily for the kingdom of Scotland, was begun a very fearful and savage war between the kings of England and France.

CLVIII.
Death of Andrew of Moray.

IN the year 1338 died Andrew of Moray, the warden of Scotland, and was buried at Rosemarky; but his bones were afterwards brought down to Dunfermline, and entombed before the altar of the Blessed Virgin, in the monastery of that place. He did a good deal for his country's freedom; and assaulted and destroyed all the castles and strongholds held by the English about the water of Forth, except Cupar and Perth. But all the country he marched through, in his wars, he reduced to such desolation and distress, that more perished afterwards, through starvation and want, than the sword devoured in time of war. He was two years and a half guardian of Scotland. The same year, Robert Stewart was made guardian of Scotland, and stood until King David's arrival.

CLIX.

The town of Perth besieged and taken.

IN the year 1339, the town of Perth was besieged by the said Robert and the rest of the magnates of the kingdom. It was held, on behalf of the English, by Thomas Otyr (Ughtred), who had with him a great many Scots that cleaved to Edward of Balliol. On the 17th of August, the aforesaid town was surrendered, on condition that the English were saved harmless in life, limb, and all their moveables. Accordingly, they left Scotland with all haste—some, by a sea-voyage, others, by a land journey—amid much jeering, after yielding their lands and possessions to the Scots, and submitting to such wrongs as had been shamelessly heaped upon the king and the natives in the time of the war. I should mention that there took part in the siege of the said town a naval commander from France, named Haupilie, with two ships laden with freebooters. At the first onslaught he made upon the English, this man lost his ship, through over-much foolhardiness and want of skill. There also took part thereat two knights from France, with their vassals, and a famous squire, named Giles de la Huse. Now the said commander, after having recovered the ship he had previously lost, was given money by the guardian, as a reward for his trouble; then, going on board ship with the knights and his own servants, hoisted the sail, and, being caught in a squall, at the outlet of Drumlie, at once went to the bottom.

But the said squire, who was on board another ship, escaped unhurt the maw of the awful gulf. I should mention, likewise, that, at the time of the siege of the aforesaid town of Perth, the lord William Bullock, a chaplain, warden of the castle of Cupar, chamberlain of Scotland, on behalf of Edward of Balliol, and lieutenant and treasurer of all the English and their adherents in the kingdom of Scotland, after having liberal compensation granted him for his lands and possessions, surrendered the above-mentioned castle to the warden, and became, with his party, King David's liege man. He, moreover, took part in the aforesaid siege with all his might, lending efficient help, and imparting useful advice. This man, who was distinguished, above all of his day, for his tact and the terse eloquence of his speech in his mother tongue, had risen suddenly from the lowest depths. First, he was chamberlain with Edward of Balliol, and treasurer to the rest of the English; and, lastly, chamberlain of Scotland with King David, the greatest among his first councillors, and renowned for shrewd and skilful advice—indeed, equally by the king and lords of Scotland, and by the king of England, he was held worthy to be praised as a second Coucy. But, after he had filled sundry different offices, and had amassed boundless wealth, he was at length suspected of treason, and suddenly dismissed from his office of chamberlain, when as he thought he stood fast; and, by the king's command, he was all at once taken by David Barclay, and kept in custody at Malimora. Thus, after much happiness and success, adversity came back to him; and he ended his life by an unhappy death. Therein was very strikingly fulfilled that saying of the poet:—

"The more man's life is strained to reach success.
The stronger the recoil to wretchedness."

CLX.

ON the 17th of April 1341, Edinburgh Castle was taken with the strong hand, no less fortunately than cleverly, by the lords William of Douglas, William Eraser, and William Bullock, with their party, after they had subdued the whole garrison of that castle. The same year—in

1341, to wit—on the 2d of June, David, by the grace of God the illustrious king of Scots, came back from France to Scotland. He and the queen were brought over by a fleet to Inverbervie, and landed safe and sound.

CLXI.

Roxburgh Castle taken by Alexander of Ramsay.

ON the 30th of March 1342—which, that year, was Easter Eve—about cock-crow, Alexander of Ramsay and his followers scaled the walls of Roxburgh Castle by ladders, and took it with the strong hand, after they had overcome all the guards, and slain some.

CLXII.

Death of this Alexander.

THE same year, on the 20th of June, Alexander Ramsay, warden of Roxburgh Castle, and sheriff of Teviotdale, summoned before him, at Hawick, all in the said sheriffdom, and repaired thither in person. But when he had been a long while awaiting, in the church of that town, the arrival of those summoned, in order that he might discharge his duty, and had not the least inkling of guile or ill-will, news was brought him that William of Douglas was on the point of coming thither. Ramsay, although he had been put on his guard about William's fierceness, suspected no evil from him, inasmuch as, shortly before, all misunderstandings had been settled, and friendship renewed afresh; so he waited in the church for William's coming. When William came in, Ramsay rose, and, greeting him peacefully, asked him to sit down beside him. But William and his men, armed as they were, ruthlessly fell upon him and three others who came to his rescue, and seized and wounded them with ghastly wounds, in the bosom, of holy mother Church. As for Alexander himself, they bound him with chains, set him on horseback, and took him away; and, when he had been brought down to Hermitage Castle (near Castleton), he is said to have lived seventeen days without any bodily sustenance; and, fortified by partaking of the

Saving Host, he paid the debt of nature on that same seventeenth day after he was taken. Ramsay had done a good deal for the king and for the country's freedom: he had felled the foe everywhere around, greatly checked their attacks, won many a victory, done much good, and—so far as man can judge—would have done more, had he lived longer. In brave deeds of arms, and in bodily strength he surpassed all others of his day; and even as he was mightier than the rest in deeds of arms, so was he luckier in his struggles. But the old enemy envied his prowess, and roused against him one who, governed by envy, not only traitorously, but also most pitifully, wrested from him, and destroyed, the badges of his virtues.

CLXIII.

Now as, from the day of the struggle at Kilblene until this Alexander's death, all things, in the result of every war, were brought to a prosperous issue, so, when he was taken away from our midst, all things which were tried for the good of the country had straightway, on the contrary, an unlucky result. For, through this Alexander's death, feuds and misunderstandings, undying—as it were—and endless, arose in the kingdom, not only among the lords, but even among the common people; so that, thenceforth, they murdered each other with mutual slaughter, and slew each other with the sword.

CLXIV.

In the year 1344 there was so great a pestilence among the fowls, that men utterly shrank from eating, or even looking upon, a cock or a hen, as though unclean and smitten with leprosy; and thus, as well as from the aforesaid cause, nearly the whole of that species was destroyed.

CLXV.

Battle of Durham fought.

In the month of October 1346, David, king of Scotland, gathered his army together, and marched, in great force, into England. On the 17th of October, a battle was fought at Durham, with the English, and King David was defeated and taken prisoner; while all his nobles were taken with him, or killed—except Patrick of Dunbar, Earl of March, and Robert, steward of Scotland, who took to flight, and got away unhurt. Together with the king, were there taken the Earl of Fife; Malcolm Flemyng, Earl of Wigtown; the Earl of Menteith, who was afterwards drawn by horses in England, and was put to death, racked with divers tortures; William of Douglas; and many other barons, nobles, valiant knights, and picked squires. The killed were John of Randolph, Earl of Moray; the Earl of Stratherne; the constable of Scotland; the marshal of Scotland; the chamberlain of Scotland; and numberless other barons, knights, squires, and good men. The same year, just after the aforesaid battle, the castles of Roxburgh and Hermitage (near Castleton) were surrendered to the English; and Lothian was consumed by fire.

CLXVI.

Robert Stewart, guardian of Scotland.

THE same year, not long after that battle took place, the chief men who were left were gathered together, and, lest the state of the commonwealth should be thrown into confusion chose unto themselves, as guardian, the lord Robert, steward of Scotland, the aforesaid king's nephew; deeming that, forasmuch as he was the most powerful of all, the general interests would be most strongly guarded by him. But how he governed in the office of warden—how he governed the kingdom intrusted unto him, his deeds show forth unto all times.

CLXVII.

Pestilence among men.

IN the year 1350, there was, in the kingdom of Scotland, so great a pestilence and plague among men (which also prevailed for a great many years before and after, in divers parts of the world—nay, all over the whole earth), as, from the beginning of the world even unto modern times, had never been heard of by man, nor is found in books, for the enlightenment of those who come after. For, to such a pitch did that plague wreck its cruel spite, that nearly a third of mankind were thereby made to pay the debt of nature. Moreover, by God's will, this evil led to a strange and unwonted kind of death, insomuch that the flesh of the sick was somehow puffed out and swollen, and they dragged out their earthly life for barely two days. Now this everywhere attacked especially the meaner sort and common people;—seldom the magnates. Men shrank from it so much that, through fear of contagion, sons, fleeing as from the face of leprosy or from an adder, durst not go and see their parents in the throes of death.

CLXVIII.

Death of the Lord David of Barclay.

In the year 1351, on Fasten's Even, that noble and mighty man, the lord David of Barclay, knight, was inhumanly and treacherously slain, at Aberdeen, by John of Saint Michael and his accomplices;—though it is reported that it was through the intrigues of the lord William of Douglas (who was then a prisoner in England), to avenge his brother, John of Douglas, whom this David had caused to be seized. The aforesaid John of Saint Michael, however, and all others, his abettors, who took part in this murder, were, after no long interval of time, destroyed one after the other, by the sword of vengeance; and not even one of them escaped death.

CLXIX.

Matilda of Bruce and her Offspring.

In the year 1353, Matilda of Bruce, sister of the lord David, king of Scotland, died at Aberdeen, on the Feast of the blessed virgin Margaret, and was buried in Dunfermline, with her father and mother. She wedded a certain squire, named Thomas Isaac, who, of her, begat two daughters. The elder, named Joan, wedded a noble and mighty man, John of Lorne, lord of that ilk; who, of her, begat sons and daughters.

Matilda's younger daughter, named Catherine, was taken away from this life at Strivelyn (Stirling).

CLXX.

Death of the Lord William of Douglas.

THE same year, in the month of August, Sir William of Douglas, a wise and most sagacious man, was, while out hunting, and crossing Ettrick Forest, unsuspicious of evil from any man, was slain by William of Douglas, lord of that ilk; who, afterwards, had other lands given him by our lord the king, and was called earl of that lordship. He was thus put to death in revenge for the death of Alexander of Ramsay and the lord David of Barclay, and because, also, of a great many other causes of unfriendliness, and many a grudge stirred up between the two Douglases by their thirst for power. His body rests at Melrose.

CLXXI.

Messengers sent by the King of France to the Nobles of Scotland.

IN the year 1355, after the Feast of Easter, there came a certain noble person, of tried skill in arms, a valiant and most dashing knight, named Eugene de Capencers (Garencières), with certain chosen knights and gallant and famous squires, to the number of sixty. He was sent by the king and council of France to the guardian and nobles of Scotland—though not empty-handed, but with huge store of pounds of gold, which was to be bestowed freely, on behalf of the lord their king, upon that same guardian and the lords of the kingdom: Provided, however, that the Scots should not maintain peace or any good understanding with the English; but should, on the contrary, bravely war them down. This, at all events, was settled and finally promised by the leading men of the kingdom, in sundry interviews and councils held in sundry places, before the aforesaid gold, which had been left behind in Flanders, came into Scotland; and the Scots, who often for a penny lose a shilling, were led away, by lust for gold, to promise to fight England to the last. But afterwards, when it came to deeds, they achieved little worthy of remembrance. So the chiefs of the kingdom shared among themselves the aforesaid gold they had got from the French; and the others, of meaner sort, they sent empty away. But from this agreement and greed of gold, there followed, soon after, the destruction of Lothian by the king of England.

CLXXII.

Conflict at Nesbit.

THE same year, in the month of August, the Earl of March and William lord of Douglas, finding it hard to brook the depredations which had lately been committed by the English on the aforesaid Earl's lands, sent a valiant man, of tried prowess—the lord William of Ramsay, knight—with a great many men, to the marches, to plunder the town of Norham and the whole of the outlying lands, and the dwellers therein. This was accordingly done. When hard pressed by the enemy, he held his ground for awhile, as best he could; but he soon made a feint of fleeing, and purposely drew them on, as had been planned, to a certain place called Nesbit, where he well knew that the aforesaid lord of Douglas was lurking with his Scots and Frenchmen, and waiting to see how things would turn out. Then, quickly putting the spur of a hill between him and the enemy, he came to the Scots, and brought them good news of the coming of the English. The Scots rose from their seats, and hastened merrily to meet them. But the English, thunderstruck at the sight of them thus unexpectedly, and knowing full well the aforesaid lord's ensigns and banners, could not now, with honour, flee; so they staked their lives upon their own prowess, and manfully fought it out with the Scots. Since, however, even the strong must needs be overcome by stronger, and the weaker side be tripped up, the Scots, thank God! prevailed against them, and they were all subdued and overthrown. A few, indeed, were slain; and the remainder, except a few who fled, were led away scathless into captivity, and kept closely guarded in divers places. These were afterwards ransomed for much gold and silver and other substance. On that day, there fell, on the side of the Scots, John of Haliburton, a brave and warlike man, who had always given the English great trouble. But on the other side were taken the lord Thomas Gray, a noble knight, with Thomas, his son and heir; and a brave and famous squire, named James Darres, with a great many other gallant English nobles.

CLXXIII.

Thomas Stewart, Earl of Angus, makes an attempt upon the town of Berwick.

THE same year, about Allhallowmas, Thomas Stewart, Earl of Angus, after having long thought of the undertaking, got together a number of ships from the several harbours of Scotland; and, with a mighty arm, and at the head of a body of stout men conveyed with him by sea, he brought up at Berwick harbour, on a still night, as had been planned between him and the Earl of March. They stealthily disembarked, and came on shore, bearing with them ladders provided for the purpose; and, bivouacking under the city walls, they lay in wait for a fit time to do what they had come for. Accordingly, in the twilight of the following morning, they set up the ladders, and brave men straightway mounted them, and manfully entered the city; and, though the watchmen on the walls had given them a great deal of trouble on their entrance, they overthrew all who strove to defend the city. At length, all in the city, being panic-stricken at the sudden coming of the Scotsmen, rose out of bed, and rushed headlong without the walls, leaving the Scotsmen gold, and silver, and boundless wealth. These, however, dealt unmercifully with what their foes had, with much time and trouble, scraped together unto themselves. Nevertheless, the Scots, though they bravely assaulted the Castle of Berwick, could not manage to take it.

CLXXIV.

The town of Berwick is surrendered to the King of England.

THE same year, in the month of February, Edward III., king of England, brooking ill the taking of the town of Berwick by the Scots, and fearing that, if he let them alone so, they would wrest the place and people from him, came to the marches, with a large force, as fast as he could (seeing that he lived so far off), and was going to lay siege to that town. The Scots, seeing this, and being unable to defend the town—because they were few, and had no provisions; and because they had a great dread of the aforesaid king's fierceness, and were hopeless of getting succour from their own nation, owing to the feuds among the chiefs—were wisely advised, and came to the best conclusion under the circumstances: they surrendered the aforesaid town to the king of England, on condition that they were saved harmless in life, limb, and all their substance; and thus every one hied him home scathless.

CLXXV.
Edward of Balliol comes to meet the King of England at Roxburgh.

I MUST not omit to state that, the same year, immediately after the town of Berwick had been made over to the aforesaid king, and while he in person was at Roxburgh, before he had advanced further into the land of Scotland, Edward of Balliol came, like a roaring lion, to meet him; and, scarce containing himself for wrath, he broke forth into these words, more bitter than death itself, and said:—"king, and best of princes! who art, I know, the mightiest of all mortals in the world in these days—I wholly, simply, and absolutely yield unto thee my cause, and all right I have, or may have, to the throne of Scotland, so that thou avenge me of mine enemies, the Scottish nation, a race most false, who have always cast me aside, that I should not reign over them." And as evidence that he did so he held forth unto him, as he spoke, the royal crown, and some earth and stones which he picked up off the ground with his own hand. "All these," quoth he, "I give unto thee as a token of investiture. Only, act manfully, and be strong; and conquer for thyself the kingdom which ought formerly to have been mine." This, moreover, should be noticed in this matter: that he gave away nothing from himself, inasmuch as he had no right, from the very first; and, if haply he had had any, he then resigned it into another's hands.

CLXXVI.
The King of England comes to Scotland.

WHEN this business had been duly gone through, as above stated, the aforesaid king, hailing Edward as his cousin, warmly thanked him for so noble and stately a gift; and, marching on thence, like a she-bear raging in the forest, when robbed of her young, he in cruel wise entered the land of Scotland, with great power and majesty, and got as far as the town of Haddington; and his fleet followed him. While he tarried there ten days, a strong wind came from the region of the desert—that is to say, from the north (for "evil will come from the north")—and caught this fleet, and sent it to the bottom. When the king was thus left without his fleet, he and his whole army were soon after suffering from want of bread; so, shifting his camp thence, after having burnt down the whole monastery of the Minorite brothers, together with their stately church (a most costly work, of wondrous beauty, and the one pride of all that country), he bent his steps through Lothian, wasting everything all around, and saving nothing. And thus he hied him home without glory; though not without loss to his men, and much danger to his own body, from an ambush laid for him in the forest near Melrose. Now his aim and purpose had been, if his ships had held their course prosperously, to demolish and destroy the kingdom of Scotland far and near—yea, to waste it utterly; but God put off to a far-off time the execution of this plan. He would, however, have doubtless been able to do this at that time, had not the Virgin Mother come to the relief of the wretched Scottish nation, in this plight. For, while that king was still at Haddington, and was, without respite, thirsting for the blood of the Scots, the blessed Virgin, the spring and source of goodness, by her pious prayers obtained from her Son,—One who said, "Without me ye can do nothing"—that boisterous wind and rough weather; so that the ships parted from one another, and could not move a step beyond the Firth of Forth, but were unceasingly tossed among the waves of the sea and the storms of the deep, so that a great many of them have never, to this day, met the gaze of living man. For some men-of-war's men, sons of Belial, had, shortly before, disembarked, and fallen upon the white kirk of the Virgin, which stands by the sea-side. There, not having God before their eyes, and being unmindful of their own salvation, they banished fear, and stripped the image of the Virgin, which no man had, with impunity, touched with evil intent, and which was decked with gold rings, necklaces, and armlets, and other ornaments wherewith the oblations of the faithful had becomingly loaded it; and two canons of the house of Holyrood, who had lately been commissioned as keepers of that chapel, they bound and dragged with them to their craft, after having carried off all the property they found in the chapel. This turned out unluckily for them, however. For, not long after, the uproar and storms above spoken of followed, in revenge for this thing; and the ship which had wrought the heinous robbery, and its crew, who had dared to lay hands on the Lady of the World, were whelmed in the gulf of the deep, in the sight of many. But the said canons had, by God's will, been shortly before shifted to other ships; and they were thus, by Our Lady's succour, snatched from the maw of the awful gulf, and allowed to cross over freely to their dwelling-place. Such was the miracle that Almighty God, through His Mother's prayers, deigned to show forth, at that time, for the salvation of the Scottish nation.

CLXXVII.

Conflict which took place at Poitiers, in France.

IN the year 1356, the king of France, named John, hearing that the fourth Edward, son and heir of the king of England, had entered the borders of his kingdom in hostile wise, with a strong and sturdy hand, in order to conquer him, and subdue the whole land of France to his power and dominion, gathered from every part of his kingdom, and from other countries which lay under his sway, a strong army, and people without end. Among others, a certain noble and mighty William of Douglas, lord of that ilk, a Scot by birth, was glad to come and lend his help to the aforesaid king of France; and he brought with him a great many Scots, strong in body, accomplished in arms, and learned in warfare. Before the shock of battle, this same king promoted him and many others, with much honour, to the belt and order of knighthood. To make a long story short—while his foes were plundering the land of France, the king, with his men, followed them from place to place, until he reached a place called Poitiers; and, pitching his tents there, he tarried some time, watching lest his adversaries, who were posted over against him, should give him the slip. At last, the English prince and his men, who were very few in comparison with the French, seeing that their position was shut in, had no hope of being able to escape; and being sore afraid of the numbers of those pitted against them, durst not, at first, openly come to blows with the French, who stood in their lines, and stirred not. So they planned a stratagem and shrewd device, in order to part them asunder. They made a feint of wishing to return to their own country by another way, near the French. But when these found this out, they thought the English had taken to flight; so, by an unlucky impulse, they straightway broke from the ranks, deeming that they would swallow up the Scots like a gnat. But, alas! great was the ruin and dismay which came of their being broken up. The marshal of France, with many of the best men of France, thinking to do bravely, burst through the hedges and vineyards, in hot pursuit of the English; and he there fell, together with all who had come with him, overcome by the archers, and the other ghastly strokes of war-craft. Thereupon, the English, gladdened beyond belief, hastened briskly and fearlessly to the former battle-ground, where the king had been standing the whole time without stirring. Here a desperate battle was straightway fought between the two sides, and the French fled miserably from before the face of the English. Their king was left on the field alone with his little son Philip, and was, without delay, seized by the enemy, stripped of his kingly ornaments, and, after some little interval of time, sent over to the king of England. But the men of the lord of Douglas, seeing what had happened in the battle, and what was in store for them, dragged their lord out of the thick of the fight, and took him away with them, against his will. A great many of the best of his men were killed in battle, and others were taken, and put to ransom.

CLXXVIII.

Release of our Lord King David, King of Scotland.

IN the year 1357, about Michaelmas, King David of Scotland was released from prison, after having been, for twelve years, kept in close confinement in sundry places in England. There were given, for his ransom, 100,000 merks sterling, to be honestly paid within the ten years immediately following, without any treaty, dismemberment or subjection of the kingdom, or any exaction whatsoever. As security that the whole of this money would be paid to the king of England, the sons and heirs of nearly all the nobles and lords of the kingdom of Scotland were given, as hostages, into the hands of the English; and a great many others—earls, and barons—long remained, in person, as hostages for their lord. The same year, the Lady Christiana of Bruce, King Robert's sister, a most noble matron, died at a good old age, and was buried at Dunfermline, with her parents and her forebears, the kings of Scotland, whose own burial-ground that is.

CLXXIX.

Great Flood of Waters.

IN the month of September 1358, on the eve of the Nativity of the Blessed Virgin, such a great flood of rain burst forth in Lothian, as had not occurred in the kingdom of Scotland from the time of Noah until now; so that the waters were swollen, and, overflowing their beds and banks, poured over the fields and towns, cities and monasteries, utterly overthrowing and sweeping away, in their rush, stone walls and the strongest bridges, hamlets and houses. Moreover, tearing up by the roots lofty oaks and sturdy trees which grew near the streams, the resistless tide washed them down to the sea-coast. The crops, also, and stubble, reaped and left out to dry where it was cut, it filched from the use of man, from all places both far and near, thereby doing great damage.

CLXXX.
King David begs a tenth from the Sovereign Pontiff.

IN the year 1359, David, king of Scotland, sent his ambassadors—namely, the lord Robert of Erskine, and Norman of Leslie, esquire, with some other men of standing—to the Apostolic See, in order to beg a tenth of all the income and rents of the whole Scottish Church, in aid of the payment of his ransom, whereto he had lately become bound towards the king of England. This prayer the sovereign Pontiff kindly granted—for three years only: Provided, however, the king did not demand or ask for more from the clergy of his kingdom, as far as his whole ransom was concerned. So the above-named messengers, thus bounteously sped with papal bulls addressed to the clergy of Scotland upon this same matter, went home again merrily. Nevertheless, when so much had been got, all the lands and temporalities held from the king, or otherwise, by Churchmen, were, by that king's directions, made to contribute, together with the barons and other freeholders of the kingdom—though the clergy made a strong stand against this.

CLXXXI.
The King of England crosses into France.

THE same year, Edward III., king of England, entered the kingdom of France, in cruel wise, about Michaelmas, in all the glory of his power, and with a countless host from the whole of England. Respecting no spot or province, he reduced to an endless waste even the noblest monasteries, and other stately places of sundry religious orders, as well as abbeys of nuns, after having destroyed all their substance upon earth. No one in the French kingdom durst lift his head against him, or fight against him in any way; but with unhindered foot went he into boroughs and fortresses, towns and cities, perpetrating countless massacres. And thus after dealing many a great blow to God's people, he, with no little gladness, reached that most noble city of Paris. But they of the city, taking heed unto themselves for the time to come, treated with the king for peace, and for the release of their king. So the aforesaid king, perceiving that the greatest advantage unto him and his kingdom, for ever, would grow out of this bargain, fell in with the more suitable plan; and, withdrawing from them, he made for England, and got back safe and sound, without loss.

CLXXXII.
The King of France in England is released.

IN the year 1360, after some little time had gone by since the English king's return from the kingdom of France, all the elders and greater nobles of the whole of France held a council; and, wishing to duly follow up the matter of their king, sent their envoys and special messengers to the aforesaid king, about the release of their prince. That king, on the other hand, deeming, with great foresight, that a practicable opening, a covenant most advantageous to his honour, was being held out to him by the other side, and having, first, earnestly talked the matter over with his wise men, determined, after mature deliberation, to close with the messengers, who had full powers. So he let their king, after giving hostages, go home again; though not without a great dismembering of the kingdom and unsettling of all property. For, by way of ransom, John invested and seised the king of England, and his successors, of the underwritten lands and domains, with many others which the writer of this Chronicle has been unable to ascertain; and he alienated them for ever from the crown of France. He granted him those of Gascony, with their pertinents, freely and without reservation, releasing him utterly from the fealty and homage at first due unto him. He also gave him the duchy of Guienne, the seignory of Berri, the city of Calais, and the city of Guines; and moreover showered upon him exceeding much gold and silver, and boundless treasure from the French treasury. But the king of England resigned, for himself and his posterity for ever, all right he had, and was toiling after, to the throne of France.

CLXXXIII.
Second Pestilence.

IN the year 1362 a death-sickness among men raged exceedingly in the whole kingdom of Scotland, like the former one, of the jubilee year, in all respects, both in the nature of the disease and in the number of those who died.

CLXXXIV.
Plot against King David.

THE same year, a great sedition and plot was set on foot and hatched, in the kingdom of Scotland, by the greater and more powerful chiefs thereof. The magnates met together against their lord the king, and formed, among themselves, the design of bending him to their views upon a demand which, as every one could see, was an unrighteous one— or banishing him; and, that none of them might draw back from that resolve, indentures were drawn up, and sealed with their several seals. Indeed, they soon showed forth, by deeds, the treason they had devised; and they manfully rose up in great numbers, with arms in their hands, to gain their ends through force or fear. Accordingly they took the king's adherents, wheresoever they could find them; and, having taken them, threw them into prison. In hostile wise fell they upon towns, and boroughs, and the whole country, and shared the spoils of the people, and wrought other damnable evils; to the end that the king, being so often pricked by the sword of compassion, should feel for the woes of the people, and the more easily bow himself unto their wishes, however unwilling he might be. But the king, acknowledging the vantage-ground of power, put forth his hand unto strength; and, wishing to check their rashness, and taking heed lest this insolence, if left unpunished, should, in time to come, turn out an example unto others elsewhere, while this great carnage would go on gathering strength, and the state of the commonwealth would seem to be impaired, he, in order that he might break down the presumption of those men, and thwart their plans, mustered his lieges from the four corners of his land, offering them much money for their pay. First, however, with his wonted forbearance, he had a proclamation published, that they and their abettors should leave off this foolishness, and be still. But as they were hardened in their stubbornness, and defended their own doings, he went after them, with some men of courage, who listed to die sooner than see the woes of their nation and the desolation of the land. The king's opponents, however, durst not openly come to blows with him and his; but when they might not carry out what they had begun, they sent an embassy, asking for terms of peace, and submitting themselves and theirs to his will and pleasure. So, being a most meek man, who would rather forgive than avenge, he formed a wise resolution for the nonce, and decided to be indulgent towards them, taking an oath of fealty from them, lest they should again take upon them to do such things, and the community should go on and suffer greater woes; and thus that trouble was set at rest. The following year, Robert Stewart, king David's nephew, swore him fealty afresh at Inchmurdach, in the form given elsewhere.

CLXXXV.

Second espousals of King David.

IN the year 1363, the aforesaid lord David, king of Scotland, took to wife, at Inchmurdach, a great lady, named Margaret of Logic, of high and noble birth, and born in his kingdom; and he endowed her with many lands and possessions, and raised her to reign in honour with him, with the royal diadem.

CLXXXVI.

IN the year 1370, on the Feast of St. Peter's Chair, David Bruce, king of Scotland, died at Edinburgh Castle, and was buried in the monastery of Holyrood. He reigned forty-eight years, and had no children. His nephew, Robert Stewart, who was then of age, succeeded him by right of inheritance, and was enthroned and crowned at Scone, that same year, on Lady Day. In the year 1373 died the lady Bridget of Sweden, etc.

CLXXXVII.

IN the year 1378, within five days before the Feast of the apostle Saint Andrew, the castle of Berwick was taken, by night, during a truce, by some of the meaner sort, who, however, slew some courtiers they found therein. But it was soon after retaken, and all the Scots who were therein were slain. In the month of December 1384, likewise, this same castle was taken by night, by means of scaling-ladders, after a brave resistance on the part of the town and tower; but it was soon after given up to the English.

CLXXXVIII.

THE same year, the bishop of Glasgow was made cardinal; and the red hat, together with the papal bulls for his appointment, was sent to Scotland. He was also ordained legate a *latere* of the Apostolic See, and made spiritual vicar of the kingdoms of Scotland and Ireland, with full powers.

CLXXXIX.

ABOUT the end of the month of May 1385, by agreement between France and Scotland on either hand, some Frenchmen to the number of eleven hundred men-at-arms, fifty of whom were knights, twenty-six bannerets, and one, only, an earl, came over to Scotland, in two hundred and forty ships. Their captain was the noble and valiant knight, the lord John de Vienne, a Burgundian by birth, and called the admiral of the king of France. These stayed for three months in sundry places in Lothian, and then, with the Scots, toiled on towards the marches; and, having destroyed some strongholds in England, they returned to the places where they were before. But, about the middle of the month of August, the king, Richard by name, then nineteen years old, came in with a great multitude; and, marching on, destroyed everything all about, saving nothing, and burning down, with the fiery flames, God's temples and holy places—to wit, the monasteries of Dryburgh, Melrose, and Newbattle, and the noble town of Edinburgh, with the church thereof. So after making great havoc in Lothian, they went home again without loss. It is worthy of remark, moreover, that the king of France, besides the wages paid to the aforesaid admiral, the paid soldiers, and the sailors, sent unto the king of Scotland and the lords thereof 50,000 francs, and fourscore suits of armour, with as many iron-headed spears, and much other costly gear. About Allhallowe'entide, the Frenchmen returned to their own land, in ships despatched by the king of France to bring them over. They bore themselves nobly, to the best of their power.

CXC.

IN the year 1383, on the 4th of February, Lawmabane (Lochmaben) Castle was taken and destroyed by the Scots, to wit, the Earl William of Douglas, and Archibald.

Printed in Great Britain
by Amazon